Detroit Studies in Music Bibliography

Editor
J. Bunker Clark
University of Kansas

Richard S. Hill: Tributes from Friends

compiled and edited by

Carol June Bradley and James B. Coover

DETROIT STUDIES IN MUSIC BIBLIOGRAPHY   NUMBER FIFTY-EIGHT
INFORMATION COORDINATORS, INC.   DETROIT   1987

Copyright © 1987   Carol June Bradley and James B. Coover

Printed and bound in the United States of America

Publisher   Information Coordinators, Inc.
1435-37 Randolph Street
Detroit, Michigan 48226

Editor   J. Bunker Clark
Book Design   Elaine J. Gorzelski
Art Director   Nicholas Jakubiak
Typographer   Colleen Osborne

Library of Congress Cataloging-in-Publication Data

Richard S. Hill—tributes from friends / compiled and edited by
Carol June Bradley and James B. Coover.
p.   cm. — (Detroit studies in music bibliography ; 58)
Bibliography: p. 58
ISBN 0-89990-035-6
1. Music—History and criticism.   2. Hill, Richard S. (Richard
Synyer), 1901-1961.   I. Hill, Richard S. (Richard Synyer),
1901-1961.   II. Bradley, Carol June.   III. Coover, James, 1925-
IV. Series: Detroit studies in music bibliography ; no. 58.
ML55.H514   1987
780'.9—dc19   87-23292

Contents

Illustrations

PART III
THE MUSIC TRADE

Tables

Prologue

He changed us. All of us. Some knew him professionally, some personally. Some worked with him or for him. Anyone today involved in music bibliography has been affected by the Music Library Association and its journal *Notes,* which was for so long Dick's magazine. He set standards for just about everything he touched. In his long, single-spaced, midnight letters to colleagues — on all kinds of subjects — were couched ideals by which many of them have since been guided. (Several of the contributors to this volume suggested that some of those now-treasured letters be reprinted.)

He was fierce about clear thinking and clear writing. He was goad and gad-fly — and encourager. His whopping revisions of articles and reviews submitted to *Notes* persuaded a few contributors to write less but prodded most to write better. If your thinking or your copy needed help, he gave it. If your ideas about food, musical comedy, music printing, periodical indexing, dodecaphony, the state of music cataloguing or the organization of IAML went askew, he helped uncurl them too. All in a gentle way. And wise you were to listen. What a delight it would be to have a sound movie of Dick holding others rapt as he talked of the myriad things of his world — in a bistro, in the halls of the Library of Congress, on a street in Paris, over lunch at the Supreme Court cafeteria, in the back of a taxi on a dark night in Cleveland — you name it, wherever he went.

It wasn't one-sided; he knew how to listen, too, and he made you feel comfortable with what you were saying — most of the time.

The topics of the papers in this celebration volume by a few of his friends would have intrigued him. Almost all of the writers knew Dick well, and all were asked to contribute something that they thought he would have liked. By no means are all of his interests covered — all of those invited to present essays were not able to do so.

His colleague for many years at the Library of Congress, William Lichtenwanger, offers prodigious research on the text of *The Star Spangled Banner,* completing a project that was one of Dick's unceasing concerns. Dena Epstein's charming picture of an American musical family and Irving Lowens' pick-and-shovel bibliographical work on a supposed piracy, though very different, would have pleased Dick immensely, we think. So too H. Earle Johnson's survey of early American music publishing in New England. A measure of Dick's intense interest in this subject is the part he plays in Johnson's essay. Dick was a scholar and was alert to scholars' needs. Even the list of auctions of music plates and copyrights, bizarre as it is, would have caught his fancy. It, like most of the papers here, he would probably have accepted for *Notes* while he was its editor—after improving each of them, of course.

Dick's vaunted bibliographical skills are a matter of record. Many of the exemplary bibliographies and catalogues we use today owe something to his expertise and imagination. He was concerned about the history of music bibliography as well as with quickening the generation of bibliographical controls. Donald W. Krummel's meticulous study of some little-known early music catalogues would have pleased him greatly. And he also would have agreed wholeheartedly, we think, with the point of Philip L. Miller's essay on the use of recordings as documents. Recordings were serious business to Dick—scholars' business. So too, he thought, was the study of what was then widely-considered "unserious" music, and he would be gratified by Frank Campbell's report on some of the scholarly attention that popular music is now receiving.

He would probably be less than comfortable with the lengthy, carefully-documented biography, the lead essay in this book, and by the numerous tributes from friends such as Gilbert Chase, Vincent Duckles, Florence Kretzschmar, Leonard Feist, and from Virginia Cunningham, another of his colleagues at the Library of Congress. Though not always a part of a *Gedenkschrift,* we think these recollections and plaudits add to an understanding of Dick, the man, and his work.

We hope that, though a bit embarrassed, he would have been pleased by this collective celebration of him, realizing that for a great many persons his was, indeed, a life of consequence. And that we are grateful.

James B. Coover

*   *   *   *   *

Richard Hill was one of the early crusaders devoted to the cause of the music library and one of the staunchest supporters of *The Music Index.* Fortunately for us, Dick's sister lived in Detroit and he visited her two or three times a year. When he did, he would always stop in the *Music Index* office to see how things were going. As they were going very badly in the first years of its existence, Dick tried to interest various foundations in giving assistance to the struggling *Index.*

In February of 1960 the Music Library Association met in New York City, the headquarters of one of the foundations that Dick wanted to reach. Attending an MLA meeting, we both lost track of the time and suddenly realized that we had a foundation appointment in five minutes but were fifteen minutes away from it. We couldn't get a cab so had no alternative but to run pell-mell through the streets. We arrived at our destination late and breathless. Despite our efforts we were again unsuccessful in raising any funds.

During one of his visits, Dick asked me if we would be interested in having *The Music Index Subject Heading List* checked by the staff of the Music Division of the Library of Congress. We wasted no time in accepting this offer. The result was a more coherent list that is being updated continuously to provide a tool for the indexer and a guide for the user of *The Music Index.*

In retrospect, it seems entirely within the realm of possibility that the very fine balance between the success and failure of *The Music Index* was tipped to success because of Dick's encouragement and unswerving support during its very difficult formative years.

FLORENCE KRETZSCHMAR

Part I

Richard Synyer Hill, 1901-61

Richard S. Hill at his desk, Library of Congress, ca. 1955

CHAPTER 1

Richard Synyer Hill, 1901-61

by

Carol June Bradley

He was the kind of person about whom people are eager to say, "He was my friend." He liked people and people liked him. He was an idea man who was able to sell his ideas to others and enlist their aid in their achievement. When friends and acquaintances speak of him now, they mention several specific characteristics and memories then invariably trail off with "He was a very special person!" One friend has described him as "one of the most unusual men ever created; he didn't fit in any pattern at all."[1]

Richard Synyer Hill was born in Chicago on 25 September 1901, the third child of Calvin Heywood Hill and Juliette Eliza Synyer Hill. Calvin was a direct descendant of a Jonathan Hill known to be living on Prudence Island, in Narragansett Bay in 1657; whether Jonathan emigrated, perhaps from Wales, or was born on Prudence Island, has not been established. Genealogical research has located Hills in Dorchester, Massachusetts as early as 1613 and on Prudence Island from 1657. Although the first American forebear has not been certified, the lineage from Jonathan to Calvin is clear.

Juliette Synyer was Calvin's second wife. His first, Naomi Smythe Childs Hill, to whom he was married on 18 December 1878, died in 1892. Together they had four children: twin boys who died at birth, Edith Naomi (1881-1975) and Frederic Keith (1882-1948). That family was born in Gardner, Massachusetts where Calvin was employed by the Heywood Brothers, later the Heywood-Wakefield Company, furniture manufacturers. Calvin became a member of the firm in 1888 and moved to Chicago in 1891 to establish a second factory. On 28 June 1894, Calvin married Juliette Synyer of Yonkers, New York. Juliette had worked as a secretary in the Gardner factory. Her family was second generation in America; her parents had come from England on a sailing vessel for their honeymoon and never returned. English genealogists believe Synyer to be a mutation of the French word "seigneur," so Juliette's

---

[1] McCullough interview. Letters between principal characters are identified by last name only; full information is cited in the list of unpublished sources, below, p. 57.

ancestry may well be French. Juliette was also the mother of four children: Phillip (1895-1970), Marian (born in 1898), Richard (1901-61), and Eunice (1904-80). All of Juliette's children bore her surname, Synyer (pronounced SIN-yer) because there were no male progeny to perpetuate it after her generation.

In May 1904, just before Eunice was born, Calvin moved the family into a new house in Oak Park, Illinois. The house was designed by Chicago architect Normand S. Patton, who made a specialty of public buildings; he designed many school, college, and public libraries in Chicago and elsewhere. The Hill house had 18 rooms, including a ballroom on the fourth floor. It featured a huge front porch, a barn with stables and servants quarters above, and a children's playhouse and sandbox fashioned similarly to a gazebo. The house wasn't quite finished when the Hills moved, but Juliette was anxious that the expected baby be born there.

Oak Park, incorporated in 1902, was an attempt to create the ideal community. Everything was considered, weighed, and voted upon before decisions were taken. The result is a community of exceptional intellectual achievement; a recent study found Oak Park "to be the hometown of almost 300 famous Americans who greatly shaped 20th Century American culture."[2] Among them are Frank Lloyd Wright, whose home and studio are now a museum, Ernest Hemingway, Edgar Rice Burroughs, Dorothy Thompson, Robert St. John, and others preeminent in the fields of literature, architecture, medicine, religion, and business. Calvin's grandson Norman describes the Oak Park of his and Dick's childhood:

> Dick grew up amid what Alexander Wollcott once aptly described as the bombazine skirts of Oak Park, Illinois. . . . Oak Park, in those days . . . was a very satisfactory place to grow up in, and it was even more satisfactory to grow up there as son — or a grandson — of Calvin H. Hill. In those days Oak Park was supposed to be the largest village in the world, and indeed it was large — over 100,000. It still, in the teens and twenties, preserved a very village-like atmosphere — tree-lined streets, a comfortable and genial air, and strictly ruled by upper middle class WASP morality, religion and tradition. By the time Dick was growing up, Calvin had attained a certain eminence: President of the Village, prominent member of the Union League Club and the South Shore Country Club, builder of the West Suburban Hospital and the Oak Park Club, and by then a wealthy, if not downright rich, man. He was an adept negotiator, and although extremely opinionated, an excellent evaluator of personalities, odds and eventualities, and superb at taking direct and positive action when the iron was hottest. He was dapper, generous, scrupulously honest, wryly amusing, and influential. He had flair.[3]

---

[2] Publicity release of the Oak Park Center of Creativity, 28-29 June 1982.

[3] Norman Hill, letter to author, 7 September 1982.

Completed May 1904,
one week before
Eunice was born —
May 8 — in the home.
Barn with stables
in rear, apartment
above for the couple
who worked for
the family.

THE HILL FAMILY HOME
312 N. Euclid Ave., Oak Park, Illinois

Hill pulling his
youngest sister Eunice
in the little red wagon.
Eunice was 2 —
born in 1904,
Dick was 5 —
born in 1901.
Phil, 11, and Marian,
8, in rear sitting in
playhouse sandbox
in back yard.

Richard driving a pony cart decorated with small teddy bears. Note the large teddy bear positioned as driver of the cart.

TWELVE-YEAR-OLD HILL AS A BOY SCOUT

The Hills lived elegantly. Every advantage was theirs. Ample live-in help cared for their physical needs. Each of the children was educated in a first-rate college or university. The boys were sent to a Keewaydin boys and girls summer camp in Timagami, Ontario, one of a group of Keewaydin camps operated by John Harland Rush, a former football coach at Princeton.

Cultural interests were plentiful. Juliette, especially, had a humanistic influence on her children. All had piano lessons from Mrs. Crosby Adams who also came to the house on Sunday nights to accompany the family and guests in a hymn sing. Sometimes one of the children would be asked to play, "panic time" for the affected child.[4] In addition to playing the piano, Mrs. Adams instructed the children in the fundamentals of theory and ear training.

Juliette had season tickets to the Chicago Symphony Orchestra and the Chicago Opera Company (to which she and accompanying family members were driven by the family's chauffeur). Calvin was a guarantor of the Chicago Opera Company; Juliette sponsored fund-raising events for it. Juliette was a friend of Marian MacDowell who stayed with the Hills when she came to Oak Park to raise money for the MacDowell Colony in Peterboro, New Hampshire. Once the entire family (Calvin, Juliette, and those of the children who were still at home) visited Peterboro and stayed in one of the artist cottages.

By the time of the Oak Park house, Marian remembers that Calvin spent less and less time at the Heywood business; he had become a vice president of the firm in 1904, and retired in 1923. Fred, the oldest son, went into the business as soon as he graduated from college. Calvin became the type of civic activist sometimes referred to as a pillar of the community—a man with the ability, time, and money to devote what would be the normal workday to efforts for the good of the community. He was president of the West Suburban Hospital Association and personally directed the construction of the hospital building. He visited the construction site every day and the hospital daily until shortly before he died. He was deeply involved in the affairs of the First Congregational Church, including its reconstruction after a disastrous fire in 1916. He served Oak Park as both village trustee and president, the latter for eight years. Efforts of men like Calvin "made Oak Park great. . . . *Dedicated* men who gave to the village for the sake of seeing it develop into a kind of place where people wanted to live and not for what they could get out of it."[5]

Calvin was also very active in his children's lives—their education, recreation, and social affairs. After Juliette died in 1919, Marian lived at home as her father's companion and escort, attending concerts and travelling with him. They spent part of the winter in Lake Wales, Florida, where Calvin owned a house.

[4] Hoch interview.

[5] McCullough interview.

Dick attended public schools in Oak Park: Oliver Wendell Holmes elementary school and the Oak Park & River Forest High School. Among his classmates were Ernest Hemingway and Theodore Geisel, who was later to be known as Dr. Seuss. Other Hemingway children and Frances Wright, a daughter of Frank Lloyd Wright, were classmates of Marian and Eunice. Dick left high school before graduation to attend Phillips Exeter Academy in Exeter, New Hampshire, where he graduated in 1920, shortly after Marian graduated from Smith College. To attend the graduations, Calvin had the family automobile put on a flat bed railroad car and brought East. The automobile was unloaded at Northampton for the family's use and then driven on to Exeter for Dick's graduation ceremonies.

In the fall of 1920 Dick entered Cornell University with a major in mechanical engineering. The fall of his junior year, 1922, his major changed to arts, but the new curriculum didn't improve his grades at all. The only A, something called Drill in the second semester of his freshman year, was balanced by a later F in economics; B's, C's, and D's are about equally represented on his college transcript. Too much time must have been spent in musical endeavors, including playing four-hand duets with his Oak Park classmate Pete Gervais. Both men maintained a life-long love of playing four- and sometimes eight-hand piano arrangements of orchestral works. In later years when Dick visited Chicago, he would rent a Steinway piano from Lyon and Healy for his hotel room so he and Pete could play together.

Dick's editorial experiences began at Cornell where he was Editor-in-Chief of two campus publications, the *Cornell Era* and the *Cornell Graphic*. The *Era* became a literary quarterly under his editorship and published "an enormous (and very fine) issue" in 1924, "then expired."[6] The *Graphic,* a picture magazine, persevered until 1926 when the costs of graphic reproduction could not be met by circulation revenue.

At Cornell, Dick was also a member of Sigma Delta Chi, a journalistic society, and the Sphinx Head, an honorary society for seniors.[7] His fraternity was Beta Theta Pi. On a Cornell questionnaire he listed his musical affiliations as Band (leader), Musical Clubs 1, 2, 3, and Orchestra.

From Cornell, Dick and Pete went to Oxford for graduate study. Dick matriculated for the B.Litt degree, and Pete pursued a one year self-designed program to broaden his musical experiences and exposure to Europe as well as study. Dick's consuming interest at Oxford became a study of the legends of Thaïs. On 14 May 1926, the Oxford Faculty of Theology approved his thesis topic, "The Legend of Taisia, the Converted Harlot," with Mr. F. Ll. Griffith

---

[6] Morris Bishop, *A History of Cornell* (Ithaca: Cornell University Press, 1962), 496.

[7] Information from Geri Solomon, Manuscript Arranger, Cornell University Libraries, to author, 18 June 1981.

The Hill Family in
its 1905 Winton car.
Calvin at the wheel,
with Edith beside him.

LEFT TO RIGHT
IN THE BACK:
Phillip, Richard,
Marian and Juliette
with Eunice on her
lap. The photo is in
the driveway of the
Hill Home, Oak Park.
Mr. Hill held Illinois
auto license no. 4
until his death in 1929.

THE FAMILY WINTON CAR, 1905

FRONT LEFT TO RIGHT:
Eunice, aged 13
Mr. Hill
Marian, aged 10

REAR LEFT TO RIGHT:
Dick, aged 16
Mrs. Hill
Phil, aged 22; he had
just received his
Commission in the
U.S. Navy as 1st
Lieutenant, and went
immediately into
Convey service
carrying U.S. soldiers
to war in Europe.

HILL FAMILY PORTRAIT, 1917

HILL MEN, ca. 1924

LEFT TO RIGHT: *Frederic with his son David;*
Calvin with grandsons Calvin II (Philip's son) and Henry (Frederic's son);
Richard, standing; Norman, Frederic's son, standing;
Phillip with his son Malcolm.

Photo in the library of the Hill Home, Oak Park, Illinois

supervisor.[8] Earlier that year he made "a trip around the shore of the Mediterranean in search of Taisia's manuscripts."[9] That search included a sojourn with the monks on Mount Athos, a trip down the Nile in a native boat stopping at the places Thaïs stopped, and extensive research and photographing in the Cairo Museum. An aspect of the research involved the study of phallic worship in Egypt. For that, Hill worked in the Cairo Museum. He clearly found a great deal of data, for correspondence from the museum after his visit offered additional pictures of items found subsequent to Hill's visit on the condition that neither the Museum nor its officials be acknowledged for their assistance—the former because "We dread the presence of this little collection becoming known," the latter because Museum employees could not "claim to distinguish cult-objects from 'smut' pure and simple."[10]

From Egypt, Hill travelled to Italy and France for additional research before returning to Oxford for two terms in succession without leave. (The Mediterranean data collection trip was taken from Christmas 1925 until April 1926, by combining two vacation periods.)[11] Part of the Italian stay was in the company of his "*belle ami,* Julie Lincoln" who was on a two-week vacation from Brentano's. Their vacation is described in an eight-page letter to Pete Gervais which is as charming and romantic an account of young Americans abroad as you'll ever read (reprinted below, pp. 389-92). By Hill's own estimate it was "one of the best letters I have ever written."[12]

Dick and Julie's itinerary included a week in Rome, "a glorious Saturday night and Sunday wandering about Orvieto," Florence, Pisa, Genoa, and then Milan, where they arrived on Saturday morning. As Hill tells it,

> The first thing we did was to rush to La Scala to get seats for that night, and what should we find to be on the bill but The Martyrdom of Saint Sebastian by d'Annunzio, Debussy, and Leon Bask (?spelling). Can you feature a better trio? And then to cap it all, St. Sebastien [*sic*] was to be played by Ida Rubenstein. I turned handsprings all over the street while Julie held my hat and cheered. I had completely given up all hope of ever seeing the thing, since it had been forbidden in Paris until last year, and there seemed to be no hope of getting it produced again even

---

[8] Hill selected the Faculty of Theology because "he admired the color of the academic gown." Charles Warren Fox, letter to author, 8 February 1983.

[9] Hill to Gervais, 31 January 1926. Gervais Letters. According to Fox, the Thaïs of Hill's thesis was the Christian saint, a reformed prostitute, whose story was written by Anatole France in 1890 and used by Massenet for his opera *Thaïs* in 1894.

[10] R. Engelbach (sp?) to Hill, 2 May 1926 and 11 June 1926. Hill Papers.

[11] Information from Hill to Gervais, 31 January 1926. Gervais Letters.

[12] Hill to Gervais during the summer of 1926 from Hotel d'Egypt, Paris. Gervais Letters.

though the ban was removed. . . . Consequently, as I have intimated, my joy knew all kinds of bounds, leaps, and skips, when I found I was going to see the thing *tout complete*. As a matter of fact, it was not quite complete — one act was omitted — but since even then it lasted for three and a half hours, I could hardly find it in me to ask for more. The scenery and costumes were excellent, the music uneven, sometimes as perfect as anything he has done and again quite unintelligible even though I was reasonably familiar with it from the piano transcription. It only occasionally reached the steady high level of *Pelleas*. And the play itself is hopeless.[13]

Tuesday night, after Julie had returned to work, Dick went again to see if his first impressions had been correct.

They were for the most part. Somebody spotted d'Annunzio in a box, and he was clapped until he gave a little speech. As a matter of fact, it was the only time during the performance that the audience got at all vociferous.

When I get back to Paris, I shall buy the play and see if it makes better reading then it does acting, but just at present I can't hand it a thing.[14]

The letter then proceeds through a two and a half page blow-by-blow account of the Italian premiére of Moussorgsky's *Kovantschina* and a detailed account of a bachelor dinner at one of his favorite hotels in Bourg, France. Again, let him tell his own tale.

When I first stepped into the hotel, I realized something had happened. The dinning [*sic*] room had been shifted to the other side of the hotel, and right opposite the main entrance were two glass doors through which the stoves with chefs busy about them could be seen. They took me to my room, a large affair with a private bath. I was on the point of telling them that I was not accustomed to such splendor, but then I says to myself, "No, Hill, you will make a night of it. This is your first night in France after three long months. You will take this room, and not even ask the price of it, for if you did, you might feel compunctions. No, you will go down and have a perfect meal, and then after your café and cognac, you will come up here, fill the tub with nice hot water, and soak for at least two hours." All of which I did. When I got to the dinning [*sic*] room, my suspicions were confirmed. Dinner had gone up over ten francs and the wine eleven. But I was feeling reckless, and by continually reminding myself that the franc had fallen

---

[13] Hill to Gervais, 11 March 1926. Gervais Letters. The Russian painter Léon Bakst designed the costumes and scenery for the theatrical production which combined aspects of both opera and ballet.

[14] Ibid.

considerably, I kept up my spirit, ordered the things I wanted, and a half bottle of Romanée for twenty francs. Everything was perfect. . . . The next morning, I went to the Church of Bron and took some pictures of the carvings on the choir stalls which had particularly delighted me on my previous visit. Then back for an excellent lunch and a cold bottle of Chablis, after which I called for the bill with fear and trembling. My splendid room and bath had cost twenty-five francs. When I considered that I had had to pay 75 piasters (which are worth more than a franc) for a room with a wash basin & pitcher in Cairo, I realized one of the greatest blessings of *la douce France*. My whole splurge had cost 139 francs, about five dollars.[15]

Life on the Egyptian trip must have been Spartan. Certainly there would have been few comforts during the stay with monks on Mount Athos. Hill once remarked that he lived for weeks on eggs because the fresh vegetables were contaminated. He bought eggs and took them to a café where they were boiled in the water used to make coffee.[16]

During the Italian weeks and the trip back to Paris, Hill's days were spent in libraries, the evenings with Julie or on trains. In Italy he sent Julie sightseeing while he worked; their evenings were devoted to reading and attending concerts. Julie, full name Juliana Armour Lincoln, was a college acquaintance of Dick's older sister Marian. Julie graduated from Smith College in 1922 and sometime thereafter took a position with the American Embassy in London. In the letter quoted above, Dick described her as working in Brentano's, without mentioning a city. A subsequent letter[17] to Pete was written in a Parisian café on his way home from visiting Julie in the American Hospital where she had had an appendectomy. The precise details of these years of their lives are not clear except that Julie made it her business to be in Europe when Dick was, whether at the American Embassy in London or Brentano's in Paris.

For Dick's activities after he returned to Oxford in April 1926, we are dependent upon his letter to Pete in which he indicated his intentions of staying in Europe until about Christmas 1926. The time would be spent writing his thesis. After the two-term stay in Oxford he returned to Paris where he visited Julie in the American Hospital; he told Pete he "expected to go to St. Malo in Brittany in another ten days . . . to park until the first of October." His father planned a trip to Europe in November, "just for the ride," and together they might go to the Riviera before returning to the United States for Christmas.

Whether those exact plans materialized is not known, but Hill did return to the United States and wintered with his father in Florida

---

[15] Ibid.

[16] Information from Fox interview.

[17] Hill to Gervais, summer 1926. Gervais Letters.

(1927). Sometime that winter or spring, Oxford rejected the completed thesis; the criticism was that a biography of Thaïs was not sufficient, it should be a psychological study. "Dick was very annoyed and very disillusioned about Oxford."[18] He began to read psychology and was reading Koffka's Gestalt psychology at the family home in Oak Park during the summer of 1927 when he remarked to his sister Edith, "I wish I knew where that man is going to be this year." "I know," replied Edith, "he's going to be at Smith."[19] So Dick became a research fellow to Kurt Koffka at Smith College for the academic years 1927-28 and 1928-29.

Edith, Dick's half-sister from Calvin's first marriage, was a full generation older than Dick, but they were very good friends. She described him as "like a dear son as well as brother."[20] Edith graduated from Smith College in 1903 and went on to Columbia Graduate School in English and history. In 1910 she was persuaded to return to Northampton and begin a quarterly journal for Smith College alumnae. At a salary of $200 a year, with a three-bank Corona typewriter and a newly-acquired style book, Edith Hill created the *Smith Alumnae Quarterly*. She resigned her editorship in 1938 but "remained the editor's counselor and the magazine's most careful proofreader until past her ninetieth year."[21]

Edith was an invalid all her life. She was born with a circulatory abnormality in her left leg: there was no pulsation to send the blood back from the foot to the heart. That congenital condition was severely aggravated when, at the age of seven, she was thrown from a horse and buggy and one of the wheels ran over the leg, and again, while a student at Smith College, a beam fell on it during a basketball game in the gym. As a result of the Smith College accident, Edith spent her entire senior year in the infirmary but still graduated with honors. While the family home remained in Oak Park, Edith would prepare an issue of the *Quarterly* in Northampton and return to Oak Park by train where she would take to her bed, cared for by nurses around the clock. The family would say "Poor Edith, this time she won't be able to go back." But the day before she was scheduled to return to Northampton she would get up and leave as planned to prepare the next issue.[22]

Dick's mother Juliette died on 29 May 1919 of cancer caused by a uterine cyst she neglected rather than submit to surgery while the children were home from college for summer vacation. By the time the surgery was performed it was too late; the cyst had become malignant. After Juliette died, Calvin gave each of his children a sum of money, reportedly $100,000, with which to start their careers.

---

[18] Hoch interview.

[19] Quotes from Edith N. Hill, letter to Charles Warren Fox, without date but shortly after Fox's reminiscence of Hill appeared in *Notes* (June 1961).

[20] Ibid.

[21] Facts and quote from the *Smith Alumnae Quarterly* 66 (August 1975): 78.

[22] Facts from Hoch interview.

"For Edith he set up a larger fund that saw her through a long, productive, and brave career at Smith.[23] In addition, a house was purchased for Edith in Northampton so it would never be necessary for her to live with any of her siblings. Several nurse-housekeepers cared for her there until she moved into an apartment and, finally a nursing home. Her advanced age—she died on the eve of her 94th birthday—and poor health made her last years a burden; she was so tired and uncomfortable she really wished to die.

Edith was a beloved personality to generations of Smith girls. Oak Park girls would find little bouquets of flowers in their rooms when they arrived for their freshman year. She would have teas and dinners for small groups of Smith girls; she knew everyone. Although she was not a musician and had no piano in her house, she and Dick shared their love of books and their similar tasks as editors of journals.

Dick's older full sister Marian used part of her money to buy a house for her young family. The summer of 1925 she had married Arthur Hoch, a Sears Roebuck salesman. The wedding took place in Paris; Dick, who was already in Europe for his Oxford study, made the arrangements. Edith, Eunice, Calvin, and Julie Lincoln, as well as several Oak Park friends in Europe for the summer, attended.

Eunice, Dick's young sister, married Harold Alyea on 14 November 1929, four days before Calvin's death. Alyea, who went by the nickname Babe, was a stock broker until the 1929 crash; after that he rebuilt large motors for a living. Eunice allowed Babe access to her money and he lost it all in the stock market. Their marriage had many troubles; Babe drank heavily and money was always a problem. Just when Eunice finally agreed to divorce him he joined Alcoholics Anonymous and devoted the last six years of his life to salvaging drunks from the streets of Detroit. Dick was especially close to Eunice and provided for her from his own estate so that after his death she received a monthly check as long as she lived.

Dick is reported to have converted his money from Calvin into U.S. government bonds.[24] Whatever he did, he didn't lose it, for it funded his European travel and education until he took gainful employment at the Library of Congress. Even there he continued to live on a scale incompatible with his salary. His brothers Fred and Phillip were businessmen who well knew how to handle money to its best advantage. Dick's use of his money and his lifestyle were a source of friction to Phil who had no sympathies in common with Dick; they were never very good friends. Phil couldn't understand what Dick was doing with his life: "He doesn't earn an honest dollar."[25] During the course of the interviews for this paper, the incompatibility of Phil and Dick surfaced several times. Their lack of understanding of each other's interests and life style is described by their sister Marian.

[23] Norman Hill, letter to author, 7 September 1982.

[24] McCullough interview.

[25] Hoch interview.

. . . I can still hear Phil mutter "Damn lazy So and So, he doesn't earn his salt!" But PHIL was a business-man de lux, and really did not appreciate the ARTS.[26]

Calvin's grandson Norman reports Phil to have been most like Calvin, Dick and Fred least so.

His first fall in Northampton, 1 October 1927 to be exact, Dick married Julie Lincoln. Julie was a native of Willimantic, Connecticut, where the wedding took place. Ted Geisel, Dick's Oak Park and Oxford classmate who later assumed the *nom de plume* Dr. Seuss, was the best man. Pete Gervais could not be best man, couldn't even attend the wedding because of a severe illness which required brain surgery. It was three years before Pete recovered sufficiently to work in his family's business, an iron fire door factory.

The attitude of other members of the Hill family isn't known, but Marian, who knew Julie from college, opposed the match and told Dick as much. Marian felt Julie lacked the intelligence and background to complement Dick; "she wasn't the mentality to understand Dick."[27] Although Marian attended the wedding and Dick and Julie subsequently spent Christmas at the family home, Dick resented Marian's attitude and relations between them were strained.

After two academic years at Smith College with Koffka, Dick returned to Cornell, intending to re-do the Thaïs biography for his dissertation in psychology. At Cornell he met and became life-long friend with Charles Warren Fox, also a psychology graduate student. The focus of both psychologists' lives altered with the arrival of Otto Kinkeldey on the Cornell campus in the fall of 1930. Kinkeldey, engaged as University Librarian and first Professor of Musicology in the United States, began his seminar in musicology that fall. Hill and Fox both attended. Kinkeldey had a provision in his contract which allowed him to admit anyone he wanted to the seminar, which met in his home on Thursdays at 4 o'clock. There was no group of musicology students from which to draw; rather, anyone from within or without the Cornell community could attend. One girl from off-campus did not have a high school diploma. For admission to the seminar Kinkeldey required only that the students "read a simple hymn tune at sight on the piano and know a little modicum of theory."[28] To give the seminar continuity, Kinkeldey would pick an example from some field of musical history as the theme for a session. All the students would work on that and it would be covered in 10-15 minutes of the next seminar. The rest of the class would be devoted to the students' papers. The "papers" were extemporaneous oral reports given from notes rather than fully written-out papers and merely read. The other students and Kinkeldey commented on each presentation.[29]

---

[26] Marian Hill Hoch, letter to author, 25 June 1981. Reproduced with her emphases.

[27] Hoch interview.

[28] Information from Fox interview.

[29] Ibid.

Fox attended Kinkeldey's seminar from 1930 to 1932, but continued his degree program in psychology, earning his Ph.D. in 1933. Hill's interest, on the other hand, "shifted from psychology to music."[30] The Thaïs research was never completed; among Hill's papers in the Library of Congress is a large manuscript box with negatives of the photographs of manuscripts, art, churches, etc., taken on the Egyptian trip. There is also a large collection of folders filled with research notes, bibliographies, translations of manuscripts, charts, etc. He sold his Egyptology library to a Washington antiquarian.

Hill attended Kinkeldey's seminar from the fall of 1930 until the fall of 1939 when he left Ithaca. To say that Hill came under Kinkeldey's influence simplifies their relationship, for they were devoted to each other. But Fox believes Hill would have said Kinkeldey was the primary influence in his (Hill's) professional life. When Pete and his bride visited Dick in Ithaca on their honeymoon, Dick arranged for Pete to meet Kinkeldey. Pete was in no mood to meet any professor and wouldn't go, which made Dick "absolutely furious. He just couldn't understand why anyone wouldn't want to meet this wonderful, great guy."[31] The letters to Pete, on which we are dependent for a contemporary account of the Cornell years, are filled with references to Kinkeldey and his scholastic requirements. An example is Hill's response to Pete's query about good histories of music.

> Actually, there is no perfect history of music in any language. You have to read around in various ones, and Kinky recommends a course in dictionary articles. If you start say on Grove and read the article on Polyphonic music, a good many names will be given. Make a list of these and look them up in several dictionaries, collecting more names as you go. . . . True, it's not predigested, but since that's dangerous anyway its not a bad idea.[32]

Hill continues by recommending Schering's *Geschichte der Musik in Beispielen* to Pete, suggesting how to purchase it and a fair price to pay. "I can't loan you mine, because Kinkey says we have to know every composition in it for our examination. . . ."[33]

Hill carried on several research projects in Ithaca. His knowledge of and interest in the music of Arnold Schoenberg first brought him and Fox together. The first time they met, Hill said "I hear you're interested in Schoenberg." Fox explains: "There were no recordings of Schoenberg at that time . . . he was practically unknown."[34] Those who knew the music gained their knowledge

---

[30] Ibid.

[31] McCullough interview.

[32] Hill to Gervais, 7 July 1932. Gervais Letters.

[33] Ibid. Hill's spelling of "Kinkey" varies in his letters to Pete.

[34] Fox interview.

from studying the scores, and a collection of Hill's Schoenberg scores, heavily annotated and/or with analyses laid in, is now in the Music Division of the Library of Congress. His first musicological publication was a Schoenberg study published in *The Musical Quarterly* of January 1936: "Schoenberg's Tone-Rows and Tonal System of the Future." That paper brought him international recognition, although he worried that it had been cut and condensed to the extent that it was "almost unintelligible."[35] Somehow Dick became friendly with Schoenberg who, on at least one occasion, sent him an unpublished manuscript to study. Dick analyzed it and found an error which he drew to Schoenberg's attention. Schoenberg responded that *he* knew about it, but he didn't think the average person would be aware of it and he wasn't going to change it.[36]

The pages of *Notes* include several Hill "reviews" of Schoenberg compositions which are, rather than reviews, analyses and essays on the evolution of atonality.

As early as 1932 Hill mentioned his forthcoming "book on Modern Dissonant Music." "Since the analyses and biographical material will be very helpful," Pete was pressed to save programs from the Chicago Symphony Orchestra as well as any others that came his way. "The book is not scheduled to appear until 1937 or 38, so that you will have a chance to collect quite a few of them."[37] And by 1936 he was building a personal library to accommodate the course he was to teach at Cornell, "Modern Music."

> The first thing I did when I started preparing the course was to go through the quarterly book lists in the Musical Quarterly, the yearly lists in Peters Jahrbuch from 1920-36, and stacks of miscellaneous book catalogues and bibliographies, culling as complete a list of books on the subject as I could put together. There's very close to four hundred books on it, believe it or believe it. The music department had twenty-five bucks left of its appropriation, and Kink allowed me another fifteen dollars of a special fund he has. Since there was practically nothing whatsoever in the library, that forty bucks barely covered the mere essentials. I had quite a few things, but—you know me where books are concerned—I figured a bit of plunging was in order. So I thinned the list down again and again, and finally made up a list for Germany, England, and France which together included 82 items.[38]

---

[35] Hoch interview. Hill makes a similar disclaimer in his 11 March 1936 letter to Pete but does mention that "Oliver Strunk of the Music Division of the Congressional Library even called it 'an extraordinarily capable piece of work.' Haven't gotten around to sending one to the Old Man himself [i.e., Schoenberg] yet, but when I do, I'm expecting something of an explosion from that direction—although it's entirely possible that it may simply make him so mad that he won't answer the letter at all." Gervais Letters.

[36] Facts from Hoch interview.

[37] Hill to Gervais, 3 June 1932. Gervais Letters.

[38] Hill to Gervais, 19 June 1936. Gervais Letters.

Those volumes were complemented by almost complete sets of programs from the Chicago Symphony, which Dick paged consecutively throughout the season, indexed and bound. He was "mainly interested in the lesser known gents" who lacked full biographies.

> One of the best ways I know of finding out about a composer — in addition to dictionary articles — is to look him up in the program notes of various big symphony orchestras.[39]

His course, a tangible result of *The Musical Quarterly* Schoenberg paper, was first offered the summer of 1936; Hill taught without pay — the idea came up after the appropriations had been allocated. By the summer of 1937, however, he was paid a salary of $100.

Sometime during the Cornell years, Hill became interested in the history of the firms which antedated and developed into the C. F. Peters music publishing house. The project is first mentioned in 1937 in a card to Pete from an unspecified European location.

> . . . I'm staying abroad longer than I planned — the chief reason being that Max Hinrichson of the Peters Verlag has taken a fancy to my Hoffmeister catalogue, and plans to publish it along with Einstein's Appendix to Köchel — so the job must be well done.[40]

He searched libraries in Berlin, Leipzig, Munich, and Vienna. Late winter 1938, he toured East Coast American libraries — Rochester, Boston, New York, and Washington — where he found more than he'd anticipated — "fifty to a hundred pieces everywhere I went, and nearly three hundred in Washington."[41] He filmed the first and last pages, or occasionally the complete opus, of the music published by Franz Anton Hoffmeister and Ambroise Kühnel, the predecessors of the Peters firm. In Germany he was literally granted *carte blanche* to film as he chose because of his sophisticated camera equipment. As he related it to Pete, the German economy was so devoted to the production of armaments that civilian technology had fallen behind. When German library authorities saw the quality equipment Dick brought, he was permitted to photograph at will.[42]

Back in Ithaca, Dick projected the images — which must have been on 35 mm slides — onto his piano rack, played them through, and at night printed copies of those appropriate to accompany his paper for the Western New York Chapter of the American Musicological Society, 12 May 1938. Even though the preparation of the paper took him away from the firm's catalogue temporarily,

---

[39] Hill to Gervais, 3 June 1936. Gervais Letters.

[40] Hill to Gervais, 27 October 1937. Gervais Letters.

[41] Hill to Gervais, 1 June 1938. Gervais Letters.

[42] Facts from McCullough interview.

he was not losing time because the work had to be done sometime for his thesis.

The paper, "The Age of Beethoven (?)," was really a concert, with commentary, from his photocopied Hoffmeister and Kühnel music. The pieces he chose illustrated that

> The Age of Beethoven is no more the Age of Beethoven than this is the Age of Schönberg. There's probably as much difference between Oginsky's celebrated "suicide" Polonaise (written because his girl ran off with another man and supposedly followed immediately afterwards by Oginsky's suicide) and Beethoven's Op. 131 as there is between Irving Berlin and Schönberg's Pierre Lunaire; and in between, there are just as many variants and types.[43]

He was pleased with the paper.

> . . . My firm represented a pretty good cross-section of the music of the period. . . . Even Kink had never heard a piece by [Joseph] Wölfl although he had long known of him as Beethoven's greatest concert rival.[44]

Kinkeldey told Harold Spivacke, Chief of the Music Division, Library of Congress, that three times during the Cornell years Hill "did work for which I was willing to give him a Ph.D. but it didn't satisfy him."[45] Fox commented that "Dick hardly ever finished anything because he would go into it so deeply it would be years and years of work."[46] Three research projects, all unfinished, date from the Cornell period: the Thaïs study, begun at Oxford and for the conclusion of which he went to Cornell in 1929, the book on modern music — including the Schoenberg study, and the history of C. F. Peters' predecessors which Hill referred to as his Cornell thesis. In later years Hill's colleagues at the Library of Congress kidded him about not finishing his dissertation, saying "He had his degree in musicology except to finish the last page."[47] Mary Rogers reports he didn't finish projects because he didn't think they were good enough; he always wanted to do more research on them.

But there were several completed pieces of work: the Schoenberg paper printed in *The Musical Quarterly,* three papers read before the Western New York Chapter of the American Musicological Society, and one before the annual meeting of the AMS and subsequently printed in its *Papers.* Three of the AMS presentations were off-shoots of his dissertation, "The History of a Series of Music-

---

[43] Hill to Gervais, 1 June 1938. Gervais Letters.

[44] Ibid.

[45] Spivacke interview.

[46] Fox interview.

[47] Rogers interview.

Sometime before 21 June 1932, Julie left Dick for Keith Pevear, the husband of Mary Case, Dick's brother Fred's wife's cousin. Julie met and fell in love with him at one of the family Christmas celebrations she and Dick attended in Oak Park. Keith was very handsome, "the glamour boy around . . . all the married women were crazy about him."[49] When Julie left Dick she went to Keith in New York City who divorced his wife and married her on 26 July 1933. Keith lived only two or three years after that; Julie died in Boston in April of 1964.

Although the divorce testimony indicated Julie deserted Dick more than one year prior to 15 June 1932, Charles Warren Fox recalls her being in the Ithaca apartment in June of 1931, after a performance of Bach's B Minor Mass by the Westminster Choir School and the Rochester Civic Orchestra.[50] Dick had a recording of the complete Mass which he played for a group of friends, including Fox, in the apartment during the afternoon. That evening they all heard the live performance and returned to Dick's apartment to replay the recording. But when the group reached the apartment, Julie was there with "a couple of her drunken friends" who "were not interested in music in the least," so the recording was not played.[51]

Dick's sister Marian felt Julie "was just bored with the whole business of being married and housekeeping," "tired of Dick being Dick"—studying and playing Bach on the piano by the hour.

Dick went back to Chicago to file for divorce; he claimed Illinois residency although he'd been in Ithaca since 1929. Marian and Pete Gervais were his witnesses; the divorce was granted in the Superior Court of Cook County on 21 June 1932. Dick "made a settlement on Julie . . . with the understanding that she would never come to him again for any more money."[52]

The divorce was difficult for Dick. Pete's wife Helena recalls that Dick "just could hardly speak to me to tell me about it. . . . He couldn't concentrate for months. He read westerns and whodunits. It took him a *long, long* time. . . . He really loved Julie, there was no doubt about that." At the same time, the Oak Park "consensus was that that was the *most* ill-matched couple that could ever

---

[48] Richard S. Hill, "Publisher—Versus Composer—Catalogues," *Bulletin of the American Musicological Society,* no. 5 (August 1941): 10.

[49] McCullough interview.

[50] Fox's recollection of the Talbott Music Festival performance was dated in *Musical America* 51 (June 1931): 32.

[51] Fox interview.

[52] Hoch interview. Although the divorce testimony indicated Julie deserted Dick more than one year prior to 15 June 1932, she was in Ithaca on 20 June 1931 according to Fox's recollection of the Bach B Minor Mass episode. Several of Dick's letters to Pete mentioned Julie's involvement in upcoming events during the year. That one statement may be no more accurate than Dick's claim of Illinois residency when, in fact, he had lived in New York since 1929.

be."[53] Even Dick seems to have reached that conclusion.

> I still think, of course, that she has her good points, but
> I'm utterly convinced that she has enough others to make
> her very bad for me. In fact, I now agree completely with
> Babe [Eunice's husband] that I got a lucky break.[54]

Yet he noted and commented to Pete nine months later: "Julie was finally married on the 26th of last month, so that's finally off my mind."[55]

Judging from Dick's letters to Pete and from Helena's reminiscence, the years Julie and Dick were together were years of partying, late hours, and heavy drinking despite Dick's academic endeavors. He seems to have enjoyed both, but by the summer of 1931 he yearned for "a period of reorganization rather than of spending, a little basking in Bach rather than evenings of pinochle rummy and alcohol."[56]

Dick's relationship with Marian returned to pre-Julie normalcy after the divorce. Between 1934 and 1945, when she moved to Elyria, Ohio, Dick regularly spent the Christmas holidays with Marian and her family in River Forest, Illinois.

In 1939 Harold Spivacke had an opening for a reference librarian. Kinkeldey suggested he appoint Hill. Spivacke didn't believe Hill would accept the position; "Dick? Can I get him?" Kinkeldey thought he could, for Hill would have no teaching position at Cornell in the fall of 1939 because the university was decreasing its staff.[57] Kinkeldey told Spivacke, " . . . I have taught in Germany and here and I never had a student who knew music history better than Richard Hill."[58] Although Hill was known to the staff of the Music Division because of his attendance at the Coolidge Festivals and his research use of the Library, he submitted the name of at least one reference in addition to Kinkeldey's: Kurt Koffka. Koffka wrote both Spivacke and Hill on 4 July 1939, encouraging Hill in his letter: "I hope you'll get the job." He did: under date of 7 July 1939 he was notified of his appointment and directed to report for work on 1 September 1939.

Spivacke's description of Hill's arrival in Washington it too colorful to paraphrase.

> And when he came, of course, he drove up in the *latest* Buick
> that even then had eight cylinders, moving electric seats,
> electric windows and everything. And he took a beautiful

---

[53] McCullough interview.

[54] Hill to Gervais, 29 November 1932. Gervais Letters.

[55] Hill to Gervais, 8 August 1933. Gervais Letters.

[56] Hill to Gervais, undated but clearly late May or early June 1931. Gervais Letters.

[57] Information from Hill to Gervais, 3 April 1939. Gervais Letters.

[58] Spivacke interview.

apartment on 16th St. in one of the new buildings of the day and people said, "Hey, you got that fellow! He's got this fancy car and I hear he's got that. . . ." And I learned to say with a straight face, "Well, I'm paying him $2,000 a year!" And walk away fast and leave them potless why they can't make out on $3,000 a year.[59]

The Buick had been bought for a projected trip to Charleston, South Carolina, with Pete and Helena Gervais. Pete had family there and Dick wanted to experience the essence of Charleston as only an entrée to native inhabitants would permit. The trip was never made, but Dick had the Buick when he got to Washington.

Dick remained in the apartment at 3200 16th St., N.W., until 1956 when he moved into the Methodist building on Maryland Ave., only a block from the Library of Congress.

In an April 1939 letter to Pete Gervais, Hill had outlined his plans for the completion of his dissertation by fall. The catalogue was nearly complete, lacking only a quick trip abroad "in order to fill out as many holes as possible . . . before I get tied down to regular hours and can't dash about the Globe collecting materials."[60] The completed catalogue would then be "boiled down into twenty-four tables" accompanied by "a lengthy historical introduction" and various indices. The Ph.D. qualifying exams were another problem. The course work for the psychology and physics minors had been done during the earlier of his nine years at Cornell so that "extensive reviewing" would be necessary. The summer, then, was to be spent finishing the dissertation and reviewing for exams to be taken in the fall when Kinkeldey returned to Cornell after teaching in Harvard's summer school.

The move to Washington dealt a death blow to the dissertation and Ph.D. The dissertation was never completed; the only publication of information from it was "The Plate Numbers of C. F. Peters' Predecessors" in the *Papers* of the American Musicological Society.[61]

Nor did Hill return to Ithaca for the qualifying exams. Once at the Library of Congress, his research went off in a completely different direction. Requests for information about the history of *The Star-Spangled Banner* were a recurring aspect of the Music Division's reference mail. Spivacke asked Hill to prepare copy suitable for a "four-page circular on *The Star-Spangled Banner*" which could be mailed instead of an individually-written letter from a member of the Reference Section. Hill tackled the project with his customary thoroughness and submitted a manuscript of which Chapter 1 was 160 pages, but "of no use" to Spivacke for his proposed circular.[62] Hill persevered on the project so that by September

---

[59] Ibid.

[60] Quotes from Hill to Gervais, 3 April 1939. Gervais Letters.

[61] (1938): 113-34.

[62] Spivacke interview.

of 1940, when William Lichtenwanger became his assistant on the Reference staff, Lichtenwanger was persuaded to accompany Hill to Baltimore to photograph various aspects of Fort McHenry, birthplace of the text.

The search for the tune's history in the United States led to songsters and newspapers where Hill looked for "To Anacreon," "Oh say can you see" and parodies on either. As Hill explained his project in 1942,

> . . . the most crying need is something to trace the history of *To Anacreon in Heaven* from its introduction into this country until *The Star-Spangled Banner* is sufficiently launched on its noble career. The sheet music editions simply do not touch this phase. To do the job properly, one should make an exhaustive study of all the parodies as they appear in the newspapers, but since this would be the work of a life-time, I have compromised on tracing their appearance in the songsters.[63]

The problem, in wartime Washington, was that

> since most of the Library's early volumes and manuscripts have been put in protective storage outside of Washington, I have had to beg favors of practically every library in this country, and I have literally written dozens of long letters to Great Britain. Everyone has been amazingly kind. . . .[64]

In addition to the letters, Hill traveled to Philadelphia, New York, Worcester, Boston, and Providence, Rhode Island, to inspect collections of songsters. Then he typed up his list of songsters and sent it to Professor S. Foster Damon at Brown University, Margaret M. Mott at the Grosvenor Library in Buffalo, and Clarence Brigham at the American Antiquarian Society in Worcester. Each supplied citations for songsters they held which were not on Hill's list. Those were subsequently borrowed on interlibrary loan or microfilmed for Hill's use in Washington. In July of 1943 Hill petitioned the Library's Reference Department and Rare Book room for access to certain materials removed from Washington because of the war emergency. Later that month he reported his progress to the Library's Publications Committee:

> By far the greater part of the research has been completed for the report, except for two things. One of these things is of such paramount importance that the writing of the report must necessarily wait until the matter can be settled one way or another, since it will condition the presentation of all the evidence on the origin of the tune. The point in question, of course, is whether or not the tune was used by

---

[63] Hill to S. Foster Damon, 14 May 1942. Hill Papers.

[64] Hill to Sam Henry, 25 January 1943. Hill Papers.

the 5th or Royal Irish Regiment of Dragoons before it was adopted by the Anacreontic Society. . . . The second point that needs additional work is the bibliography of American songsters containing the SSB.[65]

The songster information was collected or transcribed onto 5 x 8 cards, arranged chronologically. The information collected included title and imprint, location within the Library of Congress and other libraries, appraisal of the contents, and first lines and page numbers of patriotic songs. (As the project progressed, Hill had expanded his scope to include all patriotic songs, aiming towards a bibliography of "patriotic songs in general" which he hoped the Library of Congress would publish.)[66]

Hill, appalled at the number of unique songsters he found for the years between 1790 and 1840, noted that

> . . . the quantity of practically unique copies of songsters seems to be almost unlimited. One could shrug one's shoulders and say that being unlimited it was useless to try to cope with the matter. Personally I think that, considering the scarcity of these little books, it might be well to do just the opposite and make some attempt to compile a reasonably complete bibliography.[67]

Hill's cards remain in the Library of Congress, but his projected bibliography never materialized.[68]

The Library's Publications Committee set a 30 June 1942 copy deadline for *The Star-Spangled Banner* brochure. Hill conceived the idea of printing two pamphlets: one a brief explanation for mass distribution, the other longer and more detailed for restricted distribution. He worked out a scheme whereby a single printing would produce the small version which would also function as the cover of the larger when 24 or 32 pages of text were inserted. Hill did not meet the June 30 deadline. To resolve some of the unanswered questions he applied to the Beethoven Association's Sonneck Memorial Fund for a $150 grant with which to hire researchers in Great Britain. The request was approved by a committee which consisted of Spivacke, Kinkeldey, Carl Engel, and Harold Bauer. With one of the researchers in North Ireland, a Donal O'Sullivan, Hill corresponded in letters of up to 39 single-spaced pages!

The work on *The Star-Spangled Banner* history continued throughout Hill's life—indeed, it was the project on which he was working when he suffered his fatal heart attack. Several publications,

---

[65] 23 July 1943.

[66] Hill to J. S. Jackson, Brown University, 4 June 1942. Hill Papers.

[67] Ibid.

[68] The work of a colleague at the Library of Congress was published by the American Antiquarian Society in 1976. In his *Bibliography of Songsters Printed in America before 1821,* Irving Lowens acknowledges Hill's role and influence in the project.

but not Spivacke's circular, did result. Hill wrote *The Star-Spangled Banner* entry for the *Collier's Encyclopedia* (1950); a paper entitled "The Melody of 'The Star-Spangled Banner' in the United States before 1820" for *Essays Honoring Lawrence C. Wroth;*[69] and from 1955 to 1958 prepared several statements and gave testimony before the House of Representatives' Hearings on an "official" version of *The Star-Spangled Banner.*[70] In addition to the 160-page manuscript of "The 'Unsettled' Text of *The Star Spangled Banner*" printed here in William Lichtenwanger's revision (pp. 71-184 in this volume), Hill left a 1943 manuscript of some 225 pages dealing with the history of the tune of *The Star-Spangled Banner.*[71]

Although he had spent twenty years investigating the history of *The Star-Spangled Banner,* Hill was unable to finish the work to his satisfaction. As with the dissertation, "he didn't think it was good enough and he would always want to go and do one more piece of research."[72]

On the other hand, *The Star-Spangled Banner* research may have kept Hill out of the military services. In October of 1942 he received his first induction papers. Concerned about the completion of *The Star-Spangled Banner* report, Spivacke wrote to the Librarian of Congress who in turn wrote Hill's draft board requesting a month's deferment so the book could be completed. Although the second induction papers had not arrived, Hill was "about to join up . . . in spite of the fact that the book was far from finished" when President Roosevelt

> appointed a new Man-Power Board, whose first action was to issue an order that all men over 38 should stick to their jobs because it was felt that they could serve the war effort more effectively keeping civilian life going than they could puffing about with the troops.[73]

Mary Rogers recalls that she and Hill were working frantically at the Library on the bibliography of songsters when Spivacke called with news of the new ruling. Mary and Hill were in the habit of returning to the Library after dinner to work on the bibliography. Spivacke ended his call with the advice they quit for the night and go to a movie — which they did.

Mary Rogers had begun to work at the Library of Congress in 1933 as a temporary assistant addressing envelopes for the Coolidge

---

[69] (Portland, Me.: n.p., 1951); also issued separately the same year by the Library of Congress.

[70] U.S. Congress. House. Committee on the Judiciary, subcommittee no. 4. *The Star-Spangled Banner*. Eighty-fifth Congress, Second Session, 2, 22, 28 May 1958.

[71] As an aspect of the 1976 American Bicentennial celebration, William Lichtenwanger published his own history of "The Music of 'The Star-Spangled Banner': From Ludgate Hill to Capitol Hill" in *Library of Congress Quarterly Journal of Acquisitions* 34 (July 1977): 136-70.

[72] Rogers interview.

[73] Hill to T. Franklin Currier, 6 November 1942. Hill Papers.

Festival. At the time, Carl Engel's secretary Mrs. Fay was about to retire. Mrs. Fay sent Mary to take dictation from Engel so he would see how competent she was. Engel kept Mary on as secretary of the Coolidge Foundation until 1 January 1934, when she was put on the Library's payroll as Secretary of the Music Division and the Foundations.

Soon after Dick began at the Library he and Mary developed a special relationship which Dick hoped would culminate in their marriage. He pled with Mary to marry him, but she wouldn't because she was Roman Catholic and he a divorced man.[74] Mary explains that

> At that time I could not have gotten married in the Church. . . . My mother was living and she was dependent upon me; I would have had to have her live with me and it would have been very difficult. . . . I could think of the conflicts there.

Hill acceded to Mary's feelings with the remark:

> I think that you're the kind of a person who would be very happy if you could share the love of your man with the love of your religion. Then you would be happy. . . . I realize you might be very unhappy and that would make me unhappy.[75]

Rather than marriage, they continued their friendship and comradeship until the time of Hill's death.

Because of their work at the chamber music concerts sponsored by the Coolidge and Whittall Foundations, both Dick and Mary had what were called "all hours" passes to admit them to the Library at any time. Concert nights all members of the Music Division were required to be on hand. Before the war, they dressed formally; during and after, normal street attire was worn. Frequently on nights when there were no concerts Dick and Mary would return to the Library to work, first on *The Star-Spangled Banner* report, later on *Notes*. Mary recalls that Dick would go into the stacks to look for something. A little before 10 p.m., when the lights were to go off in the stacks, Mary would go to warn him. "Oh, yes," he'd say, "just one more minute" and then the lights would go off and they'd have to find their way out in total darkness. Spivacke told a story about Dick stranded in the dark in the stacks; he just sat down and waited till a guard came by to lead him out. The astonished guard and his colleagues bought Hill a flashlight with instructions not to venture into the stacks without it!

From 1941 to 1946, Edward N. Waters, Assistant Chief of the Music Division, Library of Congress, was president of the Music

---

[74] Information and terminology from Hoch interview.

[75] Quotes from Rogers interview.

Library Association. Although the normal term of office was two years, officers were frozen for the duration of the war because it was impractical to have a national meeting and election. *Notes,* the occasional journal of the Music Library Association, had been something of a stepchild since 1940 when then-president George Sherman Dickinson effectively removed the founding editor, Eva Judd O'Meara, by naming an editorial board on which she did not sit. During Waters' first term as president, there was considerable desire and agitation to renew and regularize the journal. Both Waters and John T. Windle of the Newberry Library gathered cost estimates from printers in their respective cities. Correspondence between Waters and Windle about printers' estimates, sample title-pages, content, and so forth continued until 15 November 1943 when Waters advised Windle that "*Notes* was being printed. . . . We went ahead and had the printing done here because the price was more satisfactory than the Chicago price. . . . Dick Hill is the new editor-in-chief."[76] And so it began; a particularly felicitous union of editor and journal which ended only at the death of the editor in 1961. One of the longest editorships in American musical/library history, Hill and *Notes* are inseparable. He solicited manuscripts, he wrote editorials as "Notes for *Notes,*" he cajoled commercial firms for advertisements, he commandeered friends and colleagues as aides, he paid the printing bills. He initiated membership campaigns to more nearly equate costs and distribution; he pled with readers for editorial direction, for reaction, for participation in the journal's development. From the beginning of his association with it, *Notes* seems to have been the dominant aspect of his affiliation with the MLA. Hill was never an elected officer, never served on a committee, but never neglected an MLA meeting, issue, query, or printer's bill. Although his financial involvement in *Notes* and MLA may not have been the most substantive aspect of his service, it may have been the most important for it kept *Notes* alive, and there seem to have been post-war years when everyone else was doing something else, when the periodic appearance of *Notes* was, in fact, the primary indication of MLA's existence. Hill himself complained:

> For some strange reason it always seems to me that the magazine goes out into a great void where nobody pays the slightest attention to it. I know we get a terrific volume of reference correspondence from people who are actually members of MLA, which I answer by referring them to some specific article or listing which they should have known about themselves.[77]

[76] Edward N. Waters to John T. Windle, 15 November 1943. Waters Papers. The account of Hill's appointment as editor of *Notes* is reproduced, with some variation, from the author's history of the Music Library Association written on the occasion of its 50th anniversary: *Notes* 37 (1981): 763-822.

[77] Hill to Howard Haycraft, 20 July 1948. Hill Papers.

For the first issue of the printed *Notes,* Hill designed the title logo,[78] Waters wrote an urgent "Notes for the *Notes,*" but no advertisements clustered around the Table of Contents. Funded only by its treasury, the first issue stood in somber black relieved only by Hill's logo. Doubtless only "old-timers" can recreate the feelings of professional security and pride that printed *Notes* generated; certainly none could foresee the influence it would have on one's professional life. *Notes* flourished by subscription, advertising, and Hill's generosity. Its departments reflected contemporary needs: Record reviews were summarized by Philip L. Miller and Louise Pratt Howe in 1948 and continued into the present by Kurtz Myers. Publishers' and dealers' catalogues were crucial as commercial enterprise returned to normal after the war, so Hill was at pains to make their existence known to the profession. Those who came onto the music library scene after 1960 know the name Richard S. Hill, but nothing has recreated for them the warm, personal feeling older members experience at the mention of Dick Hill. He truly kept *Notes,* and by extension its parent organization, going through thin and thinner, for *Notes* never had a thick during Hill's lifetime. He was so vital to the Association that there was general concern it might not survive his death. Although nothing dramatic occurred, some of the Association's memorable moments may have been the Yale meeting in 1964 as it became apparent the Association would live, and indeed was expanding its activities.

From today's perspective it is difficult to appreciate *Notes*' struggle to become known, both in the United States and Europe; to gain and retain advertisers; to increase its circulation. By 1947, printing costs for small runs like *Notes* had become prohibitive. Increased advertising was not feasible; wider circulation seemed the appropriate solution. MLA had conducted its first membership campaign in 1939-40. The Committee[79] had prepared an extensive mailing list of music libraries, general libraries which included music, radio station libraries, and music school and college faculty to whom were sent a letter descriptive of the MLA, a summary of its principal activities, and an enrollment blank to be returned with $2 annual dues to the secretary-treasurer. Summary articles in the *Library Journal* and *Special Libraries* emphasized the publications aspect of the MLA's activities.[80] That campaign, which brought in 104 new

---

[78] "The cover was designed by Dick Hill, and the inside layout was more or less my own idea influenced (for the better) by the printer's advice." Waters to Richard S. Angell, 16 December 1943. Waters Papers.

[79] The committee members, chosen for geographic coverage of the whole country, were Jessica Fredricks, San Francisco; Louise Chapman, Minneapolis; Isabelle S. Snodgrass, New Orleans; and Richard S. Angell, chairman, New York City.

[80] *Library Journal* 65 (1940): 344, and *Special Libraries* 31 (1940): 137. The *Special Libraries* notice specifically mentioned the codes for cataloguing music and records, the subject heading lists, *Notes,* and the papers on training for music librarianship which had appeared in the *ALA Bulletin* and the *Library Journal.*

members, was followed by others in 1942, 1944, 1947, 1948, et al. As printing costs for the Second Series of *Notes* continually exceeded MLA's available revenues, Hill nagged the membership and readers of *Notes* for help.

> For the five or six years after NOTES first began to appear in print, the number of new members and subscribers continued to grow in a very satisfactory fashion, thus making it possible gradually to increase the size of the magazine and extend the coverage of its reports and reviews of new music materials. On the theory that a still more comprehensive coverage would attract further members and subscribers, additional pages and departments were added. . . . As a consequence, the costs of publishing the magazine have increased, whereas the circulation has not. Worse still, it is becoming constantly more difficult to sign up the basic quota of advertisements, and the income from this source has dropped by several hundred dollars per issue. . . . It would seem, therefore, that the time had come when either the size of the magazine must be sharply reduced or the circulation increased. Now the magazine has always been a joint operation designed to render a service to music librarians and others in allied professions. Obviously, this purpose can only be completely realized if the magazine is kept as comprehensive as it can be made, and if the service is constantly being extended to more and more people. Of the two alternate solutions mentioned above, therefore, it goes against the grain to cut the size of the magazine, whereas an increase in circulation will work for the benefit of everyone concerned. George Schneider and his Membership Committee are doing everything in their power to bring about this happy state of affairs, but no committee can possibly reach all of the potential new members and subscribers. Surely most of the present members and subscribers, however, must each know a few individuals and institutions that could use the magazine with profit. Such new members and subscribers do not all have to be professional music librarians. They can be private record collectors, performers, music teachers, music stores — in short, anyone who likes to keep abreast of new publications, and who has the money to pay his dues or subscription. If, however, the present members and subscribers are unwilling to accept their share of the responsibility in the matter, and do not see to it that the circulation is boosted to a figure where economical operation is possible, then the only other alternative is to make future issues smaller and less comprehensive. It is up to each individual reading this paragraph to decide in which direction he or she prefers to see NOTES move. Leaving it up to George in this instance will simply not be good enough.[81]

---

[81] "Notes for *Notes*," *Notes* 8 (1950-51): 679-80.

George had, indeed, done his share. In his committee report to the December 1948 meeting in Chicago, George Schneider, head of the MGM Studio's music library, reported mailing

> over 3,000 brochures and/or pamphlets to prospective members or subscribers. We have sent "follow-up" letters to about half that number. We have attempted to cover the membership of ASCAP, MTNA, the major symphony orchestras, and NASM. The results have not been too encouraging; on the other hand, we are getting responses to some of our "blurbs" sent out at the beginning of our activity. . . .
>
> With the exception of the printing of pamphlets sent to me from Washington, occasional special delivery stamps, and the postage necessary to keep me informed as to additions to our rosters, your committee has been of no expense to the Association. We have personally paid for the printing of the brochures, attended to the addressing of the same, paid for the postage on the follow-ups, and have provided some members of the Committee with stationery.[82]

Hill prepared subscription blanks in the form of a double postcard for distribution to MLA members so they, in turn, could personally recruit three or four subscribers.

> The wider the circulation, the greater the reputation of the Association, and the higher the rates that can be charged for advertising.[83]

But increased circulation to subscribers rather than members required an adjustment of *Notes'* editorial policy; "not very many . . . will pay out good money to read about a music librarian's technical problems, association news, and shop-talk." The answer lay in the creation of another journal for "purely library news," a "supplement for members only" while the coverage of "reference functions – the reviews, bibliographies, essays, information about phonograph records, eventually perhaps a periodical index" remain in a *Notes* "designed for more general consumption."[84] The first *Supplement for Members* appeared in September of 1947; membership dues of $4.50 and subscription fees of $3 reflected the adjusted service to the membership. To save money, Hill typed the *Supplement* on his Varityper and pasted up photoready copy for the printer. The *Supplement* continued for 36 numbers before it faltered, a victim of Hill's death. *Notes* itself lost a whole year before settling down to its third phase under the editorship of Harold Samuel.

Waters remembers Hill's response to his designation as editor: "Fine; I've always wanted to edit a magazine."[85] Although one can

---

[82] *Notes: Supplement for Members*, nos. 6 & 7 (December & March 1949): 21-22.

[83] *Notes* 4 (1946-47): 228.

[84] Quotes from Hill's introduction to the first supplement: "The Whys and Wherefores," *Notes: Supplement for Members*, no. 1 (September 1947): 3-4.

[85] Waters interview.

study the issues themselves or Krummel's retrospective appraisal,[86] a great deal of Hill's philosophy and aspirations for the journal may be found in his *Notes* correspondence. He aimed at one "readable" article in each issue. While he was willing to print "lists and bibliographies that are obviously intended to be used as such," he balked at articles which were essentially bibliographies because subscribers would have "nothing to read at all."[87]

But the character of the "readable" article also had to be carefully considered:

> It seems best to avoid straight historical essays, except when they bear on the holdings of some library. . . . In order to give the magazine a character of its own, differentiating it clearly in function from the AMS Journal and the [Musical] Quarterly, we are trying to round up stuff that is bibliothecal in character. There was a group at the [MLA] meeting in San Francisco that complained heartily that *Notes* was not a music library magazine, but had begun to resemble an ordinary music magazine.[88] It might even be something that could be issued by the American Musicological Society. I am not kidding myself about this being actually true, of course, but I have been trying to aim a bit over the heads of the usual music librarian in a public library. I want to continue to do this, since the magazine goes to a lot of university libraries also, and we obviously have to take their interests into consideration. At the same time, it ought to be possible to aim at more things which both types of libraries could actually use — and by this I mean material which is not merely something that could conceivably interest them, but which contributes to their welfare and makes for better libraries and librarians.[89]

It must have been difficult for Hill to hear some of the more visible music librarians publicly faulting *Notes*. From his point of view its issues were larger than MLA could afford because ever more material was being published and, if *Notes'* review sections were to

---

[86] Donald W. Krummel, "Twenty Years of *Notes* — A Retrospect," *Notes* 21 (1963-64): 56-82.

[87] Hill to Walter H. Rubsamen, 28 July 1949. Hill Papers.

[88] At the MLA Business Meeting in San Francisco in January 1950, there were expressions of dissatisfaction with *Notes* and its *Supplement*. Some wanted information related to library problems returned to *Notes*; some wanted the *Supplement* for information about the regional chapters of MLA; some saw too little difference between the *Journal* of the AMS and *Notes*. Hill, who was admittedly aiming "just a little" over the heads of "a very large proportion of the members of MLA" to "encourage them to widen their horizons," resolved to "concentrate on articles with a bibliothecal flavor — that is, bibliographies, reports on holdings of a library or individual, etc. . . . [and] articles involving American music, since too few magazines publish such things and I have just a touch of chauvinism about me." Hill to Oswald Jonas, 4 July 1951. Hill Papers.

[89] Hill to Walter H. Rubsamen, 22 July 1950. Hill Papers.

be as comprehensive as possible, they would require increasing space. That space cost Hill more than $2,000 in 1951 "before the June issue was paid for."[90]

The mechanics of printing, pasting up page proof, and mailing have been delightfully recounted by William Lichtenwanger in "When *Notes* Was Young: 1945-1960."[91] But policy, as Lichtenwanger remarks, was always solely Dick's. In the latter years membership mumbling about the character of the journal became more and more audible to the point that elected officials were prepared to defend *Notes'* editorial policy on the floor of the business meeting of the Music Library Association, 4 February 1961. The issue, in fact, was not raised, but grumbles about "the Washington Mafia" continued until the editorship of *Notes* began to rotate among other libraries.

"Bred a musicologist," as Hill described himself,[92] he was competent and willing to question hypotheses and conclusions of articles submitted for publication. Usually he would re-research the issue himself — "out-of-hours" as Mary Rogers pointed out, hence more of those evenings in the Library. If his research reinforced his doubts about the article in question, he might send it back to the author for revision; he might ask a recognized scholar of the subject to read and comment upon the piece; or, he might reject it outright. Non-musicological articles such as bibliographies or appraisals of current interest he revised, enlarged — yes, rewrote himself. Lichtenwanger mentioned that he (Lichtenwanger) often wondered about authors' reactions when they saw what Hill had done to their contributions.

> Dick's own feeling was that editors should be read but not heard. And he didn't blink an eye over completely rewriting somebody, even high professionals in the musicology field who were frequently the ones who needed it most because their English had the least style.[93]

Indeed, Lichtenwanger indicated that as Dick's editorship matured, he became more and more unable to print anything without rewriting it.[94] Mary Rogers spoke of his saying, in response to anger from agitated authors, "Why should they be upset with me; I didn't do anything."[95] Hill reasoned that his willingness to allow rewritten authors full credit for vastly improved articles should keep them from complaining too much. In an unfinished document found in his *Notes* file, Hill articulated his editorial stance.

---

[90] Hill to Oswald Jonas, 4 July 1951. Hill Papers.

[91] *Notes* 39 (1982): 7-30.

[92] Hill to Hans Tischler, 22 November 1946. Hill Papers.

[93] Lichtenwanger interview.

[94] ". . . He (Hill) could seldom bring himself to print anything unless he had either written or rewritten it, and that got harder and harder to manage as the years went by." William Lichtenwanger to Eva Judd O'Meara, 26 June 1961. Hill Papers.

[95] Rogers interview.

Seven long years of editing a magazine have taught me quite a lot about authors. Usually those with a fair amount of experience realize that an editor's job is to help his authors, rearranging and polishing an essay with an objectivity that no author can possibly have in regard to his own writing, thus slanting it for the special audience of the magazine and making it easier for the reader to assimilate. On the other hand, there are a fair number of individuals who seem to be utterly unable to conceive that anyone can know as well as they how an idea should be expressed, and they therefore hotly resent the simplest changes, completely misunderstanding the editor's intentions. Naturally, it is a great deal pleasanter for the editor when working with the first type, and invariably the final result is better — partly because of the greater experience of the author but also because practically every passage of prose can be improved through the sympathetic cooperation of two minds. Despite this, I have long since learned to understand the feelings of the second type, and even if I can't bring myself to admire them, I invariably respect them — even to the point of coddling them. With people who I don't know and with whom I can't discuss changes, I make it a general practice to assume that they belong to the second type until I've had a chance to learn to the contrary. It makes life easier all around, and since I like people and want them to like me, it is the only safe policy. I don't claim that I've always followed the policy. I had to learn it the hard way.[96]

Using Margaret Mott's three-part "Bibliography of Songsheets: Sports and Recreations in American Popular Songs"[97] as an example, Lichtenwanger described Hill's editorial procedure.

Peggy [Mott] did the basic work and sent in her copy consisting of songs in various categories — for instance, football, baseball. But as far as I know she didn't do any work at the Library of Congress. She had a very nice collection there . . . in the Grosvenor Library, but of course the Library of Congress had tons of things in these categories that she didn't have access to and didn't know about. And I can remember night after night that Dick would go down there [to the stacks] — nearly everybody else was leaving — he'd go down to search out various candidates for addition to her lists. And I think he chose, probably, nearly all the illustrations [and] attended to having the plates made.[98]

As Lichtenwanger mused, what would be one's reaction to unacknowledged enhancement of that kind, seen for the first time after it was already in print?

---

[96] Hill to Sigmund Levarie, 4 April 1950. Hill Papers.

[97] *Notes* 6 (1948-49): 379-418; 7 (1949-50): 522-61; 9 (1951-52): 33-62.

[98] Lichtenwanger interview.

But you can hardly fault a person who paid for his "indulgences," if that's what a few agitated authors thought. Urging concision on an author, Hill remarked his concern about the length of *Notes* articles

> because it is getting to the point where I have to pay out of my own pocket for the added expense if the issue runs too long, and you can easily imagine that I can find more pleasant ways of getting my spare cash spent than by paying to publish somebody else's article.[99]
>
> Believe it or not, I don't *like* to cut articles, but I just don't have enough cash to print everything that can conceivably be said on a subject, and thus I sometimes have to cut.[100]

There was also the quality of the submitted manuscripts to consider. Articles "were so wretchedly prepared" it was "absolutely necessary to concentrate on them."[101] ("Concentrate" was Hill's euphemism for "rewrite.")

You have to wonder if the advertisers' segment of *Notes* may not have been the bugaboo. Four times a year, without prior appointments, Hill used his vacation time from the Library of Congress and his own money to travel to New York City where he pounded the pavements, hat in hand, seeking paid advertisements for *Notes*. But that wasn't even the extent of it. Once a publisher agreed to advertise in *Notes* it was a question of size of ad, frequency, and design. In the extant *Notes* files at the Library of Congress there are as many as four letters in seven calendar days between Hill and a single advertiser which address type face, border design, position within the issue, contents of a list of the publisher's recent publications, etc. Multiply that effort by the number of advertisers per issue for an idea of the work involved. It is greatly to Hill's credit that he managed the demanding New York visits with the grace and charm Feist remembers (pp. 373-74 in this volume); his own account of one New York trip varies greatly from Feist's.

> I didn't expect to get ads as easily as a year ago, but my trip to New York was even more barren of results than I had feared, and when I got back here it was necessary to send out around 70 letters to see if I couldn't round up enough to risk going to press.[102]

Yet Lichtenwanger acknowledges he

> heard from many people that Dick, in some ways, was a very different person when he was in New York. . . . He'd go out and visit with Walter and Evelyn Hinrichsen. . . . It

---

[99] Hill to Walter Rubsamen, 27 July 1949. Hill Papers.

[100] Hill to Walter Rubsamen, 2 February 1949. Hill Papers.

[101] Hill to Albert B. Earl, 10 January 1952. Hill Papers.

[102] Hill to Sydney Beck, 26 July 1948. Hill Papers.

was a release for him, really the only release he had because he didn't take the annual leave . . . in order to go up to a hotel for two or three weeks at a time like normal people did. He got his relief and fun that way.[103]

To save money, Hill obtained a complete catalogue of the printer's type faces and border type with which he designed many of the ads and positioned all so that if the number of publishers who bought quarter-page ads didn't work out properly, Hill had to resolve it some way. It was a man-killing task — and it did. In addition to carrying his full-time workload within the Music Division, Hill was intellectual monitor of the articles in *Notes,* editor of *Notes,* advertising agent, advertisement designer, copy editor, layout designer, and last, but certainly not least, the man who paid the bill. Mary Rogers, treasurer of the Music Library Association from 1946 until 1967, states unequivocally that Hill paid about half of the expenses of publishing *Notes* during his editorship.[104] And that half was actually paid out *after* Hill and the other staff members of the Music Division had donated their time and efforts to perform regular printers' tasks in order to keep the financial outlay as small as possible. Little wonder Hill felt himself

> much less the editor of *Notes* than its business manager . . .
> hence my preoccupation periodically with the advertisers. . . .
> I have to write some seventy advertisers to persuade them
> to come through with a little cash for an advertisement.[105]

But the disclaimer about his editorship vis-à-vis business manager's hat cannot be taken too seriously. Few besides editor could preempt desired volumes for review or expect to see a review of some seven and a quarter printed pages in a section where reviews half that size predominated. Most Schoenberg scores were reviewed (actually analyzed) by Hill, as were scores of many Broadway shows and song books.[106] Nor was the tone of Hill's reviews any less

---

[103] Lichtenwanger interview. The beginnings of Hill's friendship with the Hinrichsens is described below, pp. 42-43.

[104] Mary Rogers, speaking in her role as secretary/treasurer of the MLA from 1946 to 1948 and treasurer, 1946-67, elaborated on *Notes'* financial circumstances. "Anytime I needed the money I'd say we need it for such and such and I'd get a check for such and such and that would be it. I used to bawl him out and say 'Look, you're going beyond what we can do [with MLA money]' — [*Notes*] was growing too fast for what we were coming up with. He'd say, 'That's all right, I'll take care of it.' I would say that he paid very close to half of *Notes.*" Rogers interview.

[105] Hill to Walter Rubsamen, 22 July 1950. Hill Papers.

[106] Hill had a life-long love of musical shows. The Gervais letters include many reports of Hill's theater-going, none more spectacular than: "Carl Engel, Koussevitsky, Irving Berlin, Cole Porter and I saw the opening of Gershwin's 'Porgy and Bess' in Boston a couple of weeks ago" (Hill to Gervais, 14 October 1935). On another occasion Hill attended Robert Sherwood's Pulitzer prize winning play *Idiot's Delight* in the company of Nicolai Sokoloff. Sokoloff was a good friend of the Lunts, stars of the play, "so we were all taken around to their dressing rooms later" (Hill to Gervais, 3 June 1936).

straightforward or candid than his correspondence with authors and publishers. The lengthy review alluded to evaluated the fifth edition of *Grove's Dictionary of Music and Musicians* in which Hill took editor Eric Blom to task for nationalism, reprinting obsolete information, omission, and haphazard coverage of American topics. After seven pages he found that

> musicologists working in any field except that of English music will do much better to wait on *Musik in Geschichte und Gegenwart,* which is a far sounder publication on practically all counts. Naturally, in all libraries wherein the language problem is paramount, the unique position of Grove V as the only large music dictionary in English makes its acquisition mandatory, but the proportion of dead to green timber in this new edition will leave many individuals and institutions with a difficult choice to make—a choice that, for example, may not lead to the purchase of copies for all branch libraries.
>
> It should go without saying that I am more than a little sad to arrive at this conclusion.[107]

After some early criticism of the scholarly level of *Notes* reviews, Hill and his section editors were at pains to match material to be reviewed with appropriate reviewers. Only knowledgeable reviewers could achieve perspective and add "the salt of criticism" which so appealed to Hill.[108]

Notes was the first American periodical to introduce a regular department of music reviews. Beginning with the June 1945 issue, editions of early music, "because so many libraries feature them," and full scores, "by and large they are the most expensive and advice regarding their purchase will be correspondingly more valuable" were reviewed in *Notes*.[109] One can scarcely fault the quality of the reviewers Hill lined up for the new department: Lou Harrison, Harrison Kerr, Erich Leinsdorf, Nicolas Nabokov, Charles Seeger, and Virgil Thomson.

To Eva Judd O'Meara, whom he addressed as "Original Editor," he confessed perplexity about the

> sort of magazine Notes ought to be. Obviously, bibliography has to be our bread and butter, and if reviews are a form of bibliography then you can call it the roast beef as well. This doesn't leave much room for solid reading matter, and means I have to be extremely selective about it.[110]

O'Meara, who admired Hill's development of *Notes*, mentioned her desire for a

---

[107] *Notes* 12 (1954-55): 91-92.

[108] Hill to Florence Kretzschmar, 16 October 1950. Hill Papers.

[109] *Notes* 2 (1944-45): 183.

[110] Hill to Eva Judd O'Meara, 17 April 1947. Hill Papers.

question-and-answer department in "Notes." . . . I tried to
do something of the sort when I was editing "Notes," and
I will own that no one else asked any questions or answered
them except in one case. You are making so much more
of the undertaking, and there is so much more interest, it
might go if offered now.[111]

Several issues of *Notes* in the mid 1940s carried a "Notes and Queries"
paragraph as part of "Notes for *Notes*," but the department didn't
"go," as O'Meara put it.

Phonograph records were a life-long interest of Hill. During
the Cornell years he bought record-making equipment in order to
record performances of his own compositions, to record Schoenberg
performances off-the-air,[112] and to produce Christmas gifts for his
friends. Though there's no evidence of a master plan or progressive
scheme in *Notes*' development, Hill remarked his desire for a record
section as early as 1944: ". . . I have been planning on starting a
rather elaborate [record] review and discussion section. . . ."[113] Yet
he was loath to devote a great deal of space to record reviews, for
they were reviewed in many periodicals, while

> There is no one place where you can find reviews of so many
> books on music, and practically no place at all where you
> can get reasonably decent reviews of music.[114]

The solution came in the form of an idea of Gladys Chamberlain,
a staff member of the 58th St. Music Library of the New York Public
Library. Chamberlain reported to Philip L. Miller that some public
libraries were indexing record reviews and might be willing to publish
their findings. Miller passed the idea along to Hill who thought it
"divinely inspired, perfect, glorious, and [the] ideal answer. It is
something that nobody [i.e., periodical] at all does."[115] The trick,
then, was to work out details and find a willing compiler.

For the March 1948 issue, Philip L. Miller and Louise Pratt
Howe prepared an evaluative summary of record reviews printed in
eight other journals during the preceding November, December, and
January. The feature, called "Index to Record Reviews," was so
popular it has been continued to the present by Kurtz Myers, formerly of the Detroit Public Library. As 33-1/3 rpm records super-
seded 78s, acquisition librarians were required to replace existing
record collections. The process could have been quite involved were
it not for the concise information available in the "Index." That led

---

[111] Eva Judd O'Meara to Hill, 10 October 1945. Hill Papers.

[112] Information from Hill to Gervais, 11 March 1936. Gervais Letters.

[113] Hill to H. Dorothy Tilly, 16 June 1944. Hill Papers.

[114] Hill to Philip L. Miller, undated but clearly late November or early December
1947. Hill Papers.

[115] Ibid.

Hill to propose annual cumulations of the "Index" in conjunction with *Notes,* and five-year cumulations to be published commercially.

Two annual cumulations, the "Index" segments from volumes 7 and 8, were published under the aegis of the Music Library Association by Hill and the *Notes* printer. For the five-year cumulation the Music Library Association, in the person of Hill, negotiated with Crown Publishers. After a great deal of contract revision and with a great deal of hesitance and wariness on MLA's part, the appropriate officers signed the contract in February of 1954. The volume, *Record Ratings,* was to be compiled by Kurtz Myers from the twenty quarterly issues of *Notes.*

To avoid re-setting type as much as possible, the entries which would have been the third and fourth volumes of annual cumulations (*Notes,* vols. 9 and 10) had been brought together into two long series of galleys. These were in the printer's shop. Type from volume 5 of the "Index" was held to be mixed into the revised volumes 3 and 4. Volumes 1 and 2 had to be re-set because the type had been distributed. The whole procedure was further complicated by a style change in volumes 4 and 5 to which volumes 1 to 3 needed to be revised.

Hill planned for Myers to revise the galleys of volumes 3 and 4, adding additional reviews, altering cross references, and revising the style of volume 3 entries. Hill would then paste up a dummy cumulating them, and at the same time mix in the entries from volume 5. Entries from volumes 1 and 2 would then be revised by Myers and entered into the volumes 3 to 5 sequence. From the master galleys Hill would make up the page proofs from which Myers would compile the performer index.

They were scarcely started before the difficulties began. Crown's representatives consistently talked manuscript when, in fact, there would never be a manuscript. The type held by the printer of *Notes,* the re-set volumes 1 and 2, and the revisions and additions, all in type, were the only manuscript. The MLA, through its agents Hill and Myers, was

> expected to supply not only the crude copy, but also edit it, do the proof reading, paste up proof dummy, and see the whole thing through the press.[116]

Crown was to be supplied with uncut volumes ready to be bound.

The cost of "renting" the printer's type became a major issue — with Hill very much in the middle. "Crown's shenanigans have made my relations with Notes' printer strained and difficult. . . ."[117] The printer threatened to melt the type unless his fee was paid; Crown mentioned removing the type and having the book printed elsewhere.

At his end, Myers worked slower and slower so that a schedule of months became years, again with Hill caught between Crown and the printer. While attempting to mollify Crown about the pace of

---

[116] Hill to Robert Simon, 10 September 1953. Hill Papers.

[117] Hill to Robert Simon, 12 August 1956. Hill Papers.

the project, Hill had to urge all possible speed to Myers' efforts and try to maintain workable relations with the printer through various issues of *Notes*. (Myers' data was verified by Hill in the Library of Congress—in addition to the other elements of his work schedule. Verification of Myers' data frequently involved locating a copy of the record in question to identify its contents.)

When the volume was finally published, June 1956, Crown reneged on its royalties. As late as 4 August 1957, Hill wrote Crown's Robert Simon that nothing could be gained by further discussion of the royalties Crown owed.

> Myers and I worked our heads off to supply Crown with a "satisfactory" book and it is already long past the time when Crown should have paid the MLA for the use of its type, and Myers and myself for our labors. [118]

Hill sought to resolve Crown's stated causes for withholding payment by suggesting a *Supplement* to bring the coverage up-to-date and, at the same time, aid Crown in selling its remaining copies. Miraculously Hill persuaded the MLA to "re-invest" its royalties—royalties never received—in a *Supplement* on which he and Myers collaborated—at least until 2 July 1958. On that date Hill wrote Myers the "devastating" news that New York City record people felt the switch to stereo would be "as complete and thorough as the switch from the 78 rpm discs to the LPs," and that soon it would "be impossible to buy a monaural recording" (an excerpt of the 2 July 1958 letter is reprinted below, pp. 395-97). That circumstance would kill any sales of both the *Supplement* and the original *Record Ratings* because they dealt with only monaural recordings. For whatever reason or combination of reasons, *Record Ratings* and its *Supplement* disappeared from Hill's subsequent correspondence, although the "Index" continued in *Notes*.

*   *   *   *   *

Returning to the chronological account of events in Hill's life, the Second World War

> caught America unprepared in all sorts of ways. . . . Among the implements of war we lacked, not the least was printed information about enemy countries and other strategic parts of the globe. The intense effort of planning and carrying on a total war . . . placed a heavy burden on library facilities. [119]

---

[118] Hill to Robert Simon, 4 August 1957. Hill Papers.

[119] Reuben Peiss, "European Wartime Acquisitions and the Library of Congress Mission," *Library Journal* 71 (1946): 864.

Wartime acquisitions for United States Government agencies were realized through the Interdepartmental Committee for the Acquisition of Foreign Publications. The IDC, as it was called, was organized in 1941 to centralize acquisition, analysis, and distribution of foreign information. The Library of Congress requested, and received from the IDC, "several hundred thousand pieces (books, pamphlets, journals, newspapers) in the original, as well as additional hundreds of thousands of pieces on film."[120]

Another wartime source of acquisitions was the efforts of Manuel Sanchez, a Foreign Representative of the Library of Congress who toured the Iberian Penninsula, Algeria, France, and Italy between April 1943 and May 1945, buying for the Library. Sanchez' presence on the scene secured "many publications that would otherwise have been lost."

As it became apparent that the end of the war was coming, both the Library of Congress and the Association of Research Libraries looked for a way to acquire European, especially German, publications. There seem to have been two major alternatives: one, that ARL and the other library associations form their own group of representatives to go to Europe as soon as the war was over; the other, that the Library of Congress continue to use its European network to acquire books for all American libraries. In the end, the latter alternative, supplemented by the Library of Congress Mission to Germany, was used.

The first IDC office in Germany was set up in June of 1945 in Wiesbaden. From there a team of librarians — some actually members of the U.S. Army, some not — toured Germany visiting libraries, publishers, and dealers to appraise damage, availability of stock, and begin negotiations for the purchase of multiple copies for export. Army personnel were in charge of occupied Germany so Library of Congress agents worked "within the framework of the Army." A warehouse in Frankfurt was assigned for storage of materials awaiting shipment to the United States. On 15 January 1946, seven additional members of the Library of Congress Mission to Germany arrived in Frankfurt with the objective of acquiring

> a minimum of three copies of every saleable book published during the war years and up to 25 copies (and, in exceptional instances, 50 or 100) of important titles.

Military authorities agreed that

> the Library of Congress would act as the sole and central collecting agency for captured publications turned over by the Army and for purchases in countries where normal commercial channels were not yet reopened. All acquisi-

---

[120] Ibid. This summary of the devices with which the Library of Congress acquired wartime publications and the preliminaries of the LC acquisitions mission is drawn from the Peiss article.

tions would be thrown into a common pool, and distribution priorities would be worked out by a committee representing American libraries and learned societies.

The Committee to Advise on the Distribution of Foreign Acquisitions, as it was entitled, presided over the distribution of materials among some 111 American libraries. The libraries deposited funds with the Library of Congress against which the price of volumes assigned to them was charged.

The members of the Mission who arrived in Frankfurt in January of 1946 to complete the staff of the Mission were David H. Clift, associate librarian designate of Yale University; Harry M. Lydenberg, American Library Association; Don D. Travis, formerly a member of the Office of Censorship; Julius Allen, Legislative Reference Service, Library of Congress; Richard S. Hill; Daniel Shacter, previously on the staff of the IDC; and Janet Emerson, formerly on the staff of the Acquisitions Department, Library of Congress. Hill was notified of the assignment the day before Thanksgiving 1945; the group sailed from New York aboard the Queen Mary on 6 January 1946.

Initially Hill was not assigned to music acquisition. Like the other members of the Mission he was expected to spend most of his time collecting confiscated materials which would be useful for research[121] with the idea that any music materials which turned up would be cleared through him. His special assignment was to serve as liaison officer for the collection of materials in the British Zone.[122]

Hill considered his assignment "completely disastrous from the point of view of music." He foresaw an accumulation of music in which there would be

> a tremendous amount of duplication in Nazi song books and popular biographies of composers, but practically none of the important musicological studies, and very few of the larger music publications.[123]

One of Hill's first contacts in Germany was Walter Hinrichsen, son of the owner of the C. F. Peters music publishing house in Leipzig. As the Nazis' power increased, the Hinrichsens, a Jewish family, ran into trouble. Walter went to Chicago in 1934 as Peters' representative for the Western Hemisphere; he subsequently became an American citizen and married Evelyn Merrell, secretary to Luther Evans, Librarian of Congress. His brother Max emigrated to London in 1937 where he set up a separate publishing business. A third son, Hans, ran the Leipzig firm until 1938 when

---

[121] Hill to Walter Hinrichsen, 20 January 1946. Hill Papers.

[122] Luther H. Evans, "The Librarian's Page," *Library of Congress Information Bulletin* 4 (2-8 March 1946): 2.

[123] Hill to Walter Hinrichsen, 20 January 1946. Hill Papers.

the Nazis finally forced the family to "sell out," although . . .
no one in the family received any money. The father, two
daughters, and Hans died or were killed in concentration
camps during the war.[124]

Walter enlisted in the U.S. Army and happened to be in a detachment
which occupied Leipzig. Before he left the area, Walter posted a
sign on the door of his publishing house declaring it the property
of an American citizen. When the Russians took over Leipzig, they
respected the sign and eventually recognized Hinrichsen "as the
rightful owner of Peters Edition, Litolff, and associated firms."[125]

At the time Hill was in Germany, Hinrichsen was Music Control
Officer of the Office of the Director of Information Control in the
United States' Military Government for Germany. Hill immediately
threw himself on Hinrichsen's mercies, asking advice and information
about the state of music publishing in occupied Germany. Working
in conjunction with Hinrichsen, Hill was able to travel around
Germany, to talk personally with publishers, agents, book sellers,
and librarians. After March he made his headquarters in Berlin.[126]

As in the other disciplines, the desirable music materials had
to be purchased, and purchased quickly before dealers and other
institutions entered the competition. But purchase plans were difficult to execute because publishers had so few copies of anything they
were loath to part with them. In many cases, when Hill visited
publishers' stock rooms he found only archival copies, none to be
sold. But if there were a few copies, their purchase could be more
successfully negotiated with cigarettes than money. Rations were
meager and Germans held onto their remaining possessions until they
could sell them for immediate cash with which to purchase food or
cigarettes in the black market. Cigarettes were worth a mark apiece
(the mark worth 10¢) so that rather than 750 marks for a $75 score,
Hill paid a carton of cigarettes.[127]

---

[124] Hill to Reuben Peiss, 22 May 1946. Hill Papers.

[125] Walter Hinrichsen to Richard S. Hill, 9 February 1947. Hill Papers.

[126] Charles Warren Fox recounted an amusing, though potentially dangerous, aspect
of life in Berlin in 1946:

> The Russians, of course, had come in and occupied part of Berlin; Dick
> and someone who'd gone with him were out riding somewhere and they
> realized that they'd gone into the Russian part of Berlin. Some Russian
> soldiers stopped them and arrested them. Dick could not speak a bit of
> Russian but someone who'd gone over with him spoke Yiddish and one of
> these Russians happened to speak Yiddish so they got into a conversation with
> each other and the Russian said, "Well, we'll have to take you to our police"
> but the Russian, who'd just arrived there, didn't know where the police station
> was so this fellow who spoke Yiddish said, "I'll show you where it is." So
> he took them to the [police] station in West Berlin and arrested [the Russian
> soldiers].

[127] Hill's source of cigarettes was the staff of the Music Division back in Washington.
At one point he asked that a "special commission" be set up to see to it he received
two cartons a week. With those "cigarette-marks" he acquired the "rarer items" for
the Library. Information and quotes from Hill to Edward N. Waters, 4 May 1946.
Hill Papers. Since the 10¢ mark value cigarette works out to a $20 value for a carton
of cigarettes, acquiring a $75 score in such a trade was a true bargain!

As an adjunct to his official Library of Congress work, Hill bought multiple copies when possible. The second library for which he bought music scores was the University of Rochester's Eastman School of Music which

> paid, I remember, a ridiculous fee of $1 per item. Many of the things were worth a hundred times that, but just to simplify bookkeeping we paid $1 a volume.[128]

In the Sibley Music Library those volumes may be identified by a pencilled no. 119, in American script.

Although one might imagine Hill enjoyed the intense activity and myriad contacts with persons heretofore known only by name, the opposite seems to have been true. "I just don't like it here; I feel I'm more fitted for the type of work to be done in Washington than in Berlin at the moment." The exciting, romantic Germany of his Oxford days had become ". . . a horrible place now, and I'm only sorry that I have to come so close to grips with it."[129]

Nevertheless, Hill was so successful in his music work that the Mission relieved him of general duties so he could pursue his "special leads."[130] Hill's published account of his efforts appeared in the *Library of Congress Quarterly Journal of Current Acquisitions* for November of 1946, but his personal letters to Music Division staff and friends reveal the hardships, fatigue, and frustration of the seven-month assignment.[131] Of particular concern was the great delay in getting answers and instructions from Washington. Various schemes devised on the spot to facilitate his acquisitions raised questions for which Hill wrote or cabled the Music Division for guidance and answers. There was either no response or it was so long in coming that Hill was forced to proceed without it. Hill felt the people in Washington just didn't appreciate the urgency of his communiqués, the urgency of his acquisitions work: purchases had to be concluded before dealers or other institutions entered the picture to compete with the Mission; frequently individual purchases had to be negotiated on the spot or not at all; the political situation caused by the four-power occupation frightened some publishers so that they chose to sell only to the Russians in hope of favorable treatment later. In his extant letters to the Music Division, Hill complained about its lack of cooperation:

> I don't get the idea of why you guys seem to think you are helping the cause by never answering such questions — yes,

128 Fox interview.

129 Quotes from Hill to Edward N. Waters, 4 May 1946. Hill Papers.

130 Peiss, "European Wartime Acquisitions," p. 874.

131 Excerpts of several letters are printed in Dena J. Epstein, "Buying Music in War-Torn Germany with Richard S. Hill," *Notes* 37 (1980-81): 503-07. Hill's "Buying Music in Germany," which originally appeared in the *Library of Congress Quarterly Journal of Current Acquisitions*, is also reprinted, pp. 507-19.

I know you are busy, but it doesn't always have to be busy with someone else's rackets and never with mine.[132]

In addition to the European problems was his as yet unresolved relationship with Mary Rogers and the uncertainty of *Notes'* future, threatened by a proposed merger of the Music Library Association and the American Musicological Society.

At the first post-war MLA meeting, 22-23 March 1946, outgoing president Edward N. Waters raised the issue of "overlapping interests" of the MLA and the AMS. Waters credited the idea to Dr. Waldo G. Leland, director of the American Council of Learned Societies, who suggested that such a merger would "effect greater economies in operations, . . . produce a journal devoted to both library and musicological interests, . . . and give music a better chance of gaining representation in the American Council of Learned Societies itself."[133] The second point must have sent a chill into Hill's heart, isolated, un-involved, and more than three thousand miles away from his beloved *Notes*. Friends wrote counseling various actions. "Don't worry" was high on their lists. One suggested apprising Dorothy Tilly, president of the MLA, of his intention to resign as editor of *Notes* should the merger succeed. "The members of the MLA came out so very definitely for your continuing that the fact that you're considering resigning in the event of a merger would be a strong point to them."[134]

Hill ably outlined the drawbacks of a combined journal in his 4 May 1946 letter to Waters:

1. Too few American musicologists were interested in American music or in good musicological studies of American music to support the new journal.

2. Musicologists rarely bought the sort of music published in America so that the addition of their names to *Notes'* mailing list would not sell ads.

3. Librarians would drop their subscriptions to *Notes* if it became musicologically-oriented.

4. A change of editorial focus would make it impossible to expand *Notes'* coverage of library matters.

5. *Notes* would become "just another music magazine."

Meanwhile both organizations appointed committees to investigate and exchange information about the issue. In the end, MLA's committee found there to be "no desire" for a common journal but to continue a committee "to investigate and act on projects upon

---

[132] Hill to Edward N. Waters, 4 May 1946. Hill Papers.

[133] "Report of the Committee to Study Relationships with the American Musicological Society," 6 January 1947. Waters Papers.

[134] Gina [no last name used; I've been unable to identify her] to Hill, 14 May 1946. Hill Papers.

which the two societies might co-operate, with the limitation that complete merger was not to be one of [those] subjects."[135]

Hill returned to Washington on 2 August 1946, where he found an unfinished September issue of *Notes*. The March and June issues had been brought out by the other members of the *Notes* staff, i.e., the Music Division staff. The September issue, which Hill finished, included his first-hand account of the condition of the Preussische Staatsbibliothek, "The former Prussian State Library," lavishly illustrated with his own photos. (His sister Edith had sent him Kodachrome film which he returned to Rochester, New York, to be developed.) In addition to the photos published in *Notes,* Hill put together an album of his 1946 photos which he presented to the Library of Congress in 1952.

* * * * *

After preliminary meetings in Florence (1949) and Lüneburg (1950), the first General Assembly of the newly-formed International Association of Music Libraries convened in Paris, 22-25 July 1951. The goals[136] of the Association were to promote the inventory and cataloguing of music collections in schools, colleges, churches, monasteries, and private libraries; encourage microfilming of manuscripts, musical autographs, and early prints; compile a bibliography of musicians' letters; publish the catalogue of the Allgemeine Musikgesellschaft in Zurich; and compile an inventory of musical sources, a revised or updated Eitner.[137] All of these projects were to be international in scope; several were to be undertaken jointly with the International Musicological Society.

Hill was the United States' representative to the Preparatory Commission, which functioned prior to the 1951 Paris Assembly, and a member of the joint MLA-American Musicological Society committee for the inventory of musical sources. In those capacities he was one of the four official U.S. delegates to the Paris Assembly, where he spoke twice. Once, unofficially, reporting on "The U.S. position on the International Inventory of Musical sources,"[138] and again, in a formal paper which urged creation of an international code for cataloguing music, "Some pros and cons regarding an international code for cataloging practical music."[139] He must have had a

---

[135] *Notes* 4 (1946-47): 230-31.

[136] Published in three languages in the *Kongress-Bericht, Zweiter Weltkongress der Musikbibliotheken* (Kassel: Bärenreiter-Verlag, 1951), 64-72.

[137] Robert Eitner, *Biographisch-bibliographisches Quellen-Lexikon der Musiker und Musikgelehrten der christlichen Zeitrechnung bis zur Mitte des 19. Jahrhunderts . . .* (Leipzig: Breitkopf & Härtel, 1898-1904).

[138] International Association of Music Libraries, 3e Congrès International des Bibliothèques Musicales, Paris, 22-25 Juillet 1951. *Actes du Congrès . . .* (Kassel: Bärenreiter, 1953), 28-32.

[139] *Actes du Congrès . . . ,* 37-45.

profound influence on the largely European assembly, for it elected him first President of the International Association of Music Libraries. So to his national prominence as Editor of *Notes* was added an international role — and a great deal of work. Hill's report of the election described it as

> much against my better judgment and desire. Of course, in a way it's an honor, but it's an honor which I would gladly have done without. [140]

Before the Paris meeting Hill had planned to stay in France during August

> to finish up some work which should have been done on my thesis twelve years ago. I have a hunch that if I don't do it now, it will never get done. And it's silly to hold up the Peters Catalog forever when a few weeks work might clear up the blocks. [141]

Whether because of his increased organizational responsibilities or not, he didn't stay in France but returned to Washington.

The years of his IAML presidency required frequent trips to Europe for both Executive Council meetings and Congresses. The trips took a heavy toll, both on Hill and his associates who were forced to pick up extra duties in the Music Division and on *Notes*. William Lichtenwanger acknowledges his resentment toward IAML because of the amount of Hill's work he had to assume. [142] Hill came to think he held international office "purely and simply because I can get to Europe oftener than most." [143] That is clearly a false assumption, for no matter how frequently he could go, had he not functioned appropriately the Europeans would not have asked him to come, and events would have proceeded without him. Nevertheless, international travel in the 1950s wasn't the 6-7 hour jet flight of today, and 3 or 4 trips a year added up to a considerable amount of time away from all his Washington duties and a substantial financial investment in IAML.

One of the disappointments in describing Hill's IAML activities is the dearth of primary sources. Neither in the Hill Papers nor in the files of the Music Division have I or the staff of the Music Division found a cache of IAML correspondence and documents. Lichtenwanger recalls Hill typing long letters to Vladimir Fédorov,

---

[140] Hill to Florence Kretzschmar, 12 August 1951. Hill Papers.

[141] Hill to Kurtz Myers, 14 June 1951. Hill Papers.

[142] "He (Hill) knew how bitter I felt about IAML taking him practically out of the Music Division and that meaning that I had to do a lot of what was supposed to be his job in the Music Division; and it simply meant that I had to put in more of my own time, in addition always to *Notes,* in order to keep the reference letters from going entirely to smash." Lichtenwanger interview.

[143] Hill to Irene Millen, 18 June 1959. Music Department Files, Carnegie Library of Pittsburgh.

executive secretary of IAML; few have come to light. Of course it is possible that most of the IAML work was done in person at the various meetings. Language was certainly a problem. Although formal papers were read in their authors' native language, the Europeans spoke English to Hill. Of those I've seen, many of Fédorov's letters are in French despite Hill's preference for English.[144]

From the extant documentation we learn that budget problems were a great concern. The request to UNESCO, which supported the central headquarters in Paris, had to be prepared. The dues structure of member libraries and individuals had to be considered. As the national branches came into existence it became a question of allocating a portion of IAML dues to the branches or requiring them to collect their own from their members.

The Central Secretariat of the International Inventory of Musical Sources was set up as were national collection agencies for cards from libraries holding items to be reported. The first volume of the Inventory, usually referred to by the initials of its French title, *Répertoire International des Sources Musicales* (RISM), came out in 1960. The proceedings of the second World Congress of Music Libraries (Lüneburg, 1950) and of the first General Assembly of IAML (Paris, 1951) were published; the first issue of *Fontes artis musicae,* official journal of IAML, appeared in 1954.

One of the first Association proposals was that national libraries index the music periodicals published in their countries. The entries would be interfiled, world-wide, and published under UNESCO's auspices. That proposition faltered because the national libraries would not assume responsibility for the indexing. The next hope for an international index to music periodicals lay in expanding and re-directing Florence Kretzschmar's *Music Index.* Hill and Kretzschmar corresponded with Vladimir Fédorov about the projected roles of *Music Index* and IAML. In the end it was discovered that the Europeans were interested only in "serious musical studies," not the whole gamut of musical literature indexed by the *Music Index.*[145] There was also a need to avoid competition with the newly-restored *Bibliographie des Musikschrifttums,* edited by Wolfgang Schmieder.[146] Yet Kretzschmar was eager to expand the musicological side of *Music Index.* The issue, as always, came down to money. European libraries could not afford the $125 yearly subscription fee to *Music Index.* Kretzschmar was willing to print IAML's music periodical index, designed as they chose, on the conditions they provide their own editor and funds to create the index; she would be the publisher and distributor of the product. Even with UNESCO's support, the

---

[144] "I am under the impression . . . that you 'feel' better my English, though bad and inaccurate, than you 'understand' my supportable French. So I put aside all possible complexes and write you in English." Vladimir Fédorov to Hill, 22 December 1954. Hill Papers.

[145] Hill to Florence Kretzschmar, 6 March 1952. Hill Papers.

[146] Leipzig, Frankfurt am Main: Friedrich Hofmeister, 1936-39, 1950-.

necessary funds could not be raised and the project lay fallow until 1967 when *RILM Abstracts of Music Literature* began publication under the auspices of the International Musicological Society, IAML, and the American Council of Learned Societies.

Special sections devoted to the concerns of broadcast libraries, public libraries, and record libraries developed within the larger Association. In other words, the organization proved it was needed, well-designed to function, and capable of carrying out its mission.

After his four-year term as president, Hill continued to serve the Association as vice president, an office which did not, apparently, require frequent trips to Europe. The last Congress Hill attended was the 1959 Congress in Cambridge, England. He extended his stay in the British Isles to conduct research in Edinburgh and Dublin on his *Star-Spangled Banner* project. There was new urgency to his work. Charles Seeger and several others were planning a *Festschrift* in honor of the 80th birthday of Otto Kinkeldey, Hill's Cornell professor of musicology. Hill's contribution was to be his long-delayed history of the text of *The Star-Spangled Banner*.

The contributions for the "Kinkschrift," as it came to be called, were presented to Otto Kinkeldey at the Cornell Club, New York City, on 28 November 1958. Hill's wasn't finished; publication of the volume was delayed, several times apparently, while the pressure built on Hill. The final deadline was 1 March 1960; on 26 February Seeger reminded Hill: "It's getting perilously close to the March 1st deadline and no paper from you." By August, he admonished him sternly.

> For heaven's sake, stop writing these beautiful long letters and put in the time on the article. . . . We *need* your contribution and your participation in the roster of contributors. *Take a vacation and get it done.*[147]

To help save Hill's time and effort, both Seeger and Jan LaRue sent pre-typed postcards with boxes for Hill to check as his response and then drop in a mailbox. But if Hill responded at all to their queries it was by letter because the unreturned postcards are in his papers in the Music Division.

Hill's life long hesitancy to finish a piece of research, actually commit himself to a completed product, prevailed over the advice of friends and colleagues who urged an end to the project. As several colleagues have mentioned, he was always looking for more evidence, loath to decide he had all the available information. By the time of this renewed push to complete *The Star-Spangled Banner* project, he had become unable to print anything submitted to *Notes* without rewriting it. He verified the research on everything; sometimes he greatly extended the scope of an article, as with the Mott example described by Lichtenwanger; other times he found discrepancies in

---

[147] Charles Seeger to Hill, 16 August 1960. Hill Papers.

the original research and rejected the contribution altogether after spending a great deal of his own time.

The career-long habit of opening each of his letters with a description of the piles of unanswered correspondence at his desk and complaints of being far behind in his work grew from paragraph to page length.[148] In a candid, touching personal letter to Yvette Fédorov, Hill appraised his life and the circumstances in which he found himself.

> I not only approve, but think very highly indeed, of your idea of writing letters animated solely by friendly impulses and with all "business" strictly excluded. It's good for one's soul. And besides, there is no more satisfying thing in life than a good friend. I used to have a fair share of them, but I'm afraid these last years I've tested their patience and friendship sorely. It isn't that I like to do so. It's simply that without in the least intending it I seem to have taken on more jobs than I can handle properly. I used to love to give little dinner parties. Sometimes I'd spend a whole day, and occasionally even more time, concocting fancy dishes, and when the guests finally arrived, I'd serve them six and seven courses, each course with its proper wine, and everyone would relax and enjoy themselves thoroughly. I haven't had such a party in over five years. For a while, I'd try to compromise, by stopping on the way home from work to buy a steak or something that could be cooked quickly, but it wasn't the same, and I rarely attempt even that any more. I used to think it was uncivilized not to keep up with the theater and the better motion pictures, but I haven't been to the theater in Washington for years, and if I get to see a motion picture oftener than once a year, it is a red-letter day. I've got four sisters of whom I'm very

---

[148] For instance,

> . . . I want to answer your recent letter practically on receipt. By rights, this should be merely a common courtesy, instead of a feat to be proud of. . . . [I] am only a wretched human being gradually sinking under piles of unanswered letters—and acquiring in the process a reputation that I shudder to think about. If I were only a halfway sensible individual I would have budgeted things differently. Instead of putting all our revenues back into the magazine [*Notes*] in order to make it larger, I should have hired a secretary and kept the magazine small. Then perhaps the correspondence would have stayed at a reasonable level, and it could have been handled with relative ease. As it is, the larger magazine makes more work and an utterly unbelievable amount of correspondence, so that either a lot of letters automatically do not get answered or else the magazine doesn't come out. In either case, I get it in the neck. [Hill to John Davies, 25 February 1949. Hill Papers.]

And again,

> . . . If you could see my desk and the surrounding territory. . . . This has been a truly hellish year. The work piles in just as fast, if not faster, than it used to do, and I'm afraid the truth of the matter is that I'm beginning to feel my age. . . . The whole thing adds up to a backlog of uncompleted tasks and unwritten letters that is truly shocking. I'm going to have to unload some of my outside jobs or learn how to pass the buck to the younger members of the division, since obviously I can't get away with things like this indefinitely. [Hill to Charles Cudworth, 13 September 1958. Hill Papers.]

fond. When I was still in school, I used to write them all frequently, and even afterwards I almost always wrote them at least once a month. Then, five or six years ago, the letters were spaced more and more widely, and since they couldn't understand my "neglect," their letters to me were full of complaints and accusations that I didn't love them any more. Needless to say, love had nothing whatsoever to do with the case. It was purely a question of time. Probably, if I was a better manager, I would arrange things either so that I had less to do, or else simply did less, but I guess I'm just not built that way. At the Library, I've learned to write short letters which go directly to the point, since otherwise I would never get through. My longer letters are largely limited to those I write Vladimir—in hopes that occasionally I will persuade him to see things my way—or those that go to people with whom I'm involved in some business problem. If I hadn't had such a happy, normal life during the 1920s and 1930s, I'd feel downright sorry for myself now. I do nothing but work all the time that I'm awake (except for an occasional detective story, and I only indulge in them when I'm too tired to work and yet can't get to sleep). True, there is a certain satisfaction to be derived from work. I suppose that if there wasn't, I probably would have taken more desperate steps to rid myself of some of my odd jobs. But there is also the possibility of getting too much of even a good thing, and I am rapidly becoming convinced that that is exactly what I've got now. I don't quite know where I'll start cutting down, but it definitely isn't going to be long before I start cutting somewhere. Maybe then I'll be able to act more like a human being and write you and my few other friends more regularly. At the moment, I can only hope that you will believe that my heart is definitely hung in the right place, and I would give far more evidence of it if I could only somehow manage to find the time.[149]

He had proceeded from the luxury of his Oak Park childhood and carefree European years to a circumstance in which he was forced to entertain professional and business colleagues in hotels rather than his apartment. Although he lived in a fine building and owned fine furnishings, he couldn't find a cleaning lady who would work without disturbing his books and papers. The apartment was in serious need of redecoration but he had no time to pack his books and papers to satisfy the management's regulations before they sent in painters. In 1952 his first Washington apartment was painted. The accompanying travail and chaos were recounted several times to friends and

---

[149] Hill to Yvette Fédorov, 5 April 1953. Hill Papers. The only explanation for Hill's statement, "I've got four sisters . . ." is Marian's comment that "Dick was very fond of Fred's wife Emma. Maybe she was the 4th. . . . Emma was like a mother to all of us." Marian Hill Hoch, letter to author, 9 July 1984. Edith Hill, Fred, and his wife Emma were a generation older than Calvin's second family.

correspondents. After his move[150] during the summer of 1956, he found it impossible to relive that experience. Not long after that he had his telephone removed. As he explained to Kurtz Myers, he simply couldn't concentrate on non-professional affairs long enough to keep the bill paid on time.[151] He was truly living only for his work: the Library, *Notes,* IAML and the unfinished *Star-Spangled Banner* research. Mary Rogers acknowledges that he was "getting tired, not tired *of,* just tired."[152] She feels he was contemplating a change, perhaps retiring from the Library in order to continue his other activities.

In a frantic effort to complete *The Star-Spangled Banner* paper for the "Kinkschrift," Hill began to work through the night. Leading up to Thanksgiving 1960, he lived through several days and nights without going to bed at all. The frenzy took its toll. During the early morning hours of Thanksgiving Day, 24 November 1960, he suffered a heart attack: " . . . an indescribable sensation in my breastbone . . . a star-shell shooting sparks in all directions."[153] About 8 o'clock Hill called his physician who came to the apartment and had Hill taken to the Washington Hospital Center by ambulance.[154] Hill was hospitalized until the middle of January 1961, when Spivacke drove him home to prepare to fly to Florida where he would continue his recuperation.

---

[150] In June of 1956 Hill moved into the Methodist Building at 110 Maryland Ave., N.E. Increased traffic had made it difficult to drive to the Library and parking spaces there were at a premium; the Methodist Building was a block from the Library. Ed and Carrie Waters, of whom Hill was very fond, also lived there. An added convenience was its excellent cafeteria, much-frequented by the staff of the Music Division.

[151]   You won't be getting quite so many telephone calls from me in the near future, because I got mad at the telephone company and told them to take my phone out. They are utterly impossible here. They send out bills on a cock-eyed schedule to keep the clericals busy throughout the month, and then 20 days after the bill has been rendered they start phoning subscribers to tell them that their bill has not yet been paid. Naturally, I'm not ever home during the day, and so they felt perfectly free to call me at the library. I usually got my bill around the twentieth, and since I started paying bills I've always picked an evening or Sunday afternoon around the middle of the month and balanced my accounts and check book. There are simply too many things of greater importance to drop everything and pay each bill as it's received. If the telephone company had stuck to written notices, I'd probably be mad but still a subscriber, but I simply wasn't going to put up with those phone calls to the Library. Most of my time there is spent talking to some reader or fellow employee and I simply wasn't going to put up with the practice. It's a common enough problem apparently, but just the same I wasn't taking any chance that I'd be talking to some important visitor and have to explain that the telephone company was dunning me for my bill. Nobody would believe that it wasn't months in arrears, whereas actually when I was in the country it was paid like clock work every month. I protested verbally a couple of times, but when this didn't do any good, I finally told 'em to take the damn thing out. [Hill to Kurtz Myers, 2 July 1958. Hill Papers.]

[152] Rogers interview.

[153] Christmas card postmarked 25 December 1960, to Pete and Helena Gervais. Gervais Letters.

[154] Facts from ibid.

Carroll Wade, a reference librarian in the Music Division, was to accompany Hill to Keewaydin Island off the coast of Naples, Florida, where Marian and her husband Arthur were wintering. Arthur had recuperated from a heart attack by taking long walks on the beach under the care of Dr. James Craig, protégé of Paul Dudley White, Boston heart specialist; Hill was to follow a similar course. The Keewaydin resort, one of John Harland Rush's camps, had originally been a school for children whose parents were vacationing in Florida during the winter months.

Carroll stayed with Hill two weeks in a guest cottage; Marian and Arthur were in their own cottage. After Carroll's return to Washington, Hill was making arrangements for another friend to visit and share his cottage. The day of 6 February 1961 Marian accompanied Hill into Naples to see his doctor. Afterwards, as they breakfasted in Naples, Hill related the doctor's favorable findings and indications that Hill could resume normal activities. That afternoon Marian walked with him on the beach. Shelling was new to Hill and Marian recalls his joy and pleasure collecting them.

Alcoholic beverages were not served at Keewaydin but ice could be delivered to guests' cottages for pre-dinner use. Marian had guests, as well as Dick, for cocktails before dinner. After dinner, served in a common dining hall, Marian, Arthur, and their friends played bridge in a recreation hall while Hill played Bach on the piano. About ten o'clock he went back to his own cottage to work on *The Star-Spangled Banner* paper. After midnight he came to Marian's cottage in the midst of another heart attack, asking Marian to get oxygen and a doctor. There were no phones in the individual cottages, so Marian put her brother into her bed and ran to the manager's cottage to phone for help which had to come by small boat from the mainland. Meanwhile a doctor who was himself a guest at the club, endeavored to assist Hill. When Marian got back to her cottage, Dick was unconscious. The doctor attempted to dislodge the clot, to no avail; Hill died before additional help arrived.

His body was cremated in Naples and the ashes buried in the family plot in Forest Home Cemetery, Oak Park. A memorial service planned by Carroll Wade and William Lichtenwanger was held in the Chapel of the Methodist Building on 25 March 1961 for the family, colleagues from the Library, and friends and acquaintances. Announcements of the service were mailed to professional colleagues across the country. Kinkeldey came down from New York; several publishers who had advertised in *Notes* also attended.[155]

After the service the family stayed in town to break up Hill's apartment. His will, dated 19 July 1957 in New York City, gave all his books, music, and records to the Library of Congress. When they were accepted by the Library, 5 May 1961, the 7,595 pieces were

---

[155] I have not talked with anyone who remembers more about the service than Lichtenwanger's recollection that the Budapest String Quartet played the slow movement of Beethoven's Opus 135.

assessed at $5,736.10; 706 scores were considered rare. The fourth provision of Hill's will gave "to the Music Library Association, Inc., a sum equivalent to any and all unpaid printers' bills due at the time of my death" for printing *Notes*. The fifth provision put his estate in trust, the income to be paid "in convenient installments to my sister, Eunice Hill Alyea, during her lifetime." At her death the estate was to be distributed to the issue of Calvin H. Hill, Dick's father.

Carroll Wade packed the books and art works for delivery to the Reference Department of the Library. Most of Hill's research notes and the contents of his desk were packed and delivered to the Music Division where they remain essentially as Wade packed them.

The "Kinkschrift," published in 1960, carried an inserted slip which noted Hill's forthcoming contribution, "The 'Unsettled' Text of *The Star-Spangled Banner*," to appear "in the near future as a separate publication" of the American Musicological Society. Thanks to William Lichtenwanger, it is published here for the first time (pp. 71-184 in this volume).

Many letters of condolence were addressed to the "Music Division family."

> Somehow it was a surprise to learn that Dick had a family. It was natural to think that you & Ed & Mary & the others were his family, that the Music Division was his home, that his work was his life. [156]

> I don't know any of his relatives (he used to speak of a sister) and so I write to you and my former colleagues in the Division, for we surely must be counted among his relatives. [157]

> I must tell a friend of the deep shock and sorrow I feel. Naturally I turn to you . . . and the Music Division Family; I know how you all must feel, and I want you to know that I am one of the many friends who share this feeling of sadness and great loss. [158]

Paul Henry Lang wrote in his *New York Herald Tribune* column:

> There is scarcely a cultivated musician or scholar in this country who directly or indirectly did not receive valuable guidance and information from Mr. Hill. Ensconced in that magnificent library, and working day and night (he virtually worked himself to death) with single-minded devotion, he could produce an answer to our query if it was humanly possible. [159]

Three projects retained Hill's interest from his initial involvement with them until his death: *The Star-Spangled Banner, Notes* and

---

[156] John C. Haskins to Harold Spivacke, 13 February 1961. Hill Papers.

[157] Harold E. Johnson, 20 March 1961. Hill Papers.

[158] Rudolf Serkin to Edward N. Waters. Hill Papers.

[159] Lively Arts Section, 19 February 1961, p. 16.

IAML. One can speculate that he maintained his interest in *The Star-Spangled Banner* because of his location in the Nation's capital and, perhaps to lesser degree, a professional interest in completing the work begun by another Library of Congress Music Division staff member, Oscar G. T. Sonneck.[160]

The pervasive concern about *Notes,* almost that of a parent for a handicapped child, is less transparent. Hill considered himself a musicologist concerned about music library affairs, yet he found himself

> walking a very uncertain tightrope when it comes to deciding what I might properly include in the magazine and what would better fit a magazine devoted primarily to musicology.[161]

Mary Rogers remembers that

> he was always looking out for the music librarian. And I think one of the reasons for that was he had so much to do with music librarians when he wanted to look up things for his own work that he appreciated what they had done for him and he felt that they should in every way be helped.[162]

And there was the warm, reciprocal affection between Otto Kinkeldey and Hill; Kinkeldey, the first German-educated Ph.D. in Musicology in the United States, earned his living as a librarian rather than professor of musicology. While there was doubtless a germ of truth in Hill's comment to Waters that he'd always wanted to edit a magazine, functioning editorially is quite variant from the financial patron circumstance Hill assumed toward *Notes.* Whether he could have articulated his motives or concerns toward *Notes,* it seems apparent his professional interest, physical energy, and money sustained *Notes* during years when *Notes* sustained the Music Library Association. Whether the Association would have foundered without *Notes* cannot be known, but there is no doubt his vision, energy, and money contributed to its viability as a professional organization. As editor of *Notes,* 1943-61, Hill exerted incalculable influence over America's other music librarians, bibliographers, and historians.

Hill's contributions to IAML were less direct than those for *Notes;* that organization did not require the immediate, hands-on support *Notes* required. Yet there is no doubt Hill functioned as visionary in the organization and planning of IAML despite his modest disclaimers, oft repeated in apologies for his absences from

---

[160] In 1907 Librarian of Congress Herbert Putnam asked Oscar Sonneck, Chief of the Music Division, 1902-17, to prepare a history of *The Star-Spangled Banner* and several other patriotic songs. Sonneck's original report was published in 1909, and a revised and enlarged version in 1914.

[161] Hill to Hans Tischler, 22 November 1946. Hill Papers.

[162] Rogers interview.

LC, that he was the only person with the financial circumstance and the time to make the necessary repeated trips to Europe.

* * * * *

Historians work with the paper trail and personal reminiscence, yet I am not sure any of this adequately portrays the unique individual, Richard Synyer Hill. The documentation varies according to the relationship Hill maintained with the individual in question: he was someone different to each person close to his life. Florence Kretzschmar found him, although cheerful, to be a man of tensions.

> I had the feeling that I was dealing with a man who was very high-strung but he didn't give that appearance. And [he had] a very nice sense of humor.[163]

To Mary Rogers he was

> completely wrapped up in his work — completely, intense — but he could close it off like that [snap of fingers] and be just as intense with having fun.[164]

Helena McCullough commented that "You had a feeling he was making it too hard for himself."[165] To William Lichtenwanger, Hill's "worst enemy was his determination not to finish anything until it was perfect. And his biggest professional contribution, as an everyday (or on-and-off) working reference librarian, was an accumulation of many small bits. . . ."[166]

Circumstances and Hill's actions are reported faithfully; readers' interpretations will vary. In the end we can only acknowledge our debt to a privileged individual who chose to work himself to death for his profession.

---

[163] Kretzschmar interview.

[164] Rogers interview.

[165] McCullough interview.

[166] William Lichtenwanger, letter to author, 1 July 1984.

Cunningham, Virginia. Interview with author. Chapel Hill, North Carolina, 14 January 1979. Tape recording, Music Library, State University of New York at Buffalo.

Ellinwood, Leonard. Interview with author. Washington, D.C., 12 October 1981. Tape recording, Music Library, State University of New York at Buffalo.

Fox, Charles Warren. Interview with author. Gloversville, New York, 12-13 May 1981. Tape recording, Music Library, State University of New York at Buffalo. Siglum: Fox interview.

Gervais, Paul T. Letters from Richard S. Hill. Helena Gervais McCullough, Oak Park, Illinois. Siglum: Gervais Letters.

Hill, Richard S. Papers. Music Division, Library of Congress, Washington, D.C. Siglum: Hill Papers.

Hinrichsen, Evelyn. Interview with author. New York, New York, 28 October 1981. Tape recording, Music Library, State University of New York at Buffalo.

Hoch, Marian Hill. Interview with author. Elyria, Ohio, 9-10 June 1981. Tape recording, Music Library, State University of New York at Buffalo. Siglum: Hoch interview.

Kretzschmar, Florence. Interview with author. Detroit, Michigan, 17 August 1982. Tape recording, Music Library, State University of New York at Buffalo. Siglum: Kretzschmar interview.

Lichtenwanger, William. Interview with author. Berkeley Springs, West Virginia, 15-17 March 1981. Tape recording, Music Library, State University of New York at Buffalo. Siglum: Lichtenwanger interview.

McCullough, Helena Gervais. Interview with author. Oak Park, Illinois, 18 August 1982. Tape recording, Music Library, State University of New York at Buffalo. Siglum: McCullough interview.

Rogers, Mary. Interview with author. Washington, D.C., 11 October 1981. Tape recording, Music Library, State University of New York at Buffalo. Siglum: Rogers interview.

Spivacke, Harold. Interview with author. Washington, D.C., 9-11 April 1974. Tape recording, Music Library, State University of New York at Buffalo. Siglum: Spivacke interview.

Waters, Edward N. Interview with author. Washington, D.C., 3 January 1978. Tape recording, Music Library, State University of New York at Buffalo. Siglum: Waters interview.

Waters, Edward N. Papers. Music Library Association Archive. University of Maryland Library, College Park, Maryland. Siglum: Waters Papers.

Bibliography of Writings about and by Richard S. Hill

Biographical entries appear in *Baker's Biographical Dictionary of Musicians,* 5th-7th eds.; *International Cyclopedia of Music and Musicians,* 9th and 10th eds.; *Die Musik in Geschichte und Gegenwart; The New Grove Dictionary of Music and Musicians; The New Grove Dictionary of American Music;* and *Riemann Musik Lexikon, Personenteil.*

There were obituaries in *Library Journal* 86 (1961): 971, *Library of Congress Information Bulletin* 20 (6 February 1961): 79-80, *Musical America* 81 (March 1961): 66, *New York Times,* 8 February 1961, *Notes* 18 (1960-61): 193-96, *Washington Evening Star,* 8 February 1961, *Washington Post,* 8 February 1961, and *Wilson Library Bulletin* 35 (1961): 582. A very fine reminiscence by long-time friend Charles Warren Fox, *Notes* 18 (1960-61): 369-74; memorial tributes by Vincent Duckles in *Acta Musicologica* 33 (1961): 69-71, and Vladimir Fédorov in *Fontes artis musicae* 8 (1961): 1-2; and Dena Epstein's "Buying Music in War-Torn Germany with Richard S. Hill," *Notes* 37 (1980-81): 503-07, complete the writings about Hill.

Like the original compilers of the bibliography of Hill's writings, Carroll D. Wade and Frank C. Campbell,* I cannot certify that it is complete. In this printing, the same subgroups established by Wade and Campbell are used; journal volume numbers and reprint information have been added.

BOOKS AND
ARTICLES

1. "Schoenberg's Tone-Rows and Tonal System of the Future." *Musical Quarterly* 22 (1936): 14-37. [Issued separately as offprint.]

2. "The Plate Numbers of C. F. Peters' Predecessors." *Papers of the American Musicological Society* (1938), 113-34.

3. Unpublished typescript dealing with the history of *The Star-Spangled Banner* (1943), 225 pp.

4. "The First Protestant Hymn Book." *Library of Congress Quarterly Journal of Current Acquisitions* 1 (July-Sept. 1943): 32-36.

5. *A Bibliography of Periodical Literature in Musicology and Allied Fields,* no. 2, October 1, 1939-Sept. 30, 1940. Assembled for the Committee on Musicology of the American Council of Learned Societies by D. H. Daugherty, Leonard Ellinwood, and Richard S. Hill. Washington, D.C.: American Council of Learned Societies, 1943. Reprint, New York: Da Capo, 1973.

6. *Music and Libraries: Selected Papers of the Music Library Association.* Presented at its 1942 Meetings. Edited by Richard S. Hill. Washington, D.C.: Music Library Association and American Library Association, 1943.

Notes 18 (1960-61): 375-80. That volume also carried William Lichtenwanger's notice of Hill's heart attack, p. 43, and the announcement of the Music Library Association's Richard S. Hill Memorial Fund, p. 404.

7. "Military Marches in Colonial Times." *Library of Congress Quarterly Journal of Current Acquisitions* 1 (January-March 1944): 40-48.

8. "Concert Life in Berlin, Season 1943-44." *Notes* 1 (June 1944): 13-33.

9. "Not So Far Away in a Manger: Forty-One Settings of an American Carol." *Notes* 3 (1945-46): 12-36, 192.

10. "The Lyrebird Press —Paris." *Notes* 3 (1945-46): 151-53.

11. "The Former Prussian State Library." *Notes* 3 (1945-46): 327-50, 404-10.

12. "Buying Music in Germany." *Library of Congress Quarterly Journal of Current Acquisitions* 4 (November 1946): 15-25.

13. "Getting Kathleen Home Again." *Notes* 5 (1947-48): 338-53.

14. "The Plight of Our Libraries." *Musical America* 69 (February 1949): 25, 162, 301.

15. "The Ten Best." *Notes* 6 (1948-49): 217-19.

16. "A Mistempered Bach Manuscript." *Notes* 7 (1949-50): 377-86.

17. "Music from the Collection of Baron Horace de Landau." *Library of Congress Quarterly Journal of Current Acquisitions* 7 (August 1950): 11-21.

18. "Mozart and Dr. Tissot." *Notes* 8 (1950-51): 40-69.

19. *Collier's Encyclopedia* (1950-51). S. v. "Melody," "Schoenberg," "The Star Spangled Banner," "Richard Strauss."

20. "The Melody of 'The Star Spangled Banner' in the United States before 1820." In *Essays Honoring Lawrence C. Wroth,* ed. Frederick R. Goff, pp. 151-93. Portland, Me.: n.p., 1951. Issued separately, Washington, D.C.: Library of Congress, 1951.

21. "International Inventory of Musical Sources: The Joint Committee Meeting in Paris, January 1952." *Notes* 9 (1951-52): 213-25. Issued separately, Washington, D.C.: American Musicological Society and the Music Library Association, 1953.

22. "The Mysterious Chord of Henry Clay Work." *Notes* 10 (1952-53): 211-25, 367-90.

23. "The U.S. Position on the International Inventory of Musical Sources." In *Troisième Congrès International des Bibliothèques Musicales, 22-25 Juillet 1951*, pp. 28-31. Kassel: Bärenreiter, 1953. Issued separately, Kassel: Bärenreiter, 1953.

24. "Some Pros and Cons Regarding an International Code for Cataloging Practical Music." In ibid., pp. 37-45. Issued separately, Kassel: Bärenreiter, 1953.

25. "The Growing of IAML." *Fontes artis musicae* 1 (1954): 7-11.

26. "Special Announcement concerning the International Inventory of Musical Sources." *Notes* 13 (1955-56): 195-96.

27. *Record Ratings: The Music Library Association's Index of Record Reviews.* Compiled by Kurtz Myers, edited by Richard S. Hill. New York: Crown Publishers, 1956.

28. "A Proposed Official Version of *The Star Spangled Banner:* A Report of the National Music Council's Committee." *Notes* 15 (1957-58): 33-42. *National Association of Teachers of Singing Bulletin* 14 (December 1957): 16-19, 29. *National Music Council Bulletin* 18 (Fall 1957): 3-6. *Hearings before the Subcommittee No. 4 of the Committee on the Judiciary, House of Representatives— 85th Congress, Second Session* (May 1958), 42-48.

29. Arnold Schoenberg, *Quintet for Wind Instruments, op. 26.* Record jacket notes: Columbia ML5217 (1957).

30. *Die Musik in Geschichte und Gegenwart* (1959). S. v. "Otto Kinkeldey."

31. Unpublished typescript: "The 'Unsettled' Text of *The Star Spangled Banner*" (1960), 160 pp.

REVIEWS

32. Alban Berg, *Lulu* (Columbia Record SL-121). *Musical Quarterly* 39 (1953): 134-38.

33. Cecil Hopkinson, *A Bibliography of the Musical and Literary Works of Hector Berlioz. Journal of the American Musicological Society* 6 (Spring 1953): 77-84.

34. Alban Berg, *String Quartet, op. 3*; Alfredo Casella, *Five Pieces for String Quartet* (Bartók Records 906). — Arnold Schoenberg, *The Complete String Quartets, Nos. 1-4, op. 7, 10, 30 & 37;* Anton von Webern, *Five Movements for String Quartet, op. 5* (Columbia SL-188 or ML4735/37). *Musical Quarterly* 40 (1954): 435-44.

REVIEWS IN *NOTES*

35. Edgar A. Palmer, ed., *G. I. Songs.* 1 (September 1944): 63-66.

36. Paul Eduard Miller, ed., *Esquire's Jazz Book.* 2 (1944-45): 56-58.

37. Hans T. David, *J. S. Bach's Musical Offering: History, Interpretation, and Analysis.* 2 (1944-45): 167-68.

38. G. Seldon-Goth, ed., *Felix Mendelssohn Letters.* 2 (1944-45): 168-69.

39. Albert G. Hess, ed., *800 Years of Music for Recorders.* 2 (1944-45): 174.

40. Sigmund Spaeth, *Read 'Em and Weep.* 2 (1944-45): 296-97.

41. Alfred Einstein, ed., *W. A. Mozart: The Ten Celebrated String Quartets.* 2 (1944-45): 304-06.

42. Arnold Schoenberg, *Ode to Napoleon Bonaparte.* 2 (1944-45): 308-09.

43. Ernst Krenek, ed., *Hamline Studies in Musicology.* 3 (1945-46): 42-43.

44. *Transportation in American Popular Songs: A Bibliography of Items in the Grosvenor Library.* 3 (1945-46): 47-48.

45. Gilbert Chase, *The Story of Music: Broadcast Series of the NBC University of the Air*, Handbook, vol. 1. 3 (1945-46): 48-49.

46. William C. White, *A History of Military Music in America.* 3 (1945-46): 49-50.

47. *Listen to the Mocking Words,* compiled by David Ewen. 3 (1945-46): 50.

48. Igor Stravinsky, *Scènes de ballet for Orchestra.* 3 (1945-46): 70-71.

49. Henry W. Simon, ed., *A Treasury of Grand Opera.* 3 (1945-46): 361-62.

50. Gilbert Chase, ed., *Music in Radio Broadcasting.* 4 (1946-47): 77-78.

51. Dika Newlin, *Bruckner, Mahler, Schoenberg.* 4 (1946-47): 158-59.

52. *Portraits of the World's Best-Known Musicians . . .,* compiled and edited by Guy McCoy. 4 (1946-47): 174-75.

53. *The Billboard Encyclopedia of Music, 1946-47,* 8th Annual Edition. 4 (1946-47): 175-76.

54. Gilbert Chase, *The Story of Music: Broadcast Series of the NBC University of the Air,* Handbook, vol. 2. 4 (1946-47): 176-77.

55. *Tommy Thumb's Song Book . . .* by Nurse Lovechild, 1788; facsimile edition, 1946. 4 (1946-47): 177.

56. Hans Heinsheimer, *Menagerie in F sharp.* 4 (1946-47): 341-42.

57. Edward B. Marks Music Corp., *Tear Jerkers Everyone Loves.* 4 (1946-47): 365-67.

58. Alfred Einstein, *Music in the Romantic Era.* 4 (1946-47): 461-63.

59. Ralph Potter, et al, *Visible Speech.* 4 (1946-47): 468-70.

60. Victor Alexander Fields, *Training the Singing Voice.* 4 (1946-47): 470-71.

61. *The Year in American Music, 1946-47,* ed. Julius Bloom; *The Billboard Encyclopedia of Music,* 9th Annual Edition, 1947; *Hinrichsen's Musical Year Book,* vols. 4-5, 1947-48. 5 (1947-48): 98-100.

62. Kathi Meyer and Paul Hirsch, *Katalog der Musikbibliothek Paul Hirsch.* 5 (1947-48): 228-30.

63. *Catalog of Copyright Entries: Pt. 3, Musical Compositions,* new ser., vol. 41, 1946. 5 (1947-48): 230-32.

64. Harold Barlow and Sam Morgenstern, *A Dictionary of Musical Themes.* Reviewed with Charles Seeger. 5 (1947-48): 375-76.

65. Béla Bartók, *Album,* piano solo; *For Children*—little pieces for violin and piano. 5 (1947-48): 411.

66. Paul Nettl, *Luther and Music.* 5 (1947-48): 568-69.

67. Sigmund Spaeth, *A History of Popular Music in America.* 5 (1947-48): 154-56.

68. Frank Shay, *American Sea Songs and Chanteys. . . .* 6 (1948-49): 156-57.

69. David Ewen, ed., *The Year in American Music,* 1948 edition. 6 (1948-49): 309-10.

70. George Frederick McKay, *Lincoln Lyrics: That All Men May Aspire, A Choral Suite;* Bert Reisfeld, *A Lincoln Song Book for Young America.* 6 (1948-49): 491-92.

71. *Hinrichsen's Musical Year Book,* vol. 6, 1949-50. 6 (1948-49): 614-15.

72. Ernest Glen Wever, *Theory of Hearing.* 7 (1949-50): 116-17.

73. Henry W. Simon and Abraham Veinus, *The Pocket Book of Great Operas.* 7 (1949-50): 119.

74. Arnold Schoenberg, *A Survivor from Warsaw.* 7 (1949-50): 133-35.

75. Alexander Scriabine, *Ten Sonatas for Piano.* 7 (1949-50): 437-38.

76. Ludwig van Beethoven, *Notturno for Viola and Piano,* and *Rondo à Capriccio for the Piano, op. 129.* 7 (1949-50): 441-42.

77. René Leibowitz, *Schoenberg and His School: The Contemporary Stage of the Language of Music.* 7 (1949-50): 474-76.

78. Arnold Schoenberg, *String Trio, op. 45.* 8 (1950-51): 127-29.

79. Arnold Schoenberg, *Style and Idea.* 8 (1950-51): 167-68.

80. Henry G. Farmer, *Military Music* and *Handel's Kettledrums and Other Papers on Military Music.* 8 (1950-51): 348-50.

81. *Kongress-Bericht: Zweiter Weltkongress der Musikbibliotheken— Lüneburg, 1950.* 8 (1950-51): 705-06.

82. C. P. E. Bach, *Sonatine D-Moll* and *Sonatine Es-Dur für Cembalo, 2 Flöten, 2 Violinen, Bratsche und Bass.* 8 (1950-51): 740-41.

83. Helen Traubel, *The Metropolitan Opera Murders.* 9 (1951-52): 135.

84. *The Rodgers and Hart Song Book.* 9 (1951-52): 401-02.

85. John Vincent, *The Diatonic Modes in Modern Music.* 9 (1951-52): 411-12.

86. Arnold Schoenberg, *Three Songs: Sommermued, Tot, Maedchen-lied.* 9 (1951-52): 503-04.

87. Daniel McNamara, ed., *The ASCAP Biographical Dictionary of Composers, Authors, and Publishers,* 2nd edition. 9 (1951-52): 606-07.

88. Richard Rodgers, *The King and I.* 9 (1951-52): 646-47.

89. Arnold Schoenberg, *Phantasy for Violin with Piano Accompaniment, op. 47.* 9 (1951-52): 647-48.

90. Hellmuth von Hase, ed., *Der kleine Köchel . . . Zusammengestellt auf Grund der dritten, von Alfred Einstein bearbeiteten Auflage,* and Karl Franz Müller, ed., *W. A. Mozart: Gesamtkatalog seiner Werke.* 10 (1952-53): 278-80.

91. Arnold Shaw, *The Money Song.* 10 (1952-53): 286.

92. Margaret B. Boni, ed., *The Fireside Book of Favorite American Songs.* 10 (1952-53): 323-25.

93. Arnold Schoenberg, *Five Pieces for Orchestra, op. 16,* new version. 10 (1952-53): 328-29.

94. Association Internationale des Bibliothèques Musicales, *Troisième Congrès . . . Paris, 22-25 Juillet 1951*. 10 (1952-53): 444-46.

95. Alexander Weinmann, *Vollständiges Verlagsverzeichnis Artaria & Comp.* 10 (1952-53): 449-50.

96. C. P. E. Bach, *Konzert G-Moll (W. Nr. 6)* and *Konzert F-Dur (W. Nr. 33) für Cembalo und Streicher.* 10 (1952-53): 484-85.

97. Arnold Schoenberg, *De Profundis (Psalm 130), op. 50B.* 10 (1952-53): 682-83.

98. George Kinsky, comp., *Manuskripte, Briefe, Dokumente von Scarlatti bis Stravinsky: Katalog der Musikautographen Sammlung Louis Koch.* 11 (1953-54): 119-20.

99. Albert Dietrich, Robert Schumann, and Johannes Brahms, *F-A-E Sonate für Violine und Klavier.* 11 (1953-54): 274-75.

100. Noël Coward, *The Noël Coward Song Book.* 11 (1953-54): 285-86.

101. *A Treasury of Hymns,* selected and edited by Maria Leiper and Henry W. Simon. 11 (1953-54): 286.

102. *Index Bibliographicus,* Directory of Current Periodical Abstracts and Bibliographies, vol. 2: Social Sciences, Education, Humanistic Studies; *Guide des centres nationaux d'information bibliographique,* and *Vocabularium bibliothecarii— English, French, German,* begun by Henri Lemaître, revised and enlarged by Anthony Thompson. 11 (1953-54): 447-49.

103. Wolfgang Schmieder, ed., *Bibliographie des Musikschrifttums.* 11 (1953-54): 555-57.

104. *Grove's Dictionary of Music and Musicians,* 5th edition, ed. Eric Blom. 12 (1954-55): 85-92.

105. Josef Rufer, *Composition with Twelve Notes Related Only to One Another;* George Rochberg, *The Hexachord and Its Relation to the 12-Tone Row.* 12 (1954-55): 223-25.

106. Stephen F. Keegan, ed., *The Musicians' Guide,* 1st edition. 12 (1954-55): 239.

107. Percy Scholes, *God Save the Queen: The History and Romance of the World's First National Anthem.* 12 (1954-55): 445-46.

108. Frederic V. Grunfeld, ed., *Music and Recordings, 1955.* 13 (1955-56): 77-78.

109. Erwin Stein, *Orpheus in New Guises.* 13 (1955-56): 80.

110. Jerome Kern, *The Jerome Kern Song Book.* 13 (1955-56): 338-39.

111. Arthur Edwards, *The Art of Melody;* Joseph Smits van Waesberghe, *A Textbook of Melody.* 13 (1955-56): 646-48.

112. Alban Berg, *Wozzeck.* 13 (1955-56): 688-89.

113. Leonard B. Meyer, *Emotion and Meaning in Music;* Victor Zuckerkandl, *Sound and Symbol: Music and the External World.* 14 (1956-57): 253-55.

114. *The World's Encyclopaedia of Recorded Music,* Third Supplement, 1953-55, compiled by F. F. Clough & G. J. Cuming. 14 (1956-57): 357-59.

115. Franz Niemetschek, *Life of Mozart.* 14 (1956-57): 371.

116. *Mozart: L'Année Mozart en France; Mozart en France.* 14 (1956-57): 371-72.

117. Frank Loesser, *The Most Happy Fella.* 14 (1956-57): 438-39.

118. James J. Fuld, *A Pictorial Bibliography of the First Editions of Stephen C. Foster.* 15 (1957-58): 105-06.

119. *The Musician's Guide,* 1957 edition. 15 (1957-58): 111-13.

120. David Ewen, *Panorama of American Popular Music.* 15 (1957-58): 115-16.

121. Alexander Weinmann, *Wiener Musikverleger und Musikalien-händler von Mozarts Zeit bis gegen 1860. . . .* 15 (1957-58): 396-97.

122. *The British Union-Catalogue of Early Music Printed before the Year 1801 . . . ,* ed. Edith B. Schnapper. 15 (1957-58): 565-68.

123. Henry G. Farmer, *History of the Royal Artillery Band, 1762-1953.* 15 (1957-58): 572-73.

124. Antonio Soler, Sonatas in various editions. 16 (1958-59): 155-57.

125. Duane D. Deakins, *Cylinder Records.* 16 (1958-59): 243-44.

126. *The Rodgers and Hammerstein Song Book.* 16 (1958-59): 311-12.

127. Karlheinz Stockhausen, *Nr. 7 Klavierstück XI.* 16 (1958-59): 322.

128. Cecil Hopkinson, *A Bibliography of the Works of C. W. von Gluck, 1714-1787.* 16 (1958-59): 385-87.

129. J. S. Bach, *Clavier-Büchlein vor Wilhelm Friedemann Bach . . . ,* facsimile with a preface by Ralph Kirkpatrick. 16 (1958-59): 459-60.

130. Duane D. Deakins, *Comprehensive Cylinder Record Index, Part III.* 17 (1959-60): 58.

131. *Catalogue of Printed Books in the British Museum.* Accessions: Third Series-Part 291B: Books in the Hirsch Library, with supplementary List of Music. 17 (1959-60): 225-27.

132. Victor Zuckerkandl, *The Sense of Music.* 17 (1959-60): 243-44.

MISCELLANEOUS

133. Abstracts in the *Bulletin of the American Musicological Society:*

"Greek Theory of Melody," read before the Western New York Chapter, 8 October 1936, *Bulletin* no. 2 (June 1937): 18-20.

"The Age of Beethoven (?)" read before the Western New York Chapter, 22 May 1938, *Bulletin* no. 4 (September 1940): 19-21.

"Publisher—versus Composer—Catalogues," read before the Western New York Chapter, 4 March 1939, *Bulletin* no. 5 (August 1941): 10-12.

134. "Notes for *Notes*," *Notes* 1-18 (March 1944-September 1960).

135. "The Gateway to Honor," *Notes* 4-5 (June 1947-March 1948).

136. Annual Reports of the Music Division in *The Library of Congress Quarterly Journal of Current Acquisitions* 5 (November 1947): 35-47; 6 (November 1948): 28-36; 7 (November 1949): 34-44; 10 (November 1952): 33-44; 11 (November 1953): 15-26; 12 (November 1954): 37-51.

Part II

Americana

PROPOSED OFFICIAL VERSION OF "THE STAR SPANGLED BANNER"

PLATE 1.
The Star Spangled Banner. Text and melody recommended for an official version by Richard S. Hill's National Music Council Committee. Reproduced from Hill's report in the *National Music Council Bulletin* 18 (Fall 1957): 3.

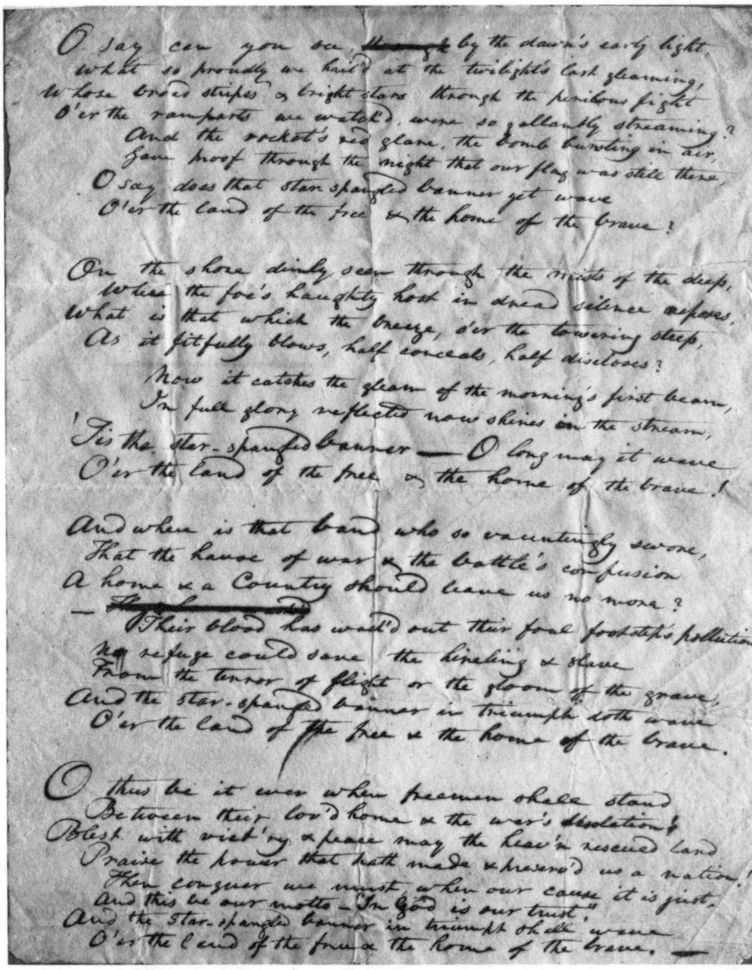

O say can you see ~~through~~ by the dawn's early light,
What so proudly we hail'd at the twilight's last gleaming,
Whose broad stripes & bright stars through the perilous fight
O'er the ramparts we watch'd, were so gallantly streaming?
And the rocket's red glare, the bomb bursting in air,
Gave proof through the night that our flag was still there,
O say does that star-spangled banner yet wave
O'er the land of the free & the home of the brave?

On the shore dimly seen through the mists of the deep,
Where the foe's haughty host in dread silence reposes,
What is that which the breeze, o'er the towering steep,
As it fitfully blows, half conceals, half discloses?
Now it catches the gleam of the morning's first beam,
In full glory reflected now shines in the stream,
'Tis the star-spangled banner — O long may it wave
O'er the land of the free & the home of the brave!

And where is that band who so vauntingly swore,
That the havoc of war & the battle's confusion
A home & a Country should leave us no more?
— ~~They have~~ Their blood has wash'd out their foul footstep's pollution.
No refuge could save the hireling & slave
From the terror of flight or the gloom of the grave,
And the star-spangled banner in triumph doth wave
O'er the land of the free & the home of the brave.

O thus be it ever when freemen shall stand
Between their lov'd home & the war's desolation!
Blest with vict'ry & peace may the heav'n rescued land
Praise the power that hath made & preserv'd us a nation!
Then conquer we must, when our cause it is just,
And this be our motto — "In God is our trust,"
And the star-spangled banner in triumph shall wave
O'er the land of the free & the home of the brave. —

PLATE 2.
Francis Scott Key's earliest known complete draft of his poem (to which he gave no title), completed on the evening of 16 September 1814. At the Maryland Historical Society, Baltimore.

CHAPTER 2

Richard S. Hill and "The 'Unsettled' Text of The Star Spangled Banner"

by

William Lichtenwanger

I. A REFERENCE LIBRARIAN AT WORK

"R-r-ruckets r-r-red glare. Bumps boorsteen kgin in air. Meester Hill iss expert on Schoenberg's method; at Rochester I have heard him talk extemporé but goot." [From here on the reader must imagine for himself the booming bass voice with its Central European accent emanating from a human fireplug named Yury Arbatsky.] "Why does he spend much time on a nationalistic song which not so many of his countrymen even can sing?" Arbatsky was a visitor to the Library of Congress whom I knew only through his interest in certain "ethnic" musics. What he wanted this time, however, when he found Mr. Hill engaged with a Congressman on a *Star Spangled Banner* matter, was to see an obscure book that turned out to be in one of the Library of Congress's weakest collections: medicine. "Oh," I said, "he's a reference librarian, and reference librarians have to be a bit expert on a great many topics. Is your main field medicine?" "Jah," was the laconic reply. "I didn't know that; what's your specialty?" I asked as we squeezed between some ladies crowded around a shelf in a reference alcove off the Main Reading Room. "Zee peenis" boomed the reply in full voice — whether in truth or in jest I never learned.

Arbatsky's reaction to hearing that Mr. Hill was busy on a matter he considered *nicht musikwissenschaftlich* was a reaction not uncommon among Dick's acquaintances during his early years at the Library. Some knew him from his undergraduate days as a student at Cornell under Professor William Strunk. Some knew him as the postgraduate student at Oxford (in the Department of Theology, whose colors he liked) who had spent some time and considerable money delving into Egyptology (and, of course, into Egypt) trying to trace the Thaïs legend. Leland Hall and others in New England knew him first as an assistant in psychology to Kurt Koffka at Smith College. More got to know him when he returned to Cornell in the thirties as a doctoral candidate under Otto Kinkeldey, working on a dissertation far from the misty sands of Egypt: "The Plate Numbers of C. F. Peters and His Predecessors."

Such peregrinations through various subject areas are not uncommon among young people searching for their true niche. What set Dick apart from most of the others was that when he, at the age of thirty-eight, finally settled into his first real job he went right on adding to his varied roster of specialties. He became the chief music reference librarian in an institution with the largest and most varied collections, and the broadest spectrum of users, of any in the world. It was a job that required great zest for tackling new and often complicated problems both in music and in other fields. It required a nice balance between patient thoroughness and practical efficiency under pressure from the clock and the calendar. Obviously it called for both intelligence and learning as well as for common sense. Zest and intelligence and learning Dick had in abundance. His lump of common sense, of knowing when to fish and when to cut bait, was also sizable, although there were times when his zest and determination won out over the clock or some other practical consideration.

All of these qualities were ever-present in Dick's twenty-year courtship of *The Star Spangled Banner* (like Oscar Sonneck, Hill disdained the hyphen between "Star" and "Spangled"). The affair began in 1940 as a simple reference assignment from Harold Spivacke, chief of the Music Division, to his reference librarian. With the war in Europe, more and more Americans were writing the Library for information about their national anthem and its origin; Spivacke asked Hill to prepare a 500-word pamphlet that would reduce the number of individually-prepared replies necessary. Dick had never given the anthem much thought, but he set to work with great enthusiasm. My personal introduction to the project came on a beautiful Saturday in September 1940, my second Saturday as Hill's assistant in the Music Division. (Ironically, in view of our concern just then with a British attack on Baltimore, it was the day before that crucial Sunday of 15 September 1940 that saw the climax of the Luftwaffe's attack during the Battle of Britain.) I being the younger by fourteen years, Dick had me clambering over fences and rooftops along the eastern bank of the Patapsco River's estuary, south of Dundalk in Baltimore, taking pictures of Fort McHenry from points that were as near as we could get on land to the area where Dick calculated Francis Scott Key's cartel ship was anchored when he saw "that our flag was still there" over Fort McHenry.

Photographs were easy to come by. Unfortunately the same was not true of answers to the crucial questions of where the tune of *The Star Spangled Banner* originated and what should be considered the authentic or proper or official text of the song. Over the next three years Dick cleared up most of the other questions that he thought should be answered by his "pamphlet" (which soon became a good-sized monograph and eventually a mountain of typescript), but those two baffled him: the first because of insufficient evidence, the second because of too much evidence — dozens and dozens of variant texts. Then in 1943 Dick was appointed the first editor of the Music Library Association's journal *Notes* in its new quarterly and printed form. Inquiries about the national anthem continued to flow in, and Dick answered each one individually (sometimes at great length) because it went against his whole nature to publish even an information sheet with those two great questions unanswered. Here Dick's perfectionism was a practical drawback, for an information sheet would have saved him many a weary hour.

During the twelve years from 1943 to 1955, Dick had little time to devote to continued research on the source of the tune and the proper text. The tune Key had in his mind while he was thinking up his words was of course "To Anacreon in Heaven," the song of the Anacreontic Society of London, *ca.* 1766 to *ca.* 1792; the question was where *its* tune originated. Dick could neither prove nor disprove the prevailing theory that it was composed by one John Stafford Smith. Smith lived until 1836, when both songs had been printed dozens of times with only a single and questionable attribution to Smith.[1] Hill became obsessed with the idea that the tune originated in Ireland; he visited Dublin at least once, on his way back from a IAML meeting in Europe, and he even hired investigators to search possible Irish sources. Nothing came of it. As for the text, he continued to identify and record new versions when they came to his attention, but that was about all.

Then, in 1955-57, three things happened to bring the *SSB* back to prominence in Dick's mind. First was a request from a constituent of Rep. Joel T. Broyhill of Virginia for "a copy of the official version of the national anthem." When Mr. Broyhill read the reply Dick drafted for him, saying there was no official version, he became interested in the matter, asked his assistant Mr. Homer Krout to go into the situation with Dick, and ended by assuming the adoption of an official version as one of his "causes" in the Congress. Second, the approach of Otto Kinkeldey's eightieth birthday (27 November 1958) led the American Musicological Society to plan a commemorative volume for which Dick Hill agreed to write a chapter on the text of the *SSB*. Third, *Record Ratings* (an offshoot from Kurtz Myers's index of record reviews in *Notes* and a joint product of Myers and Hill) finally reached print via Crown Publishers of New York.

Getting that volume off his shoulders lulled Dick into a momentary feeling of freedom, a state of euphoria in which he envisioned unlimited stretches of time (apart from his LC duties, *Notes,* IAML — he was chairman of the United States committee on RISM — and a few other "minor" obligations) in which he could prepare a comprehensive treatise on the text of *The Star Spangled Banner,* leaving the music to be similarly treated at some future time. Thus was conceived "The 'Unsettled' Text of *The Star Spangled Banner,"* the idea and the adjective both derived from O. G. Sonneck's summation on page 93 of his centennial report (Washington: Government Printing Office, 1914) on *The Star Spangled Banner:*

---

[1] See Lichtenwanger, "The Music of 'The Star-Spangled Banner': From Ludgate Hill to Capitol Hill," *Library of Congress Quarterly Journal of Acquisitions* 34 (July 1977): 136-70 (separately issued by the Library of Congress, 1977); reprinted with slight changes as "The Music of 'The Star-Spangled Banner': Whence and Whither?," *College Music Symposium* 18 (Fall 1978): 34-81.

In course of time verbal inaccuracies would creep from one song book into the other. Also the compilers themselves have sometimes felt justified in improving Key's text. The result of all this has been, of course, that gradually Key's text became unsettled. . . . Hence, very properly, the cry for an authoritative text has been raised.

Through Congressman Broyhill's intervention the cry for an authoritative—and officially recognized—version was finally heeded and an effort made in 1957-58. The National Music Council was one of various organizations whose advice was sought by Mr. Broyhill, and it appointed a committee with Richard S. Hill as chairman. The committee was to work out the most proper and effective versions of both words and melody, which the NMC would then recommend to Mr. Broyhill as the basis for his bill to be introduced into the Congress. The committee did its work (with Hill, after much research and consultation, proposing and the whole committee disposing with much give and take by all hands). The National Music Council put forth this "preliminary version," questions were raised in various quarters, some changes and improvements were made, and the final version recommended to Congressman Broyhill who submitted a revised bill (House Joint Resolution 558) on 4 March 1958.

This version was almost identical in tune and text with that printed in the December 1957 issue of *Notes* and elsewhere (see plate 1 at the head of this article). Four other members of the House of Representatives submitted bills with their own suggested versions, and on 21, 22, & 28 May 1958, hearings on all these bills were held by Sub-Committtee No. 4 of the House Committee on the Judiciary. A transcript of all the testimony and exhibits tendered at the hearings was published by the Committee,[2] but no legislative action was taken. Many of the statements and questions at the hearings lower one's respect for "the peepul" and for their ability to listen and learn. Dick Hill was a chief witness for the Broyhill bill, but neither he nor the Congressman could disabuse their opponents of the ridiculous belief that "they're trying to change our beloved national anthem!" Mr. Broyhill continued to resubmit his bill in future Congresses, but nothing came of it.

Perhaps the most worthy result of the whole episode was that Dick Hill had been forced, in order to do a proper job of selecting the proper text to recommend to the NMC and Mr. Broyhill, to sift carefully through all of the early manuscript and printed versions of the *SSB* text, to determine what changes Francis Scott Key himself had made in his original poem, and thus to "settle" the "unsettled text." His original deadline for handing in his contribution to the

---

[2] U.S., Congress, House of Representatives, Committee on the Judiciary, *The Star-Spangled Banner: Hearings before Subcommittee No. 4,* 84th Congress, 2d sess., H. J. Res. 17, H. J. Res. 517, H. Rept. 10542, H. J. Res. 558, and H. Rept. 12231, May 21, 22, and 28 1958, serial 18.

"Kinkschrift," as it was affectionately called, must have been some-time early in 1958 if the volume was to have been in being for presentation to Kinkeldey on 27 November 1958. Dick was surely not the only one who failed to make that deadline, so there were later deadlines.

I have no recollection now of when they were, or of how near completion his contribution was on, say, 27 November 1959. My recollection is that it was not until somewhere around June 1960 that guilt at holding up the entire volume forced him to start neglecting as many other responsibilities as he dared in order to work on it continuously (a relative term, of course, for the Library of Congress, *Notes, RISM*, and other responsibilities could not be shrugged off entirely). What I remember most clearly about Dick's last six months of work, when he enjoyed finally getting to grips with all of the textual problems, is that his joy was darkened by the shadow of all his responsibilities then being neglected even as he battled to finish the Kinkeldey piece, already more than two years overdue. He finished typing his Notes on page 160 of his draft early on the morning of Thanksgiving Day, 24 November 1960, his heart attack already under way.

Even under all these pressures, Dick's professional ethic did not permit skimping on sources, or taking things for granted, or summa-rizing quickly off the top of his head. In terms of extent, detail, close reasoning, and even of its expository style, the draft could be considered close to complete and ready for editing. It was, in fact, too long and too lavishly written. Dick, for instance, was not content to summarize briefly the comings and goings of some fifty ships of the British fleet in the Chesapeake Bay; he got copies of the log books and muster rolls of many of the ships from the Public Record Office in London and devoted pages to their movements in August and September of 1814. The one thing he was barely able to start on — though it was well-formed in his mind — was a variorum edition of the *Star Spangled Banner* text showing the likenesses and differences among many dozens of manuscript, sheet music, newspaper, and other editions, word by word and apostrophe by apostrophe. This edition was to have been printed on a fold-out chart so large it might have constituted one of the seven wonders of the book world.

Dick was out of the hospital and (we dared think) recuperating in Florida when the fatal heart attack struck him early in the morning of 7 February 1961. At the AMS meeting in California during the last week in December, I had gone over Dick's situation with Charles Seeger and others responsible for the Kinkeldey volume, describing the size of the Hill contribution and the amount of work still to be done. The Society decided it had better wait no longer, and the commemorative volume was published as its *Journal,* three issues in one, for 1961; Dick's contribution would be published as a separate AMS monograph when it was ready. After Dick died, five weeks later, there was talk of the editing and final preparation for publica-tion being undertaken by Irving Lowens; he had often eaten late evening meals with Dick in the final weeks of work on the draft and knew better than anyone else Dick's thinking about the many problems involved. But the job would have required many weeks of work taken from Irving's own tight schedule, and Irv was himself a survivor of a near-fatal heart attack; and, somehow, without Dick's own particular zest for the project and his dogged determination to settle the unsettled text, the project seemed to fade into a "someday" limbo. Then with the publication in 1972 by the Maryland Historical Society (Baltimore) of *Star-Spangled Books,* an exhibition catalog prepared by P. W. Filby and the late Edward G. Howard, Sonneck's 1914 report was in most respects more than brought up to date. A short chapter was devoted to the text, comparing eighteen of the earliest versions.

When I was asked to contribute to the present volume, however, it struck me that perhaps I could use Dick's typescript to serve two purposes: to publicize the most important of his findings and conclusions about the various textual sources, and at the same time pay tribute to his inimitable character as a reference librarian — for to me this "settlement project" exemplifies that inimitable character in terms larger than life. The project was studied from various angles and a plan of attack determined before he got down to the operational level; it reveals the breadth and depth of his concerns and his mastery of many unlike sources; it is not quite complete but it contains many answers to various pertinent questions; and, perhaps most unusual, it evidences the author's expert viewpoints but at the same time shows sympathy with the views, wrong-headed though they may sometimes be, of ordinary citizens. Not every expert-author on matters of history or art or (weasel word!) sociology can lay claim to all of these characteristics; but a good reference librarian has to. Dick Hill was, before all else, a good reference librarian.

Instead of beginning at the chronological beginning of the text of *The Star Spangled Banner,* Dick wisely began his account by laying the foundation for his work, showing the need for a major study to settle the long-since unsettled poem by Francis Scott Key. He quotes Public Law 823 of the 71st Congress, signed into law by President Herbert Hoover under date of 3 March 1931: ". . . the composition consisting of the words and music known as *The Star Spangled Banner* is designated the national anthem of the United States of America." After twenty years of haggling and disagreement among various factions (some wanting "My Country, 'Tis of Thee," some "America the Beautiful," some "Hail, Columbia," some wanting no official anthem at all) the *SSB* faction, led by Marylanders both in and out of the Congress, had finally pushed that bill through. To have tried to get agreement on a specific version of both words and tune would have killed that minimal effort and left the designation of a national anthem in cacophonous chaos.

From 1931 Dick Hill then looks back to America's entry into World War I. At that time President Woodrow Wilson by executive order designated *The Star Spangled Banner* as the national anthem, just as the Navy had done as early as 1893 (article 147 of the *Naval Regulations* of that year) and the Army sometime after. None of these executive fiats had designated any particular version of words or music, but by 1917, with the greatly increased number of perform-

ances after the United States entered the war, authorities in several
areas felt moved to reach agreement so as to avoid both musical and
jurisdictional conflicts. Writes Dick:

**Two semi-official committees had established versions of
the song that differed one from the other in a number of respects,
although both agreed in omitting the third [anti-British] stanza
of Key's poem. In one case, the Navy Department's and the War
Department's Commissions on Training Camp Activities had
merged their interests and appointed a joint civilian National
Committee on Army and Navy Camp Music. With the assistance
of this Committee, three pocket-sized song books were issued
for free distribution to all officers and men in the Army, Marine
Corps, and Navy. The contents of all three song books were
very nearly identical, except that starting with pages 17 a few
pages were devoted to songs suited to the particular service. All
of the books started with the melody and three stanzas of *The
Star Spangled Banner* in the version prepared by the Committee.
There was also a set of part books issued early in 1919 with
"Band Accompaniments to Songs of the U.S. Army, Navy and
Marine Corps," in which the same version, arranged for band
by Wallace Goodrich, was given in two keys—B-flat for service
and ceremonial occasions and A-flat for singing. All four publications could be distributed only to service personnel; and the
Committee seems to have joined with two other groups for the
preparation of arrangements to be issued by commercial
publishers—the Oliver Ditson Company of Boston, Chas. H.
Ditson & Co. of New York, and Lyon & Healy of Chicago. The
sheet music edition brought out in 1918 has the following note
at the head of page 2:

> *Service Version,* prepared for the Army and Navy song
> and band books, and for School and Community Singing
> by a Committee of Twelve Consisting of John Alden
> Carpenter, Frederick Converse, Wallace Goodrich, and
> Walter R. Spalding, representing the War Department
> Commission on Training Camp Activities; Peter W.
> Dykema, Hollis Dann, and Osbourne McConathy, repre-
> senting the Music Supervisors' National Conference; C.
> C. Birchard, Carl Engel, William Arms Fisher, Arthur
> Edward Johnstone, and E. W. Newton, representing
> music publishers; Chairman—Mr. Dykema.

Almost simultaneously, another edition, described as "A
Standardized Version of the Melody," was published by G.
Schirmer of New York and Boston. The cover of the sheet music

---

** Throughout this chapter, material presented in SANS SERIF TYPEFACE is text of
Richard S. Hill, whereas SERIF TYPEFACE is text of William Lichtenwanger.

edition says that it was harmonized by Walter Damrosch, and page 2 gives the heading:

> Version prepared at the request of the U.S. Bureau of Education by the following committee: Will Earhart (Chairman), Walter Damrosch, Arnold J. Gantvoort, O. G. Sonneck, and John Philip Sousa.

The committee that established the Education Version had Mr. Sonneck as one of its members, and since he was the one man on the committee who must have been thoroughly familiar with the sources for Key's text, it is logical to see him as the chief influence in giving that version a text that comes far closer to Key's original autograph than does the text of the Service Version. For one thing, the Education Version gives the line ''Praise the power that hath made and preserv'd us a nation'' with a small ''p'' on the word ''power.'' Key had written it so in his earliest extant autograph. On the next day, however, when the poem was first set in type at the shop of the *Baltimore American* by the fourteen-year-old apprentice Samuel Sands, the lad's exuberance got the better of him and he added capitals to seventeen words that Key had given in their lower-case forms. [Among them was the capital on "Power" in verse 4, line 4. In this one instance the matter of capital versus lower-case has more than a trivial significance, one that has generally been misunderstood, and Dick later devotes a paragraph to it (see p. 103).]

It might reasonably be supposed that the variety of the versions submitted at those hearings in May 1958 would demonstrate with ample clarity the need for some common denominator in the form of an official version. Instead, rather curiously, the most striking development was the number of people who came at their own expense to testify that we already had a commonly accepted version of both words and music. One witness thought that Thomas Carr's first sheet music edition might be used, because ''Key himself had read proof on it''—an utterly false assumption. Others supposed that President Wilson must surely have had a specific version in mind when, in his 1917 revision of the regulations of the armed services, he authorized use of the song as a national anthem. One lady believed it would be only proper to use the version played for the Congress by the Marine Band when, in 1931, Public Law 823 making the song the national anthem was on its way to being passed.

The text of the Carr edition is so very corrupt that one wonders what form of myopia could possibly make it appear acceptable; no one seemed able to produce President Wilson's version (naturally, since no particular version was specified in his regulation), and no one could identify what the Marine Band had played in 1931. Such problems did not seem to disconcert the witnesses in the least. They came to the hearings convinced that a nefarious attempt was being made to ''change'' the national anthem, and nothing said seemed to convince them that the intent was rather to get rid of the innumerable changes that

had already been made and to settle on a version that the
majority could accept.

In partial justification of these witnesses perhaps it should be said that the unsettling process has at no time reached a point where it renders Key's poem unrecognizable. Omission of the third stanza is fairly common, but no line of any stanza has been so extensively altered as to make it unidentifiable. The changes that have become widespread affect a few words and certain phrases, but most of the inconsistencies and awkwardnesses apply to matters of case, capitalization, spelling, and punctuation. The general populace is usually quite unaware of all these minutiae — unless and until, that is, they have to tell school children whether to sing "in the stream" or "on the stream," or have to prepare a text to be printed in the *Ladies' Club Weekly,* or have to direct their choir whether "that" in "that Star-Spangled Banner" is to be sung on one quarter note or two eighth notes. Then, like Congressman Broyhill's constituent, they want and deserve to know which is *right* and which is *wrong*. Further uncertainties bedevil mostly professional musicians: how far can a citizen rightfully go in personalizing a performance (before a ball game, for instance), in slowing down or hurrying up the tempo, in crooning, or bellowing, or putting strange emphasis on certain words?

It is not any great esthetic or political problem we are dealing with here, not any extensive rewriting or ''changing'' of Key's poem, but a multiplicity of small alterations and deviations. Considered individually they may appear insignificant; it is their total and cumulative effect that becomes the great problem. That this cumulative effect is indeed pervasive may be seen from the variorum chart of the poem at the end of this paper. It shows that not a single one of the thirty-two lines in the poem has remained entirely unchanged over the years from the text given in Key's earliest extant autograph.

If, under these circumstances, the cry for an authoritative text heard by Mr. Sonneck in 1914 still remains unanswered, the blame should nevertheless not be laid wholly on the shoulders of Congress. For one thing, the Congress has never assumed that its functions call on it to serve as an Institut de France; and with so many conflicting voices anxious to advise it, the inherent problem becomes incredibly difficult to solve. Do we accept the exact reading of Key's earliest surviving manuscript without reference to the many changes that he himself introduced in his four later autograph copies of the poem? Or do we accept certain alterations introduced by others and sanctioned today by their very wide usage? So far as the melody is concerned, it would be unthinkable to go back to the form that Key himself knew in September 1814; and if the ''folk'' are to be allowed to introduce changes in the music, why not also in the words? Finally, if a judicious selection of readings is to be made according to a combination of these different principles, then who is to be the judge of what is right? Obviously, before any of these questions can be answered — if they can be answered at all — we must first determine as exactly as possible the various sources of the changes in the text in order that we may know who made which alteration when, and thereby determine how suitable and acceptable each change is.

That task is simpler to state than to perform. We probably know as much as we need to know about a few of the pertinent documents, but the two most crucial sources—Key's earliest extant autograph and the first known printing of the poem—are still shrouded in uncertainty. A few editors even in 1814 recognized that they had in their hands a superior patriotic creation; yet no one seems to have suspected that the poem was to become a national symbol. As a consequence, no one involved set down the details of its publishing history at a time when these would have been fresh and clear in the minds of many. By the middle of the nineteenth century, when the first accounts begin to appear, the inevitable psychological drive to simplify and dramatize events of the distant past had taken over and even the accounts of firsthand observers become imprecise. Still later, when the third-hand and fourth-hand recitals of "family traditions"* are stirred into the pot, it seems almost impossible to sort out the few actual ingredients of the original stew. Mr. Sonneck attempted to present all the accounts fairly and objectively in his 1914 report, but he soon found himself in such a morass of contradictions that he was able only to eliminate a few of the more obviously false claims. He did not even try to establish a firm, documented, chronological sequence of events.

Since 1914 a few hitherto unknown sources on the early history of the text have come to light, and they relieve us of the need to involve ourselves so tiresomely with "family traditions"; we can come close to limiting this present reconstruction of events to the firsthand accounts plus one widely-accepted secondhand source. In addition there are a goodly number of military, naval, and historical documents surviving from September 1814. Few of these so much as mention Key's poem, but they do provide a structure of day-by-day events against which the later and more pertinent account may be measured. Even so, we are left with far too many areas of conjecture, but at least we can advance farther than before toward a more realistic determination of what happened to Key in Baltimore and the Chesapeake Bay in September 1814, and in particular we can establish a more reasonable chronological sequence of events. In what follows, the documents—both new and old—will be discussed in connection with the principal figures in the story, in the hope that this organization will make it easier for the reader to follow and evaluate the arguments.

---

* Dick refers here to traditions among the descendants of Thomas Carr, first publisher of the music, of Judge Hopkinson, who really played no part at all, and indirectly of Chief Justice Taney. — WL

Key himself left no written account at all of his writing of his poem. A leading lawyer of the Washington-Baltimore-Frederick area, he had the good sense to recognize that his poetical efforts were the product of an amateur. He was almost painfully modest, and he seems always to have been genuinely surprised when anyone thought one of his poems good enough to publish. He also seems never to have raised any public objection when the printed product failed to correspond very closely to his manuscript. True, he had very few opportunities (aside from the many printings of *The Star Spangled Banner*) to see any of his poems in print. His earlier parody on the *Anacreontic Song*, using the same tune as the original version of *The SSB*, was *When the warrior returns from the battle afar.* Key himself sang it at a dinner in Georgetown, D.C., in 1805, a celebration in honor of Charles Stewart and Stephen Decatur upon their return from putting down the Barbary pirates; the poem was printed in a few newspapers and perhaps ten songsters. His hymn ''Lord, with glowing heart I'd praise Thee'' is found in quite a large number of hymn books. Miller & Osbourn of Philadelphia in about 1832 issued a sheet music edition of Key's *The Home of the Soul,* a sentimental parody fitted to the melody of *Home, Sweet Home*. The majority of his poems, however, had to wait for publication until fourteen years after his death, when the Rev. Henry V. D. Johns gathered all the Key manuscripts he could find among the poet's relatives and friends. With them Johns issued *Poems of the Late Francis S. Key, Esq., Author of ''The Star Spangled Banner,'' with an Introductory Letter by Chief Justice Taney* (New York: Robert Carter & Brothers, 1857). One of Key's daughters, Mrs. Charles Howard, made a revealing comment on her father's attitude toward poetry in a letter to George Henry Preble dated ''Baltimore, 25 April 1874'':[3]

> . . . I do not think I ever had an autograph of the Star Spangled Banner. My father gave his children from the time they could speak the habit of committing poetry to memory, and in that way only has the song been preserved by me. Except one or two words, Mr. Keim's version as you have it is the one I have ever remembered. . . .

With a similar absence of pretension Key seems to have trusted to his own memory, not only for the text of his one famous poem but also for the events surrounding the writing of it. Fortunately it was an excellent memory, so that years later when the poem had thoroughly established itself on the national scene and friends asked for copies of it in his own hand, he could write

FRANCIS SCOTT KEY
(1779-1843)

---

[3] Printed under "Notes and Queries," *The New England Historical and Genealogical Register* 28 (Oct.-Dec. 1874): 469-70.

out the complete poem in a form that in most respects comes closer to his 1814 autograph than does the broadside printed very shortly after the poem was written.

At a political dinner in Frederick, Maryland, on 6 August 1834, a toast was drunk to Key as the author of *The Star Spangled Banner,* and in his reply to the toast he went so far as to admit his technical authorship. With typical modesty, however, he immediately claimed that his was only a small and insignificant contribution, since he had merely described the heroic deeds of others; and he ended by proposing another toast to "The real authors of the song" — the citizen-soldiers of Baltimore who had so gallantly defended Fort McHenry. The little speech contains some fine oratorical conceits, but unfortunately no facts at all; hence it is of no service in the present quest.[4]

Further under the heading "Francis Scott Key," Hill devotes eighteen typewritten pages to a discussion of Key's character ("Key was a nervous and excitable man"), his family and its disposition during the anxious weeks of August-September 1814, his own goings and comings caused by the attack on Washington and the expected attack on Baltimore, his commissioning by John Mason (Commissary General of Prisoners for the United States during the War) to visit the British fleet and try to secure the release of "old Dr. Beanes." Dr. William Beanes, 1749-1828, was a prominent citizen and the leading physician of Upper Marlboro, Maryland, some 15-18 miles east of the Capitol. He must have had a fine house, for it was selected as the headquarters of Admiral Cockburn as the British moved overland from the Patuxent to Washington. Both sides apparently were courteous; the British placed a guard around the house to prevent their troops from plundering.

The trouble did not arise until after Admiral Cockburn and party had withdrawn from Dr. Beanes's enforced hospitality and were making their way back to their ships, leaving the capitol and White House in flames. Some British stragglers, finding the Beanes home no longer protected, took to looting and treating Dr. Beanes as an enemy. The good doctor reacted by forming a small party of armed Americans which pursued some of the stragglers and made prisoners of them. When this news reached Admiral Cockburn back on his ship, he reacted angrily in turn and sent a detachment to free the British prisoners, capture Dr. Beanes, and throw him into the flagship's brig for transportation to Halifax, Nova Scotia, the North American headquarters of the fleet. Apparently they viewed him not as a prisoner of war but as a gentleman who had broken his word to them.

---

4 Hill's note: The dinner was fully covered in the local papers and Key's speech was reprinted by the Rev. Henry V. D. Johns in his edition of *Poems of the Late Francis S. Key, Esq.* (New York: Robert Carter & Brothers, 1857). The speech is also discussed and quoted from in Victor Weybright's *Star Spangled Banner* (New York: Farrar & Rinehert, 1935), 260-65, and in Edward S. Delaplaine's *Francis Scott Key — Life and Times* (Brooklyn, N.Y.: Biography Press, 1937), 378-81.

Hill quotes from several letters written by Key in this period, including one to his friend John Randolph of Roanoke, Virginia, that was written *after* his sojourn with the fleet but does not even mention his poem (both Key and Randolph had actively opposed this country's going to war with Great Britain):

> . . . You will be surprised to hear that I have . . . spent eleven days in the British Fleet—I with a flag to endeavour to save poor old Dr. Beanes a voyage to Halifax in which we fortunately succeeded—They detained us til after their attack on Baltimore, & you may imagine what a state of anxiety I endured. Sometimes, when I remembered it was there the declaration of this abominable war was received with public rejoicings, I could not feel a hope that they would escape—and again, when I thought of the many faithful, whose piety leavens that lump of wickedness, I could hardly feel a fear.
>
> To make my feelings still more acute the Admiral had intimated his fears that the town must be burned: I was sure that, if taken, it would have been given up to plunder. I have reason to believe that such a promise was given to their soldiers.—It was filled with women & children!—I hope I shall never cease to feel the warmest gratitude when I think of this most merciful deliverance. It seems to have given me a higher idea of the ''forebearance, long-suffering & tender mercy'' of God than I had ever before conceived.
>
> Whether this gentle paternal chastisement we have been suffering will be sufficient for us is yet to be seen.— I have my fears.—Never was man more disappointed in his expectations than I have been as to the character of British officers.—With some exceptions they appear to be illiberal, ignorant & vulgar, & seem filled with a spirit of malignity against every thing [*sic*] American. Perhaps, however, I saw them in unfavorable circumstances. [Apparently, Hill remarks, on re-reading his letter Key felt that he may have spoken too harshly of the British officers, and crowded this sentence in between the two paragraphs as a second thought.]
>
> There is a great clamor in the City [Washington] & George Town about the removal of the Seat of Government. I am so uncertain about my own movements that I care but little about those of the Government. If the war lasts (as I think it will) I cannot see how I can live in George Town; & perhaps if the great folks move off little people can live cheaper.—As to the disgrace of abandonning [*sic*] the seat of Government & acknowledging that the Conquerors of Canada cannot defend their own Capitol, it would be a serious thing to a people not already in the very dust and mire of ignomy. If I continued to live in Geo-Town I don't know but I should like to get clear of them—As it is, the *Seat* of Government may *sit* (as Holland says) where it pleases.

On the remaining pages under his heading of "Francis Scott Key," Hill deals at length with the chronology of the trip to the fleet, the sojourn with the fleet, and the return to Baltimore after the British retreat. His primary reason for devoting considerable space to this chronology was that some of the "family traditions" to which he earlier referred had telescoped and over-simplified these phases, with the result that Key was supposed to have written his poem on Wednesday, 14 September, taken it to Baltimore on 15 September, and had it printed and widely distributed by the sixteenth. Anyone of reasonable intelligence and knowing the geography of the Chesapeake Bay together with the dates of the land and naval actions around Baltimore should have recognized such "traditions" as impossible, but certain Marylanders became so caught up in local chauvinism that even a chief justice of the Supreme Court of the United States had the song being printed and popularized all within an hour. Here I shall try to restrain myself and keep to the bare facts—though the reference librarian in Dick had so much fun figuring out the courses and locations on different days of the fifty-plus ships that made up the British force that one is tempted . . . but no: facts, important facts, facts only.

Fact No. 1 is that Key met John S. Skinner in Baltimore on Sunday, 4 September, and that the two started south on their cartel ship on the morning of the fifth. That ship was one of several similar sloops owned by a Baltimorean; its name has never been proven despite various guesses. In the log book of the British frigate *Surprize,* where the crew of the sloop were guests from the morning of the 8th to late on the 11th, Dick found the names of John Ferguson, master; James Gramahe, mate; and eight seamen: Thomas Harrison, James Butler, Miles Marton (or Morton), Fred Wilkinson, John Porter, Richard Carol, Michael Walker, and Jonathan Mercer. Also listed is "David Baines, Surgeon," actually the 65-year-old Dr. William Beanes who in due course was out of the brig and treated as a run-of-the-mill guest.

Skinner and Key, as official representatives of their government, were treated as distinguished guests. Skinner technically was a purser in the Navy, but he was commissioned by General John Mason to take charge of arrangements concerning the exchange of prisoners, the delivery of mail (primarily to the British fleet), and other matters requiring a go-between with the enemy. Skinner sent a dispatch to his Commissary General just before they embarked, saying that they expected to find the British flagship in the Patuxent estuary, discharge their business, and be back in Baltimore on the evening of the seventh.

Fact No. 2 is that by the time Key and Skinner left Baltimore the British flagship *Tonnant,* eighty guns, had left the Patuxent. When the cartel ship finally caught up with her she was twenty-some miles south of Point Lookout (where the north bank of the Potomac meets the west bank of Chesapeake Bay) and it was the afternoon of the seventh. The *Tonnant*'s log, according to Dick Hill, recorded their coming aboard between two and four, and shortly afterwards the two Americans were invited to dinner.

Fact No. 3 is that the dispatches and letters handed over by Skinner to Admiral Sir Alexander Cochrane, the Commander-in-Chief, told of good treatment by the Americans of wounded British officers and men who had been left behind at Bladensburg and Washington. This news mollified the British command (including General Robert Ross, in charge of the land forces, who would be killed the following Monday at the very beginning of the land attack on Baltimore) and disposed them toward releasing the impetuous "old Dr. Beanes"—at least *de jure*. *De facto,* however, Beanes and all the Americans presented a problem. At dinner and throughout the seventh the British had spoken freely in front of their visitors about their decision to turn back north and capture (at the very least) Baltimore. Both strategy and tactics, plus timing and troop strengths, had been discussed. The British of course did not want to send the cartel sloop on its way and let it warn Baltimore and the American command. The muster book of the frigate *Surprize* showed Dick that early on the morning of 8 September Dr. Beanes (the spelling "Baines" is a reminder of the pronunciation of that day) and the sloop's crew of ten were put aboard the *Surprize* which took the sloop in tow; Key and Skinner, however, remained on board the flagship.

Fact No. 4 is that by 8 September the ships of the fleet were scattered all over the Bay and its tributary rivers, especially the Potomac. Not having radio or even a motor launch to distribute the new orders, the *Tonnant* had to round her flock up like a mother hen. By Sunday morning, 11 September, the *Tonnant* and *Surprize* were in the Patapsco off Baltimore, but it was late the next day before most of the ships were in their places. On the eleventh the Americans from the *Surprize* and Skinner and Key from the *Tonnant* were put aboard the cartel ship (with a marine guard to ensure that they did not slip away to warn Baltimore). The first part of the two-pronged attack (by land from the northeast and by water from the southeast) then got under way.

Fact No. 5: The smaller ships and transports began putting their troops ashore at North Point (where the Patapsco meets the west side of the Bay) on 11 September, their idea being to circle well east of the city and then attack from the northeast where there were few defenses except entrenchments recently dug (see map, plate 14). The encircling movement started early on Monday the twelfth and met with immediate though flexible resistance. The god of battles showed early that he had changed sides since the fiasco at Bladensburg: General Ross, spurring his horse ahead to see where the American fire was coming from, was an easy target for two Baltimore marksmen and died before he could be taken back to a ship. The so-called Battle of North Point on that Monday took place mostly on the neck of land between the swampy beginnings of Bear Creek and the upper reaches of Back River. It took the British that day and the next to push their way to a front extending northwest from Philadelphia Road to Belair Road. That was as far as they got; the Baltimore citizen-militia were much better prepared and officered than those at Bladensburg three weeks before.

Fact No. 6: Five bomb ships and a rocket ship easily made their way up the estuary toward Fort McHenry, but the various frigates with their greater draughts could not get close enough—because of the uneven depths and also because the Americans had sunk a barrier of old ships and hulks across the mouth of the Ferry Branch and the North West Branch so that no vessel of any size could brazen its way past the Fort to attack it from the rear or to fire on the city. It was seven in the morning of Tuesday, 13 September, before the second prong of the attack on Fort McHenry and Baltimore could get under way.

The bombardment itself did not commence until the morning of Tuesday, the 13th, and continued throughout most of the day and at intervals during the night. By seven on the morning of the 14th the British were convinced that it would be too costly to take the city (even supposing that they could do so at all) and their withdrawal was begun.

Fact No. 7: The remainder of his general section under "Key" is devoted by Dick to refuting the Baltimore legend that prevailed for more than a century, with the British leaving on the 14th, the same day that began with Key writing his poem and ended with him in Baltimore polishing it off preparatory to its being printed the next morning, Thursday, 15 September. From the *New York Gazette* Dick quotes an eyewitness report that Skinner (hence also Key) arrived in Baltimore between eight and nine o'clock on Friday evening, the 16th; it was not until late that afternoon that the last of the British ground troops were onloaded and the thirteen Americans were allowed to head for Baltimore. It was not until 10:30 on Saturday morning, the 17th, that all the ships were ready and began to draw anchor and head south down the Bay.

JOHN STUART
SKINNER (1788-1851)

In his ten typewritten pages under this heading, Hill first sketches Skinner's personality and career. He considers Skinner has been slighted in the Baltimore legend of the anthem, possibly because he was somewhat aggressive and not a popular figure and his name never acquired the social sheen that the names of Judge Nicholson and Mr. Justice Taney did. Yet Skinner was the only participant to publish a firsthand account of "what happened on the sloop," an account in the form of a letter to the *Baltimore Patriot* correcting some errors made by Charles Jared Ingersoll in his *Historical Sketch of the Second War between the United States of America and Great Britain* (Philadelphia: Lea and Blanchard, 1844 & 1849). Skinner's letter was printed in the *Patriot* for 29 May 1849, and then was reprinted in the *National Intelligencer* for 4 June 1849. It is important primarily for its testimony as to the chronology of events, and Dick prefaces it with some remarks about the shifting channels caused by the tide in the Patapsco estuary and the fact that some of the British ships could take no part in the bombardment of Fort McHenry; Admiral Cochrane shifted his flag to the smaller *Surprize,* but even the smaller frigates and brigs had to stand down so far (probably in the area just north of the mouth of Curtis Creek) that they took little part in the bombardment. That was the job of the rocket ship and five bomb ships — hence the references by Key to bombs and (Congreve) rockets rather than to heavy shot from the ships' ordinary guns. Hill quotes only the most pertinent passages from Skinner to the *Patriot,* one of which corrects Ingersoll's errant pronouncement that "It was during the striking concussions of that night [i.e., 13-14 September] that the song of *The Star-Spangled Banner* was composed in the admiral's ship." Writes Skinner:

> Now it is not unworthy of that noble inspiration that its circumstances should be more exactly known. The author of the Star-Spangled Banner was never on board the admiral ships [*sic*] after we were in sight of Baltimore. We had been invited during our detention to take up our quarters with the admiral's son, Sir Thomas Cochrane, on board the Surprize Frigate, the admiral expressing regret that his own, the Flagship, was so crowded with officers that he could not accommodate us all as he wished; but promised that his son (which he well redeemed) would make us comfortable until after the denouement of the expedition then going forward.
>
> Dining every day with the admiral and a large party of army and navy officers, his objects and plans were freely spoken of, and thus when we arrived in sight of the city, the undersigned again demanded an answer to his despatches, to which Sir Alexander answered, smilingly, "Ah, Mr. S., after discussing so freely as we have done in your presence, our purposes and plans, you could hardly expect us to let you go on shore now in advance of us. Your despatches are all ready. You will have to remain with us until all is over, when I promise you there shall be no further delay." Seeing no help for it, I demanded that we should then be returned to our own vessel — one of Ferguson's Norfolk packets, under our own "Star-Spangled Banner," during the attack. It was from her deck in view of Fort McHenry that we witnessed through an anxious day and night, "The rockets red glare, the bombs bursting in air," and the song which was written the night after we got back to Baltimore, in the hotel then kept at the corner of Hanover and Market Streets, was but a versified and almost literal transcript of our expressed hopes and apprehensions, through that ever-memorable period of anxiety to all, but never of despair. Calling on its accomplished author the next morning, he handed it to the undersigned, who passed it to the *Baltimore Patriot,* and through it to immortality.

Dick Hill based his approach to the entire SSB problem on the principle of avoiding family traditions and of taking testimony from firsthand witnesses such as Skinner — and here his witness gets Key and himself back to Baltimore in exemplary fashion but then tops his story off with a truly dangling participle in a statement that cannot be true: that he passed the poem to the *Baltimore Patriot* and so to immortality. It was to the *Baltimore American* shop that he took it, where it was set in type as a handbill by fourteen-year-old Samuel Sands and then, from the *American* handbill, printed in the *Patriot* of 20 September. Hill does not believe that Skinner's memory went wrong but rather that, in a letter addressed to the *Patriot,* which was in fact the first newspaper (and second source of any kind) to print it, Skinner chose to overlook the claim of the rival paper on behalf of its handbill. With some justice, that handbill seems to have been regarded in most quarters as a printing but not as a formal publication.

Hill quotes from Skinner's letter one more bit of evidence showing that on Friday, 16 September, the British were still finishing their preparations for leaving the Baltimore area: recovering all land troops that could be recovered, orders sent to other ships regarding their next destinations (some of those that had ventured within range of Fort McHenry's guns required repairs before they could reach the fleet's North American base at Halifax, Nova Scotia; and some, after makeshift repairs, were sent directly back to England). And, of course, Skinner was still awaiting the despatches and mail to prisoners that he was to take back with him. He writes:

> . . . The first thing Admiral Cockburn said to the undersigned, the next morning after their retreat [of the land forces back to their ships], when he waited on Admiral Cochrane for his answer to the despatches, was—even before the usual salutations, and having in view his previously expressed exulting anticipations—"Ah, Mr. S., if it had not been for the sinking of those ships across the channel, with the wind and tide we had in our favor, we should have taken the town; as it was, we flurried you, any how." "A miss, Sir George, is as good as a mile."

ROGER BROOKE
TANEY (1777-1864)

Judge Taney (pronounced *taw-ny*) was married to Francis Scott Key's sister Anne. His home was in Frederick, Maryland, and he was chief justice of the U.S. Supreme Court, 1836-64. He was not a participant in the defense of Baltimore, but he saw Key at Georgetown just before Key left for the fleet, and he saw him again at Frederick a week or so after Key was released by the British. It is his account, written to Key's son-in-law Charles Howard on 17 March 1856, that until recently was the commonly accepted source on the early days of Key's poem. Hill points out that Taney's story not only was secondhand but also was not written down until forty-one years after he heard Key's story. Even a chief justice is susceptible to foreshortened memory and confusion of the *dramatis personae,* and Dick points out that the story was written not as history but as "family tradition." Taney was so rash, for instance, that in his pride he wrote: "in less than an hour after [Key's poem] was placed in the hands of the printer, it was all over Town—and hailed with enthusiasm—and took its place at once as a national song." Oscar Sonneck, in his 1914 report, remarks that such time-shortenings as that belong in the "realm of unwholesome fiction" (p.76). (It is saddening to realize that the piece of writing for which Justice Taney is most often remembered is rather worse than "unwholesome fiction." A year later, on 6 March 1857, he handed down the Supreme Court's pro-slavery decision in the Dred Scott case. That decision was the high-water mark of governmental approval of slavery; no doubt it encouraged many Southern pro-slavers as to the righteousness of withdrawal from the Union.)

Since what Key told Taney a week or so after the event is as close as we have to Key's own account, Dick Hill quotes the two most pertinent paragraphs from Taney's letter to Charles Howard (which is in the Manuscripts Division of the Library of Congress):

> He then told me that under the excitement of the time he had written a song, and handed me a printed copy of "*The Star Spangled Banner.*" — When I had read it and expressed my admiration, I asked him how he had found time in the scenes he had been passing through to compose such a song? He said he commenced it on the deck of their vessel in the fervor of the moment when he saw the enemy hastily retreating to the safety of their ships, & looked at the flag he had watched for so anxiously as the morning opened: that he had written some lines — or brief notes that would aid him in recalling them to his mind — upon the back of a letter which he happened to have in his pocket: and for some of the lines as he proceeded he was obliged to rely altogether on his memory: and that he finished it in the boat on his way to the shore, and wrote it out as it now stands, at the Hotel on the night he reached Baltimore, & immediately after he arrived. He said that on the next morning he took it to Judge Nicholson to ask him what he thought of it: and that he was so much pleased with it that he immediately sent it to a printer, and directed copies to be struck off in handbill form, and that he Mr. Key believed it had been favorably received by the Baltimore public.
>
> Judge Nicholson you know and Mr. Key were nearly connected by marriage — Mrs. Nicholson and Mrs. Key being sisters. The Judge was a man of cultivated taste — had at one time been distinguished among the leading men in Congress, and was at the period of which I am speaking, the Chief Justice for the Baltimore Circuit, and one of the judges of the Court of Appeals of Maryland. Notwithstanding his judicial character which exempted him from military service, he accepted the command of a volunteer company of Artillery. And when the enemy approached & an attack on the Fort was expected he and his company offered their services to the government to assist in its defence. They were accepted and formed a part of the garrison during the bombardment. — The Judge had been relieved from duty and returned to his family only the night before Mr. Key showed him his song — And you may easily imagine the feeling with which at such a moment he read it, and gave it to the public. It was no doubt, as Mr. Key modestly expressed it, favorably received. . . .

This last paragraph introduces a new character on the stage, Judge Joseph Hopper Nicholson. Hill, faced with two different accounts as to who took the poem to the printer, sifted meticulously through copies of military orders of the period until he determined that because of the serious illness of Major Armistead, nominal commander of Fort McHenry, and also of an intermediate superior, Capt. Nicholson was forced to act a role higher than that of a mere captain of an artillery company. That role, Hill says, required him to remain on duty from Monday, 12 September, when the attack on North Point began, until the evening of Tuesday, 20 September, when the handbill was already in print and the poem had also been printed that day by the *Patriot*. It was on the 21st that *Key* visited *Nicholson* and presented him with one of the handbills already set in type by Samuel Sands. Thus Hill is forced to conclude that Taney suffered another case of memory shrinkage, in which Taney's memory substituted the well-known and well-loved Judge Nicholson for the relatively unknown Mr. Skinner.

Key might have been visited on the morning of 17 September by Skinner (as Skinner says), but Key could not possibly have called on Judge Nicholson, since Nicholson was not at home. He was occupied with far more weighty affairs. Indeed, once one has arrived at a proper appreciation of Judge Nicholson's character and of his position in Baltimore, it becomes just a little frivolous to visualize him as rushing about the streets seeking a printer open for business. Surely it is far more appropriate to leave whatever honor is involved in so ordinary an act to that bustling and energetic young man, John S. Skinner. Besides, for once there is an unbiased witness of record—and not only one but two.

SAMUEL SANDS
(1800-91)

In September 1814 Samuel Sands was a printer's devil in the print shop of the *Baltimore American*. He apparently was, because of his age, the only worker on duty throughout that week, although issues of the *American* testify that on several days there was enough staff to put out the paper. There was a time, early in this century, when one Benjamin Edes was a contender for the honor of having been the first printer of *The Star Spangled Banner,* but Oscar Sonneck had shown in 1914 (pp. 76, 81) that a much better claim was that of Samuel Sands. Sonneck, however, had no basis for deciding between Nicholson and Skinner as the one who took the poem to the *American* on the morning of Saturday, 17 September 1814.

Mr. Sonneck prints on page 82 of his report a substantial extract from a letter Samuel Sands wrote to General Brantz Mayer on 1 January 1877. In 1910 [when Sonneck saw it] that letter was in the hands of a book dealer in Washington; it turned up once more in the elaborate portfolio housing the Cist copy of Key's autograph when the autograph was acquired (in 1941) by the Library of Congress. Mr. Sonneck seems willing enough to go along with the basic claim advanced by Sands in his letter; but Mr. Skinner's letter to the *Patriot* had not been rediscovered in 1914 and Mr. Sonneck, like everyone else, accepted the role in which Taney had cast Judge Nicholson. Even Sands himself was overawed by the aura of Chief Justice Taney. In his letter to General Mayer and also in an article published in his own magazine, the *American Farmer,* for June 1874 (pp. 220-21), he seems to doubt his own memory. In his preface to the article he writes:

We never professed to *know* who had brought it to the *American* office, yet from some cause we had it fixed upon our mind, that it was Mr. Skinner. An introductory letter to the volume alluded to above [the Johns 1857 edition of Key's *Poems*], however, written by the late Chief Justice Taney, relating the circumstances connected with the writing of the song, shows that Mr. Key, when he reached the city, after the enemy had retired from our waters, handed it to Judge Nicholson, a connection by marriage, to advise with him as to its publication. The Judge being much pleased with it, "sent it to a printer," says Judge Taney, "and ordered copies to be struck off in handbill form, which were distributed to the public," and adds that Mr. Key "believed it to have been favorably received by the Baltimore public."

No allusion is made in this narrative of Judge Taney as to the office to which it was sent for publication; but Mr. Lossing, in his *Historical Record* alluded to above, attempts to supply the omission by saying that Judge Nicholson "took it to the office of Captain Benjamin Edes, on the corner of Baltimore and Gay Streets," and that "his apprentice, Samuel Sands, who was living in Baltimore a few years ago, set up the song in type, printed it, and distributed it among the citizens."

There are other circumstances given in connection with its first publication, which induce us to believe that the copy Mr. Lossing had before him was not one of the originals, but was subsequently printed after it had issued from the office of the *American*. In the first place, we were never connected with the office of Mr. Edes, nor do we remember that the office of that gentleman was ever at the corner of Baltimore and Gay streets, as stated by Mr. Lossing; we were at the time an apprentice at the office of the *American,* which was then located at No. 4 on the east side of Harrison Street, but several years afterwards it was removed to the southwest corner of Gay and Baltimore streets. Captain Edes' office at one time, we remember, was at the northeast corner of Baltimore and Calvert streets.

If the facts given to the editors of the *American* by Sands in 1872 were correctly reported, then he did once "profess to know" that it was Skinner who brought Key's manuscript to the shop. The problem is—where did he pick up this information? As an apprentice of fourteen, Sands was not likely to have been personally acquainted with Skinner and to have recognized him as he came into the shop, especially since Skinner at that time was not a regular resident of Baltimore. Besides, Sands says that it was Mr. Thomas Murphy who accepted the job from Skinner and passed it along to Sands, so it is by no means certain that Sands came in direct contact with Skinner during the episode in 1814.

There was no need for Sands to come into direct contact with Skinner. Skinner no doubt handed the poem to Editor Murphy in the office and told him the circumstances that Murphy then put into his introductory note, including the tune Key had in mind. By the time Murphy finished drafting that introductory note Skinner probably had gone, but Murphy took Key's poem, with the "annexed note" attached, out into the printshop and gave it to Sands, quite naturally telling Sands who had brought the poem and what to do with it.

We are obviously on more solid ground, however, when it comes to Sands's testimony with regard to his own part in the affair. Here he was not allowing himself to be talked down by anyone, Chief Justice or not, and he apparently felt he had so well disposed of the seeming conflict involving two different printers that he does not refer to that matter again in his letter to Brantz Mayer. But there is one aspect of the Mayer letter that is significant since in it Sands proceeds to dispose of one other and unlikely element in the mid-century accounts and to delimit his own part in the affair:

> When it was brought up to the printing office my impression is, and ever has been, that I was the only one of those belonging to the establishment who was on hand, and that it was put in type and what the printers call "galley proofs" were struck off previous to the renewal of the publication of this paper, and it may be and probably was the case that from one of these proof slips handbills were printed and circulated through the city.

This statement requires some explaining. Earlier in the letter Sands had told of being alone in the office while the others had been "bearing arms," but he also states that Mr. Thomas Murphy had returned to open the counting room before the manuscript was brought to the office, and hence by that time he was not quite alone. In fact, there must have been a touch of memory-shrinkage here, since by the seventeenth (when Skinner brought Key's autograph) enough of the staff had returned to get out reduced issues of the paper on the fifteenth and sixteenth. The compositors and pressmen would have been very much in short supply, and hence it would have been logical and reasonable to turn a small odd job over to the apprentice. Then in the last sentence Sands must again be speaking loosely. In the way he puts it, the proof slips or galley proofs run off by him from the type he set served as copy for a second setting of type for the handbills. That operation would have introduced a needless complication and would leave us without a typesetter for the handbill. The type did have to be reset for the poem's reappearance in the regular issue of the *American* on 21 September, for Sands's original lines were too long for the narrow columns of the newspaper; but surely no intermediate type setting was necessary for the handbills. The type as set by Sands surely must have been used for the handbills.

At the same time, the point Sands is apparently trying to make is both sound and logical. All he did was to set the type (by hand) and pull a few galley proofs; he did not print the handbill or have a hand in circulating it. Sonneck has already poked fun at Mr. Justice Taney for writing of Key's song that "in less than an hour after it was placed in the hands of the printer it was all over town." Even with a modern Linotype and electrical rotary presses it is improbable that such a feat could be accomplished. A master printer who has himself set considerable type by hand estimates that an hour would be the very least an expert type-setter would need for setting the complete text of the Key poem, and that it might easily take somewhat longer. This, furthermore, is only the first and much the shorter of the two steps in the printing process. Mr. Jacob Kainen of the Smithsonian Institution's Cultural History Division believes that nothing but a Ramage press could have been available in Baltimore in 1814, and this press is operated entirely by hand. First the type would have to be fixed firmly into the type-bed. Then, since the roller for applying ink had not yet been invented, the ink-ball (a mallet-like device with a composite head saturated with ink) would be struck against the type several times before each impression. Damp paper would then be dropped over the type and the whole slipped under the press proper, for pressure to be applied by a turnscrew. With this clumsy apparatus Mr. Kainen says that two expert printers could make perhaps two hundred and fifty impressions (in this case, copies) in an hour, but he grants that the printers would have to be fairly strong and expert to continue this rate for any length of time.

No one to my knowledge has ever attempted to estimate the total number of handbills that were printed. But there is plenty of evidence that a copy was given to every member of the Fort McHenry garrison—apparently on 19-21 September—which would mean about one thousand copies; and there is evidence that copies were distributed freely elsewhere in the city, bringing the total perhaps into the neighborhood of two thousand. As an instance of "job printing" the handbill was certainly an odd job; but Hill points out in some detail that the printing was part of an extraordinary affair and cannot be viewed in any other way. When the mighty British flotilla headed south on 17 September, many were skeptical and expected a new attack from some other quarter; but when days passed and reports verified that the British were still sailing southward (and then north to Halifax) the town went wild with relief and the jubilation of victory.

One can imagine Sands's patron [editor and boss] Mr. Thomas Murphy taking a hand in the technical production of these issues [the *American* for 15 and 16 September] but obviously with the equipment at hand he could not possibly have produced them by himself. There must have been other men gradually drifting back from the entrenchments on Loudenslager's Hill east of the city, even if Sands had no specific memory of them. Still others would be turning up on the seventeenth and nineteenth with their patriotic fervor undimmed. And with the general agreement that no papers should be issued "for some days" it hardly seems unreasonable to suppose that two of the pressmen might work off some of their fervor printing from time to time as many copies of the handbill as anyone wanted to distribute. The general moratorium at least makes conceivable the performance of an act that we know must have been executed sometime, and other limiting circumstances do not leave too much choice as to the exact date. Skinner brought the manuscript to the office of the *American* on Saturday morning, 17 September. No printing was ever done on Sunday, which eliminates the eighteenth. The first issue of the *American* after the break appeared on 20 September. This leaves us with only Saturday afternoon, the seventeenth, and most of Monday, the nineteenth, as the more probable times for the printing of the handbill.

THOMAS MURPHY
(1780-1860)

In his search for all of the published evidence by Samuel Sands, Dick Hill came across an account of the song's first printing that in its way is more palpable, more convincing, than any of the others because it is by a participant in the affair whose part was crucial but yet who had no particular axe to grind. Sands mentions in his letter to Brantz Mayer that he had on a former occasion given "sundry items" of information to the editors of the *Baltimore American* for their Centennial issue, which Dick located under date of 12 September 1872 — an issue standing thirty inches high, with three columns down the center of the front page containing excerpts from issues of 1814 accompanied by commentary. Near the foot of the third column is a story about Key and his poem and how it was published. Dick quotes the following paragraph of that story, a story unsigned but certainly written by Thomas Murphy, in 1814 the editor of the *American:*

. . . This song was first brought to Baltimore and given to the publishers of *The American* by John Skinner, Esq., who at the time of which we speak had been appointed by President Madison to conduct some negotiations with the British forces relative to the exchange of prisoners. It was in this way that Mr. Skinner chanced to meet Mr. Key on the flag-of-truce boat, and obtained from him a copy of the song. Mr. Key having, as above stated, gone down under a flag-of-truce to procure the release of a friend who had been captured by the enemy. Mr. Skinner having furnished the manuscript to *The American* after the fight was over, it was there at once put in type and published. Immediately the song became a favorite with the people and was in great demand. It was also printed in slips in addition to being published in *The American,* and was extensively circulated. Strange to say, the "printer's boy" who was then employed in the office of *The American* and put this famous song in type still survives, and in full vigor, too, being none other than our respected friend, the editor and publisher of the *American Farmer,* Samuel Sands, Esq.

Since Thomas Murphy died in 1860, his account obviously was written for some earlier occasion and reprinted in the centennial issue in 1872. His information about how Key and Skinner met came from hearsay and is not quite right, but his information about the printing is unimpeachable. Hill was bothered by Murphy's putting the newspaper printing ahead of the handbill printing, forgetting that the editor of the paper naturally would think of that first — and then Hill himself has pointed out that the handbills probably were run off a batch at a time, some of them quite possibly after the 21 September issue of the *American* with the poem on its front page (differently set) had appeared. Indeed, one could say that the handbill constitutes a printing but not a publication in the formal sense; and that is the way it seems to have been viewed by Skinner, Murphy, and even Sands. At any rate, Hill concludes, "The words are surely those of the editor of the *American*."

One other block of words vital to the first printing of Key's poem surely can be attributed only to Murphy: the title and the introductory paragraph plus the naming of the tune (see the facsimile, plate 8). Key's extant autograph bears no title and it is not likely, from the evidence, that he applied one to the fair copy from which Sands worked. The editorial note does not read like Key, and neither Key nor Skinner would have confused the Potomac with the Patuxent River. Sands had neither the words, the knowledge, nor the authority. Judge Nicholson, to whom it used to be attributed in the Baltimore legend, is shown by Hill to have been at his immediate job as one of the acting commanders at the Fort — and if he had written the introductory note one can be sure Mrs. Nicholson would have saved it along with the autograph and the handbill (both of which were presented to the Nicholsons by Key when he called at the Nicholson home on September 21st). Hill for some reason overlooks Murphy completely, and others have said he lacked the knowledge. But when Skinner gave the manuscript to Murphy he certainly would have briefed him on the writing of the poem and on the tune to which Key had written it. Skinner would have been told by Key, and he no doubt heard the poet in his hotel room that morning singing snatches of his poem. In 1814 the Anacreontic Song was past its period of greatest popularity in London, but on the east coast of the United States it was in its heyday. One can cite no less an authority than Richard S. Hill for the fact that by 1820 some 85 parodies using that tune had been published over here, two of them by Key. In 1805 in Georgetown, Key had written (and publicly sung) his first one to honor the return of Stephen Decatur and Charles Stewart from putting down the Barbary pirates: "When the warrior returns from the battle afar."[5]

---

[5] See Richard S. Hill, "The Melody of 'The Star-Spangled Banner' in the United States before 1820," in *Essays Honoring Lawrence C. Wroth,* ed. Frederick R. Goff (Portland, Maine: n.p., 1951), 151-93; issued separately by the Library of Congress, 1951; see pp. 18-19.

The Sands handbill or broadside (there really is no satisfactory delimiting term for it) represents the beginning of the printing history that engendered the "unsettling" of the text that Sonneck referred to. Dick Hill tried valiantly to chart its every detail and then to "settle" it by means of his report and the variorum edition he meant to append to it — and, of course, by the proposed official version that he continued to hope would eventually be recognized by the Congress of the United States. Before going on with the printing history, however, we must at least glance at the autograph manuscript history so far as we know it. Key made, it has been assumed, at least seven autograph manuscripts of his poem:

(1) *Rough Draft.* Such a draft, based on his first inspirations and the notes he told Taney he made on the old letter in his pocket, could have been finished anytime from Wednesday night to Friday evening, 14-16 September — although Taney quotes Key as saying he "finished it" on the boat going into Baltimore on Friday evening. Skinner wrote in his letter to the *Patriot* in 1849 that the song "was written the night after we got back to Baltimore, in the hotel. . . ." The two statements do not necessarily clash. Key could have meant that on the boat he finished the poem in his memory and in his notes; but that at the hotel, having eaten, having found suitable paper and a calmer milieu, he wrote out his first complete draft — the manuscript now at the Maryland Historical Society.

(2) *The Nicholson — Maryland Historical Society copy.* This manuscript is so "clean" as drafts go that Hill assumed Key, presumably bone-tired and exhausted from the ordeal he had been through, could not possibly have written it out until after a good night's sleep at the hotel. He apparently did not take seriously Skinner's remark that Key had finished "it" on the sloop. But what was "it?" The really rough draft that no one has seen? If so, then next morning Key had to make (in Hill's view) not one but two copies: the fair copy that Skinner took to the *American,* and the Nicholson — Maryland Historical Society copy. All writers have agreed — and the reader may judge for himself — that the latter copy bears no telltale ink smudges inevitable in print shops (at least before the word processor!), and also that it was not used as a model for any of the known printings from the early days. It bears no idiosyncracies that link it with the Sands, *Patriot,* or *American* printings.

What this manuscript does bear are evidences of four afterthoughts that resulted in changes made on the manuscript. In line one, Key started to write "through the dawn's early light," but before he had written down even the next word, *the,* he changed "through" to "by"; it was not a change he made after beginning the second stanza with a line using "through" in the same place. That would have required "by" to be written in above and at the end of the crossed-out "through." Then, in line four of the third stanza it appears that Key started to write "They have washed out" but then realized that the accent would fall awkwardly on "wash'd"; so he crossed out "They have wash'd" and began the line again with a much stronger inspiration: "Their blood has wash'd out. . . ."

The remaining two changes are in stanza two, line six, where Key first wrote "on" and then put the "i" and its dot on top of the "o"; and in the last stanza, line six, where Key forgot and first wrote "god" and then changed to "God." These changes admittedly *could* have been made in the course of writing out and improving an earlier copy—possibly some of the sketches on the old letter—but they at least prove that this manuscript preceded the copy used by Sands. The printer's boy committed one of the cardinal sins in type setting by failing to follow copy on many details of punctuation and capitalization; but he would never have changed "through" to "by" or added "Their blood has wash'd out"—which are in Key's hand on the extant autograph.

Do these changes not point to this manuscript as Key's first and only complete draft, the result of fifty-some hours of emotional release while still pent up physically? That was time enough for him to have made several drafts, had he worked that way. But the wording of Skinner and of Key as reported by Taney point to only one draft, made in the hotel room on the night of 16 September and preceded only by the notes and remembered passages that he completed on the sloop during the journey from the fleet into Baltimore harbor. The notes were discarded and the complete draft given to his sister-in-law and Judge Nicholson when he visited them on 21 September, according to Taney's letter. Some have suggested that there might have been two fair copies, one taken to the *Patriot* by Skinner, the other taken to the *American* by Nicholson. Would Key have bothered to write out two such copies on that Saturday morning? We have seen evidence from his daughter that with Key the poem was the thing, the manuscript mattered little. Could the existence of a second fair copy have gone unremarked all these years? Finally, while it is true that the editor of the *Patriot* added his own short introduction to his printing of 20 September, he followed that with the identical editorial note borne by the Sands handbill. The existence of a second fair copy seems most unlikely. Dick Hill, at least, never even considers such a possibility.

(3) *The Printer's Copy.* If the copy used by Sands was the only fair copy Key made, what became of it? Much ink (both writers' and printers') would have been saved had Editor Murphy been prescient and foreseen that this local and topical efflorescence would become a part of his country's national anthem; or if only as a matter of temporary sentiment he had taken the copy back from Sands and put it away in some safe place where it might have come to light years later when the poem's illustrious career had become evident. Apart from its sentimental value, it could at least answer the question as to how many of the sixty-three differences between it and the Key draft were due to Sands's carelessness or overenthusiasm, and how many emanated from Key himself, changes made as he continued to polish his poem while copying it from the draft. As it was, no one

realized the historical importance of Key's manuscript, so it probably fell to the floor and was swept up and burned with the trash.

(4) *The Later Autographs: the Cist Copy*. So far as we know today, Key wrote out no further copies of his poem during the years immediately following its composition. By the early 1840s, however, the tribe of autograph collectors and souvenir hunters had decided that the poem had merit, and at different times Key wrote out at least four copies of his poem upon request. Accompanying this article are reproductions of the 1814 and four later autograph manuscripts (the Maher in transcribed form), the entire group reproduced together for the first time. Since the texts are available to the reader, it will suffice here to give a brief word about the history of each manuscript.

It has already been remarked that Key was amazingly consistent when it came to writing out the text so long after the poem had been composed. This does not mean, unfortunately, that these late autographs represent an attempt to refine and polish the text. Key apparently felt no impulse in that direction. In the case of one line, to be mentioned later, he does seem to have made a rather fumbling attempt at improvement, but he could also get mixed up and write in the Cist copy "whose bright stars and broad stripes" without bothering to correct the transposition. In all four copies, he changes one of his most often quoted phrases "through the perilous fight" to the innocuous "through the clouds of the fight." In short, where changes have been made they are likely to be for the worse rather than for the better; only very rarely do they clarify his original intention. Indeed, the four late copies are probably most valuable when they make no change at all, since then at least they confirm the earlier readings. Key wrote them as souvenirs of a notable inspiration, and it is surely a mistake to view them as anything more than that.

The earliest of the four copies is dated "Washington, October 21, —40," and is signed with the close-packed "FSKey." It does not bear the name of the collector for whom it was written, but during the middle of the last century John Jay Smith published a facsimile of it which states that the original was "in possession of Lewis J. Cist." Smith's facsimile appears as Plate 55 in the second series that he engraved himself and published at New York in 1860 under the title *American Historical and Literary Curiosities*.

Lewis J. Cist (1818-85) was one of the first great autograph collectors in this country, and when his collection was dispersed after his death it took four large volumes full of brief entries to list his holdings. The Library of Congress owns a set of these catalogs, which for the most part give the prices fetched by the various lots: but Key's autograph was not sold at this time and the interim owner unfortunately has not been established. Ten years later the manuscript turns up as Item 273 in Stan. V. Henkels' Catalogue No. 738 (Philadelphia: The Bicking Print,

1895). The item is briefly listed but with a full facsimile, so that positive identification can be made. But Mr. Henkels was disposing of the holdings of at least two collectors, one of them not identified by name; and his son reports that his father's records for this early period were not preserved, so neither the seller nor the buyer has been identified. Mr. Sonneck in 1914 was unable to determine the "present whereabouts" of the copy.

Not until 1935 does the Cist manuscript come to light again, this time at an auction of the American Art Association. A number of the autographs at that sale had once belonged to Dean Sage, but he had died in 1902 and the last of a succession of heirs could not remember where he got it. Hill tried to investigate through the auction house, but by that time the house had gone out of business. A brief note on the sale of the manuscript, in the *Baltimore Evening Sun* for 13 November 1935, states unequivocally that "The manuscript is one of the principal items in a collection of autograph letters and manuscripts formed by the late Dean Sage, of Albany, N.Y.," but whether the reporter had access to privileged information or was simply assuming more than the sale catalog would warrant is difficult to say. At that time, in 1935, the manuscript was knocked down for $5,500 to the Philadelphia dealer George Grasberger, who was acting as agent for a Philadelphia collector, Mr. Louis J. Kolb. At Mr. Kolb's death in 1941, the house of William D. Morley, Inc., of Philadelphia sold (for $7,750) the autograph to Mr. Gabriel Wells, from whom the Library of Congress Music Division acquired it shortly thereafter.

(5) *The Later Autographs: the Keim Copy.* The history of the next autograph copy is simple and clear. It bears no date, but is inscribed in Key's hand "To Gen Keim." George May Keim's title derives from his commission as a major general of the Pennsylvania state militia, and his death in 1861 occurred while he was drilling a volunteer company he had raised for home defence in the Civil War. In 1838, Keim had been appointed to the seat in the U.S. Congress left vacant when H. A. Muhlenberg was appointed minister to Austria-Hungary. Thereafter the General was twice elected to the House of Representatives from Pennsylvania, serving until 1843. While he was in Washington his ready wit and his ability to improvise in verse opened the doors of all literary circles to him.[6] Since he apparently acquired only two autograph manuscripts during his entire life—the one from Key and another of "Home, Sweet Home" from John Howard Payne—both with personal inscriptions—it seems safe to assume that he was a friend of both authors.

---

[6] Hill's note: The few facts about Keim given above have been taken from the detailed account in Ernest Spofford's *Encyclopedia of Pennsylvania Biography* (New York: Lewis Historical Publishing Co., 1928), 17:298.

On his death, General Keim left the two manuscripts to his children, who on 21 November 1876 presented them to the Historical Society of Pennsylvania in Philadelphia. There they remain, bound with the letter of presentation from Henry May Keim in a handsome leather folder. The copy of "Home, Sweet Home" has a lengthier presentation inscription than Key allowed him. Both manuscripts probably were requested by the General at about the same time (Payne's inscription is dated 18 August 1841), and since the readings in Key's manuscript indicate that it falls between the Cist copy of 1840 and the Maher copy of 1842, it seems safe to give it the date of [1841?].

(5a) *The Later Autographs: "The supposed Howard copy."* Sonneck lists on page 92, as his third autograph manuscript, "The supposed Howard copy, ca. 1840." To avoid confusion it seems best to deal with it next. The story is long and unedifying, and does not bear repeating except in brief, especially since Sonneck gives the necessary citations.

For the Sanitary Fair held at Baltimore in 1864, General Brantz Mayer persuaded John P. Kennedy and Alexander Bliss to issue a handsome volume of facsimiles, *Autograph Leaves of Our Country's Authors*. The very first item in the volume is a facsimile of a Key autograph of *The Star Spangled Banner*. Benson John Lossing borrowed the first stanza of the facsimile for his *Pictorial Fieldbook of the War of 1812* (1st ed., 1868), and since *Autograph Leaves* does not identify the manuscript it reproduces Lossing apparently felt that a good authority was needed; he states in a note that the facsimile was reproduced "by permission of its owner (Mrs. Howard, daughter of the author)." George Henry Preble accepted and repeated the identification in his *Three Historic Flags* (1874), but this time both Mrs. Howard and General Keim saw that attribution and wrote to Preble, the first to say that she had never had an autograph of her father's poem (the passage quoted on p. 81) and the latter to say that the autograph used had been his. Preble retracted the ascription, and this could easily have been the end of the matter.

Mr. Sonneck, however, noted three striking, if somewhat superficial, differences between the Keim autograph and the facsimile in *Autograph Leaves*. The latter gives the poem a title but has no presentation inscription, whereas the Keim autograph lacks a title but bears the note "To Gen Keim." In the Keim autograph the stanzas are arranged three on the first page and the fourth on a second page; but the facsimile balances them, two to a page. These differences led Mr. Sonneck to reject the Keim autograph as the source of the facsimile, and he ends his discussion: "Though, therefore, Mrs. Howard disclaimed ownership of this particular autograph, yet it must have existed and is, to judge by the facsimile, genuine."

The solution, of course, is very simple. Mr. Sonneck seems to have been unfamiliar with the nineteenth-century practice of doctoring facsimiles—a practice he would naturally have found abhorrent—and made the mistake of assuming that the reproduction had to be exact. The preface of *Autograph Leaves* claims only that the facsimiles were "executed with admirable fidelity to the originals," and at that time this phrase could mean only that the document had been copied onto the lithographic stone by hand, not by photolithography (an art that was still in its infancy in 1864). For the purposes of Kennedy and Bliss the poem had to be given a title, so the lithographer modeled his "Th" on the letters starting the "That" at the beginning of the second line of the third stanza of the Keim autograph. For the rest he followed with admirable fidelity the "Star-Spangled Banner" as Key wrote the words in the seventh line of the second stanza. Indeed, the fidelity is sufficiently admirable to make it possible to say that the title could have been copied only from that line and not from the similar line in the other three stanzas (see plates 4-5). The inscription to General Keim was no doubt omitted so that the facsimile would have a more universal appeal, and the rearrangement of the four stanzas would have been done to provide a more balanced and artistic visual effect. As for the poem itself, the facsimile fits the Keim autograph in every whorl of every letter and even in the slips of the pen. Hence there is no need to hypothecate any other autograph than the one written for General Keim. Should anyone wish to check this derivation and not have access to a copy of *Autograph Leaves,* Joseph Muller reproduced the fictitious facsimile as the frontispiece in his *The Star-Spangled Banner Words and Music* (New York: G. A. Baker & Co., 1935), and this can be compared with the reproduction of the Keim autograph accompanying this article.

(6) *The Later Autographs: the Maher Copy.* This manuscript, its present whereabouts unknown, is or was nonetheless genuine and deserves mention. Key wrote it out and presented it to a man who is described in the *National Intelligencer* for 31 March 1866, as "the late James Maher, for more than thirty years the gardener of the Executive Mansion, well known for his extraordinary enthusiasm on the subject of American victories over the British." The handwriting of the autograph had been certified by several friends of Key before it was placed on exhibition in the window of the Philip & Solomons Metropolitan Book Store at 332 Pennsylvania Avenue, N.W., between Ninth and Tenth Streets in Washington. With Maher recently dead and the manuscript on exhibit in a book store, one presumes it was being offered for sale; but who bought it—if indeed anyone did buy it—remains a complete mystery, since from that day to this there is no mention of the whereabouts of the manuscript in the known literature on the *SSB*. Perhaps someday it may still turn up, but the chances are surely minimal by now. Its absence leaves us dependent entirely on a transcription of the text printed in the *National Intelligencer* of 31 March 1866, p. 2, col. 6, a source that obviously must be used with some care.

According to that transcription, the copy was dated 7 June 1842, and the date is confirmed approximately by the fact that its readings fit into the sequence of the other autographs. The gentleman who prepared the edition for printing took pains to note the points where the manuscript varies from some of the printed sources of the day, and thus gives us the first variorum edition of the poem. Even in 1866 it was recognized that the text was "unsettled." Unfortunately the editor could know nothing of Key's 1814 autograph (still hidden away in the keeping of Judge Nicholson's family), nor did he have any other version on which he could base a really useful comparison. Instead, he chose the versions found in two large and popular anthologies, whose compilers in turn had attempted to cover such a wide and variegated area that they could spend little time on the selection or editing of any one poem. Even so, it is useful to know what an intelligent citizen considered significant differences as early as 1866, and therefore the entire article and transcription of the poem as given in the *National Intelligencer* are here reproduced in facsimile (see plate 6). In the newspaper it was of course printed in a single column, but here it has been enlarged and divided into two sections to fit this format and make easier reading.

The "Dana" in the notes stands for Charles Anderson Dana's *Household Book of Poetry*. The third edition has been the earliest available, and in it the New York publishing house of Appleton has a printed copyright notice of 1857, although the preface is dated August 1858 and the title page imprint date is 1859. The collection reached an eleventh edition in 1867. In the third edition, *The Star Spangled Banner* is on pages 380-81. The "Griswold" stands for Rufus Wilmot Griswold's *The Poets and Poetry of America*. First issued in 1842, the book had its seventeenth edition in 1856 (all editions at Philadelphia). Both Griswold and Dana were the sort of editors who felt they had not earned their pay unless they had left their mark on a text, and Griswold particularly seems to have had a very real genius for picking unusual readings. His two principal sources were the *American Melodies* edited by George P. Morris (New York & Philadelphia, 1840-41) and William McCarty's *Songs, Odes, and Other Poems, on National Subjects* (Philadelphia, 1842). He probably used still other sources, since both of these give the reading "Power" whereas Griswold gives "power." Dana also gives the lower-case "power" from one of the standard *Patriot*-type versions, but he adds to this basic structure a number of the more unusual readings from the Reverend Johns's edition of Key's complete *Poems*.

The editor of the variorum edition in the *National Intelligencer* does not seem to have had a very sharp eye for these unusual readings, and passes by without comment even such striking variants as Dana's and Griswold's substitution of "for our cause" in place of "when our cause it is just." Or, if he comments his footnote may miss the point. Maher, Dana, and Griswold all give the reading "on the stream" without (apparently) realizing that the real choice is between "in" and "on the stream"; the editor in his third note says that several versions give "o'er the stream." I have found the reading "o'er" in a single edition, and a British one at that (see Muller No. 26); it appears extremely doubtful that the editor of a variorum edition could discover many others, since so odd a concept as a reflection appearing above a sheet of water could hardly have gained wide currency (except perhaps as a mirage in the desert). But Key had a poet's eye and saw accurately. In his 1814 draft, he first wrote "on" and then changed it to "in," knowing that a reflected object appears at the same depth below the reflecting surface as the object is above it. After the more prosaic editor of the *Baltimore Patriot* had changed the preposition to "on," it became so widely popular that Key himself wrote "in" only in the manuscript for General Keim; in the other three late manuscripts he substituted "on." The substitution surely is not one of his better revisions.

Similarly, despite the fact that the text as transcribed in the *National Intelligencer* gives the capital "P" on "Power" whereas Dana and Griswold use the lower case, the editor does not comment on the difference. It is always possible, of course, that he simply did not notice the variation. It is also theoretically possible that there might be a different explanation: if Key, as he had always done before, had written the word as "power" in the Maher copy, then no difference would have existed between the autograph and the printed versions in Griswold and Dana, and the editor would have had no occasion to enter a note. In that case the capital in the transcript might have been introduced by the typesetter, who might have seen sufficient examples of this spelling elsewhere to make him think he was merely correcting a mistake in the editor's copy. Almost certainly, the typesetter must have pluralized "bombs" in the first stanza, since *all* of the other autographs give "bomb." But when the last (to date) of the late autographs was discovered recently it turned out that in it Key had changed to the capital on "Power." With the two manuscripts written only a few months apart, it seems possible that he had changed to "Power" in the Maher copy as well. It may never be known for certain, but it is this sort of thing that makes the use of even a *careful* transcription of an autograph so dangerous, and prevents the transcription in the *National Intelligencer* from being regarded as a basic document. Some of the variants, both those the editor notes so carefully and those he passes over in silence, will be dealt with elsewhere in connection with more solid evidence; but a few others are as inconsequential as "o'er the stream" and will not be mentioned again.

(7) *The Later Autographs: the Espy Copy.* Having disposed of the "supposed Howard copy," it is a pleasure to be able to replace it with a genuine autograph that came to the writer's [Hill's] attention only a short time ago. The pleasure is some-

what tempered with chagrin, because the "new" autograph has rested since 1897 in the archives of Georgetown University, less than two miles from the Key house by the Potomac River near the west [actually, north—WL] end of Key Bridge and from where Key practiced law in Georgetown—and just across town from the Library of Congress. It is true that some rumors, vague rumors, of an autograph of Key's poem being somewhere in Georgetown had been heard; but facsimiles often give rise to such rumors, and since Mr. Sonneck obviously had sniffed out no such rumor of an autograph so near his home base nothing had been done about it. On 30 April 1960 (p. A16), however, the *Washington Post & Times-Herald* carried an interview with Georgetown University's archivist, Father W. C. Repetti, S.J., in which the autograph was mentioned along with a number of other notable treasures. An expedition of exploration to that far land was arranged in conjunction with Frederick Goff, chief of the Library's Rare Book Division. The result proves conclusively that researchers should look beneath their noses as well as toward distant libraries across the sea.

For the manuscript is indubitably a genuine Key autograph, signed by him and dated "Washington/Augt. 29, —42." Perhaps the most convincing evidence of its authenticity can be seen in its readings. These belong to the family of late autographs, but—as with the others—there are some unique readings. A very few variants agree with and confirm those in the Maher transcript, but far more of them derive from the other late autographs—a fact that is rather surprising considering the brief lapse of time between the last two. Differences between any of the autographs are of course numerous, especially in view of the more than a quarter of a century between the 1814 manuscript and the others. It is interesting to find Key, even after all that time, still experimenting with the first line of the third stanza. In 1814 the line read: "And where is that band who so vauntingly swore," with the linking section in the four late copies successively altered to "is the host that," "are the foes that," "is the foe that," and, lastly, "is the host that." Perhaps there are those who wish Key had had even more time to experiment, but of the lot surely the last is the best (see plate 7).

The one awkward aspect of the Georgetown autograph is that, having become known in the *SSB* literature so late and without documents disclosing its early history, it poses a mystery so far as its origin is concerned. There is no presentation inscription, which probably means that Key wrote it for someone with whom he was not personally acquainted. Archivist Father Repetti at Georgetown University has done everything possible to help track down the manuscript's history, and he has made available the two letters that accompanied the autograph on its arrival at Georgetown. One letter was sent with the manuscript, under date of 16 February 1897, to Father Gillespie of St. Aloysius Church on North Capitol Street at I Street, N.W., Washington, D.C., by Mrs. J. A. Nunn of Fort Madison, Iowa:

Your most kind and welcome letter should have been acknowledged before this time. I must more than thank you for your kind words spoken of my father. I have just been writing to, I might say, a life long friend of his in Washington, Dr. John McCalmont, and thought I would write you a few lines. I have just mailed to you a picture which please accept and know you will appreciate its meaning.

I also send the original manuscript of the Star Spangled Banner. It was my father's. I found it among his papers and thought perhaps you might like to have it. Its delapidated [sic] condition was caused by my taking it to school when a child. I have forgotten how he came by it, although I heard him tell about this often when a child. . . .

Say a Hail Mary for your distant relative, Mrs. J. A. Nunn.

Father Gillespie had no suitable library at Saint Aloysius for keeping such a manuscript, and therefore sent it along to Georgetown on 10 March 1897, with the following note:

Please put it in your case of rare manuscripts. It will please her very much, I am sure. I have already written to her that I was going to present it to Georgetown in her name.

The editor of the *Georgetown College Journal* apparently felt that the new acquisition was worthy of reproduction, but not of any verbal commentary. He published a facsimile on a separate plate between pages 216 and 217 in the issue of the *Journal* for February 1901 (vol. 29, no. 5). The plate has not even a brief title, there is no editorial comment, and no entry for the plate appears in the table of contents nor in the annual index to the *Journal*. It is small wonder that news of the autograph spread slowly.

With everyone known to have been involved in the 1897 transfer now dead, with no published record of the autograph known in the literature, there seemed to be little chance of amplifying the scant information [in Mrs. Nunn's letter to Father Gillespie. A reference librarian, however, is not without a variety of resources, important among which are other reference librarians.] A letter to Mrs. Rita Benton, administrative head and chief reference librarian of the School of Music at the University of Iowa, Iowa City, promptly produced a positive reply from Ms. Ada M. Stoflet, reference librarian and genealogy expert in the main University Library there. Ms. Stoflet cited two references[7] containing biographical information about a Mrs. Joseph A. Nunn

---

[7] (1) *Biographical Review of Lee County, Iowa* (Chicago: Hobart Publishing Co., 1905), 394-96; (2) *Portrait and Biographical Album of Lee County, Iowa* (Chicago: Chapman Brothers, 1887), 586.

of Fort Madison, Iowa, who had been born on 22 February 1841, as Elizabeth McCalmont Espy in Franklin, Pennsylvania. She was the daughter of Thomas Stevenson and Mary Ann McBride Espy, who had been married at Meadville, Pennsylvania, on 12 May 1840. Thomas Espy had five children; Elizabeth Nunn had ten. If all these children had been as fruitful as their parents, the search for a descendant with some knowledge of the Georgetown autograph could take a lifetime. This obvious avenue for research is not exhausted yet; neither has it so far produced results.

It was Thomas Stevenson Espy, however, who had come by the autograph in some manner his daughter forgot. At the Library of Congress Dick Hill easily located, in its genealogical collections, a *History and Genealogy of the Espy family in America,* compiled by Florence Mercy Espy and published privately for her at Fort Madison, Iowa, in 1905. The entry for Thomas Espy on pages 72-73 tells us that he was born on a farm at Espyville, Pennsylvania (on the north bank of the Susquehannah River, to the northeast of Sunbury).[8] The date was March 26, 1814, and he was

> Educated at Gambel's Academy, Jamestown, Pa., and Roberts' Select School, Andover, Ohio; studied law with, and afterwards became a partner of, Judge Alexander McCalmont, Franklin, Pa.; came to Fort Madison, Iowa, in 1844, where he practiced his profession; operated a flour mill, distillery and foundry; failed in business in 1858. In 1863, he removed to St. Louis, Mo., and became one of the foremost lawyers of the city, but failing health caused him to return to Fort Madison in 1881. He was school director of Madison Township, 1846-56; State Senator 1848-52; was appointed General of the State Militia in 1851. He was always a busy and influential man and died honored by all that knew him, Dec. 24, 1895.

There seems to be nothing in Thomas Espy's career other than the practice of law to suggest a connection in 1842 with Washington and Francis Scott Key, and some such connection is obviously necessary unless Thomas obtained his autograph either by correspondence or secondhand.

Florence Mercy Espy is my authority for the statement that the only Espy ever to really amount to something was James Pollard Espy, who published his *Philosophy of Storms* at Washington in 1841 and was a leading government meteorologist in Washington. The two branches of the family were connected only distantly, however, so it would be a mistake at this point to build too much on the family name and some association with Washington, where Francis Scott Key passed his final

---

[8] A visit to Espy, PA, in 1983 yielded a courteous reception but absolutely no information about the Espy family.

IV. THE UNSETTLING OF THE TEXT IN PRINT

All of the many hundreds of printings of the text that have appeared since 16 September 1814 are descended ultimately from the small handbill (see plate 8) whose origin has already been told. It in turn was a setting of a Key manuscript that has not survived, that probably disappeared with other debris from the print shop of the *Baltimore American* as the departure of the British force was joyfully perceived to be genuine, not a ruse, and as normal life gradually replaced the anxious life of the front line. That manuscript inevitably was a copy, presumably a fair copy (cleaner and less tentative than a draft) made on Saturday morning, 17 September 1814, as Key sat in his room at the Indian Queen Hotel on the corner of what are now Baltimore and Hanover Streets. The evidence, both positive and negative, indicates that the fair copy was preceded only by Key's first draft of his poem, written out the night before from notes (the "rough" draft) and remembered phrases accumulated by Key's imagination during some sixty hours passed on the flag-of-truce sloop between learning that the British attack had failed and the sloop's berthing at last on the shore near Fort McHenry (Filby-Howard, p. 37). That first (and only) complete draft is the autograph manuscript now at the Maryland Historical Society in Baltimore. It shows no signs of ever being handled by ink-begrimed hands in an old-fashioned print shop, and none of the prints suggest direct descent from it by any idiosyncracy of thought or word.

The handbill owes its character as well as its existence to the military situation around Baltimore about midday on that Saturday, 17 September 1814. No doubt John S. Skinner gave the manuscript to Thomas Murphy, owner-editor of the *American,* with the thought that it be published in an early issue of the paper; but uncertainty among the American commanders about the British intentions resulted in uncertainty as to when enough employees would be able to come back to work to get out the next issue of the paper. Murphy did have, however, one immediate means of action: fourteen-year-old Samuel Sands, three years into his apprenticeship, was too young to bear arms and could at least set the poem in type that Saturday afternoon. As older workers on temporary leave from the "front" drifted back singly or in small groups, they could help with the more laborious job of inking the type, tightening the turnscrew, and pulling each sheet through the press one by one. When Murphy took Key's manuscript from Skinner he also, one can be sure, got a short oral account of how the poem came to be written. His memory erred only in confusing the Potomac River with the Patuxent. He also learned from Skinner the name of the tune that Key had in mind when he fitted his words to it, the name Skinner would have learned from Key, who probably sang the first stanza (if not more) to Skinner, thus kindling Skinner's enthusiasm.

So Murphy, being the editor, performed the perfectly ordinary editorial function of prefixing Key's poem with a brief introduction (see plate 8), naming the tune, and naming also the poem (to which Key had put no title, at least in his draft) with a phrase, "The Defence of Fort M'Henry," that required no great deliberation. It epitomized to Murphy in very specific terms what the poem—which Key had worded much more generally—was about. Who else could have performed this editorial function in just this way? Key and Skinner would not have erred about the rivers and would not have written with the same flat, third-person air. Nicholson? As Hill's evidence shows, Nicholson was by force of circumstances one of the acting commanders at the Fort; with a part of the fifty-odd British vessels still visible in Baltimorean waters, he would hardly, as Hill says, have been running around the city looking for a printer. Besides, had he written the editorial note one can be sure that Mrs. Nicholson would have preserved his manuscript along with Key's and a copy of the handbill, those being the copies now with the Maryland Historical Society.

Certainly it was Murphy who gave the Key poem to Sands—who, by the way, was more than a mere employee to Murphy; he was living in Murphy's home as one of the family (Filby-Howard, p. 157)—and told him to set it in type, probably also prescribing the size paper and print column to use (22 picas, about 3-5/8", much wider than the *American*'s usual columns). Filby and Howard (p. 55) sought advice from printing experts and were told that "a capable apprentice of 1814 could have set the handbill by himself in three to five hours. . . ." That was the easier of the two phases of the job, but with the printing Sands no doubt had a great deal of help on the 17th and 19th, from Murphy and from other workers on temporary leave from the "front."

In fact, from a letter by Sands and another presumed to be from Murphy, quoted by Hill from the *Baltimore American*'s centennial issue of 12 September 1872 front page, it appears that Sands only set the type; that he pulled a few "proofs," but that the time-consuming press work was done by other employees during their temporary leaves from the "front" on the 17th, 19th, and perhaps later. (Hill assumes that the shop's doors were always tightly closed on Sundays, but with an emergency of this kind one wonders.) It appears to Hill that perhaps more than two thousand copies were pulled, since each of the approximately one thousand men at the Fort was given one (Filby-Howard, p. 157); the same may have been done for those in the entrenchments, and others no doubt went to citizens not under arms. It is therefore remarkable, as Hill writes, that

Today, copies of the broadside have become exceedingly scarce. Considering the number of copies that must have been printed, this present scarcity would be odd were it not for the fact that the document is indubitably plain and unprepossessing. It is easy to see why anyone unaware of its textual and historical significance might discard it. By the time the history of the poem had become a subject for discussion, no copy of the broadside is mentioned as known to exist until Mrs. Edward Shippen, Judge (and Captain) Nicholson's granddaughter, discovered it and the Key autograph (both now at the Maryland Historical Society) in a desk that had come down to her through her father, James Nicholson, from his mother, Joseph Nicholson's widow. For another fifty years Mrs. Shippen's copy remained the only one known. Then Jesse L. Cassard of Baltimore discovered another copy in an old scrapbook and offered it to the Library of Congress. After extended negotiations to determine a price for it, the broadside was finally purchased by the Library at the very nominal figure of $350 on 17 October 1940. At present writing[9] the two copies are the only ones known to survive.

Scarcity alone will rarely make a document significant, but this little sheet of paper takes on a quite extraordinary significance when we realize two points—first, that it is the ultimate source of nearly all subsequent printings (a few have been based on the 1814 autograph since it became known); and, second, that it introduced sixty-three points of difference from the Maryland Historical Society autograph. Most of these alterations are relatively minor ones, and a fair number of them do not change the sense of the poem in the least. Examples in the latter category are two places where Key gave an apostrophe instead of "e" and Sands spelled out the words as "hailed" and "washed." Similarly, in his extant autograph Key wrote out the word "and" five times at the beginning of lines, but in eleven other instances in the middle of a line he used an abbreviation that could be taken as a Greek alpha but obviously is an ampersand. In the broadside all eleven of these abbreviations are spelled out as "and"—a matter to which no sensible person could object, despite the fact that they do not reproduce Key's autograph accurately.

In the foregoing paragraph and on some other occasions, Dick in his haste and intensity forgets that there is no reason to suppose that Sands ever saw the extant autograph; that there is every reason to believe that he worked from a fair copy made by Key that same Saturday morning. One of the factors distinguishing a fair copy from a draft is that such shorthand devices as ampersands are written out, capitals and punctuation are tidied up, a word is replaced here and there. As Hill continues with his analysis of the sixty-three discrepancies he does remember and mention the fair copy. He points out, for instance, that the early Key autograph has an exclamation point at the end of line 2 in the last stanza, whereas Sands's printing does not. Sands's mind, Hill says, was certainly not subtle enough to have been bothered by this superfluous exclamation point, whereas Key surely would have found it too much of a good thing; hence he is by far the more likely person to have made this correction. (The reader may compare the two versions by their reproductions in plates 2 and 8 or in the variorum chart at the end of this article.)

---

[9] As in 1960, so also in 1987.

Of the gratuitous capitals that Hill supposes Sands to have added out of sheer exuberance (this was apparently the first chance he had had in a couple of days to do something of his own related to the "war-effort"), Hill points to the "Power" in stanza 4, line 4, as a change that has predominated down to the present. When the Hill-Broyhill official version of the anthem was proposed in 1958 it followed Key's first three surviving manuscripts by referring to "the power that hath made and preserved us a nation."

At first thought, the difference seems to be extremely minute and unimportant; but, actually, its significance has broad implications. With "power" we have an attribute of God; but with "Power" the word becomes a synonym for God Himself. Presumably Key knew which he intended. He was a deeply religious man and had committed long passages of the King James version of the Bible to memory. It would appear that he used the word as a literary allusion to the line from The Lord's Prayer: "For Thine is the kingdom, and the power, and the glory, forever," where all three attributes are given in lower-case forms. Besides, he was building in that fourth stanza to his climax on "And this be our motto—'In God is our trust.'" It should be obvious that an anticipatory reference to God as a "Power" would weaken that affirmation. Nonetheless, the ladies who have banded together in a variety of patriotic associations were loud in their protests that Mr. Broyhill was "taking God out of the national anthem." And since they have a highly developed system of communication, their mimeographed protests started flowing in from all parts of the country.

Two other of the sixty-three discrepancies, Dick points out, mar the very accuracy of Key's lines: the change from "rocket's" to "Rockets'" and from "bomb" to "Bombs" in stanza one, line five:

The two capitals are a bit of nonsense that may be safely disregarded, but the plural forms of the two nouns, like the capitalization of "power," are more significant than at first they appear. They introduce an historical inaccuracy, and tend to give an impression diametrically opposed to the one Key was trying to create. At that point in his poem Key was not describing a continuous fireworks exhibit which would keep the flag constantly illuminated all the night through. Rather he was trying to recreate in his readers' minds that feeling of painful tension that grew throughout the night precisely because he feared the Fort had fallen, and only the flare of an occasional rocket or the bursting of an occasional bomb reassured him by revealing that the flag was still there. By turning a dark and threatening night into a Fourth-of-July celebration, Sands neatly removes the major dramatic element in the stanza.

Thereupon Dick's reference librarian's sense of getting to the bottom of a matter to convince a reader, rather than simply making a statement without evidence, leads him to describe the mechanisms of those particular rockets and bombs and to study the logs of each of the five bomb ships and one rocket ship that got reasonably close to Fort McHenry. He reports that a total of 1,049 bombs were fired at the Fort from the five bomb ships (a count for the rocket ship *Erebus* apparently is included in this figure) between 7:30 a.m. and 9:00 p.m. on Tuesday, 13 September. After a hiatus of four hours the firing began again, with the immediate purpose of drawing attention away from some small craft that at 1:00 a.m. on the 14th began trying to push their way through the line of sunken hulks with which the Americans had blocked the way into the Ferry Branch of the Patapsco River, closer to Baltimore itself and to try to lure the defenders outside the Fort to leave their trenches. The ruse was not successful, so firing from the six ships was discontinued at 4:00 a.m. Dick figured from the logs that 220 bombs (and rockets?) were fired in those three crucial hours, averaging about fifty seconds between bursts.

So slow an average rate, reduced still further by bombs that did not explode at all or exploded too far from the flag to cast any light upon it, should have given Key plenty of time to build up tension between some of the explosions. The singular form he gave rocket and bomb surely reflects that experience more sensitively than Sands's blithe plurals. Whether the citizenry of the United States can ever be persuaded to sing of *a* rocket's red glare, of *a* bomb bursting in air, is something else again. One thing is certain. If they can be persuaded to sing "bomb" at all they will find it infinitely easier to negotiate on a fleeting eighth note than the sibilant "bombs."

Unless another Key autograph of his poem someday turns up, showing inky traces of having been used in either the *American* or the *Baltimore Patriot* print shop, we shall never know for sure how many of the sixty-three discrepancies between autograph draft and handbill are the work of Sands rather than of author Key—or editor Murphy. At least, Hill writes, Sands as a typesetter was no tyro, for only one clearly typographical error can be found: in stanza two, line six, Key's "now shines," balancing the "now" in the preceding line, came out as "new shines," confusion between "e" and "o" being common in hand-set type because of their similar appearance and the closeness of their trays. One other change is perhaps moot: line three in stanza three changes Key's conditional "should" to the third-person imperative future, "shall." Whether it resulted from another failure to "follow copy" or from a typographical error (we don't know what his manuscript looked like at that point, and even a fair copy sometimes contains write-overs), the reading has come in handy for all those who have tried to trace the various versions from source to source.

Among these "genealogists" Richard S. Hill is surely the most determined and the most meticulous in his tracing of the various streams or families of texts, and beyond them the subfamilies, the hybrids, the hopelessly miscenegated, and even a few genealogical sports. Thus far we have quoted or summarized from pages 1-90 of his typescript (and Dick's special elite machine could put twice as many words on his nearly marginless pages as an ordinary pica machine with normal margins). In his remaining pages, 91-160, he deals with the unsettling of the text as it was printed in various forms from 1814 through 1865. His emphasis is on the earliest songsters and especially on the fifty-four sheet music editions (plus variants) described, with many facsimile reproductions, by Joseph Muller in his 1935 volume.[10] In his enthusiasm Dick assumed, I think, that the reader might well have Muller at hand; and he certainly assumed that the reader would follow his minutest tracings with an enthusiasm matching his own. His huge variorum edition at the end was to present the more "unsettled" readings as they appear in sixty-some sheet music versions, thirty-six songsters (but with statistics based on ninety-four), a dozen newspapers, plus some early magazines and poetry or song collections; such an edition would have at least provided the reader with a battlefield map of the war of the words down to the end of the Civil War.

For this volume such an undertaking is out of the question. (It would have been out of the question for the American Musicological Society volume as well, but Dick planned to subsidize it to the extent necessary. In our last talk together, when I reported the AMS decision to go ahead with the Kinkeldey volume without waiting for his contribution to be finished, he admitted he had realized the necessity of a separate volume on account of size, apart from time and expense.) For this volume, on the other hand, it seems to me that in 1987 Dick's plan of dealing only with the text as it was before 1865 is no longer the best solution. Whether to choose an official text or merely to understand the history of the national anthem, one needs to know something of what happened to the text between 1865 and the actions of Hill's National Music Council committee. We have therefore provided a more modest variorum chart (pp. 147-84) but one that bridges the time gap and also provides the complete text of each edition chosen.

Before we take up that variorum chart, however, we must continue with Dick's pages 91-160 and either quote or summarize his chief findings on the unsettling of the text in print over its first fifty years. With the songsters and especially the sheet music, those findings are reached through such a multitude of closely packed detail that the inimitable Hill style will have to be bypassed more often than I should like.

Since we are still under the subheading of "Broadsides" I should mention that here Dick understandably puts all his eggs into one basket, the Sands handbill. In truth, handbills or broadsides did not play an important part in the printing history of *The SSB* once the very first one was past history. Nonetheless (to use one of Dick's favorite idea-bridging adverbs) Filby-Howard cites several, one of which (Hb-7 in the chart) can rightly be called a "sport." It is apparently unique, printed on satin with the text enclosed within highly ornamental borders, and presenting a curious mixture of textual variants. The side borders consist of quasi-Doric columns

---

[10] Joseph Muller, *The Star Spangled Banner: Words and Music Issued between 1814-1864. An Annotated Bibliographical List with Notices of the Different Versions, Texts, Variants, Musical Arrangements, and Notes on Music Publishers in the United States* (New York: G. A. Baker & Co., 1935).

supporting at the top an ornamental arc under which the title encloses an eagle with a shield and standing on a globe. The date suggested is 1815-20.

By this point, the major sources for Key's text have all been presented. In what follows the aim will be not so much to discuss the original readings but rather to diagram the spread of the poem in different media. It would only serve to confuse the reader and take an inordinate amount of space if all the variants were set down in each case, and there would be useless duplication with the variorum text at the end of the article. In this running commentary, therefore, only such crucial readings will be mentioned as tend to differentiate whole families. The goal will be to choose those variants in such a way that through two or three carefully selected ones the ultimate source of the version can be identified. No one, however, should be misled into thinking that the few selected variants are all that will be found typical of that particular family.

It happens that the first three printings of the poem—Sands's broadside and those in the *Baltimore Patriot* of 20 September and the *Baltimore American* of 21 September—can be differentiated through the use of only two cue variants. Key wrote as his 19th line: "A home & a country should leave us no more." Among other things, Sands changed the "should" to "shall," but both of the newspapers returned the reading to "should." The use of "shall" in any later edition points directly to the broadside as the ultimate ancestor, and (since the 1814 autograph was not then available) the use of "should" points to one of the two newspapers.

In the 14th line, Key wrote "shines in the stream." The broadside follows this reading as does the *American,* but the *Patriot* introduces "on the stream." Thus, wherever "in" and "shall" are found in the same version, that version must ultimately stem from the broadside and the family can be quickly [named] the "in-shall" version. The *American* is characterized by "in-should" and the *Patriot* by "on-should." An occasional exception may be found to this basic trifurcation where a hybrid has drawn on the readings from two or more versions; but, curiously, whenever an "on-shall" reading turns up it can almost invariably be shown to be a mixture by examining the other readings associated with the basic variants. Nevertheless, it is surprising how long these three simple patterns persisted in relatively pure form, and indeed they may still be found quite commonly to this day.

Because of the persistence of these three basic patterns, it may be as well to note in this one instance some of their associated characteristics. The broadside, or handbill, has already been discussed in detail and need not be mentioned again except to contrast it with the two newspaper printings. On the whole, editor Murphy of the *American* followed the broadside very closely, even to omitting (in the second stanza) the hyphen in "star-spangled" and the comma after "free" that divides the last line of each stanza into two segments. Nonetheless, the editor of the *American* did not follow the broadside slavishly. He added a comma after "night" to produce "Gave proof through the night, that our Flag was still there." On the model of the first stanza, he stepped up the broadside's comma after "stream" (end of line 14) to a semicolon, apparently on the theory that the final couplet of the stanza needed to be separated more firmly from the body of the stanza. And somebody, presumably the typesetter, in trying to fit "And this be our motto—'In God is our trust'" onto one line reduced the double quotation marks to single ones and dropped the final period entirely.

One other change, made presumably by the editor, involves a curious problem in meaning. In the extant 1814 autograph, Key opens the last stanza with

> O thus be it ever when freemen shall stand
> Between their lov'd home & the war's desolation!

If Key intended "home" to stand for the freemen's homeland or country, it is perfectly possible for many freemen to share such a large territory and fight to protect it from the desolation of war. This is what the majority of editors during Key's lifetime supposed he meant, and this is the reading they allowed to stand. The time-encrusted image ordinarily evoked by this rather standard patriotic phrase, however, has nothing to do with a homeland: it refers rather to the embattled individual citizen defending his own front door. Taken in this sense, "home" cannot be used as collective noun, and the freemen obviously cannot all stand in front of a single embattled front door. The plural "homes" must necessarily be used. Key certainly used the singular in the extant 1814 autograph, and it might have been difficult to know whether this was an odd use of a familiar poetic image or merely a slip in grammar made by a bone-weary (though tremendously excited) man were it not for the fact that Key wrote "homes" in all four of his late autographs. The editor of the *American* showed considerable prescience in realizing that Key must have meant "homes" and in changing to that plural in his version. Sands, however, had followed Key's copy, and the *Patriot* for once followed Sands. Editor Murphy of the *American* followed Sands in most other respects, however, and perhaps for this reason his reading was rarely used by later editors so his one good reading was lost. Key could not have been under pressure to make the change because of printed editions, for during his lifetime not one in a hundred printed editions used the plural; so his change to the plural in the late autographs must have represented his final choice. The reading did not become at all common until the Civil War decade, and it still does not predominate even today. Key, however, clearly preferred the plural four to one.

The *Patriot* had already caught Key's other grammatical slip involving a singular noun that should have been plural. In line 4, stanza 3, he wrote ''Their blood has wash'd out their foul foot-step's pollution.'' Key never did realize his mistake; he repeated it in all four of the late autographs. It has been suggested that Key used ''footstep's'' as a collective noun, but the explanation is much too simple. In the proper context one can say that an army marches on its stomach without calling up the picture of soldiers crawling forward stomach to ground, but I can think of no context that would allow ''an army marches on its foot.'' (Dick goes on for over half a page about the British army and a one-legged soldier, the problems presented by certain apostrophes, etc., etc., and giving the *Patriot* editor kudos for being a good, professional editor who moved the apostrophe to its proper place following the "s." I myself perceive "footstep's" to be a perfectly acceptable collective noun; an army can leave a collective footstep just as easily as it can march on a collective stomach. As sometimes happened, Dick turned up his nose at a simple, prosaic explanation and went in search of one more *outré:* that Key was subconsciously avoiding a dangling apostrophe.)

The transposed apostrophe gives the *Patriot* family one more distinctive reading in addition to ''on-should,'' but even more important is that someone, editor or typesetter, got rid of ten of Sands's exuberant capitals. The remainder of the twenty-nine points of difference between the *Patriot* and the handbill are a miscellany, the most characteristic being the *Patriot*'s addition of pointless commas in ''On the shore, dimly seen'' and ''What is that, which the breeze,'' commas that subsequent editors printing from the *Patriot* often omitted; but where they are still present, they identify the origin absolutely.

If we stop to consider the three printings described so far, it should be amply apparent that neither the broadside nor the *American* supplies an acceptable text. The *Patriot*'s text is not very much better, and in fact its ''now shines on the stream'' (rather than ''in the stream'') is a positive stride away from an acceptable text. At the same time, its punctuation changes are usually inconsequential when they are not minor improvements, and any reduction in Sands' capitals is unquestionably a move in the right direction. The editor (or typesetter) of the *Patriot* had, of course, no autograph to follow, and it is therefore rather surprising to note the number of times when, through sheer intuition and elementary good taste, he altered the readings to conform to Key's 1814 autograph. Thus, though it still cannot be characterized as a *good* text it is of these three the emphatically preferred version. In the rough and tumble selection of alternate versions during the succeeding decades, its basic principles came actually to be preferred more often than any other version, and eventually it managed to achieve, in a considerably modified form, a position of relative predominance.

The surviving runs of newspapers from this period tend to be broken and scattered. A very large number of daily and weekly papers were being published, so it has not been practical to make a comprehensive search of all of them to determine how the poem spread out from the broadside and the two Baltimore newspapers. A few such printings, however, have come to my attention in one way or another, and several of them may as well be briefly mentioned.

The first of all printings to identify Key as the author of the poem was the *Frederick-Town Herald* of 24 September 1814. The *Herald* might be called Key's "home town paper" and it might be thought that Key himself was responsible for the printing and the identification. Were that the case, however, the textual readings surely would have been close to Key's still-extant autograph, whereas a glance at the key readings shows that the poem was printed from the *Patriot*, no doubt carried to Frederick by some unknown party. The next known printing (N-12) appeared in the *National Intelligencer* of Washington two days later, 26 September. Key's authorship of the poem was still unknown there, since after giving the explanatory paragraph on how the poem came to be written the editor adds: "Whoever is the author of these lines, they do equal honor to his principles and his talents." The heading states "From a Baltimore Paper," and the readings again clearly identify that paper as the *Patriot*.

The *Maryland Gazette and Political Intelligencer* of Annapolis had been having trouble getting press men, as had the Baltimore papers. It was only supposed to be a weekly, but even so managed to get out four issues (in much reduced format) between 8 September and 6 October. On 13 October it returned to its former size, and in that issue Key's poem was printed, apparently from a copy of the broadside since it gives the readings "in-shall." It also continues the typographical error of "new" for "now" (line 14) and outdoes Sands by repeating all 17 of his capitals and adding three more of the same sort: "Land" and "Free" (but not "home" and "brave," line 16) and "Banner" (line 23).

On the following day, 14 October, the third of Baltimore's newspapers, *The Federal Gazette & Baltimore Daily Advertiser,* finally got around to printing Key's poem. The lateness is peculiar, since ordinarily the *Gazette*'s editor William Gwynn paid more attention to music, poetry, and the theater than did the editors of the other papers. Perhaps, having lost the services of three of his press men, two of whom were seriously wounded, his shop was so seriously disorganized that he had no time to bother with poetry until after his two competitors had already published the poem. In that case he may have decided to omit it entirely. Only when the popularity of the song continued to increase may he have then changed his mind and run the poem to celebrate the passing of a month since the day of victory.

When it did appear, the *Gazette* text was taken directly from the handbill, including the title, the introductory paragraph, the line specifying the tune, and the "in-shall" and "new" for "now" readings. Even so, Mr. Gwynn did some extensive editing of the text, and there are 35 points of difference between the *Gazette* and Sands's broadside. Some of these changes exhibit good sense: fifteen of Sands's capitals are lower-cased, leaving only "Heav'n" and "Power" in the last stanza, and six wholly unnecessary commas are removed. Mr. Gwynn was not altogether consistent in this last regard, since he added five other commas that are equally unnecessary and changed five other punctuation marks to little or no purpose. Having followed the broadside in spelling out "hailed" (line 2), he altered the broadside in the name of consistency by also spelling out "watched" (line 4). By the time he reached the third stanza, however, the principle had been forgotten, and he changed "washed" to "wash'd" (line 20) and later made "rescued" into "rescu'd" (line 27). This last example shows how strong the impulse to use the apostrophe must have been in this period, since here the "e" is not only a part of the participial ending but also serves to modify the sound of the "u." When the apostrophe is asked to serve both functions, we get a word that even a cow might renounce, since it can only be properly pronounced "res-cud." Nevertheless, the spelling proved popular and found its way into nearly a third of the songster printings.

Indeed, there is some indication that these features combined with one other rather unusual reading may point to the *Gazette* as the source of all those printings, at least in part. In the penultimate lines of the last three stanzas Key simply used the article in referring to "the star-spangled banner"; but in the first stanza he used the more emphatic demonstrative "that." The *Gazette* gives only "the." Here Hill pauses to describe two hybrid families of Baltimore songsters printed and reprinted during 1817-31, which in 1831 — after nine printings — still show both "rescu'd" and first-stanza "the" (in place of "that"). This suggests to Dick that the *Gazette*, perhaps through still unlocated newspaper printings, was their ultimate ancestor. The theory is supported by the very absurdity of the two readings, particularly in combination. They might be *copied* by later printers giving no thought to editing prior printings; but who would perpetrate both together again in preparing a new printing?

THE SHEET MUSIC EDITIONS

Thanks to Joseph Muller's *The Star Spangled Banner*, the sheet music editions can be covered much more comprehensively and at the same time more easily than any other. He gives complete facsimiles of seventeen distinctive editions, and anyone so minded can from Muller's notes fit these into the main series of fifty-four editions (with their many different states). As a bibliographer, however, Muller was more interested in establishing different editions than in describing their textual relationships. Something of the latter sort, therefore, must be attempted here. Most editions will be identified by their Muller numbers; only when an edition starts a new and significant subgroup of variant texts will there be any attempt at a fuller description. In the course of collating various texts and fitting editions into their historical background it has been possible to establish a few of the dates more precisely. In a few instances we can rearrange Muller's order—but there has been no tampering with Muller's numbers.

Since the appearance of Mr. Muller's bibliography, however, no one has risen to question his determination that the Joseph Carr edition with the subtitle ''A Pariotic Song'' (an obvious but convenient error for ''Patriotic'') was in fact the first of all the sheet music editions. It has one further important distinction. It gives the title of the song as ''The Star Spangled Banner,'' without any reference to Fort McHenry or its defense, and provides what is apparently the ''first known use'' of this title in print. There is no reference to the author of the words by name or even by place of domicile. At the foot of the first page, however, there appears the note ''(Adap^d. & Arr^d. by T. C.).'' The initials stand for Thomas Carr, Joseph's youngest son. In 1814 Thomas was 34 and may already have taken over active direction of the business, which he was to inherit five years later.

At any rate, he prepared a very musicianly arrangement of the music with a descending bass line to accompany the opening phrase of the melody, ending with a momentary modulation into the dominant. Whether he personally devised this modulation (with the fourth of the scale raised half a step in the melody, on the second syllable of ''early'') or whether he merely followed a practice that had become common in performances of ''The Anacreontic Song,'' he was at any rate the first musician to print the alteration in any known British or American edition. Since the modulation immediately became standard in all subsequent editions of the music, Carr deserves some if not all the credit for the slight but immensely appealing change.

That point settled, Dick Hill takes up the vexed question of the edition's date of issue. It was vexed for Muller fifty years ago and for Filby-Howard a decade and more ago. There is still no certain proof known to me, but with the help of a harmless "probably" Hill was able to dispose of the matter to his own satisfaction. We can be sure that the edition had been published by 19 November 1814, because on that date editor William Gwynn of the *Federal Gazette* writes of Thomas Carr having prepared and engraved the music and that Carr "has it for sale, at his music store, in the city. . . ." For the earliest possible publication date Dick Hill adopts as a working hypothesis the assumption . . . that the Carr first edition was available on October 19th when Mr. Hardinge first introduced the song at the Baltimore Theatre.

Carr did not stop with the first issue of his first edition. He also issued a rather striking revision of it, in which the text and the music were still printed from the same plates but with a radically changed heading. Muller felt that, because of the missing ''t'' of ''Patriotic'' in the subtitle, Carr if only from embarrassment must have issued the revision immediately. Unfortunately for that theory there is nothing to show that Carr was in the least sensitive about his typographical errors. As late as 1821 he brought out a ''New Edition'' of the song that still repeats the typograhical error of ''new'' for ''now'' (line 14) and continues to give all the other mistakes of the earlier edition. Furthermore, although both the original and revised printings of the first edition are exceptionally scarce for a song that has enjoyed so much popularity, there are approximately three times as many copies of the original edition extant as of the revised edition. It would be unsafe to assume that the sales remained constant from 1814 to 1821; but at the same time, if a new edition was needed after only seven years, there is likewise no reason for supposing that sales had sharply dropped.

Some elapse of time seems needed to account for the fresh, if inaccurate, information that Thomas added to the revised half-title. In the revision this reads: "A Celebrated Patriotic Song, / The / Star Spangled Banner / Written during the Bombardment of Fort McHenry on the 12th & 13th Septr. 1814, by / B Key Esqr." Since he was close to the action, one would like to think that Thomas Carr would have remembered that the bombardment took place on the 13th and 14th of September, that it was the Battle of North Point that took place on the earlier days.

As to the mistake in Key's name, the Carrs had given no identification of the author of the words in their first edition. Since Thomas had taken the text from a copy of the broadside, there was no need for any contact between the two men, and the lack of any indication of Key's participation in the first edition would make it seem very likely that Carr did not know his name in 1814. Indeed, Key's name is rarely given in the earliest printings and creeps in very gradually as word got about. We already know of the one newspaper attribution in 1814, and "Francis S. Key, Esq." is given as the author for the first time in any songster in *The American Star,* published at Richmond, Va., in 1817. Out of 29 songsters checked, however, that is the only one before 1820 to name the author. Indeed, after Carr in 1821 the next sheet music edition to name the author of the text is that of Atwill in 1843 (Muller 15). For several reasons, that is the most remarkable sheet music edition of the song ever published, but even it gives the author as "Francis S. Keys Esq."

Hill devotes one more paragraph to the Carr revised edition, and then remarks: Before we proceed to other matters, a curious document related to the Carr edition must be disposed of. That is a statement written in 1894 by Mary Jordan Carr Merryman, daughter of Thomas Carr, who claims that her father selected the music for the song "by Mr. Key's request in his presence from his manuscript" (see Muller, pp. 42-46). Her fulminations were inspired by what she considered a lack of proper credit given her father in articles dealing with *The Star Spangled Banner.* They in turn inspired similar fulminations even in the halls of the Congress of the United States, at intervals extending even past the death of Dick Hill — for I was once asked to brief a member of a House committee on "what this Carr business is all about." Dick in two and a half pages deals calmly and kindly with her absurd claims. Then he proceeds to another "curious" matter, "a freak sheet-music edition with Key's words" but not the familiar tune of the Anacreontic song.

Muller discusses this edition on page 35; but, since the music is different, he felt no need for treating it as fully as the other editions. It nevertheless includes the full text of Key's poem, and it is the text that is our concern here.

The music was composed by the elder James Hewitt in 1816. He felt that so fine an American poem should have American music to go with it. Unfortunately, he was not the man to compose it. Hewitt published the song himself at his Musical Repository in New York; the plates at his retirement in 1819 went to the Geibs and then Geib and Walker; E. Riley even engraved a new set of plates in 1829. But the melody lacked vitality and was even harder to sing than *To Anacreon in Heaven,* so that Hewitt's good idea eventually came to a dead end.

Hill traces in considerable detail the text Hewitt used from the original Carr edition through a G. E. Blake (Philadelphia) edition issued in late 1814 by adding a sheet with Key's handbill text to a reissue of Blake's *The Battle of the Wabash* (music by Joseph Hutton). The most significant variant Hill finds in Hewitt's text is his singular "mist" instead of "mists" in line 9, a variant that was to show up much later in the Atwill edition. The change is so unobtrusive, not to say meaningless, that when it later turns up in combination with the misplaced question mark in the same stanza, it will almost surely mean that the Hewitt text has crossed over into the main line of editions even if Hewitt's music has had to be left behind. The change is meaningless, but the elimination of the one sibilant does make the line easier to sing.

Returning finally to the main line, Hill takes up two sheet music editions published between the first (1814) and second (1821) Carr editions and clearly based on the handbill by way of Carr: Muller 2, by A. Bacon & Co. of Philadelphia, and Muller 3, by Geib & Co. in New York. One of these clearly was copied from the other, and Hill gives a convincing argument that Bacon copied from Geib rather than vice-versa as Muller had guessed. The point of Hill's argument is that Bacon corrects a number of errors deriving from Sands-Carr, and it would not make sense for Geib to copy from Bacon but introduce those same errors again. Bacon copied from Geib, but corrected some of the errors Geib had taken over without change. Proof that the two editions are closely related comes from the last note in the bass at the end of the first full measure of the piano introduction: the eighth note repeats G instead of passing down through F as Carr wrote it, an engraving error that could hardly be coincidence. Hill reads Muller's dating evidence to mean that both editions were issued in 1816, the Geib somewhat earlier in the year than the Bacon.

Mr. Muller speaks repeatedly of a "Carr-type edition," and the expression is entirely legitimate in the sense that certain of Carr's musical innovations proved very persistent, notably his raised fourth of the scale in the melody's second measure. But it is curious to note that, with the exception of his own "New Edition" (Muller 4), only the Geib edition out of all of Muller's fifty-four editions was based directly on a Carr edition. This situation is even more true of Carr's New Edition (Muller 4), since apparently not a single later edition drew on any of its readings. Carr's methods for distribution and sale outside of Baltimore must have been extremely inefficient or primitive—a conclusion confirmed by the great scarcity of his editions today. On the other hand, whole families evolve from the Geib and Bacon prototypes. Since both the Geib and Bacon editions contain many readings not found in either of the Carr editions, it is easy to demonstrate that all subsequent editions stem either from Geib or Bacon, and hence bear no direct relation to the original Carr edition.

Although it is comparatively easy to examine those subsequent editions and trace the branches by which they evolved, the picture that develops is not very edifying. One would be inclined to suppose that, since sheet music editions are generally more elaborate than newspaper and songster printings, some care would be devoted to the preparation of the text. Nothing of the sort happened with Key's poem. We started out with a particularly corrupt text; and, although some of Sands's influence was soon eradicated, the eradication seems to have been accomplished with a casual, smudged hand. There is rarely the slightest indication of an active, inquiring mind at work, so the sheet music editions will prove unfertile ground for anyone wishing to establish a sound text for Key's poem.

The music publishers in this country before the Civil War apparently attached little importance to texts and were satisfied if they could provide a usable copy of the music. One contributory cause may have been the presence of so many Germans in the engraving plants. Few of them would have had any feeling for the English language, and were no doubt happy if they could reproduce their copy accurately, mistakes and all. All too often one is astounded to note how some obvious slip, which almost anyone might have caught and corrected from the general sense of the poem, is instead reproduced literally in dozens of later editions. Here Hill cites some examples, such as the four question marks for which Thomas Carr, in preparing Muller 1, lacked the proper engraving punch; the question marks are still lacking fifty years later in Muller 53 and 54. The early sheet music editions, based ultimately on Sands's broadside, repeat his mistake of "shall" for "should" in line 19. The newspapers promptly corrected the error, but the sheet music editors paid no attention or had a less keen ear for the conditional mode and passed "shall" on into eternity. It is to be found in 31 of the 54 editions, with "should" appearing only in Muller 26 (which was published in England!) and in No. 52. To find out what happened to the word in the remaining 21 editions, we must turn to the one version bringing a fresh breeze over this calm sea of mediocrity.

The edition in question was published by Joseph F. Atwill at New York in 1843. Its title-page includes the legend: "The Symphonies and Accompaniments Composed & Arranged and Respectfully Inscribed to The Officers of the Army and Navy of the United States by Francis H. Brown." Muller 15 is a complete facsimile. Brown was one of the more proficient American composers of the period. He lived in Providence, R.I., where he was connected with Brown University. It should surprise no one to learn that his musical setting is an extremely elaborate one; but a good many people still do not know that it was apparently he who introduced two changes in the melody—they are at least seen for the first time on record in this edition—that are now found in all modern editions. Until 1843, every known edition of the melody begins the first and third lines with repeated notes on the tonic [just as John Stafford Smith wrote it *ca.* 1776]. Brown changed the beginning to the now-familiar descending triad from dominant to tonic. He also was first to introduce the passing tone eighth note on the third beat of the penultimate line, which previously had always been a repeated quarter note. In the key of C, "C C CBA A A" replacing "C C C A A A." Both changes seem insignificant, but they add materially—like Thomas Carr's raised fourth—to the sparkle and dash of the tune.

But Dick soon leaves Mr. Brown, who apparently had nothing to do with the text of this landmark edition. For seven pages Dick tracks various Atwill readings—it was Joseph Atwill who attended to the text—from edition to edition and even over into the songster domain; for Atwill was one editor who examined and selected rather than taking pot-luck. He started with Muller 10, his own earlier edition borrowed mostly from George Willig, but he took Hewitt's singular "mist" (which Hill views only as a typographical error) and from songsters he took a variety of readings. Most interesting is the answer he provided to the "shall" or "should" problem. In lines 18-19 Key wrote "That the havoc of war & the battle's confusion / A home & a Country should leave us no more?" With the substitution of only three words Atwill changes that to "And where is that band who so vauntingly swore, / 'Mid the havoc of war and the battle's confusion, / A home and a country they'd leave us no more?" Hill admires the word-juggling so greatly that he thinks it "rather beyond Atwill's dexterity" and is pleased when he finds that change in the *American Melodies* (Philadelphia & New York, 1840) of a bona-fide poet, George Pope Morris (best known for "Woodman! Spare That Tree!"). Also, Dick is sad to note, Atwill took from Morris the chauvinistic change from "when our cause it is just" to "for our cause it is just."

Dick Hill continues to swoop brilliantly from reading to reading, spotting readings appropriated by Atwill and then Atwill readings appropriated by others. (Musically there was little of the latter for several decades—because, Dick supposes, the Brown music was so easily identified and was registered for copyright.) At last Dick begins to run out of variant readings and feels the need of summation:

Thus far, 37 of Muller's basic editions have been dealt with, and since the subject can be none too easy to grasp on first reading it may be as well to repeat the numbers associated with the four main families. The Carr family consists only of Nos. 1 and 4, although No. 1 is fairly closely related to Geib's No. 3. With the Geib, a distinct family is started, most easily identified through its vestigial traces of Sands's capitals. It consists of Nos. 3, 11, 19, 23, 30, 32 = 36, 37, 39, 40, 42, 46, 51, and 52. Bacon based his edition on Geib (Muller 3), but removed all of Sands's capitals except "Pow'r" and a great deal of the punctuation—even some that would ordinarily be considered essential. The Bacon family (as presented so far) consists of 2 = 5, 7 = 13, 8 = 24, 9 = 20, 10, 12, 14, 17, 33, 43, and 53 = 54. As for Atwill, from his Bacon-type No. 10 he derived part of his 15, the plates of which were subsequently used in printing nos. 22 = 29 = 41. No. 26, published in London without any effect on American editions, is disregarded. A last word remains to be said about two of these editions, 19 and 45. For them and the sixteen editions still to be mentioned, Table 1 (pp. 124-25) of selected readings has been prepared to show the infiltration of the Atwill wording and punctuation.

After commenting on the great variety in the patterns of symbols, reflecting the great variety in hybrids, Hill continues for six pages to comment on the details of many of the hybrids and to gasp in awe at certain errors that kept being repeated in edition after edition. Bacon (Muller 2), for instance, whether with intent or by accident, changed Key's "flag was still there" (line 6) to "flag still was there"; that reading was repeated by the Bacon family in eleven succeeding editions as late as Muller 45. John Cole of Baltimore, in Muller 7 (1825), decided "whose broad" (stripes) was too much to sing on an anacrusis of two eighth notes and simply omitted "broad" so that "whose" could be sung on a quarter note. Twelve members of the Bacon family, including a couple of hybrids, followed suit (even Muller 53 = 54 where it appears as "Whose stripes"). In trying to intercalate plate numbers of the two firms of Miller & Beacham and William Hall & Son, Dick discovered that these two firms, at least, and probably others, followed a seasonal pattern. Apparently during the winter months they could get sufficient new works, on which a copyright could be obtained, to keep the engraving shop reasonably busy. During the summer, however, they took the opportunity to fill out their catalogs by making new plates of old works and by issuing pirated editions of works published abroad (not until 1891 was there any protection over here for works published abroad).

If these examples [writes Hill, referring to the Bacon and Cole editions just mentioned] seem to show a rather remarkable degree of faithful transcribing of an earlier source, other examples can be found to show that the urge to tinker, found in too many editors [careful, Mr. Editor Hill!], was not always held in check. It would certainly be unfair to blame all of the editors indiscriminately, since some of them were honestly attempting to repair the obviously faulty readings introduced by some predecessor; and, having no authoritative text to guide them, they did the best they could. However the multiplicity of readings came into existence, their very number is the clearest possible evidence of the sorry state into which the text of Key's poem had fallen fifty years after it was written. No comment on Table 2 (p. 127) is

TABLE 1

COMPARISON OF HYBRIDS CONTAINING READINGS FROM NO. 15

Line	Readings from No. 15 = x	Muller Numbers							
		19	50	44	47	48	45	16	18
1	Oh! say...see	x			x		x	y	y
4	streaming,	x	x	y	y	y	?	y	
5	rockets	R's	R's	R's	R's	R's	R's	y	y
6	thro'	x	x	y	y	y	x	x	x
	there?		;	x		x	: —	x	x
8	brave?	y	y	y	y	y	!	x	x
9	mist	y	y	x	x	x	y	x	x
12	discloses,	;	;	y	y	y	y	y	y
14	stream?	x	;	y	y	y	;	y	y
15	banner! oh,	−oh,	,O	y	y	y	,Oh!	y	y
18	'Mid	y	x	x	x	x	y	x	x
19	they'd	y	x	x	x	x	y	x	x
	no more?	y	,—	x	x	x	x	x	x
20	footstep's	y	ps'	y	y	y	x	y	y
	pollution!	y	•	y	y	y	x	y	y
24	brave!		y	y	y	y	x	y	y
27	heav'n	y	y	y	y	y	x	y-	y-
29	for our cause	y	y	y	y	y	y	y	y
30	trust."	;	−"	"	"	"	;	y	y
31	wave	y	y	y	y	y	y	y	y
32	free,	x	y	y	y	y	x	y	y
	brave!	y	y	y	y	y	y	y	y
	No. of x-readings	5	4	5	5	5	8	7	7

TABLE 1
COMPARISON OF HYBRIDS—*Continued*

21	25	27	28	31	34	35	38	49	43	Other Readings = y
	y		y	y	x	y		x	x	Oh! say,...see,
•	y	y	y	y	y	y	y	y	y	streaming;
x	y	y	y	y	y	y	x	y	x	rocket's
x	x	x	x	x	x	x	x	x	x	through
	y	y	x	y	!	!	y	!	y	there.
x	y	x	y	y	y	x	x	!	B?	brave.
y	x	x	x	x	x	x	x	x	x	mists
;		y	y		;	y	y	y	y	discloses?
;	y	y	y	y	!	y	y	y	•	stream:
,O!	y	y	y	y	x	y	y	Oh!	,oh!	—Oh!
x	x	x	x	x	x	x	x	x	x	That
x	x	x	x	x	x	x	x	x	x	shall
y	x	x	x	x	x	x	x	x	x	no more,
y	y	y	y	y	x	x	y	x	y	footsteps
	y	y	y	y	x	y	y	y	y	pollution;
y	y	y	y	y	x	x	y	x	y	brave.
y	x	y-	y	x	x-	x-	y-	x	H'n	heaven
x	y	y	y	y	x	y	y	y	y	when
;"	y	y	y	y	x	y	y	y	y	trust,"
y	x	x	x	x	x	x	x	y	y	wave,
x	y	y	y	y	x	y	y	y	F,	free
y	y	y	y	y	x	x	y	x	B.	brave.
7	7	7	7	7	16	11	8	10	7	

needed, since the variant readings of just a few selected words, with the Muller numbers of the editions in which they will be found, speak for themselves; Mr. Sonneck's term "unsettled" begins to seem entirely inadequate.

FIRST MAGAZINE PUBLICATION

The period was not without its intelligent, lively, and serious journals, somewhat on the order of *Harper's* and the *Atlantic Monthly* today. One of these, *The Analectic Magazine,* found Key's poem worthy of publication in its issue for November 1814 (vol. 4, pp. 433-34). The editor explained his reasons in a note:

> These lines have already been published in several of our newspapers; they may still, however, be new to many of our readers. Besides, we think that their merit entitles them to preservation in some more permanent form than the columns of a daily paper.

The occasion is worthy of attention, not merely because this printing is generally reputed to be the earliest magazine publication of the poem but also—to return the editor's compliment—because it is an almost impeccable job of editing. After lambasting the sheet music editors for letting the text disintegrate in their hands, I find comfort in an editor with a sense of order and a discriminating taste who through sheer intuition was able to repair some of the damage the poem had suffered at the hands of Samuel Sands.

Not that he could repair everything. He could correct Sands's obvious extravagances, but there was no conceivable way for him to get back to Key's original text. He necessarily had to start with one of the early printings, and he fortunately chose the better of the first two newspaper printings—that of the *Patriot*. This gave him one extraneous reading, "shines on the stream"; but it also gave him a plural "footsteps" (line 20). To this he added an extra fillip by introducing a hyphen, ending up with "foul foot-steps' pollution." As a matter of fact, the hyphen is also present in the *Patriot,* but there it is required because the righthand margin was reached and "footsteps" had to be divided. The preservation of the hyphen when it was not needed for so practical a purpose suggests a mind on the finicky side. So also does the archaic spelling of "the *havock* of war" (line 18), which the editor introduces. Judged against the total effect, however, two such points are nothing to hold against an editor.

It would be too much to expect him to go back to Key's singular forms of "rocket's" and "bomb," and he does not. He does at least remove their capitals, as well as five others (see the variorum chart). The editor of the *Patriot* had already removed the other capitals, including the one on "power" (line 28), so all of Sands's capitals are eradicated for a second time (the editor of the *Federal Gazette* having done that job himself).

Such improvements are perhaps obvious, but the editor did not stop with them. He went on to systematize the punctuation in a very neat fashion, removing a number of improper commas

TABLE 2

127

VARIANT READINGS

Rockets'	1 3													
Rockets	4					37	40							
Rocket's		11	19	23	30 32	36	39	42	44	46-8	50-1			
rockets	2 5-10	12-15 17	20-22 24	29		38	41			49	52-4			
rocket's		16 18	25-8	31	34-5			43	45					
rockets'				33										

footsteps	1-14 16-21 23-25	28 30-32	36-7 39-40	43-4 46-8	51-2							
footstep's	15 22	26 29	33-5	41-2 45	49	53-54						
foot-steps		27	38									
footsteps'				50								

vic'try				43							
vict'ry	1-6 8 10	14-16 18	22 24-25 27-9	31 34-5	38 40-1	45-6	49	53-4			
victory	7 9 11-13	17 19-21 23	26 30 32-3	36-7 39	42 44	47-8 50-2					

Heav'n rescued	1 4		26			43			
heav'n rescued	2-3 5-6 8 10	12 14-15 17	22 24-25	29 31		41	45		
heav'n- rescued				34-5					
heaven rescued	7 9 11 13	19-21 23	28 30 32	36-7 39-40	42 44				
heaven-rescued		16 18	27	38					
Heaven rescued				33					
Heaven rescu'd							53		

Pow'r	1-5 11	14 19	23	30 32 36	39	43		51 53-4			
Power	6-7 9-10 12-13	15-18 20 22	25 27-9 31	33-5	38	41-2	49				
pow'r	8		24 26				45				
power		21			37 40	44 46-8	50 52				

and (for the first time since Key) regularizing the punctuation of the final couplets in each stanza. Also, the natural caesura after "free" in the last line of each stanza had attracted a comma in some, though never in all, stanzas. *The Analectic Magazine* gives no commas in any of the four stanzas after "wave," but adds the comma systematically after "free" in all four stanzas. It is a particular pleasure, after wallowing in the incompetence of so many other editors, to find one who knows how to be logical even in small matters.

It seemed a shame that so good an editor should be left unidentified, even if not unsung, but *The Analectic Magazine* does not name its editor—only its publisher. A little research turned up the name. It was Washington Irving.

Dick Hill enjoyed his little surprise so much that I had not the heart to expunge it. But Irving's *Letters* (Boston: Twayn Publishers, 1978-82, 4 vols., several eds.), show that from 2 September until December 1814 Washington Irving was aide-de-camp to the Governor of New York, Major General Daniel D. Tompkins, and spent most of his time at Sacket's Harbor and elsewhere in New York. It is theoretically possible that Irving did edit, or help to edit, this November issue or perhaps at least the Key poem; but it is more likely that the job was done by his assistant or temporary replacement. His successor as editor, Thomas Isaac Wharton, apparently did not take over until sometime in 1815.

THE SONGSTERS

An almost bewildering array of songsters began publishing Key's poem very shortly after it was written. The flood appears to dry up in 1819, but this was only because a serious depression hit the country in that year and the number of songsters published dropped to an insignificant level. As prosperity gradually returned during the 1820s and the number of songsters increased again, *The Star Spangled Banner* definitely was still there—quite often as the first song in the book. The texts in well over a hundred songsters have been collated for this study. Every known songster before 1820 was checked,[11] and an extensive if not quite so thorough a search was made for the songsters published during the 1820s. If in the process any songster was found from the 1830s it was automatically included, but from the 1840s and later a songster had to offer something special or it was rejected. By eliminating most reeditions of substantially the same text, the number was whittled down to 94, and the statistics offered later on are generally based on this sampling. But the total was still far more than could be covered comfortably or sensibly here, and the list of titles below was finally cut to thirty-six.

---

[11] Hill's comprehensive treatment of the early songsters was possible only because of the great help he received from the late Irving Lowens, whose *Bibliography of Songsters Printed in America before 1821* was published in 1976 by the American Antiquarian Society, Worcester, Mass.

The list in Table 3 (pp. 130-31) is still so long that the entries must be kept as brief as possible and most of the songsters' long and florid titles reduced to a few words. The symbols consist of the last two digits in the year of publication plus a letter derived by alphabetizing all the songster titles dating from that year and giving each a letter from A to G, S, etc., in alphabetical order. ["Imp." = imperfect.] There are gaps due to the cutting down to thirty-six. No attempt has been made to gather complete location symbols, and often the only symbol is for the copy used—though if other copies are known a fair sampling is supplied.

Even with this select group of songsters, the number of different versions of Key's poem to be found in them is far too great to allow the organization and analysis given the sheet music—and, of course, the songsters have no Muller. The editors of the songsters were not as limited in their choice of sources as the sheet music publishers seem to have been: they drew on the broadside, many of the newspapers, *The Analectic Magazine,* and any sheet music that came to hand. Some editors were entirely too enterprising and created their own versions, although the majority simply copied some other songster. Of all the sheet music editions, Blake's *Battle of the Wabash* (Muller 1, amended) with the text supplied by Mr. Hardinge was used most frequently, especially in the Philadelphia area. It was one of the sources for 17E and started off two sizable families with 28B and 17B (the latter probably in combination with the *Patriot* or *Analectic Magazine*). Of the early newspapers, the *American* (whose print-shop started it all off with Sands's handbill) seems to have been used the least, turning up only in 17F and 18H. The *Federal Gazette,* in combination with 17E, seems to have been responsible for easily the most distinctive—if also most corrupt—of all the songster families. That version starts with 17D and was still going strong in 1845.

As one might suspect, the *Patriot* and *Analectic Magazine* prove to be by far the most influential sources. Their family began with 17A = 18A, 24A, and 30B and included at least twenty-eight other songsters, not counting the many separate editions that some of them achieved; it continued right down to the Civil War and beyond. These two basic sources, fortunately for Key's text, were involved in several other series as well, and the combination of printings gradually put this general type into a predominant position in the songster medium. With the sheet music offering such a sorry mess of distortion and corruption, it was probably the lowly songster that kept a reasonably pure version of Key's poem alive. Eventually it was this text that came to be selected by the editors of the more elegant anthologies of poetry, such as those compiled by Griswold and Dana. Then, when after the Civil War the editors of music editions finally became aware that Key's poem would be improved through the judicious use of a question mark, it would have been from the anthologies that they got an improved text. The songsters, unimpressive as they often seem, thereby rendered a most valuable service.

TABLE 3
EARLY SONGSTERS

14A The American Muse: or, Songster's Companion. New York: Smith & Forman. 216 p. MB, NjP, RPB.

14B American Patriotic and Comic Modern Songs. Newburyport: W. & J. Gilman. 49 p. MB, RPB.

14C The Columbian Harmonist, or Songster's Repository. New York: Smith & Forman. 288 p. MH, MWA, RPB, ScU. (A copy with this title, but with the contents of 14A is at MiUC.)

14D National Songster; or, a collection of the most admired patriotic songs. Hagers-Town: John Gruber and Daniel May. 40 p. CSmH, CtY, DLC, MWiW-C, NHi, PHi.

15A The Columbian Harmonist, or Songster's Repository. Albany: G. J. Loomis & Co. 180 p. CtY, MWA, RPB.

16A American Patriotic and Comic Modern Song-Book. Newburyport: W. & J. Gilman. 53 p.(?). DLC, MSaE (both imp.)

16B The Modern Songster. Second Baltimore Edition. Baltimore: William Warner. 216 p. MWA, TxU.

16C The Patriotic Songster. Alexandria: Benjamin L. Bogan. 156 p. RPB (imp.), ViU.

16D The Sky-lark. Hartford: B. & J. Russell. 96 p. RPB (imp).

16E The Star Spangled Banner. Wilmington, Del.: J. Wilson. Issued in two sizes: RPB, 108 p.; DLC, 144 p.

16F The Syren. Washington: W. Cooper. 120 p. NHi. (Reissued as 18I, RPB.)

17A The Aeolian Harp. Vol.I (of two). New York: M. Swaim & J. Howe. 128 p. RM PP (imp.), RPB. (Reissued as 18A, ICN, MWA, NHi.)

17B The American Star. Second Edition. Richmond: Peter Cotton. 216 p. DLC, MB, MWA, etc.

17C The Diamond Songster. Baltimore: Fielding Lucus, Jr. 156 p. MdHi, NBuG, RPB.

17D A Mess of Salmagundi. Philadelphia: published for the subscribers. 144 p. MWA, NN.

17E The New American Songster. Philadelphia: D. Dickinson. RPB (imp.).

17F The Star. Pittsburgh: Butler & Lambdin. 175 p. RPB (imp.). (Reissued as 18H, 179 p., NHi).

17G The Star Spangled Banner. Second Edition. Wilmington, Del.: J. Wilson. Issued in two sizes: MiU-C, MWA, PCC — all 108 p.; DeWI, DLC, NBuG, NHi — all 144 p.

18F Seven Good Songs. Lancaster, Pa.: Wm. Dickson. 12 p. DLC.

18G Songs for the Parlour. New Haven: J. Babcock & Son; Charleston, S.C.: S. & W.R. Babcock. 128 p. RPB.

20B The Songster's Magazine. Vol.I (all seen). New York: J. B. Jansen. 144 p. DLC.

NOTE: *To give a brief taste of Dick Hill's typewriter and of his typing personality, Table 3 is a reproduction of Hill's own typescript.*

TABLE 3

EARLY SONGSTERS—*Continued*

131

138

21C The Nightingale. Philadelphia: M. Carey & Son. 198 p. PPL.

23B The Songster's Hobby. Philadelphia: Freeman Scott. 72 p. MH.

24A The Vocal Standard, or, Star Spangled Banner. Richmond: John H. Nash. 264 p. NHi.

27A The Muse; or Flowers of Poetry. By Samuel W. Cole. Cornish, Maine: Published and sold by the author. 216 p. RPB.

27B The Southern and Western Songster. Second edition, greatly enlarged. Philadelphia: John Grigg. 306 p. DLC, MB. (Copyright claim for 1826 presumably refers to first edition, but no copy has been located. Somewhat revised and increased to 324 p., with Grigg's name added to title, the collection was reissued many times down to 1847.)

28A The Flowers of Melody. Selected and arranged by John Graham. In two volumes. Vol. II. New York: Clayton & Van Norden. 389 p. RPB.

28B The Minstrel. Philadelphia: William W. Weeks. 353 p. RPB.

29A The Vocal Companion. Philadelphia: J. W. Smith. 72 p. MB.

30B The New-England Pocket Songster. Windsor: n.p. 160 p. DLC.

32B The Singer's Own Book. Philadelphia: Key, Mielke & Biddle. 320 p. RPB. (Reissued as 39D and without date.)

34B The Free-and Easy Song Book. Philadelphia: James Kay, Jun. & Brother; Pittsburgh: John I. Kay & Co. 272 p. DLC.

35A Jack Downing's Song Book. Providence: Weeden and Cory. 256 p. RPP. (Second Edition, 36C, DLC.)

36E The Parlour Companion, or, Polite Song Book. Philadelphia: A. I. Dickinson; New York: Atwill's Music Saloon. 306 p. (plus advertisements). NN

40A American Melodies, edited by George P. Morris. New York: Linen & Fennell; Philadelphia: Henry F. Anners. 286 p. DLC.

42E Songs, Odes, and other Poems, on National Subjects; compiled...by Wm. McCarty. Part First — Patriotic. Philadelphia: Wm. McCarty. 468 p. DLC.

Even with this selected group of songsters, the number of versions of *The Star Spangled Banner* to be found in them is far too great to be analyzed and organized as were the sheet-music editions. The editors of the songsters were not as limited in their choice of sources as were the editors of the sheet-music editions, and they drew on the broadside, many of the newspapers, *The Analectic Magazine*, and any sheet music that came to hand. Some editors were entirely too enterprising, and created their own versions, although it is true that the majority simply copied some other songster. For

And that service was not always easy to render, since the enthusiasts and wilful corrupters were constantly at hand. Some of these gentlemen contributed readings that outdid in ridiculousness anything the sheet music editors could conceive of; and yet in the long run it was just the inherent silliness of those readings that drove them out of the picture. It may be amusing to observe that the editor of 17F replaced Key's "the havoc of war" with "the bustle of war," or that the editor of 16E thought that the band should swear "wantonly" instead of "vauntingly," but such absurdities carry their own death within them. For the record, one wholly outrageous version begun in 17D was repeated in some eighteen later songsters. Its variants include a careless "whose proud stripes" (line 3), in its line 11 the flag is glimpsed "o'er yon low'ring steep," and it happens that this version is also the first to perpetrate the still tempting chauvinism of "*for* our cause it is just" (line 29). As such it deserves to be publicly pilloried. (Dick had his share of patriotism, but blind chauvinism—whether pro or anti American—went hard against his grain.)

Here Dick Hill turns from the horrors to the good things and to both narrative and statistical accounts of various readings he has met with in the songster maze. He counts, for instance, sixteen possible different ways of presenting Key's "reasonably natural" two-word phrase of "heav'n rescued"; in the songsters he finds fourteen, the two missing patterns being "Heav'n rescu'd" and "Heaven rescu'd." He has statistics for even the title of the song, which of course Key did not supply though he presumably was pleased with it since he is not known to have expressed opposition to it. In the songsters Dicks counts thirteen variants, given here with the number of times he found each:

The star Spangled Banner	1	The Star Spangled Banner	9
The original Star		The Star-Spangled Banner	5
Spangled Banner	1	Star Spangled Banner	3
The star spangled Banner	1	THE STAR SPANGLED BANNER	13
Star-spangled Banner	1	THE STAR-SPANGLED BANNER	15
The Star spangled Banner	2	STAR SPANGLED BANNER	14
The Star-spangled Banner	6	STAR-SPANGLED BANNER	16

THE COMPLETE POEMS

When a poet's works are gathered together after the poet's death and published complete, or as near complete as possible, one expects them to be authoritatively edited. When the Rev. Henry V. D. Johns of Baltimore did the last honors for Key he saved a great deal of rather mediocre, previously unpublished poetry from total loss, but what he did to Key's one famous poem shows the hand of the true meddler. His version has had to be included in the variorum edition, and this brief note written, purely for the sake of the record, but neither should be taken as implying any merit in the editing.

In essence, the text is that of *Analectic Magazine*, and Johns follows it in giving a comma after "On the shore" (line 9) but not after "What is that" (line 11). To his credit it should be noted that he chose to give "now shines in the stream" (line 14). Since that reading appears in very few separate printings of the poem, it came in all probability from the autograph copy Key had made for General Keim. This was apparently the only autograph he knew, and he seems not to have trusted it very far. The Keim autograph gives "And where are the foes that" instead of "And where is that band who. . . ." Johns compromises with "And where are the foes who. . . ." Johns also accepts the Keim reading of a plural "homes" (line 26), but spells the preceding word "loved" rather than "lov'd." On the other hand he does not accept the Keim singular "rocket's" and "Bomb," but gives both in the plural. Rather fortunately he does not accept Key's late experiment with "through the clouds of the fight" (line 3) nor his singular "footstep's." These takings and rejectings, however, do not end by giving him a consistent version of any sort, and he makes matters worse by introducing quite a few changes on his own authority. "Star Spangled Banner" is given three capitals in each stanza; he moves the first question mark from the fourth to the second line and replaces the fourth question mark with a bare colon; each of the last three stanzas ends with an exclamation point. There are other unusual features about the edition; but this should be enough to convey its flavor, and it is worth no more.

EPILOGUE

Given the strength of ten, perhaps someone might carry this inquiry through to the present day and in the process discover further foolish versions. Some spot checks have been made through the later decades, however, and nothing significantly new has been discovered. Few poems have ever been printed so often during a mere century and a half, and printed under less control. Key's poem was taken over almost immediately by the people at large, not by a few careful scholars. And if it was made to suffer at the eager hands of some of the people, so also was it made to flourish in a way no poem, kept in an ivory tower, could ever flourish. What we have seen is essentially the evolution of a folk song, with each step recorded in print. Even to a folklorist it is probably not a particularly edifying sight, since although one small portion of the folk has the good taste to polish a text, the folk in general are massive eroders with far too many different personalities to leave anything the way it was. Mr. Sonneck is wholly correct in saying that the text of *The Star Spangled Banner* had become "unsettled," but in saying this, he says little more than any folklorist has often said about the variant texts of *Barbara Allen*.

The real point at issue, therefore, is not whether the folk can and will unsettle an unprotected text, but whether a text so unsettled can properly serve as a joint national symbol. Since a national anthem must usually be performed spontaneously by people coming together from all walks of life and with all sorts of musical backgrounds, this is one occasion where the usual prerogatives of private enterprise can only end in confusion or worse. Almost any thoughtful person will admit that the present state of affairs is not desirable, and the only problem comes when a group of people gathers to decide what should be done to cure it. With so many variants still flourishing in the hundreds of editions of the anthem currently available, and with plenty of proponents intent on making their own favorite changes in melody and text, the problem seems almost insuperable.

But is it? Looking back, it sometimes seems as if Humpty Dumpty had fallen from his wall on the day Samuel Sands set the first broadside and that no one would ever get all of the pieces fitted back together again. Before the week was out, however, the *Patriot* had made a fair stab at the job and the *American* had actually corrected one of Key's own slips. A month later, William Gwynn in the *Federal Gazette* had gotten nearly every chip of the shell reassembled once more. Within six weeks, Washington Irving had finished the job started by the editor of the *Patriot,* and if only Key's manuscript had been available to serve as a guide, the two versions in the *Federal Gazette* and *The Analectic Magazine* would have supplied between them almost all of the readings needed to make Humpty Dumpty a complete personage once more. And so it has gone, with one group tearing down the text and another group appearing to repair the damage. Some hard things have been said of Samuel Sands. One cannot help but wonder what the future history of the text would have been had Sands not presented to the world in his first broadside a text that invited changes, in fact, demanded them. If a printer with the taste of Washington Irving had been the first to set Key's poem in type, would the history of that text have been different? In the long run, the difference would probably have been imperceptible, since if Sands had not come first, he—or someone like him—would certainly have appeared in due course.

Finally, despite all of this breaking down and reassembling, it is a curious fact that all of the variants that produce serious problems today already existed in the first three printings. The lesson to be learned from that is simple. An early variant stands a chance of being frequently reproduced, spread, and incorporated in one of the main versions, whereas a later variant is more likely to be submerged by the hundreds of competing editions already in existence and gradually forgotten. Under these circumstances, is it wise to allow ourselves to be deflected from the main purpose by the multiplicity of later variants? The song, like the estuary of the Patapsco, unquestionably has an ever widening mouth with treacherous shoals on all sides. But running through the middle there has always been, whether we knew it or not, a clear and relatively safe channel extending from Baltimore to the Bay. It is hoped that the variorum edition offered here may help to provide a similar service for Key's poem, and by charting all the shoals and mud-banks leave the safe channel standing clear.

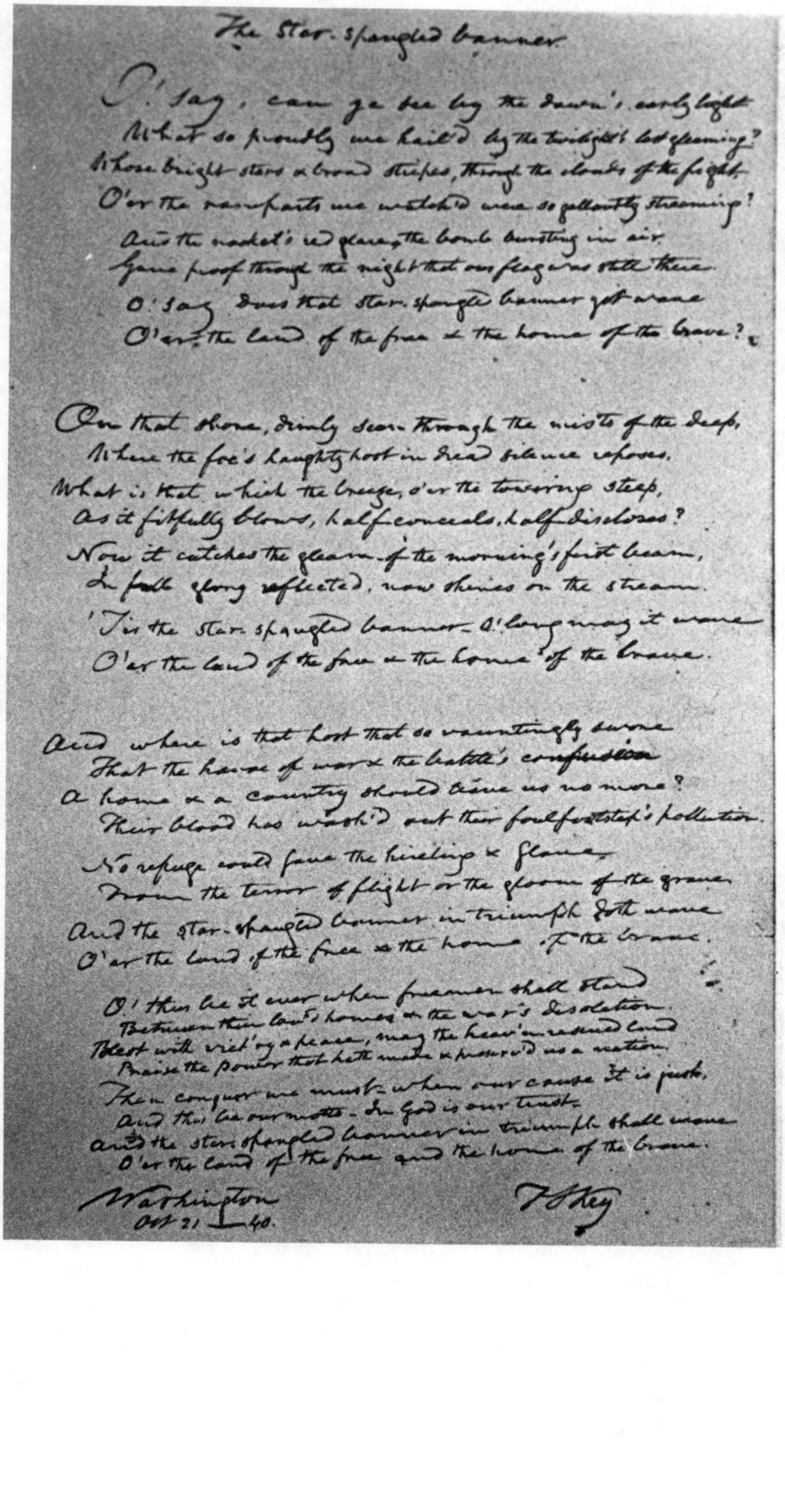

PLATE 3.
Key's manuscript
written out for
Lewis J. Cist
on 21 October 1840.
In Music Division,
Library of Congress.

O say can you see by the dawn's early light
What so proudly we hail'd at the twilight's last gleaming,
Whose broad stripes and bright stars, through the clouds of the fight,
O'er the ramparts we watch'd were so gallantly streaming?
And the rocket's red glare—the bomb bursting in air
Gave proof through the night that our flag was still there—
O say, does that star-spangled banner yet wave
O'er the land of the free & the home of the brave?—

On that shore, dimly seen through the mists of the deep,
Where the foe's haughty host in dread silence reposes,
What is that, which the breeze, o'er the towering steep
As it fitfully blows, half conceals, half discloses?
Now it catches the gleam—of the morning's first beam,
In full glory reflected, now shines in the stream,
'Tis the star-spangled banner—O long may it wave
O'er the land of the free & the home of the brave!

And where are the foes that so vauntingly swore
That the havoc of war & the battle's confusion
A home and a Country should leave us no more?
Their blood has wash'd out their foul footstep's pollution.
No refuge could save—the hireling & slave,
From the terror of flight, or the gloom of the grave,
And the star-spangled banner in triumph doth wave
O'er the land of the free & the home of the brave.

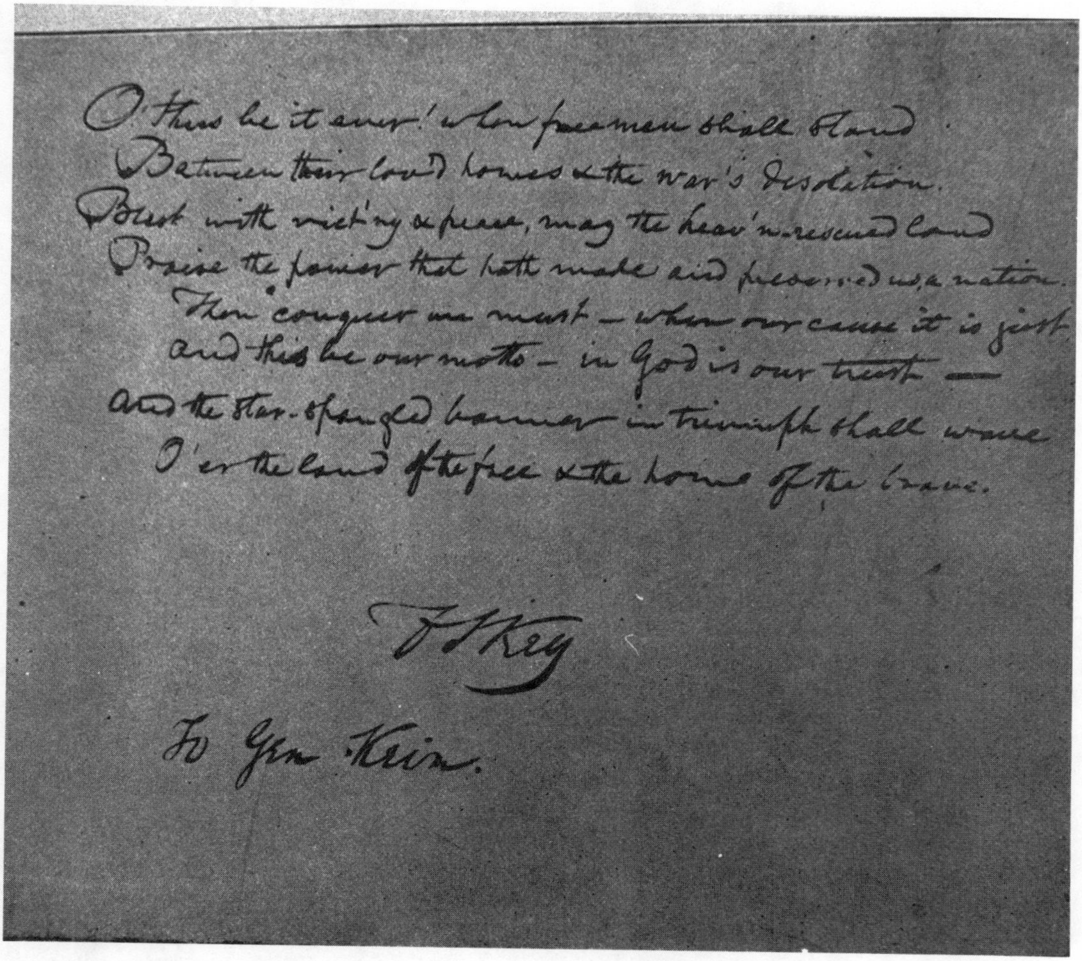

O thus be it ever! when freemen shall stand
Between their lov'd homes & the war's desolation.
Blest with vict'ry & peace, may the heav'n-rescued land
Praise the power that hath made and preserved us, a nation.
   Then conquer we must — when our cause it is just
   And this be our motto — in God is our trust —
And the star-spangled banner in triumph shall wave
   O'er the land of the free & the home of the brave.

F S Key

To Gen Keim.

PLATES 4, 5. Key's manuscript written out for General George Keim, probably in 1842.
At the Historical Society of Pennsylvania, Philadelphia.

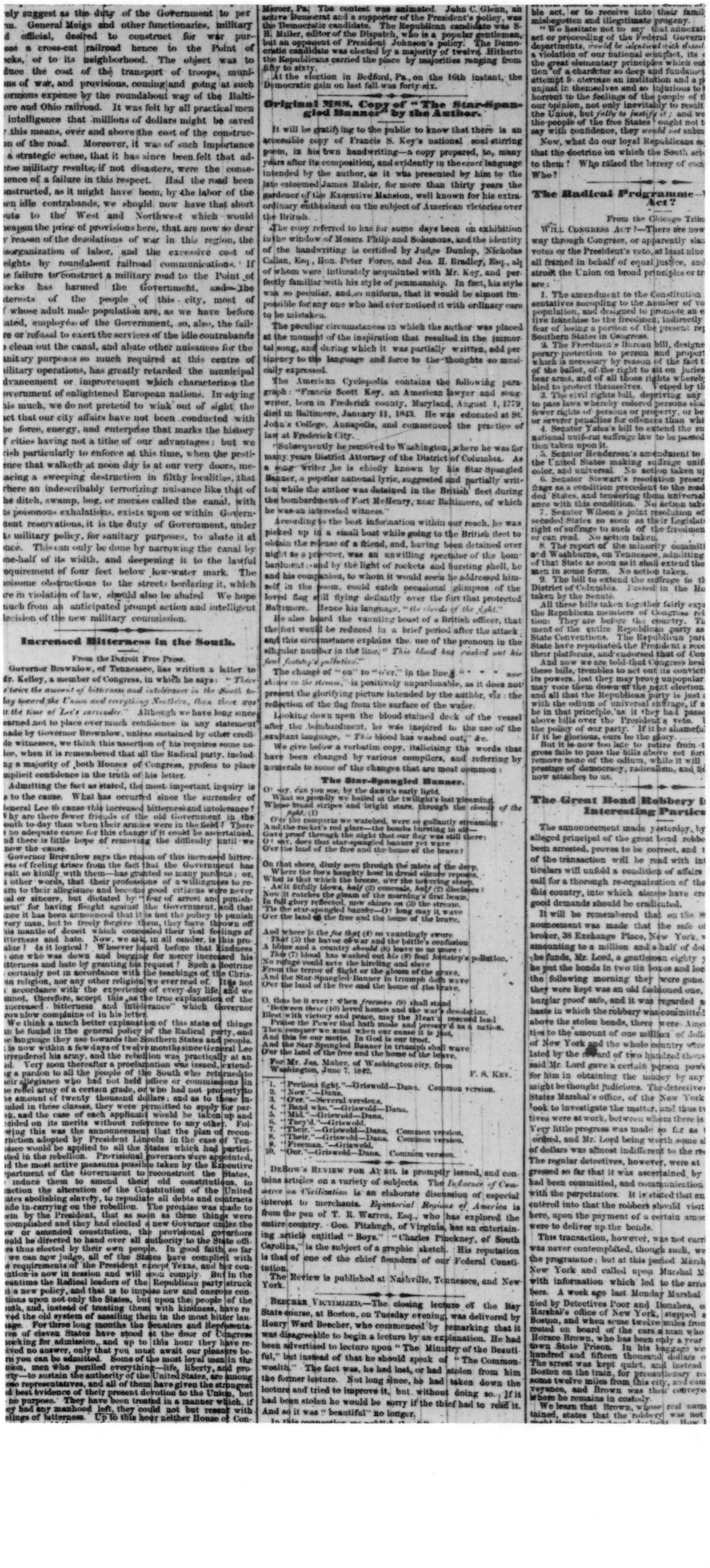

PLATE 6.
Printed version
(from the *National
Intelligencer*,
Washington,
31 March 1866)
of Key's manuscript
written out
7 June 184[2?]
for James Maher,
long-time gardener
at the White House.

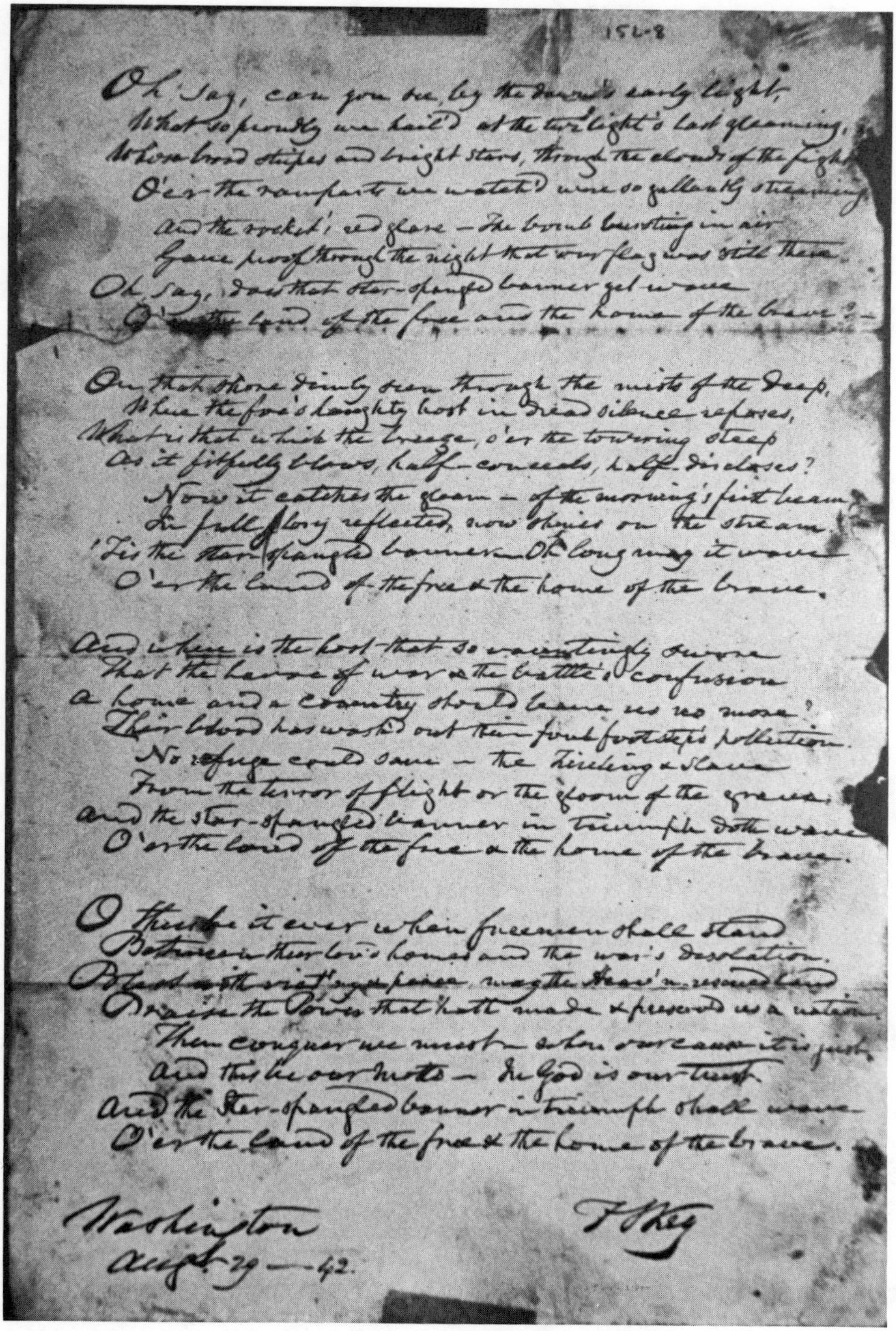

PLATE 7. Key manuscript written out at Washington, 29 August 1842.
Acquired by Thomas Stevenson Espy, of Pennsylvania,
Iowa, and Missouri under circumstances unknown.
Since 1897 in the Library of Georgetown University, Washington.

DEFENCE OF FORT M'HENRY.

The annexed song was composed under the following circumstances—
A gentleman had left Baltimore, in a flag of truce for the purpose of getting released from the British fleet, a friend of his who had been captured
at Marlborough.—He went as far as the mouth of the Patuxent, and was
not permitted to return lest the intended attack on Baltimore should be
disclosed. He was therefore brought up the Bay to the mouth of the Patapsco, where the flag vessel was kept under the guns of a frigate, and
he was compelled to witness the bombardment of Fort M'Henry, which
the Admiral had boasted that he would carry in a few hours, and
that the city must fall. He watched the flag at the Fort through the
whole day with an anxiety that can be better felt than described, until
the night prevented him from seeing it. In the night he watched the Bomb
Shells, and at early dawn his eye was again greeted by the proudly waving
flag of his country.

Tune—ANACREON IN HEAVEN.

O ! say can you see by the dawn's early light,
    What so proudly we hailed at the twilight's last gleaming,
Whose broad stripes and bright stars through the perilous fight,
    O'er the ramparts we watch'd, were so gallantly streaming?
And the Rockets' red glare, the Bomb bursting in air,
Gave proof through the night that our Flag was still there;
      O ! say does that star-spangled Banner yet wave,
      O'er the Land of the free, and the home of the brave?

On the shore dimly seen through the mists of the deep,
    Where the foe's haughty host in dread silence reposes,
What is that which the breeze, o'er the towering steep,
    As it fitfully blows, half conceals, half discloses?
Now it catches the gleam of the morning's first beam,
In full glory reflected new shines in the stream,
      'Tis the star spangled banner, O ! long may it wave
      O'er the land of the free and the home of the brave.

And where is that band who so vauntingly swore
    That the havoc of war and the battle's confusion,
A home and a country, shall leave us no more?
    Their blood has washed out their foul footsteps pollution.
No refuge could save the hireling and slave,
From the terror of flight or the gloom of the grave,
      And the star-spangled banner in triumph doth wave,
      O'er the Land of the Free, and the Home of the Brave.

O ! thus be it ever when freemen shall stand,
    Between their lov'd home, and the war's desolation,
Blest with vict'ry and peace, may the Heav'n rescued land,
    Praise the Power that hath made and preserv'd us a nation!
Then conquer we must, when our cause it is just,
And this be our motto—" In God is our Trust ;"
      And the star-spangled Banner in triumph shall wave,
      O'er the Land of the Free, and the Home of the Brave.

PLATE 8. The famous handbill, first printing of the poem.
Set in type by apprentice Samuel Sands in the print shop of the *Baltimore American,*
probably on 17 September 1814.

THE PARTERRE.

Defence of Fort M'Henry.

[☞ The following beautiful and animating effusion, which is destined long to outlast the occasion, and outlive the impulse, which produced it, has already been extensively circulated. In our first renewal of publication, we rejoice in an opportunity to enliven the sketch of an exploit so illustrious, with strains, which so fitly celebrate it.]

ED. PAT.

The annexed song was composed under the following circumstances—A gentleman had left Baltimore, in a flag of truce for the purpose of getting released from the British fleet a friend of his, who had been captured at Malborough. He went as far as the mouth of the Patuxent, and was not permitted to return lest the intended attack on Baltimore should be disclosed. He was therefore brought up the bay to the mouth of the Patapsco, where the flag vessel was kept under the guns of a frigate, and he was compelled to witness the bombardment of Fort M'Henry, which the Admiral had boasted that he would carry in a few hours, and that the city must fall. He watched the flag at the Fort through the whole day with an anxiety that can be better felt than described, until the night prevented him from seeing it. In the night he watched the Bomb-Shells, and at early dawn his eye was again greeted by the proudly-waving flag of his country.

Tune—ANACREON IN HEAVEN.

O! say can you see, by the dawn's early light,
　What so proudly we hail'd at the twi-
　　light's last gleaming,
Whose broad stripes and bright stars through
　the perilous fight,
　O'er the ramparts we watch'd, were so gal-
　　lantly streaming?
And the Rockets' red glare, the Bombs burst-
　ing in air,
Gave proof through the night that our Flag
　was still there;
　　O! say, does that star-spangled Banner
　　　yet wave,
　　O'er the Land of the free, and the home
　　　of the brave?

On the shore, dimly seen through the mists of
　the deep,
　Where the foe's haughty host in dread
　　silence reposes,
What is that, which the breeze o'er the tow-
　ering steep,
　As it fitfully blows, half conceals, half dis-
　　closes?
Now it catches the gleam of the morning's
　first beam,
In full glory reflected now shines on the
　stream.
　　'Tis the star-spangled banner. O! long
　　　may it wave
　　O'er the land of the free and the home
　　　of the brave.

And where is that band who so vauntingly
　swore
　That the havoc of war and the battle's con-
　　fusion,
A home and a country should leave us no
　more?
　Their blood has wash'd out their foul foot-
　　steps' pollution.
No refuge could save the hireling and slave,
From the terror of flight or the gloom of
　the grave;
　　And the star-spangled banner in tri-
　　　umph doth wave,
　　O'er the land of the free and the home
　　　of the brave.

O! thus be it ever when freemen shall stand,
　Between their lov'd home, and the war's
　　desolation,
Blest with victory and peace, may the Heav'n-
　rescued land,
　Praise the power that hath made and pre-
　　serv'd us a nation!
Then conquer we must, when our cause it
　is just,
And this be our motto—"In God is our
　Trust!"
　　And the star-spangled banner in tri-
　　　umph shall wave,
　　O'er the land of the free and the home
　　　of the brave.

BY THE LATE MAILS.

PLATE 9.
First formal
publication of
Key's poem, in the
Baltimore Patriot of
20 September 1814,
p. 2.

PLATES 10, 11. First publication of Key's poem with the tune to which he wrote it, adapted & arranged by Thomas Carr of the Baltimore music publisher Joseph Carr.

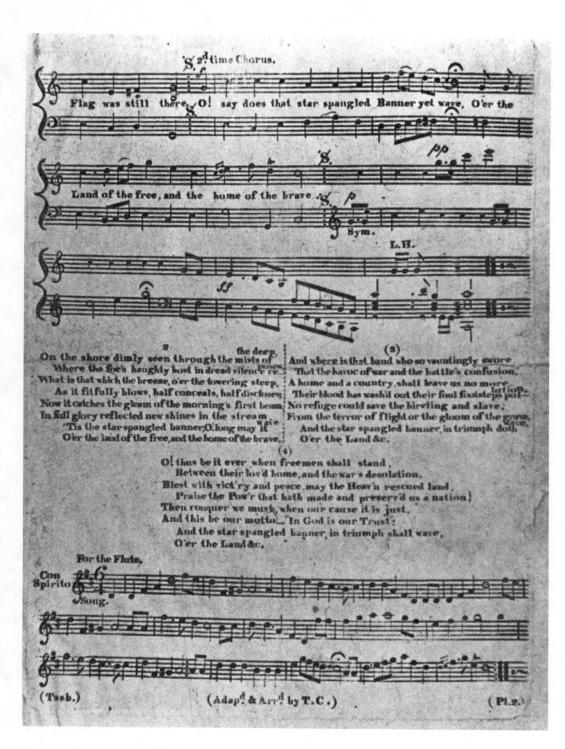

to Baltimore, in a flag of truce for the purpose of getting released from the British fleet a friend of his who had been captured at Marlborough.—He went as far as the mouth of the Patuxent, and was not permitted to return lest the intended attack on Baltimore should be disclosed. He was therefore brought up the Bay to the mouth of the Patapsco, where the flag vessel was kept under the guns of a frigate, and he was compelled to witness the bombardment of Fort M'Henry, which the Admiral had boasted that he would carry in a few hours, and that the city must fall. He watched the flag at the fort through the whole day with an anxiety that can be better felt than described, until the night prevented him from seeing it. In the night he watched the Bomb Shells, and at early dawn his eye was again greeted by the proudly waving flag of his country.

Tune—Anacreon in Heaven.

O! say can you see by the dawn's early light,
What so proudly we hailed at the twilight's last gleaming,
Whose broad stripes and bright stars through the perilous fight,
O'er the ramparts we watch'd, were so gallantly streaming?
And the Rockets' red glare, the Bombs bursting in air,
Gave proof through the night, that our Flag was still there;
O! say does that star-spangled Banner yet wave,
O'er the Land of the free, and the home of the brave?

On the shore dimly seen through the mists of the deep,
Where the foe's haughty host in dread silence reposes,
What is that which the breeze, o'er the towering steep,
As it fitfully blows, half conceals, half discloses?
Now it catches the gleam of the morning's first beam,
In full glory reflected now shines in the stream,
'Tis the star spangled banner, O! long may it wave
O'er the land of the free and the home of the brave.

And where is that band who so vauntingly swore
That the havoc of war and the battle's confusion,
A home and a country, should leave us no more?
Their blood has washed out their foul footsteps pollution.
No refuge could save the hireling and slave,
From the terror of flight or the gloom of the grave,
And the star-spangled banner in triumph doth wave,
O'er the Land of the Free, and the Home of the Brave.

O! thus be it ever when freemen shall stand
Between their lov'd homes, and the war's desolation,
Blest with vict'ry and peace, may the Heav'n rescued land,
Praise the Power that hath made and preserv'd us a nation!
Then conquer we must, when our cause it is just,
And this be our motto—'In God is our Trust'
And the star-spangled Banner in triumph shall wave,
O'er the Land of the Free, and the Home of the Brave.

FROM THE NATIONAL INTELLIGENCER.

WASHINGTON, Sept. 16.

Copy of a letter from Capt. C. Morris to the Secretary of the Navy, dated Portland, Sept. 8, 1814.

SIR—It is with regret that I inform you we were compelled to destroy the Adams at Hampden, on the morning of the 3d inst to prevent her falling into the hands of the enemy.

All the officers effected their escape, and I believe the crew, with the exception of very few, who were unable to travel. Their precise number cannot yet be ascertained, as we were obliged to pursue different routes, for the purpose of obtaining provisions through the woods between the Penobscot and Kennebeck.

I am now engaged collecting and forwarding the men with the utmost dispatch to Portsmouth, from which place I hope soon to forward a detailed account of our proceedings.

In the mean time, I request you to believe that the officers and crew of the ship neglected no means in their power for her defence.

Very respectfully, your ob't serv't.
C. MORRIS.

The Hon. *W'm. Jones.*
Secretary of the Navy.

We are pleased with the opportunity of presenting to the public the two following articles, which have fallen into our hands, and will serve, the one to correct an inadvertent error, and the other to do justice to a gallant soldier and his brother officers of the Marine Corps, than which there is not in the public service a corps meriting higher praise or more distinguished honors. Always in front of danger, it has since the commencement of the war profusely shed its blood in our country's service.

Copy of a letter from a Staff Officer to the Editors. *Washington, Sept. 14.*

Gentlemen—In Com. Porter's statement of the defence of the battery at the White House, he has, by mistake, inferred that Lt. Spencer of the corps of Artillery was second in command at Fort Warburton when that place was abandoned. I deem it my duty to inform you that Lieut. Spencer was not attached to the command at Fort Warburton, but was at the time of its abandonment in Baltimore; having reached this on the 28th, and volunteering his services, he was, on the arrest of Captain Dyson, put in command of his company, which was then on Mason's Island, and with it proceeded down the river and acting under com. Porter to his entire satisfaction —

Copy of a letter from Com. Barney, to capt. Sevier of the Marine Corps, dated Farm Elkridge, Sept. 10.

SIR—It was not until 3 days after my report was made to the secretary of the navy, that maj. Stuard called at my house and informed, that in the retreat after the battle of the 24th ult. he overtook you, wounded in the neck, and that he lent you his horse. My situation prevented me from obtaining a knowledge of the situation of many of my brave [illegible]. Lastly mentioned those I saw sir, my wishes for your speedy recovery, and present my respects to lieuts. Rickardson, Nicholl, Lord and Brooke, who so ably assisted on that memorable day.

I am, sir, with respect, your obedient servant,
JOSHUA BARNEY.

Capt. A. Sevier,
Marine Corps, Washington.

WASHINGTON, Sept. 20.

Both Houses of Congress yesterday formed a quorum, and appointed a joint committee to inform the President that they were formed and ready to receive any communication he might have to make. It is probable therefore that the Message will be delivered to-day.
Nat. Int.

We had yesterday no additional information of an authentic character from the neighborhood of Plattsburg, which is now the theatre of the most interesting operations.

The glorious victory obtained by our naval force on Lake Champlain is the counterpart of that achieved just a year before on Lake Erie, and was perhaps equally important in its consequences. The battle of Erie led to the capture of one British army, and secured the tranquility of our western border, and the battle of Champlain preceded and in fact accomplished the defeat of another which threatened a formidable invasion of our northern frontier, by an incursion into the most populous state in the Union. The recent victory has every where diffused heart-felt joy, and been received with welcome salutations. So long as history prolongs to posterity the recollection of other times, the names of PERRY and MACDONOUGH will be remembered together and the tenth and eleventh of September be recorded as fortunate days in the calendar of the Republic.—*Ib.*

CONGRERS UNITED STATES.

MONDAY, SEPT. 19.

This being the day assigned by the Proclamation of the President for the Meeting of Congress, the Members assembled at the apartments prepared for their accommodation at the usual hour. These rooms, though far from being as commodious as those heretofore occupied by the two houses, are yet much more comfortable than could have been expected from the exterior appearance of the building in which they are situated, and have been very neatly and expeditiously fitted up under the direction of the Superintendant of the city.

IN SENATE.

The Vice President not having arrived, the Hon. John Gaillard, of South Carolina, resumed the Chair as President *pro tempore* of of the Senate.

The roll having been called, it appeared that the following members were present, viz.

From New Hampshire—Mr. Thompson.
Massachusetts—Mr. Varnum.
Rhode Island—Mr. Howell.
Vermont—Mr. Robinson.
Pennsylvania—Messrs. Lacock and Roberts.
Delaware—Mr. Horsey.
Virginia—Messrs. Brent and Giles.
North Carolina—Mr. Turner.
South Carolina—Mr. Gaillard.
Georgia—Mr. Tait.
Kentucky—Mr. Biedsoe.
Tennessee—Messrs. Anderson and Wharton.
Ohio—Messrs Worthington and Morrow.
Louisiana—Messrs. Brown and Fromentin.

The Senate proceeded to business, directed the Chief Clerk in the Secretary's office (Samuel Turner, Esq.) to act as Secretary pro tempore until a successor to Mr Otis, deceased, should be appointed, and adopted some other preliminary orders; and then adjourned on learning that the House had not formed a quorum.

HOUSE OF REPRESENTATIVES.

The Speaker (Hon. Langdon Cheves) took the chair and at 12 o'clock; and the roll being called, it appeared that the following members were present, viz.

From New-Hampshire—Mr. Vose.
Massachusetts—Messrs. Ely, Hubbard and King.
Connecticut—Messrs. Champion, Davenport, Mosely, and Sturges.
Rhode Island—None.
Vermont—Messrs. Bradley, James Fisk, Rich, and Skinner.
New-York—Messrs. Avery, Comstock, Denoyellet, Jona. Fisk, Geddes, Grosvenor, Kent, Lovett, Markell, Moffit, Oakley, Post, Sag.
New-Jersey—None.
Pennsylvania—Messrs. Anderson, Bard, Brown, Conard, Davis, Glasgow, Ingersoll, Ingham, Lyle, Piper, Rea, Seybert, Tannehill, Udree, Thos. Wilson.
Delaware—Mr. Cooper.
Maryland—Messrs. Archer, Hanson, Jos. Kent, and Stuart.
Virginia—Messrs. Barbour, Bayly, Breckenridge, Burwell, Caperton, Eppes, Gholson, Goodwyn, Hawes, Kerr, Lewis, M'Coy, Newton, Pleasants, Roane, John Smith, and and White.
North Carolina—Messrs. Alston, Culpeper, Forney, Gaston, Macon, Murfree, Pearson, Yancey.
South Carolina—Messrs. Cheves, Evans, Farrow, Gourdine, and Kershaw.
Georgia—Mr. Troup.
Kentucky—Messrs. Clarke, Desha, Johnson, Montgomery, Ormsby, and Tharp.
Tennessee—Messrs. Bowen, Harris, Humphreys, Rhea and Sevier.
Ohio—Messrs. Alexander, Caldwell, Creighton, M'Clean.
Louisiana—None.
Mississippi Ter.—Mr. Lattimore.

It appearing that there was not a quorum present, the house separated by general consent till 5 o'clock in the evening; when, several other members appearing, among whom were Mr. Brigham, of Mass. Mr. Boyd of N. Y. Mr. Forsyth of Geo. Mr. Hawkins of Ky. and others, a quorum was formed, and a committee appointed to join the committee appointed by the senate to wait on the President, to inform him that the two houses were formed, and ready to receive any communication he might have to make.

Gen. P. B. PORTER is appointed by the governor of N. York a Maj. Gen. by brevet of the militia of that state, for the gallantry displayed by him on the Northern frontier during the present campaign.—*Nat Int.*

Singular Accident—A day or two ago in digging up the earth thrown up be the explosion at the city fort during the invasion of the city by this officer of each day's march, a list of all the principal officers, a statement of the entrenching tools, disbarked, &c. but no statement of the number of men employed in the expedition.—*Ib.*

BOSTON, Sept. 15.

INCREASE OF APPETITE.

When the war commenced, the enemy, promised to respect Eastport; but they afterwards took it, and then declared they meant to trouble no place to the westward of it.—They have however now taken Castine, and claim all from Passamaquoddy to Penobscot, but utter assurances that they mean to molest no other part of Maine, and these assurances will probably be found as sincere as former ones.

The territory between Penobscot and Passamaquoddy, which the Governor and Admiral from Nova Scotia have, by proclamation, (see last page,) declared their intention to take possession of, and have commenced by occupying Castine, includes about 40 towns belonging to the State of Massachusetts. Among these towns are Addison, with about 400 inhabitants, Calais, 400, Cherryfield, 200, Columbia, 500, Harrington, 500, Jonesboro, 600, Machias 1600, Steuben 600, Lubec, Robinston, Bluehill 700, Buckstown, 2500, Castine 1100, Deerisle 1600, Eden, 700 Frankfort 1500, Orrington 1400. Sedgwick 1400, Isleboro 600, Mt. Desert 1100, Trenton 600, Sullivan 800, Goldsboro 500, Penobscot 1400, &c.

By Lt. Gen. John C. Sherbrook, K. B. Commanding a body of His Britannic Majesty's Land Forces, and Edward Griffith, esq. rear admiral of the white, Commanding a squadron of His Majesty's ships, now arrived in the Penobscot:

WHEREAS, it is the intention of the British Commanders to take possession of the country lying between the *Penobscot River* and the *Passamaquoddy Bay*; the peaceable inhabitants of that District are hereby informed, that if they remain quietly at their respective homes, and carry on their usual occupations, every protection will be afforded them so long as they comply with such regulations as may be established for their conduct and guidance by the authority of the British Commanders.

All persons taken in arms, or employed in conveying intelligence to the enemy, or in assisting him in any way, shall be treated accordingly.——Such of the inhabitants as may wish to avail themselves of the terms offered in the preceding part of this Proclamation, will be required to give up their army, and to demean themselves in a quiet and peacable manner; and those who may be willing to supply the British forces with provisions, &c. will be regularly paid for the articles furnished, and shall receive every encouragement and protection in so doing.

CHARLES MARTY, *Naval Sec'ry:*
T. F. ADDISON, *Military Sec'ry.*

BRITISH THREATS.

HALIFAX, Aug. 27.

It is understood, that the grand expedition preparing at Bordeaux for America under the gallant Lord Hill, is destined for the Chesapeake direct. Our invincible little army in Canada will, at the same instant be directed to make a movement in the direction of the Susquehanna; and both armies will therefore, in all probability, meet at Washington, Philadelphia, or Baltimore. The seat of the American government, but *more particularly Baltimore*, is to be the immediate object of attack. In the diplomatic circles it is also rumored that our Naval and Military Commanders on the American station have no power to conclude any armistice or suspension of arms. They carry with them certain terms which will be offered to the American government at the point of the bayonet. The terms of course are not made public, but we have every reason to believe that America will be left in a much worse situation as a Naval and Commercial power than she was at the commencement of the war.

NEW YORK, Sept. 18—12 o'clock.

The Steam Boat Car of Neptune, has just arrived from Albany, by which we have the following—

Names and force of vessels engaged in the late memorable battle on lake Champlain.

AMERICAN.	guns.	BRITISH.	guns.	
Saratoga,	26	La Confidance,	35	Taken.
Superior,	20	Bg. name unk'n	16	
Ticonderoga,	18	Growler,	11	
President,	10	Eagle,	11	
	74		73	
6 Row Gallies,	12	12 Row Gallies,	24	Escaped.
4 do. do.	4	3 do. do.	5	
	90		102	

A gentleman from Burlington who left there on Wednesday, informs, that governor Prevost with his army, had effected his retreat without receiving any material check subsequent to general M'comb's communication.

Gen. Izard and suite, had arrived at Sacket's Harbor, where 50 row boats carrying one long gun each, and capable of taking on board 150 men each, were ready. An attack on Kingston or Fort George was contemplated.

On Friday afternoon, at 5 o'clock, a duel was fought at Bath, opposite Albany, between Lt Sheldon, of the rifle corps, and Lt Bloomfield of the ordnance department. They exchanged 5 shots, when the ball from Shelden passed through the body of his antagonist, who soon expired.

PHILADELPHIA, Sept. 19.

VIDETTE INTELLIGENCE.

Received on Saturday evening.

WILMINGTON, Sept. 17, 1814.

Sir—I have just been informed by sailing master John Kitts, of the U. S. navy, that two heavy ships were at anchor in the Delaware, also three standing towards them. The above intelligence came by a whale boat from Cape Henlopen. Kitts is from New Castle this morning.

Your humble servant,
EDWARD TWELLS, Vidette.

Charles Biddle, Esq. Chairman of the Committee of Defence.

Vidette Out-Post, Port Penn,
Sept. 17, 1814—half past 5 A. M.

Sir—A pilot boat stopped here this morning and reported a razee and frigate at anchor inside of the Light House. They are said to have come in yesterday about 1 o'clock.——

AMERICAN
AND
Commercial Daily Advertiser.

BALTIMORE: *WEDNESDAY, Sept. 21.*

EXTRACT TO THE EDITORS—DATED
"*Washington, Sept. 19.*

"The two houses of Congress did not form quorums and proceed to business until five o'clock this evening. There was this morning a sufficient number of Senators, but not of Representatives, for the purpose. A joint committee was this evening appointed to notify the President that Congress was ready to receive his communication, which will no doubt be sent in to-morrow.

"The glorious events which have taken place on Lake Champlain and at Plattsburgh, as well as the repulse of the enemy at Baltimore, appear to have infused new life into every person, and into the Members of Congress especially. The famous Mr. Hanson committed an assault this morning on the person of Mr. Alston, a member from North Carolina, in the hall of the House of Representatives. I was not present, and cannot therefore relate particulars; but this may be said with propriety, that if Mr. Hanson would take up arms and fight in defence of his country, instead of acting the bully towards individuals, and in place of reviling the government and the gallant population of Baltimore, he would give the world much more convincing proofs than he has yet given them, of his courage and patriotism too.

"It is not so certain as has generally been believed here, that Mr. Monroe has been appointed Secretary of War. The hopes of peace cherished here have very much diminished."

It afforded us much satisfaction to see the target firing of the Rifle Companies just arrived from Pennsylvania. A number of bullets were within the size of the heart of a man, and there was not one, it was believed, which would not have done execution in the field, even against a single man as an object. We learn, that nearly 1000 out of the 5000, independent of the volunteers, are riflemen. A number are from the Mountains, whose sports in the field, make them worthy of the title of *Sharp Shooters.* We should like to see John Bull's men met at North Point, by such troops and others of the same stamp among us. By the time they would reach the environs of the city, *officers* would be *wanting* and *men* would be *missing*.

We are happy to state that the brave Com. BARNEY is exchanged, and has so far recovered from his wound as to be able to resume his command, and will act in the future defence of Baltimore. He yesterday visited Forts *M'Henry*, *Covington*, the *Lazaretto*, &c. where he was received with the hearty welcome and animated cheers of the respective garrisons. That this heroic commander, who has won the warmest applause from his countrymen, and coerced the liberal encomiums of the enemy, by his able and dauntless conduct, is yet able and at liberty to act with those who properly estimate his services, is a circumstance which adds to the impulse of gratitude for our recent successes.—*Patriot.*

FROM THE AURORA.

In support of our righteous cause, an idea is suggested of establishing an asylum society, for the giving aid and comfort to honest emigrants from the British army and navy.

Each society to consist of one or more gentlemen from each county in Ireland, England and Scotland.

Committees to frame addresses, to which those names should be affixed, with prices of provisions and liquor, rates of land and labor;

Committees to correspond with all such emigrants, provide immediately for their accommodation, and in whatever line they wish employment, to provide for them accordingly;

To have hand bills posted through the woods wherever they approach, or are expected, to this effect;

BRITONS, LIBERTY! NOW OR NEVER.
Your passages are paid.
Plenty and Happiness await the honest Emigrant.
Come Brethren, and enjoy.
LIBERTY is your pass-word. Every man you meet will assist you.
YOUR CHILDREN
Will be educated and become respectable.

Committee of Vigilance and SAFETY.

City of Baltimore, 20th Sept. 1814.

Subscriptions received at the Mayor's office, since the 9th inst. to be appropriated to such objects as the Committee of Vigilance and Safety may authorise and direct,

Cornelius Howard	$20
Jacob Miller	20
Charles Diffendeffer	20
John Schulz	10
Joseph Escaiville	10
Andrew Crawford 8 bbls. Navy bread	40
Keiler & Forman	50
John Wright 10 bbls flour	60
Nicholas Brice	70
Frederick Leypold	25
Thomas Tenant	200
Hugh & Wm. Young	50
A. Fonerden	10
Clotworthy Bernie	20
A Citizen	25

Boston, Sept. 15.—Ar. sch. Dolphin, Hail, of Bath. On Monday last was chased into Portland by an English armed brig.

A valuable ship laden with copper, &c. from Sumatra, Oxford prize master, prize to the letter of marque ship Hyder Ali of this port, arrived off the mouth of Penobscot a few days since, and on discovering the enemy's ships at Castine, attempted to get into a port to the westward; but several barges from the enemy's ships were dispatched after her, and they succeeded in boarding her: while in that act Capt. Oxnard with the pilot, jumped into the pilot boat along side, and put off for the shore. The enemy on gaining the deck, immediately commenced firing on them. The pilot was killed, and Captain Oxnard received a wound in his thigh; but succeeded in getting ashore, and has arrived at Portland.

Whiskey, Gin & Corn.
300 barrels Rye Whiskey
40 pipes of Gin
5800 bushels of Corn
For Sale by

PLATE 12. The poem as published on page 2 of the *Baltimore American* for 21 September 1814, based on the *American*'s own handbill but with editorial changes.

PLATE 13. First music page of the elaborate and important sheet music edition issued by Joseph Atwill, New York, 1843, "the Symphonies and Accompaniments composed and arranged by Francis H. Brown." This edition introduced the descending eighth notes on "Oh!" at the very beginning, a distinct improvement over the tonic quarter note inherited from John Stafford Smith's *Anacreontic Song.*

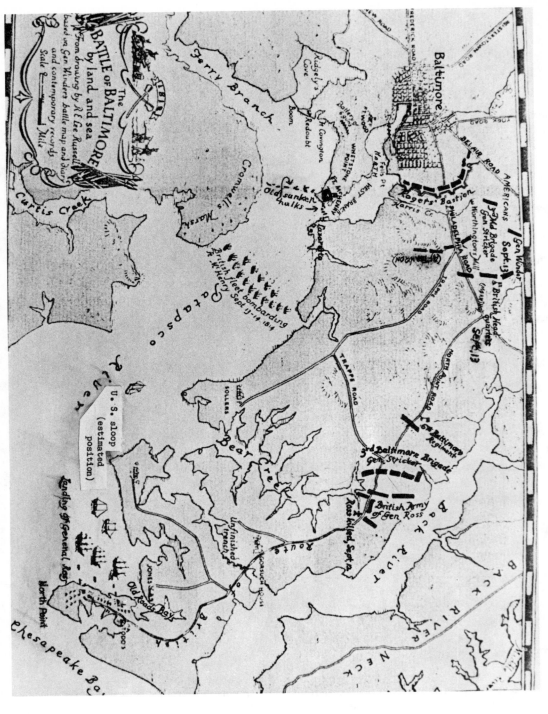

PLATE 14. MAP OF THE BATTLE AREA, 11-17 SEPTEMBER 1814
Reproduced with minor additions from a sheet map by R. E. Lee Russell.
Maryland Historical Society, Baltimore

TABLE 4
VARIORUM CHART

147

COMPARING FORTY-FIVE VERSIONS OF TEXT OF THE
Star Spangled Banner

(1) Maryland Historical Society MS. The earliest extant version of the poem in Key's hand, thought to be his first complete draft, finished in his Baltimore hotel room on the evening of Friday, 16 September 1814. A fair copy made by Key the next morning was the basis of the first and all subsequent printings, but that manuscript is not known to have survived its use in the *Baltimore American* print shop (see pp. 96-97 and plate 2). No title.

(2) Cist copy, now in the Music Division, Library of Congress. Dated "Washington, October 21, —40" and signed "FSKey." Presented by Key to Lewis Jacob Cist (1818-85; see pp. 98-99 and plate 3). Title: The Star-spangled banner.

(3) Keim copy, now at the Historical Society of Pennsylvania, Philadelphia. Undated, but thought by Hill to date from 1842. Presented by Key to General George Keim of Reading, Pa. (see pp. 99-100 and plates 4-5). No title.

(4) Maher copy, not known since 1866 but printed in the *National Intelligencer,* Washington, D.C., of 31 March 1866 (see pp. 101-03 and plate 6). The unknown editor who prepared the printed transcript gives some alternate readings from other sources, thus implying that the transcript follows Key's autograph exactly; but a comparison with the four known Key manuscripts discloses some wordings not likely to have originated with Key himself. According to the *Intelligencer* printing, the autograph was inscribed "For Mr. James Maher of Washington city, Washington June 7, 184—." Title: The Star Spangled Banner.

(5) Espy copy, now in the Georgetown University Library, Washington, D.C. Signed "Washington / Aug! 29 —42, F. S. Key" and presented to Thomas Stevenson Espy (see pp. 103-07 and plate 7). No title.

MANUSCRIPTS

(6) The first printing, a small handbill set in type on 17 September 1814 by Samuel Sands (1800-91), an apprentice in the print shop of the *Baltimore American* (see pp. 107-11 and plate 8). Only two copies out of the more than a thousand printed are known to survive, one at the Maryland Historical Society in Baltimore, the other in the Music Division of the Library of Congress. The title, "Defence of Fort M'Henry," probably was supplied on the spur of the moment by the owner-editor of the *American,* Thomas Murphy (1780-1860).

HANDBILLS OR
"BROADSIDES"

(7) "The Decorated Broadside," set on satin, dated 1815-20 by Filby and Howard.[12] Only known copy at the Maryland Historical Society, Baltimore (see pp. 112-13). Title: THE STAR SPANGLED BANNER.

(8) A broadside even more gaudy than No. 7 though set on plain paper; produced by H. De Marsan at New York, probably sometime during the Civil War. The text is framed with red and blue ribbon. At bottom left is a uniformed officer in red pants and blue coat, at right a black man in loincloth; both presumably are freemen protecting their "lov'd homes." Title: THE STAR-SPANGLED BANNER.

NEWSPAPERS   (9) The first regular publication of *Defence of Fort M'Henry*, on page 2, column 1, of the *Baltimore Patriot & Evening Advertiser* for Tuesday afternoon, 20 September 1814 (see pp. 113-15 and plate 9).

(10) The second newspaper publication, from page 2, column 1, of the *Baltimore American & Commercial Advertiser* of Wednesday morning, 21 September 1814 (see pp. 113-15 and plate 12). Title: DEFENCE OF FORT M'HENRY.

(11) The first publication naming Key as the author of the text, in his erstwhile home-town paper, the *Frederick-Town* (MD) *Herald*, Saturday, 24 September 1814, page 3, column 5 (see p. 116). Title: Defence of Fort M'Henry.

(12) *Daily National Intelligencer*, Washington, D.C., Monday, 26 September 1814, page 2, column 2 (see p. 116). Title: Defence of Fort M'Henry.

(13) *Maryland Gazette & Political Intelligencer*, Annapolis, 13 October 1814, page 4, column 1. Title: Defence of Fort M'Henry.

(14) *Federal Gazette & Baltimore Daily Advertiser*, 14 October 1814, page 2, column 1 (see pp. 116-17). Title: Defence of Fort M'Henry.

SHEET MUSIC   (15) First publication of the text with the tune, the latter composed in 1775 or 1776 by the Londoner John Stafford Smith to accompany Ralph Tomlinson's words for *The Anacreontic Song*, the

---

[12] P. William Filby and Edward G. Howard, comps., *Star-Spangled Books: Books, Sheet Music, Newspapers, Manuscripts, and Persons Associated with "The Star-Spangled Banner"* (Baltimore: Maryland Historical Society, 1972).

TABLE 4

VARIORUM CHART — *Continued*

149

official song of the Anacreontic Society of London. By the end of the century the tune was highly popular in the United States as a basis for parodies. Key himself in 1805 had written and sung such a parody using the Smith melody, celebrating the return of Stephen Decatur and Charles Stewart after defeating the "Barbary Pirates." Hence the tune was in his mind (as he told Skinner) while he was working out the poem off Baltimore and later in Baltimore, 14-16 September 1814. Thomas Carr carelessly omitted the first "t" in "patriotic" in his subtitle of his first edition (thus making identification of that edition painfully simple), but he did supply a workmanlike piano accompaniment for the tune and introduced one lasting improvement in it: the raised fourth of the scale on the third beat of the second full measure. For Hill's discussion of the publication date and other matters, see pages 118-19 and plates 10-11. Title: THE / STAR SPANGLED BANNER / A PARIOTIC SONG. The publisher was Joseph Carr of Baltimore, but at the bottom of both pages Joseph's son, Thomas Carr, is given credit for the adaptation and arrangement.

(16) *"FORT McHENRY,* OR, THE STAR SPANGLED BANNER / Sung with great applause by Mr. Hardinge, at the Theatre Baltimore. Air, Anacreon in Heaven." The text, without music, printed on a single page supplemental to a reissue of *The Battle of the Wabash,* words by Joseph Hutton put to the Anacreontic Song, published (Hill thinks in late 1814) by G. E. Blake of Philadelphia (see p. 120).

(17) Key's poem as set to music by James Hewitt and published at the J. Hewitt Musical Repository, New York, in 1817. Hewitt thought that Key's fine words should be sung to music by an American; but he, alas, was not the right American. His setting is dull (see pp. 119-20). Title: THE STAR SPANGLED BANNER.

(18) Geib and Company's edition at New York (*circa* 1816 according to Hill; see pp. 120-21). Title: *The STAR SPANGLED BANNER.*

(19) A. Bacon & Company, Philadelphia (late 1816, thinks Hill), the text based on Carr by way of Geib but with a number of corrections and improvements (see pp. 120-21). Title: *STAR SPANGLED BANNER.*

(20) An elaborate and important edition issued by Joseph Atwill of New York in 1843. The music was arranged by Francis H. Brown, who here introduced the descending eighth notes on the initial "Oh" which until then had been sung on John Stafford Smith's single quarter note on the tonic (see pp. 121-23 and plate 13). Title: *THE STAR SPANGLED BANNER!*

(21) Single page song sheet published by George Willig of Baltimore, probably in 1823 or 1824. Title: STAR SPANGLED BANNER.

(22) Edition of John Cole, Baltimore, 1825 (Hill), with a picturesque caption engraving showing a gun crew in action with the star spangled banner in the background. Title: THE STAR SPANGLED BANNER.

(23) F. D. Benteen of Baltimore issued this edition in 1844, basing the text on the Atwill and Cole editions (see pp. 121-23). Title: *THE STAR-SPANGLED BANNER.*

(24) W. C. Peters & Sons edition published at their headquarters in Cincinnati, copyright date 1856. Reissued from the same plates, with changes in the imprint data, by Peters's St. Louis office around 1860. This is the earliest publication of the song noted from west of the Mississippi. Title: *STAR-SPANGLED BANNER.*

(25) Oliver Ditson of Boston published this "song and chorus" edition in its series of "National Music" in 1861, at the beginning of the Civil War. Added to Key's four stanzas is one of two stanzas written by the elder Oliver Wendell Holmes. Title: THE STAR SPANGLED BANNER / SONG & CHORUS.

(26) Another in a series of "National Melodies" published as the Civil War began, this one by S. Brainard & Company of Cleveland, 1861, with the last two lines of each stanza arranged for four-part chorus. Title: *T*H*E S*T*A*R S*P*A*N*G*L*E*D B*A*N*N*E*R / AMERICAN NATIONAL HYMN.*

(27) G. André & Company of Philadelphia issued (1862) this alleged "50th Edition" of the song with a handsome cover lithograph showing a Union soldier boy holding a large star spangled banner by a staff. The piano arrangement, by Charles Voss, has an introduction of forty-eight measures (counting repeats) and a postlude of four, but it smacks suspiciously of a waltz. The text is full capitals. Title: THE / STAR SPANGLED BANNER.

(28) The Service Version of 1918, published in sheet music form by Oliver Ditson of Boston, Charles H. Ditson of New York, and Lyon & Healy of Chicago (see p. 77). Title: The Star Spangled Banner: Service Version. . . .

(29) The "Education Version" published in 1918 by G. Schirmer of New York and Boston. Title: The Star-Spangled Banner: A Standardized Version of the Melody . . . (see pp. 77-78).

TABLE 4

VARIORUM CHART — *Continued*

151

(30) The "combined version" of 1942. Title: "The Star-Spangled Banner: Service Version." Despite the subtitle, this edition was the product of a joint committee representing the educators as well as the armed services. This 2-page octavo sheet (which, like the 1918 and other more recent editions, omits the third or "anti-British" stanza) was freely distributed by the U.S. Office of Education and by other national organizations.

(31) *The Analectic Magazine* (Philadelphia) 4 (November 1814): [433]-34 (see pp. 126-28). Title: Defence of Fort M'Henry.

MAGAZINES

(32) *Dwight's Journal of Music* 19 (4 May 1861): 37. Six lines from Oliver Wendell Holmes's two additional stanzas are interpolated between lines six and seven of Key's text. Title: The Star Spangled Banner.

(33) "A Proposed Official Version of THE STAR SPANGLED BANNER," as printed in *Notes* 15 (December 1957): 41-42. This represents, with half a dozen minor differences apparent from comparing this with no. 45, the text and melody as proposed in the bills introduced into the U.S. House of Representatives by Congressman Joseph T. Broyhill of Virginia during 1958-67 (see pp. 73-75 and also plate 1, reproduced from the *National Music Council Bulletin* 18 [Fall 1957]: 3). The version was the result of long and careful deliberations by a committee representing the National Music Council, Richard S. Hill, chairman. The heading in quotation marks above is that of Dick Hill's article accompanying and explaining the version on pages 33-42 of *Notes* for December 1957.

(34) Rufus W. Griswold, *The Poets and Poetry of America, to the Middle of the Nineteenth Century,* 10th ed. (Philadelphia: Carey and Hart, 1850), 549 (see p. 102). Title: THE STAR-SPANGLED BANNER.

SONG & POETRY COLLECTIONS

(35) Henry V. D. Johns, ed., *Poems of the Late Francis S. Key, Esq.* (New York: Robert Carter and Brothers, 1857), 31-33 (see pp. 81, 132-33). Title: The Star Spangled Banner.

(36) Charles A. Dana, *The Household Book of Poetry,* 11th ed. (New York: D. Appleton and Company, 1867), 378 (see p. 102). Title: THE STAR-SPANGLED BANNER.

(37) J. P. McCaskey, ed., *Franklin Square Song Collection, No. 1* (New York: Harper and Bros., 1881), 65. Title: THE STAR-SPANGLED BANNER.

TABLE 4
VARIORUM CHART — *Continued*

(38) Helen Kendrick Johnson, *Our Familiar Songs and Those Who Made Them* . . . (New York: Henry Holt & Co., 1889), pp. 593-95. Title: The Star-Spangled Banner.

(39) *Boy Scout Song Book* (New York: Published for and Approved by the Boy Scouts of America by the Hall-Mack Co., 1913), no. 31. Title: The Star-Spangled Banner.

(40) F. W. Westhoff, *The Ideal Music Series: Book Three* (Normal, IL: McKnight & McKnight, 1927), p. 212. Title: The Star-Spangled Banner.

(41) *Army Song Book.* Compiled by the Adjutant General's Office in Collaboration with The Library of Congress . . . (Washington, D.C.: U.S. Army War Office, 1941), pp. 2-3. Title: The Star Spangled Banner.

(42) John W. Beattie et al., eds., *The American Singer: Book Four,* 2nd ed. (New York: American Book Co., 1954), pp. 200-01, student's ed. Title: The Star-Spangled Banner.

(43) Margaret B. Boni, ed., *The Fireside Book of American Songs* (New York: Simon and Schuster, 1952), p. 272. Title: The Star Spangled Banner.

MISCELLANEOUS (44) Frederick N. Colston, *The Battle of North Point / The Bombardment of Fort McHenry / The Birth of "The Star-Spangled Banner." Maryland Day, Jamestown* [VA] *Exposition, Sept. 12, 1907* [Baltimore, MD: Printed by J. H. Furst Co., 1907], pp. 20-21. Title as above.

(45) *House Joint Resolution 26 of the 90th Congress, 1st Session,* submitted by Congressman Joseph T. Broyhill of Virginia, 10 January 1967 (see no. 33 above, and pp. 000-000). Virtually identical bills had been introduced by Mr. Broyhill in 1958, 1959, 1961, 1963, and 1965. Hearings were held in May 1958 by a subcommittee of the House Committee on the Judiciary, but no action was taken either then or later. Title: THE STAR-SPANGLED BANNER.

NOTES Only wordings, spellings, or punctuation differing from the readings last above them are recorded. Empty space below a reading indicates an identical reading.

A horizontal line (—) indicates that the word it replaces was omitted in that version.

TABLE 4
VARIORUM CHART — *Continued*   153

STANZA 1, LINE 1

Label	#	O	say	can	you	see	by	the	dawn's	early	light	#
MSS-	1	O	say	can	you	see,	by	the	dawn's	early	light,	1
	2	O!	say,		ye	see					light	2
	3	O	say!		you							3
	4	O!	say,			see,					light,	4
	5	Oh!										5
Hb-	6	O!	say			see						6
	7	Oh										7
	8	O!	say,									8
N-	9		say			see,						9
	10					see						10
	11					see,					light	11
	12					see					light,	12
	13											13
	14		say,								light," [sic]	14
ShM-	15		say								light,	15
	16	O,										16
	17	Oh										17
	18	O!										18
	19	O									light	19
	20	Oh!									light,	20
	21	O									light	21
	22										light,	22
	23	Oh!	say,			see,			dawns			23
	24											24
	25		say			see					light	25
	26	Oh							dawn's		light,	26
	27	O										27
	28	Oh,	say!									28
	29	O				see,						29
	30											30
Mag-	31	O!	say									31
	32	Oh,	say,									32
	33	O	say			see					light	33
S&P-	34	O!	SAY,			see,					light,	34
	35	O	SAY,									35
	36	Oh!	say			see					light	36
	37	Oh,	say,			see,					light,	37
	38	Oh!				see						38
	39	O				see,						39
	40	Oh,										40
	41		say!			see						41
	42		say,			see,						42
	43		say									43
Misc-	44	Oh!	say,									44
	45	O	say									45

TABLE 4
VARIORUM CHART — *Continued*

STANZA 1, LINE 2

	What	so	proudly	we	hail'd	at	the	twilight's	last	gleaming,	
MSS- 1	What	so	proudly	we	hail'd	at	the	twilight's	last	gleaming,	1
2						by				gleaming?	2
3						at				gleaming,	3
4					hailed						4
5					hail'd						5
Hb- 6					hailed						6
7					hail'd					gleaming;	7
8											8
N- 9										gleaming,	9
10					hailed						10
11											11
12											12
13											13
14											14
ShM-15					hail'd						15
16											16
17										gleaming;	17
18										gleaming	18
19											19
20										gleaming,	20
21										gleaming	21
22								twilights		gleaming,	22
23								twilight's			23
24											24
25											25
26											26
27										gleaming;	27
28										gleaming,	28
29					hailed						29
30					hail'd					gleaming?	30
Mag-31										gleaming,	31
32					hailed					gleaming?	32
33										gleaming,	33
S&P-34					hail'd					gleaming;	34
35					hailed,					gleaming?	35
36										gleaming —	36
37					hail'd					gleaming,	37
38											38
39					hailed						39
40										gleaming?	40
41					hail'd					gleaming,	41
42					hailed						42
43										gleaming?	43
Misc-44											44
45										gleaming,	45

TABLE 4

155

VARIORUM CHART — *Continued*

STANZA 1, LINE 3

		Whose	broad	stripes	&	bright	stars	through	the	perilous	fight	
MSS-	1	Whose	broad	stripes	&	bright	stars	through	the	perilous	fight	1
	2		bright	stars		broad	stripes,			clouds of the		2
	3		broad	stripes	and	bright	stars,				fight,	3
	4											4
	5											5
Hb-	6						stars			perilous		6
	7											7
	8										fight	8
N-	9										fight,	9
	10											10
	11											11
	12											12
	13											13
	14											14
ShM-	15				&			thro'				15
	16				and							16
	17										fight:	17
	18										fight,	18
	19				&						fight	19
	20				and		stars,					20
	21				&		stars					21
	22		——		and						fight,	22
	23		——				stars,					23
	24		——									24
	25		——									25
	26		broad				stars					26
	27		——	stipes [*sic*]								27
	28		broad	stripes			stars,					28
	29							through				29
	30							thro'				30
Mag-	31						stars	through				31
	32						stars,					32
	33						stars					33
S&P-	34						stars,					34
	35						stars					35
	36											36
	37						stars,	thro'				37
	38		——									38
	39		broad									39
	40											40
	41											41
	42											42
	43											43
Misc-	44						stars	through				44
	45										fight	45

STANZA 1, LINE 4

MSS- 1	O'er	the	ramparts	we	watch'd,	were	so	gallantly	streaming?	1
2					watch'd					2
3										3
4					watched,					4
5					watch'd					5
Hb- 6					watch'd,					6
7					watch'd					7
8									streaming;	8
N- 9					watch'd,				streaming?	9
10										10
11										11
12										12
13										13
14					watched,					14
ShM-15					watch'd,				streaming,	15
16					watch'd				st[ream]ing,	16
17						where			streaming	17
18						were				18
19										19
20									streaming,	20
21									streaming	21
22					watch'd,				streaming,	22
23									streaming;	23
24										24
25										25
26					watch'd					26
27										27
28									streaming?	28
29					watched					29
30					watch'd,				streaming!	30
Mag-31									streaming?	31
32					watched,				streaming;	32
33									streaming?	33
S&P-34					watch'd,					34
35									streaming;	35
36					watched,				streaming!	36
37					watch'd,				streaming?	37
38									streaming;	38
39					watched,				streaming?	39
40										40
41					watch'd					41
42					watched					42
43										43
Misc-44					watched,				streaming;	44
45									streaming?	45

TABLE 4

STANZA 1, LINE 5

	#	And	the	rocket's	red	glare,	the	bomb	bursting	in	air,	#
MSS-	1	And	the	rocket's	red	glare,	the	bomb	bursting	in	air,	1
	2											2
	3					glare—	the				air	3
	4							bombs			air—	4
	5					glare—	The	bomb			air	5
Hb-	6			Rockets'		glare,	the	Bombs			air,	6
	7			rocket's			&	bombs		in the		7
	8						the			in —		8
N-	9			Rockets'				Bombs				9
	10											10
	11			rockets'				bombs				11
	12			Rockets'				Bombs				12
	13											13
	14			rocket's				bombs				14
ShM-	15			Rockets'				Bombs			air	15
	16			rockets				bombs			air,	16
	17											17
	18	&		Rockets'								18
	19	and		rockets		glare					air	19
	20	And				glare,					air,	20
	21	and				glare					air	21
	22	And				glare,					air,	22
	23			rocket's								23
	24											24
	25											25
	26			Rocket's								26
	27			rockets								27
	28			rocket's								28
	29											29
	30			rockets'								30
Mag-	31											31
	32											32
	33			rocket's				bomb				33
S&P-	34							bombs				34
	35			rockets'								35
	36			rocket's							air	36
	37			rockets'							air,	37
	38			rocket's								38
	39			rockets'								39
	40			rocket's								40
	41											41
	42											42
	43											43
Misc-	44			rockets'								44
	45			rocket's				bomb				45

TABLE 4
VARIORUM CHART—*Continued*

STANZA 1, LINE 6

	Gave	proof	through	the	night	that	our	flag	was	still	there,	
MSS- 1	Gave	proof	through	the	night	that	our	flag	was	still	there,	1
2											there.	2
3											there	3
4											there;	4
5											there.	5
Hb- 6								Flag			there;	6
7								flag				7
8												8
N- 9								Flag			there:	9
10					night,						there;	10
11					night							11
12					night,							12
13					night							13
14								flag				14
ShM-15								Flag			there	15
16								flag				16
17			thro'								there,	17
18								Flag			there.	18
19								flag	still	was	there	19
20									was	still	there!	20
21									still	was	there	21
22											there,	22
23									still	was	there?	23
24									was	still	there.	24
25											there!	25
26								Flag			there,	26
27											there.	27
28								flag				28
29			through									29
30			thro'									30
Mag-31			through								there—	31
32											there:	32
33											there,	33
S&P-34											there;	34
35											there:	35
36											there;	36
37			thro'								there.	37
38											there!	38
39											there.	39
40												40
41												41
42												42
43												43
Misc-44			through									44
45											there,	45

TABLE 4 159
VARIORUM CHART — *Continued*

STANZA 1, LINE 7

	#	O	say	does	that	star spangled	banner	yet	wave	#
MSS-	1	O	say	does	that	star spangled	banner	yet	wave	1
	2	O!				star-spangled				2
	3	O	say,							3
	4	O!								4
	5	Oh,								5
Hb-	6	O!	say				Banner		wave,	6
	7	Oh				star spangled	banner			7
	8	O!	say,		the	star-spangled		still		8
N-	9				that		Banner	yet		9
	10		say							10
	11						banner			11
	12						Banner			12
	13									13
	14		say,		the		banner			14
ShM-	15		say		that	star spangled	Banner			15
	16						banner			16
	17	Oh								17
	18	O!								18
	19									19
	20	Oh!							wave	20
	21	O!							wave,	21
	22	O							wave	22
	23	Oh!	say,			star-spangled				23
	24					star spangled				24
	25								wave,	25
	26	O	say						wave	26
	27					Star Spangled	Banner			27
	28	Oh,	say,			Star-spangled				28
	29	O——	say,			Star-Spangled				29
	30	O								30
Mag-	31	O!				star-spangled	banner			31
	32	Oh,				Star-Spangled	Banner			32
	33	O	say			star-spangled	banner			33
S&P-	34	O!	say,							34
	35	O,				Star Spangled	Banner			35
	36	Oh				star-spangled	banner			36
	37	Oh,								37
	38	Oh!				star spangled			wave,	38
	39	O				star-spangled			wave	39
	40	Oh,								40
	41					Star Spangled	Banner			41
	42					Star-Spangled				42
	43	Oh—	say			star spangled	banner			43
Misc-	44	Oh!	say,			star-spangled				44
	45	O	say							45

TABLE 4
VARIORUM CHART — *Continued*

STANZA 1, LINE 8

		O'er	the	land	of	the	free	&	the	home	of	the	brave?	
MSS-	1	O'er	the	land	of	the	free	&	the	home	of	the	brave?	1
	2													2
	3													3
	4							and						4
	5													5
Hb-	6			Land			free,							6
	7			land			free							7
	8													8
N-	9			Land			free,							9
	10													10
	11			land										11
	12			Land										12
	13												brave.	13
	14			land									brave?	14
ShM-	15			Land									brave	15
	16			land									brave.	16
	17						free						brave?	17
	18						free,	&					brave.	18
	19						free	and					brave	19
	20						free,						brave?	20
	21						free						brave.	21
	22													22
	23												brave?	23
	24												brave.	24
	25												brave!	25
	26												brave.	26
	27			Land			Free			Home			Brave.	27
	28			land			free			home			brave?	28
	29													29
	30													30
Mag-	31						free,							31
	32						free							32
	33													33
S&P-	34													34
	35													35
	36						free,							36
	37						free						brave.	37
	38												brave!	38
	39												brave?	39
	40												brave!	40
	41												brave?	41
	42													42
	43													43
Misc-	44													44
	45													45

TABLE 4

161

VARIORUM CHART—*Continued*

STANZA 2, LINE 1

	On	the	shore	dimly	seen	through	the	mists	of	the	deep,	
MSS- 1	On	the	shore	dimly	seen	through	the	mists	of	the	deep,	1
2		that	shore,									2
3												3
4												4
5			shore									5
Hb- 6		the										6
7								midst				7
8			shore,					mist				8
N- 9								mists				9
10			shore									10
11			shore,									11
12			shore									12
13												13
14												14
ShM-15												15
16						thro'						16
17								mist				17
18								mists				18
19												19
20					seen,			mist				20
21					seen			mists				21
22												22
23	on							mist				23
24	On				seen,							24
25					seen							25
26								mists				26
27												27
28			shore,									28
29			shore									29
30			shore,									30
Mag-31												31
32		that										32
33		the	shore									33
S&P-34			shore,								deep	34
35		that									deep,	35
36		the										36
37			shore									37
38			shore,					mist			deep	38
39			shore					mists			deep,	39
40			shore,		seen,							40
41					seen							41
42												42
43			shore					mist				43
Misc-44			shore,			through		mists				44
45			shore									45

TABLE 4
VARIORUM CHART — *Continued*

STANZA 2, LINE 2

		Where	the	foe's	haughty	host	in	dread	silence	reposes,	
MSS-	1	Where	the	foe's	haughty	host	in	dread	silence	reposes,	1
	2										2
	3										3
	4										4
	5										5
Hb-	6										6
	7									reposes;	7
	8									reposes,	8
N-	9										9
	10										10
	11										11
	12										12
	13										13
	14										14
ShM-	15										15
	16									reposes;	16
	17									reposes,	17
	18										18
	19									reposes	19
	20									reposes,	20
	21									reposes	21
	22			foes						reposes;	22
	23			foe's						reposes,	23
	24										24
	25			foes							25
	26			foe's							26
	27									reposes;	27
	28									reposes,	28
	29										29
	30										30
Mag-	31										31
	32										32
	33										33
S&P-	34										34
	35										35
	36										36
	37										37
	38										38
	39										39
	40			foes							40
	41			foe's							41
	42										42
	43										43
Misc-	44									reposes.	44
	45									reposes,	45

TABLE 4
163

VARIORUM CHART – *Continued*

STANZA 2, LINE 3

	What	is	that	which	the	breeze,	o'er	the	towering	steep,	
MSS- 1	What	is	that	which	the	breeze,	o'er	the	towering	steep,	1
2											2
3			that,							steep	3
4			that							steep,	4
5										steep	5
Hb- 6										steep,	6
7						breeze					7
8						breeze,				steep	8
N- 9			that,			breeze				steep,	9
10			that			breeze,					10
11			that,			breeze					11
12			that			breeze,					12
13											13
14											14
ShM-15											15
16											16
17						breeze					17
18						breeze,					18
19										steep	19
20										steep,	20
21										steep	21
22											22
23										steep,	23
24											24
25											25
26											26
27										steep	27
28										steep,	28
29										steep	29
30										steep,	30
Mag-31						breeze					31
32	Where[*sic*]					breeze,					32
33	What										33
S&P-34						breeze				steep	34
35						breeze,				steep,	35
36											36
37											37
38											38
39											39
40											40
41											41
42											42
43											43
Misc-44											44
45											45

TABLE 4
VARIORUM CHART — *Continued*

STANZA 2, LINE 4

	#	As	it	fitfully	blows,	half	conceals,	half	discloses?	#
MSS-	1	As	it	fitfully	blows,	half	conceals,	half	discloses?	1
	2									2
	3									3
	4									4
	5					half-conceals,		half-discloses?		5
Hb-	6					half	conceals,	half	discloses?	6
	7						conceals			7
	8						conceals,			8
N-	9									9
	10									10
	11									11
	12									12
	13									13
	14									14
ShM-	15								discloses;	15
	16								discloses:	16
	17						conceals		discloses,	17
	18						conceals,		discloses;	18
	19				blows		conceals			19
	20				blows,		conceals,		discloses,	20
	21				blows		conceals			21
	22				blows,		conceals,		discloses;	22
	23								discloses?	23
	24								discloses	24
	25								discloses?	25
	26								discloses:	26
	27								discloses;	27
	28								discloses?	28
	29									29
	30									30
Mag-	31									31
	32					now		now		32
	33					half		half		33
S&P-	34					half-conceals,		half-discloses?		34
	35					now	conceals,	now	discloses?	35
	36									36
	37					half		half		37
	38									38
	39						conceals			39
	40									40
	41				blows		conceals,			41
	42				blows,					42
	43									43
Misc-	44									44
	45									45

TABLE 4

165
VARIORUM CHART—*Continued*

STANZA 2, LINE 5

	Now	it	catches	the	gleam	of	the	morning's	first	beam,	
MSS- 1	Now	it	catches	the	gleam	of	the	morning's	first	beam,	1
2					gleam —of						2
3					—					beam	3
4					gleam	of				beam,	4
5					gleam —of						5
Hb- 6					gleam	of					6
7											7
8											8
N- 9											9
10											10
11											11
12											12
13											13
14					gleam,						14
ShM-15					gleam					beam	15
16										beam,	16
17											17
18											18
19											19
20											20
21											21
22								mornings			22
23								morning's			23
24											24
25											25
26											26
27											27
28											28
29											29
30											30
Mag-31											31
32											32
33										beam	33
S&P-34										beam;	34
35										beam,	35
36											36
37											37
38											38
39											39
40											40
41											41
42											42
43											43
Misc-44											44
45											45

STANZA 2, LINE 6

		In	full	glory	reflected	now	shines	in	the	stream	
MSS-	1	In	full	glory	reflected	now	shines	in	the	stream,	1
	2				reflected,			on		stream.	2
	3							in		stream,	3
	4							on		stream.	4
	5										5
Hb-	6				reflected	new		in		stream,	6
	7							on			7
	8					now				stream;	8
N-	9									stream.	9
	10							in		stream;	10
	11							on		stream.	11
	12							in		stream,	12
	13										13
	14				reflected,	new				stream;	14
ShM-	15				reflected					stream,	15
	16									stream:	16
	17					now				stream?	17
	18					new				stream,	18
	19					now					19
	20	Its						on		stream?	20
	21	In						in		stream,	21
	22				reflected,					stream —	22
	23				reflected					stream:	23
	24				reflected,						24
	25					new					25
	26				reflected	now				stream,	26
	27				reflected,					stream —	27
	28				reflected			on		stream.	28
	29										29
	30									stream;	30
Mag-	31									stream —	31
	32							in		stream:	32
	33									stream	33
S&P-	34	Its						on		stream;	34
	35	In						in		stream:	35
	36				reflected,			on		stream;	36
	37									stream:	37
	38							in		stream;	38
	39				reflected			on		stream:	39
	40									stream.	40
	41									stream;	41
	42									stream.	42
	43				reflected,					stream;	43
Misc-	44										44
	45				reflected			in		stream,	45

TABLE 4

VARIORUM CHART—*Continued*

167

STANZA 2, LINE 7

	'Tis	the	star-spangled	banner—O	long	may	it	wave	
MSS- 1	'Tis	the	star-spangled	banner —O	long	may	it	wave	1
2				—O!					2
3			Star-spangled	— O					3
4			star-spangled	— O!					4
5				—Oh					5
Hb- 6			star spangled	banner, O!					6
7				Oh				wave,	7
8			star-spangled	O!				wave	8
N- 9				banner					9
10			star spangled	banner,					10
11			star-spangled	banner.					11
12			star spangled	banner,					12
13			star-spangled	Banner,					13
14				banner—O!				wave,	14
ShM-15			star spangled	banner; O!				wave	15
16	Tis			banner,				wave,	16
17	'Tis			Oh!					17
18	Tis			O!					18
19	'Tis			banner				wave.	19
20			star-spangled	banner! oh,				wave	20
21			star spangled	banner O!				wave,	21
22				banner,					22
23			star-spangled	banner— Oh!				wave	23
24									24
25			star spangled	banner Oh!				wave,	25
26				banner, O					26
27			Star Spangled	Banner, Oh!					27
28			Star-spangled	oh,				wave	28
29			Star-Spangled	Banner—O,					29
30				Banner, O					30
Mag-31			star-spangled	banner, O!					31
32			Star-Spangled	Banner; oh,				wave,	32
33			star-spangled	banner O				wave	33
S&P-34	'T is			banner, O!					34
35	'Tis		Star Spangled	Banner; O					35
36	'T is		star-spangled	banner; oh,					36
37	'Tis			banner: oh,					37
38			star spangled	banner, Oh!				wave,	38
39			star-spangled	banner: O				wave	39
40				banner, oh,					40
41			Star Spangled	Banner, O					41
42			Star-Spangled	Oh,					42
43			star-spangled	banner! Oh					43
Misc-44	'T — is			oh,					44
45	'Tis			banner— O					45

STANZA 2, LINE 8

	O'er	the	land	of	the	free	&	the	home	of	the	brave!	
MSS- 1	O'er	the	land	of	the	free	&	the	home	of	the	brave!	1
2												brave.	2
3												brave!	3
4							and					brave.	4
5							&						5
Hb- 6							and						6
7													7
8												brave!	8
N- 9												brave.	9
10													10
11													11
12													12
13			Land			Free							13
14			land			free							14
ShM-15						free,							15
16													16
17						free							17
18						free,							18
19													19
20								——				brave!	20
21								the				brave.	21
22													22
23													23
24													24
25												brave!	25
26												brave.	26
27			Land			Free,			Home				27
28			land			free			home			brave!	28
29													29
30													30
Mag-31						free,						brave.	31
32						free						brave!	32
33													33
S&P-34												brave.	34
35												brave!	35
36						free,							36
37						free						brave.	37
38												brave!	38
39													39
40													40
41													41
42													42
43													43
Misc-44													44
45													45

TABLE 4   169

VARIORUM CHART — *Continued*

STANZA 3, LINE 1

		And	where	is	that	band	who	so	vauntingly	swore,	
MSS-	1	And	where	is	that	band	who	so	vauntingly	swore,	1
	2					host	that			swore	2
	3			are	the	foes					3
	4			is		foe					4
	5					host					5
Hb-	6				that	band	who				6
	7									swore,	7
	8				the					swore	8
N-	9				that						9
	10										10
	11										11
	12										12
	13										13
	14									swore,	14
ShM-	15									swore	15
	16									swore,	16
	17							——			17
	18					band,		so		swore	18
	19					band				swore,	19
	20				the						20
	21				that						21
	22										22
	23										23
	24										24
	25										25
	26					band,				swore	26
	27					band				swore,	27
	28	[stanza 3 omitted]									28
	29	′′ ′′ ′′									29
	30	′′ ′′ ′′									30
Mag-	31	And	where	is						swore	31
	32			are	the	foes					32
	33			is	that	band				swore,	33
S&P-	34				the						34
	35			are		foes				swore	35
	36			is	that	band					36
	37									swore,	37
	38										38
	39	[stanza 3 omitted]									39
	40	′′ ′′ ′′									40
	41	′′ ′′ ′′									41
	42	′′ ′′ ′′									42
	43	′′ ′′ ′′									43
Misc-	44	And	where	is						swore	44
	45									swore,	45

TABLE 4
VARIORUM CHART – *Continued*

STANZA 3, LINE 2

	That	the	havoc	of	war	&	the	battle's	confusion	
MSS- 1	That	the	havoc	of	war	&	the	battle's	confusion	1
2										2
3										3
4						and				4
5						&				5
Hb- 6						and			confusion,	6
7			havock						confusion;	7
8			havoc						confusion,	8
N- 9										9
10										10
11										11
12										12
13										13
14										14
ShM-15										15
16										16
17									confusion:	17
18									confusion,	18
19										19
20	'Mid									20
21	That									21
22								battles		22
23	'Mid							battle's		23
24										24
25										25
26	That								confusion	26
27									confusion,	27
28	[stanza 3 omitted]									28
29	''	''	''							29
30	''	''	''							30
Mag-31	That	the	havock						confusion	31
32			havoc		war,				confusion,	32
33					war				confusion	33
S&P-34	'Mid								confusion,	34
35	That				war,					35
36					war				confusion	36
37									confusion,	37
38	'Mid									38
39	[stanza 3 omitted]									39
40	''	''	''							40
41	''	''	''							41
42	''	''	''							42
43	''	''	''							43
Misc-44	That	the	havoc						confusion	44
45										45

TABLE 4
171

VARIORUM CHART—*Continued*

STANZA 3, LINE 3

	A	home	&	a	Country	should	leave	us	no	more?	
MSS- 1	A	home	&	a	Country	should	leave	us	no	more?	1
2					country						2
3			and		Country						3
4					country						4
5											5
Hb- 6					country,	shall					6
7					country					more,	7
8						should				more?	8
N- 9											9
10					country,						10
11					country						11
12					country,						12
13						shall				more!	13
14					country					more?	14
ShM-15					country,					more.	15
16										more	16
17					country					more,	17
18					country,						18
19					country						19
20						they'd				more?	20
21						shall				more,	21
22											22
23						they'd				more?	23
24											24
25											25
26					country,	shall				more,	26
27					country					more —	27
28	[stanza 3 omitted]										28
29	"	"	"								29
30	"	"	"								30
Mag-31	A	home	and	a	country	should				more?	31
32											32
33					Country						33
S&P-34					country	they'd					34
35						should				more:	35
36										more?	36
37											37
38						they'd					38
39	[stanza 3 omitted]										39
40	"	"	"								40
41	"	"	"								41
42	"	"	"								42
43	"	"	"								43
Misc-44	A	home	and	a		should					44
45					Country						45

TABLE 4
VARIORUM CHART — *Continued*

STANZA 3, LINE 4

MSS- 1	Their	blood	has	wash'd	out	their	foul	footstep's	pollution.	1
2										2
3										3
4	This[*sic*]	blood		washed		his				4
5	Their	blood		wash'd		their				5
6				washed				footsteps		6
7				wash'd				footstep's	pollution;	7
8				washed					pollution.	8
N- 9				wash'd				footsteps'		9
10				washed				footsteps		10
11				wash'd				footsteps'	pollution	11
12				washed				footsteps	pollution.	12
13									pollution	13
14				wash'd					pollution.	14
ShM-15										15
16									pollution	16
17									pollution:	17
18		brood[*sic*]							pollution;	18
19		blood							pollution	19
20								footstep's	pollution!	20
21								footsteps	pollution,	21
22				washed					pollution!	22
23									pollution;	23
24				wash'd						24
25								footstep's		25
26				washed				footsteps	polution; [*sic*]	26
27				wash'd			——	footstep's	polution [*sic*]	27
28	[stanza 3 omitted]									28
29	″ ″ ″									29
30	″ ″ ″									30
Mag-31	Their	blood	has	washed			foul	foot-steps'	pollution.	31
32				wash'd				footsteps'	pollution;	32
33				washed				footstep's	pollution.	33
S&P-34			hath	wash'd				footsteps'	pollution;	34
35			has	washed						35
36									pollution.	36
37				wash'd						37
38									pollution;	38
39	[stanza 3 omitted]									39
40	″ ″ ″									40
41	″ ″ ″									41
42	″ ″ ″									42
43	″ ″ ″									43
Misc-44	Their	blood	has	washed					pollution,	44
45									pollution.	45

TABLE 4 173
VARIORUM CHART – *Continued*

STANZA 3, LINE 5

MSS- 1	No	refuge	could	save	the		hireling	&	slave	1
2										2
3				save	— the					3
4				save	the					4
5				save	— the					5
Hb- 6				save	the			and	slave,	6
7								or		7
8								and	slave	8
N- 9									slave,	9
10										10
11										11
12										12
13										13
14										14
ShM-15										15
16							hireling,			16
17							hireling			17
18										18
19										19
20										20
21										21
22										22
23										23
24										24
25									slave	25
26									slave,	26
27									slave	27
28	[stanza 3 omitted]									28
29	'' '' ''									29
30	'' '' ''									30
Mag-31	No	refuge	could						slave,	31
32										32
33									slave	33
S&P-34										34
35										35
36										36
37										37
38										38
39	[stanza 3 omitted]									39
40	'' '' ''									40
41	'' '' ''									41
42	'' '' ''									42
43	'' '' ''									43
Misc-44	No	refuge	could							44
45										45

TABLE 4
VARIORUM CHART — *Continued*

STANZA 3, LINE 6

	From	the	terror	of	flight	or	the	gloom	of	the	grave	
MSS- 1	From	the	terror	of	flight	or	the	gloom	of	the	grave,	1
2											grave.	2
3					flight,						grave,	3
4					flight							4
5											grave;	5
Hb- 6											grave,	6
7											grave;	7
8											grave,	8
N- 9											grave;	9
10											grave,	10
11											grave;	11
12											grave,	12
13												13
14											grave;	14
ShM-15											grave,	15
16											grave:	16
17						——					grave.	17
18							the				grave,	18
19											grave	19
20					flight,						grave.	20
21					flight						grave	21
22					flight,						grave;	22
23											grave,	23
24												24
25					flight							25
26											grave	26
27					flight,						grave;	27
28	[stanza 3 omitted]											28
29	"	"	"									29
30	"	"	"									30
Mag-31	From	the	terror	of	flight							31
32					flight,							32
33					flight						grave,	33
S&P-34					flight,							34
35											grave;	35
36					flight							36
37											grave:	37
38											grave,	38
39	[stanza 3 omitted]											39
40	"	"	"									40
41	"	"	"									41
42	"	"	"									42
43	"	"	"									43
Misc-44	From	the	terror	of							grave;	44
45											grave,	45

TABLE 4

175

VARIORUM CHART — *Continued*

STANZA 3, LINE 7

	And	the	star-spangled	banner	in	triumph	doth	wave	
MSS- 1	And	the	star-spangled	banner	in	triumph	doth	wave	1
2									2
3			Star-spangled						3
4			Star-Spangled	Banner					4
5			star-spangled	banner					5
Hb- 6								wave,	6
7			star spangled				shall		7
8			star-spangled				doth	wave	8
9								wave,	9
10									10
11									11
12									12
13				Banner					13
14			star spangled	banner				wave	14
ShM-15				banner,				wave,	15
16				banner					16
17									17
18				banner,					18
19				banner				wave	19
20			star-spangled					wave,	20
21			star spangled					wave	21
22								wave,	22
23			star-spangled					wave	23
24									24
25			star spangled					wave,	25
26				banner,			shall		26
27			Star Spangled	Banner			doth		27
28	[stanza 3 omitted]								28
29	" " "								29
30	" " "								30
Mag-31	And	the	star-spangled	banner				wave	31
32			Star-Spangled	Banner					32
33			star-spangled	banner					33
S&P-34									34
35			Star Spangled	Banner					35
36			star-spangled	banner					36
37									37
38								wave,	38
39	[stanza 3 omitted]								39
40	" " "								40
41	" " "								41
42	" " "								42
43	" " "								43
Misc-44	And	the	star-spangled					wave	44
45									45

TABLE 4
VARIORUM CHART — *Continued*

STANZA 3, LINE 8

	O'er	the	land	of	the	free	&	the	home	of	the	brave.	
MSS- 1	O'er	the	land	of	the	free	&	the	home	of	the	brave.	1
2													2
3													3
4							and						4
5							&						5
Hb- 6			Land			Free,	and		Home			Brave.	6
7			land			free			home			brave.	7
8													8
N- 9			Land										9
10						Free,			Home			Brave.	10
11			land			free			home			brave.	11
12			Land			Free,			Home			Brave.	12
13													13
14			land			free			home			brave.	14
ShM-15	O'er the Land &c. [remainder of line omitted]												15
16	O'er	the	land	of	the	free							16
17													17
18						free,							18
19													19
20												brave!	20
21												brave.	21
22													22
23						free		——					23
24								the					24
25												brave!	25
26						free,						brave.	26
27			Land			Free			Home			brave	27
28	[stanza 3 omitted]												28
29	''	''	''										29
30	''	''	''										30
Mag-31	O'er	the	land			free,			home			brave.	31
32						free						brave!	32
33												brave.	33
S&P-34													34
35												brave!	35
36						free,						brave.	36
37						free							37
38													38
39	[stanza 3 omitted]												39
40	''	''	''										40
41	''	''	''										41
42	''	''	''										42
43	''	''	''										43
Misc-44	O'er	the	land										44
45													45

TABLE 4
VARIORUM CHART — *Continued*   177

STANZA 4, LINE 1

	#										#
MSS-	1	O	thus	be	it	ever	when	freemen	shall	stand	1
	2	O!									2
	3					ever!					3
	4	O,									4
	5	O				ever					5
Hb-	6	O!								stand,	6
	7	Oh									7
	8	O!								stand	8
N-	9									stand,	9
	10										10
	11										11
	12										12
	13										13
	14										14
ShM-	15										15
	16					ever,				stand	16
	17	Oh				ever				stand,	17
	18	O!									18
	19	O									19
	20	Oh!									20
	21	O				ever,					21
	22					ever					22
	23	Oh!				ever,				stand	23
	24										24
	25	oh				ever					25
	26	O!								stand,	26
	27	Oh						Freemen		stand	27
	28	Oh,						freemen			28
	29	O,				ever,					29
	30	O				ever					30
Mag-	31	O!									31
	32	Oh,				ever,					32
	33	O				ever					33
S&P-	34	O!				ever,					34
	35	O									35
	36	Oh!									36
	37	Oh,				ever					37
	38	Oh!									38
	39	O									39
	40	Oh,				e'er					40
	41					ever					41
	42										42
	43					ever,					43
Misc-	44										44
	45	O				ever					45

TABLE 4
VARIORUM CHART — *Continued*

STANZA 4, LINE 2

	Between	their	lov'd	home	&	the	war's	desolation!	
MSS- 1	Between	their	lov'd	home	&	the	war's	desolation!	1
2				homes				desolation.	2
3									3
4			loved		and				4
5			lov'd						5
Hb- 6				home,				desolation,	6
7				homes				desolation;	7
8			loved	home		——			8
N- 9			lov'd	home,		the	war's	desolation,	9
10				homes,					10
11				home,					11
12				homes,					12
13				home,					13
14				home				desolation;	14
ShM-15				home,				desolation,	15
16								disolation, [sic]	16
17				home		——		desolation,	17
18				home,		the			18
19							wars		19
20				home			war's		20
21				home,			wars		21
22								desolation;	22
23			loved	home			war's		23
24									24
25									25
26			lov'd					desolation,	26
27				home,			wars	desolation;	27
28			loved	homes			war's	desolation!	28
29			lov'd	home					29
30			loved	homes					30
Mag-31			lov'd	home				desolation,	31
32			loved	homes				desolation!	32
33									33
S&P-34				home				desolation;	34
35				homes					35
36								desolation!	36
37				home		wild		desolation;	37
38						the			38
39						wild			39
40				homes		the		desolation!	40
41			lov'd						41
42									42
43			loved					desolation,	43
Misc-44								desolation;	44
45				home				desolation!	45

TABLE 4
VARIORUM CHART—*Continued* 179

STANZA 4, LINE 3

		Blest	with	vict'ry	&	peace	may	the	heav'n	rescued	land	
MSS-	1	Blest	with	vict'ry	&	peace	may	the	heav'n	rescued	land	1
	2					peace,			heav'n-rescued			2
	3											3
	4			victory					Heav'n	rescued		4
	5			vict'ry					Heav'n-rescued			5
Hb-	6				and				Heav'n	rescued	land,	6
	7					peace	this		heaven			7
	8	Bless'd		victory		peace,		the	Heaven-rescued		land	8
N-	9	Blest		vict'ry					Heav'n-rescued		land,	9
	10								Heav'n	rescued		10
	11								Heav'n-rescued			11
	12								Heav'n	rescued		12
	13											13
	14									rescu'd	land	14
ShM-	15									rescued	land,	15
	16								heavn		land	16
	17			VICT'RY		PEACE			heav'n		land,	17
	18			vict'ry		peace,						18
	19											19
	20										land	20
	21										land,	21
	22			victory					heaven			22
	23			vict'ry					heaven-rescued		land	23
	24								heav'n	rescued		24
	25											25
	26			victory					heaven			26
	27			vict'ry					Heaven	rescu'd	land,	27
	28								heav'n-rescued		land	28
	29											29
	30											30
Mag-	31											31
	32			victory					heaven-rescued			32
	33			vict'ry		peace			heaven	rescued		33
S&P-	34	Bless'd				peace,			heaven-rescued			34
	35	Blest		victory					heav'n-rescued			35
	36											36
	37			vict'ry								37
	38								heaven-rescued			38
	39								heav'n-rescued			39
	40								heav'n	rescued		40
	41											41
	42								Heav'n-rescued			42
	43	Blessed							heav'n	rescued		43
Misc-	44	Blest							heaven-rescued			44
	45					peace			heaven	rescued		45

TABLE 4
VARIORUM CHART — *Continued*

STANZA 4, LINE 4

		Praise	the	power	that	hath	made	&	preserv'd	us	a	nation!	
MSS-	1	Praise	the	power	that	hath	made	&	preserv'd	us	a	nation!	1
	2											nation.	2
	3							and	preserved	us,			3
	4			Power					preserv'd	us			4
	5							&					5
Hb-	6							and				nation!	6
	7			power									7
	8								preserved				8
N-	9								preserv'd				9
	10			Power									10
	11			power									11
	12			Power									12
	13												13
	14												14
ShM-	15			Pow'r									15
	16			pow'r								nation:	16
	17												17
	18			Pow'r								nation.	18
	19												19
	20			Power					preservd			nation!	20
	21								preserv'd			nation	21
	22								preserved			nation:	22
	23											nation.	23
	24												24
	25												25
	26			Pow'r		has			preserv'd				26
	27					hath			preserved			nation:	27
	28											nation!	28
	29			power									29
	30			Pow'r					preserved			nation.	30
Mag-	31			power					preserv'd			nation!	31
	32			Power					preserved				32
	33			power									33
S&P-	34			Power								nation.	34
	35											nation!	35
	36			power								nation.	36
	37			pow'r					preserv'd			nation!	37
	38			Power					preserved			nation.	38
	39			pow'r								nation!	39
	40			Pow'r									40
	41												41
	42												42
	43			pow'r								nation	43
Misc-	44			power								nation.	44
	45			Power								nation!	45

TABLE 4 181
VARIORUM CHART — *Continued*

STANZA 4, LINE 5

	Then	conquer	we	must,	when	our	cause	it	is	just,	
MSS- 1	Then	conquer	we	must,	when	our	cause	it	is	just,	1
2				must—when							2
3											3
4				must	when						4
5				must—when							5
Hb- 6				must,	when						6
7											7
8											8
N- 9											9
10											10
11										just	11
12										just,	12
13											13
14											14
ShM-15											15
16											16
17											17
18											18
19											19
20					for					just!	20
21					when					just,	21
22											22
23											23
24											24
25											25
26											26
27	And [hereafter, this line identical with 26, but misplaced by André as line 6 of stanza]										27
28	Then										28
29											29
30					for						30
Mag-31					when						31
32											32
33											33
S&P-34					for						34
35					when						35
36					for					just;	36
37					when					just,	37
38											38
39											39
40				must							40
41				must,							41
42											42
43											43
Misc-44											44
45											45

STANZA 4, LINE 6

	And	this	be	our	motto	"In	God	is	our	trust	
MSS- 1	And	this	be	our	motto —	"In	God	is	our	trust,"	1
2					motto—	In				trust—	2
3						in					3
4					motto,	In				trust.	4
5					motto —	In					5
Hb- 6					motto—	"In				Trust;" [sic]	6
7					motto.	*"In*	*God*	*is*	*our*	*trust!"*	7
8					motto —	In	God	is	our	trust!"	8
N- 9										Trust!"	9
10					motto—	'In				Trust'	10
11					motto—	"In				Trust!"	11
12					motto—	*'In*				Trust'	12
13					motto—	"In				Trust,"	13
14										trust;"	14
ShM-15										Trust";	15
16					motto—	"in	god			trust;" [sic]	16
17					motto,	"IN	GOD	IS	OUR	TRUST."	17
18					motto—	In	God	is	our	trust;	18
19											19
20					motto,	"In				trust."	20
21					motto	"In					21
22					motto—	"In				trust"_	22
23					motto,	"In				trust,"	23
24											24
25											25
26						In	God	is	our	trust;	26
27					motto—	"In			Our	Trust" [mis-placed as line 5]	27
28					motto:	"In			our	Trust."	28
29					motto—	"In					29
30					motto:	"In				trust."	30
Mag-31					motto—	"In				trust!"	31
32					motto,					trust."	32
33					motto	"In				trust,"	33
S&P-34					motto,	"In					34
35										trust;"	35
36					motto—	"In				trust" —	36
37					motto:	"In				trust!"	37
38					motto,	"In				trust,"	38
39					motto:	"In				trust!"	39
40											40
41					motto,	"In				trust."	41
42					motto:	"In				Trust."	42
43					motto,	"In				trust!"	43
Misc-44										trust."	44
45					motto	"In					45

TABLE 4   183

VARIORUM CHART — *Continued*

STANZA 4, LINE 7

Source	#	And	the	Star-spangled	banner	in	triumph	shall	wave	#
MSS-	1	And	the	Star-spangled	banner	in	triumph	shall	wave	1
	2			star-spangled						2
	3									3
	4			Star-Spangled	Banner					4
	5			Star-spangled	banner					5
Hb-	6			star-spangled	Banner				wave,	6
	7			star spangled	banner					7
	8			star-spangled					wave	8
N-	9								wave,	9
	10				Banner					10
	11				banner					11
	12				Banner					12
	13									13
	14				banner					14
ShM-	15			star spangled	banner,					15
	16				banner					16
	17									17
	18									18
	19									19
	20			star-spangled					wave	20
	21			star spangled					wave,	21
	22									22
	23			star-spangled						23
	24								wave	24
	25			star spangled					wave,	25
	26									26
	27			Star Spangled	Banner					27
	28			Star-spangled					wave	28
	29			Star-Spangled						29
	30									30
Mag-	31			star-spangled	banner					31
	32			Star-Spangled	Banner					32
	33			star-spangled	banner					33
S&P-	34									34
	35			Star — Spangled	Banner					35
	36			star-spangled	banner					36
	37									37
	38								wave,	38
	39								wave	39
	40				banner,					40
	41			Star Spangled	Banner					41
	42			Star-Spangled						42
	43			star-spangled	banner					43
Misc-	44								wave,	44
	45								wave	45

TABLE 4
VARIORUM CHART—*Continued*

STANZA 4, LINE 8

		O'er	the	land	of	the	free	&	the	home	of	the	brave.	
MSS-	1	O'er	the	land	of	the	free	&	the	home	of	the	brave.	1
	2							and						2
	3							&						3
	4							and						4
	5							&						5
Hb-	6			Land			Free,	and		Home			Brave.	6
	7			land			free			home			brave.	7
	8													8
Hb-	9													9
	10			Land			Free,			Home			Brave.	10
	11			land			free			home			brave.	11
	12			Land			Free,			Home			Brave.	12
	13													13
	14			land			free			home			brave.	14
ShM-	15			Land&c. [remainder omitted]										15
	16			land			free,						brave!	16
	17						free						brave.	17
	18						free,							18
	19						free							19
	20						free,						brave!	20
	21						free						brave.	21
	22													22
	23													23
	24													24
	25												brave!	25
	26						free,						brave.	26
	27			Land			Free			Home				27
	28			land			free			home				28
	29													29
	30												brave!	30
Mag-	31						free,						brave.	31
	32	While					free	is					brave!	32
	33	O'er						and					brave.	33
S&P-	34													34
	35												brave!	35
	36						free,						brave.	36
	37						free							37
	38	While						is						38
	39	O'er						and						39
	40													40
	41												brave!	41
	42												brave.	42
	43												brave!	43
Misc-	44													44
	45												brave.	45

CHAPTER 3

Amphion: *Another Piracy from Andrew Law?*

by

Irving Lowens

Some years ago, while browsing through volume 1 of the *British Union-Catalogue of Early Music,* I was brought up short by the following entry in column 2 of page 28:

> Amphion or the Chorister's Delight, containing a select number of psalm tunes hymns and anthems, from the most approv'd authors, in three and four parts, fitted to the psalms used in the churches in general: Besides the necessary rules of psalmody. [Compiled engraved and printed by J. Burger Junr and C. Tiebout]. pp. 32. *I. Burger Junr and C. Tiebout: New York* [c. 1780] *obl.* 4°. L*. (Call no.: British Library: A.828)

It had been some time since I had done any active work on the bibliography of American tune books I had been preparing in collaboration with Richard Crawford and Allen P. Britton of the University of Michigan, but *Amphion* was a title I could not recall having seen mentioned before in the literature — after some 27 years of searching — and neither had they. I quickly ordered a microfilm of this mysterious New York tune book.

Looking at the engraved title-page on the microfilm proved to be something of a shock, for it was the familiar plate engraved by Joel Allen for the 1779 edition of Andrew Law's famous *Select Harmony,* which (in turn) was a copy of Henry Dawkins' very familiar title-page for James Lyon's 1761 *Urania.* Had I accidentally, serendipitously, stumbled upon yet another piracy from Andrew Law?

In my "Andrew Law and the Pirates,"[1] fairly conclusive evidence had been advanced that Law's *A Select Number of Plain Tunes Adapted to Congregational Worship* (ca. 1777) had evoked a piracy in the form of the anonymously compiled *A New Collection of Psalm Tunes Adapted to Congregational Worship* (ca. 1781), and that Law's 1779 and 1782 editions of the *Select Harmony* had each been pirated

---

[1] *Journal of the American Musicological Society* 13 (1960): 206-23.

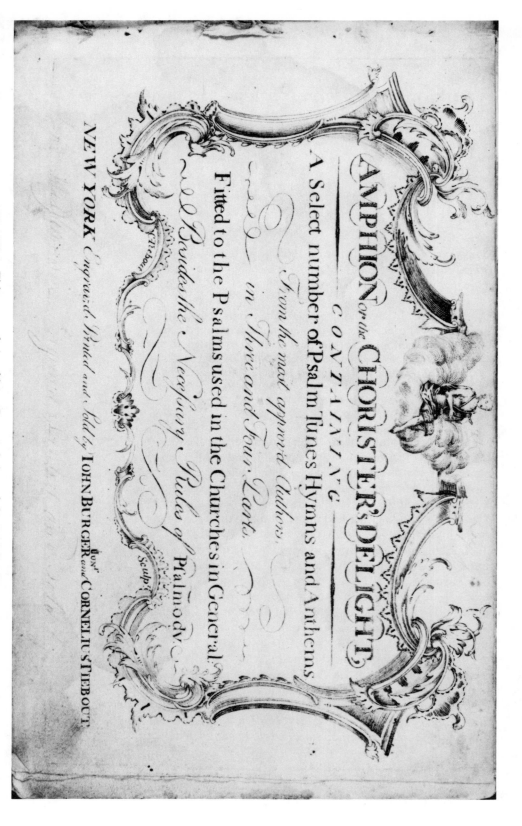

PLATE 1. Title-page of *Amphion*. By permission of the British Library.

PLATE 2. Title-page of Law's *Select Harmony*

PLATE 3. Title-page of James Lyon's 1761 *Urania*

by Daniel Bayley of Newburyport. Since Law was continually fussing about other compilers raiding his preserves, I even raised the question of additional piracies of Law's tune books, although I then considered such a possibility extremely dubious. Now, suddenly, from England, a new candidate for the dubious honor had appeared. (See plates 1-3.)

If title-page designs were all that mattered, then clearly another Law piracy had surfaced. But *Amphion*'s contents raises considerable doubt that it was a piracy of a *single* tune book, although plainly the composers had borrowed materials from Andrew Law.

The description of the title-page as given in *BUCEM* is not quite accurate. It should read (see plate 1):

> AMPHION *or the* CHORISTER's DELIGHT, / *CONTAINING* / A Select number of Psalm Tunes Hymns and Anthems / *From the most approv'd Authors, / in Three and Four Parts.* / Fitted to the Psalms used in the Churches in General; / *Besides the Necessary Rules of* Psalmody. / *C. Tiebout Sculp.* / *NEW YORK Engrav,d* [sic], *Printed and Sold by* IOHN BURGER JUN^r *and* CORNELIUS TIEBOUT.

The small volume is in the oblong format customary for American tune books and contains 2 p.ℓ., 32, [4] p. Except for the recto and verso of the 2nd p. ℓ. and the last three unnumbered pages (the fourth unnumbered page is blank), *Amphion* is engraved rather than typeset. Unfortunately, the British Library copy lacks pages 9-10, and the index (rather amateurishly set up) raises a certain amount of doubt as to the exact number of compositions included. Not counting the lacking pages 9 and 10, *Amphion* contains 33 compositions, of which 16 were American and 17 non-American. Only a single tune, LENOX on page 26, contains a composer attribution — "By Edson." So far as it can be determined, *Amphion* contains no first printings of any tunes, and 23 of the 33 are included in Richard Crawford's "Core Repertory," an index which lists the tunes published most frequently by American tune-book compilers.[2]

According to the *Amphion* index on the verso of the 2nd p.ℓ., pages 9 and 10, lacking in the British Library *unicum,* contain five tunes of British provenience: AYLSBURY, WELLS, ANGELS HYMN, KINGSBRIDGE and ST. MARTIN'S, thus bringing the total number of tunes in the original tune book to 38. The engraver (or engravers)

---

[2] Professor Crawford has compiled an extraordinarily useful index of the tunes printed in the Colonies and the United States, and has been kind enough to check the *Amphion* tunes in it for me. The most popularly reprinted tunes he refers to as the "Core Repertory." Of the *Amphion* tunes, no less than 23 of the 33 are included, an extremely high percentage. He has also made available to me his notes on *Amphion,* and has cooperated in every possible way to help solve some of the riddles it poses. [Since this was written, Crawford's book has appeared: Richard Crawford, *The Core Repertory of Early American Psalmody,* Recent Researches in American Music, 11-12 (Madison, Wisc.: A-R Editions, 1984).]

of the music used text-underlay only with the two anthems included. Texts set in type for five tunes: SOPHRONIA, THE AMERICAN HERO (A Saphic [*sic*] Ode, by Nathan Niles), MILFORD, DENMARK, and MIDDLETOWN, appear on pages [33]-[35].

In analyzing the contents of the tune book, I have made use of only the tunes which stood before me. It is likely that the five additional tunes on pages 9-10 were similar in type to the others, but they do not figure in my comparative statistics. Of the 33 actual tunes in the British Library exemplar of *Amphion,* 29 are harmonized in four parts and only 4 in three.

The prefatory remarks on the recto of the 2nd p.ℓ. addressed "To the Patrons of Genius and Lovers of Divine Music" are in some ways unique in the history of 18th-century American tune books and deserve full quotation:

> The Subscribers, after a series of incessant application to the study of the art of Engraving and Copperplate Printing, have acquired, without the aid of a teacher, a knowledge of those useful branches of business, which hath enabled them to lay before the Public, the following COLLECTION of CHURCH MUSIC. In selecting the tunes, they have depended but little on their own judgment, nor on the judgment of any particular person; this they have submitted to the taste of a number of approved Musicians. Musical Books in general are either large and high priced, or extremely small and entirely destitute of such tunes as are absolutely necessary for the use of congregations. The Editors therefore, in order to recommend this edition, have attended to such Music only as is now in general use in this state.
>
> The price of this Book being set as low as possible, and the proprietors (who are not yet arrived at an age of maturity) having been at great pains and expence, in acquiring their present knowledge of engraving and printing, flatter themselves their ingenuity and industry will meet the patronage of their fellow citizens.
>
> That this little work may be useful to both old and young, they have annexed not only the rules and groundwork of singing, but a few general observations, necessary for the attention of all performers, viz.
>
> It ought to be the care of all singers to accustom themselves to the greatest ease possible. — It adds much to the beauty of Vocal Music, to pay careful attention to the accent and pronunciation of words — Words in general ought to be pronounced as Gramarians [*sic*] pronounce them in common conversation, and so distinctly articulated, that whatever is sung may be perfectly understood — this adds a peculiar beauty to the music. It ought likewise to be the care of every performer to behave with decency and solemnity, especially, in singing sacred words, and to avoid all aukward [*sic*] gestures, such as distorted faces, &c. which frequently disgust the hearers. — The best general rule that can be given, is to aim entirely at ease, to let the voice flow freely, but not harshly.

We are with great submission, the Public's Humble Servants,

J O H N   B U R G E R, Jun.

C O R N E L I U S   T I E B O U T

N.B. Any person may be furnished, at a trifling expence, with Copies of any number of Tunes, contained in this book, by applying to the Subscribers, at No. 207, Queen street. They will also, on application, engrave and print any favorite anthem, &c.

The names of Cornelius Tiebout and John Burger, Jr. have not been prominent in the history of early American music, and it is fascinating to learn from their preface that at the time they engraved, printed, and sold *Amphion,* they had "not yet arrived at an age of maturity," which probably meant they were not yet 20 years old.[3] For youngsters still in their teens, *Amphion* is a most remarkable production, particularly if you accept their testimony that they "have acquired, without the aid of a teacher, a knowledge of those useful branches of business, which hath enabled them to lay before the Public, the following COLLECTION of CHURCH MUSIC," which should probably be interpreted to mean that they were self-taught in music.

Who, then, were Cornelius Tiebout and John Burger, Jr., whose musical fates were tied together in *Amphion?*

Cornelius Tiebout appears to have been born in New York City about 1773,[4] son of Tunis Tiebout and Elizabeth Lamb.[5] He was descended from "a Huguenot family that came to this country from Holland, and held lands on the Delaware River as early as 1656; they also owned property in Flatbush, Long Island, in 1669."[6] He was apprenticed to the New York silversmith John Burger, Sr. at a very early age, and in later years had "the distinction of having been the first American-born professional engraver to produce really meritorious work."[7] As early as 1789, while still apprenticed to Burger, he brought out a dated *Plan of the City of New York* (Stauffer 3222) signed *Tiebout sculp!,* a most creditable piece of work for a 16-year-old.[8]

---

[3] According to the 1790 Census, a new age classification was started at age 20, when presumably an individual male had graduated from apprentice to journeyman or master status.

[4] George C. Groce and David H. Wallace, *The-New York Historical Society's Dictionary of Artists in America, 1564-1860* (New Haven: Yale University Press, 1957), 630.

[5] Cornelius Henry Tiebout, *The Ancestry and Posterity of Cornelius Henry Tiebout of Brooklyn* (n.p.: Privately printed, 1910).

[6] David McNeely Stauffer, *American Engravers Upon Copper and Steel* (New York: Grolier Club, 1907; reprint, New York: B. Franklin, 1964), 1:271-72.

[7] Stauffer, 1:271.

[8] Mantle Fielding, *American Engravers upon Copper and Steel* (Philadelphia: Privately printed, 1917; reprint, New York: B. Franklin, 1964), 3:7; Stauffer, 2:530.

John Burger evidently had a high regard for his apprentice, and in 1790 he asked Tiebout to engrave for him a fancy trade card, the sole remaining copy of which is located in the Landauer Collection of the New-York Historical Society. Unfortunately, the curator of the Landauer Collection, Wendy Shadwell, was unable to locate the trade card for reproduction with this paper, but according to Martha Gandy Fales, "the New York Mechanical Society used as its insignia a raised hand wielding a hammer, with the motto 'By hammer and hand all Arts do stand.'"[9] Burger used the same motto to decorate the top of his fancy trade card.

In 1793, Tiebout left the U.S. for England where he studied engraving with James Heath of London, returning to New York as an accomplished master of his trade in 1796. His name disappears from the New York City directories in 1799[10] and reappears in the Philadelphia directories in 1801, when he was listed as an "engraver." He was active there until about 1825, joining the firm of Tanner, Kierney, and Tiebout, engravers, in 1817.[11] After a business disaster, he emigrated to New Harmony, Ind. and died there in 1832.[12]

The date of John Burger, Sr.'s birth is not known, but it is recorded that he married Sarah Baker on 20 January 1767, in New York; at least three sons were born to the couple: David, Thomas, and John, Jr. It is known that he was active as a silversmith as early as 1780, practicing the trade at 153 Water Street, southeast of Cherry Street. In 1786, he joined the Gold and Silversmith's Society and the Geneva Society of Mechanics and Tradesmen. In 1789, he moved to 207 Queen Street, noting in his advertisements that he was "late at 153 Water Street" and soliciting "orders at large."[13] By 1791, he had moved to 151 Queen Street and was listed in the directories as a "copperplate printer." He seems to have moved almost yearly, and the last entry under his name in the New York directories dates from 1796 and shows him at 167 William Street. Although the firm is not listed in the directories, in 1805 John Sr., David, and Thomas Burger had a silversmithing shop at 62 James Street.[14]

---

[9] Martha Gandy Fales, *Early American Silver* (New York: Excalibur Books, 1970), 194. Fales, honorary curator of silver at the Essex Institute in Salem, Mass., has been most helpful in running down this very elusive John Burger trade-card, as has been Shadwell of the New-York Historical Society and Stephanie Munsing of the Prints and Photographs Division of the Library of Congress.

[10] George L. McKay, *A Register of Artists, Engravers, Booksellers, Bookbinders, Printers & Publishers in New York City, 1633-1820* (New York: New York Public Library, 1942), 71.

[11] H. Glenn Brown and Maude O. Brown, *A Directory of the Book-Arts Trade in Philadelphia to 1820, Including Painters and Engravers* (New York: New York Public Library, 1950), 117-18.

[12] See Groce and Wallace, 630.

[13] Stephen G. Ensko, *American Silversmiths and Their Marks,* 3 vols. (New York: Privately printed, 1927-48; reprint, New York: Dover, 1983), see entries under John Burger.

[14] McKay, 15.

PLATE 4. St. Tamany [*sic*] as engraved by John Burger, Jr. in the May 1790 *New York Magazine.*

John Burger, Jr. makes his first appearance on the stage of history "in the *New York Magazine* for May, 1790, [where] a plate of well-engraved music is signed Burger ^{Jun} Sc^t., [and] one of the plates engraved by C. Tiebout in 1790 is signed as 'printed by I. Burger Junr.' . . . probably the music engraver noted above."[15] (See plate 4.) Then, in the 19 June 1790 *New-York Weekly Museum*, the following interesting notice appeared:

> Burger & Tiebout. — Copper Plate Printing and Engraving, are performed at Mr. Burger's No 153 Water-street, near the Crane-Wharf. The engraving by Cornelius Tiebout, The printing by John Burger, Jun. A specimen of their abilities may be seen at their shop. It is presumed that this undertaking will meet with the encouragement of all those who wish the increase of the useful arts in this country.
>
> N. B. Bills of exchange and lading, message and shop cards, large maps and music, are neatly executed and printed at a reasonable price and may be had at the shortest notice.[16]

It seems fairly self-evident that John, Jr. and Tiebout, formerly John, Sr.'s apprentice, had taken over the shop vacated by John, Sr. in Water Street and had gone into business for themselves. And one cannot avoid the suspicion that the passage of the first Federal copyright law on 31 May 1790 may have had something to do with the enterprise of the two youngsters.

Obviously, the partnership must have ceased when Tiebout left the country in 1793; the 1794 New York directory shows that John Burger, Junr., of 67 Fair Street, was engaged in copperplate printing in 1794. He was joined by his father, John Burger, Sr., in the business in 1795, but apparently the father and son did not hit it off too well. In 1796 John, Sr. moved to 167 William Street, only to be rejoined by John, Jr. at that address in 1797. John, Jr. parted company with his father permanently in 1798, when he opened shop at 192 William Street, and remained in business as a copperplate printer at least through 1820.[17] The date of his death is unknown.

It would seem from all this data that *Amphion* must have been a joint venture that Tiebout and Burger entered into in 1790, when they opened their shop at 153 Water Street. Unfortunately, this is contradicted by fact — the back endpaper, from which the former owner's name was carefully excised, contains the following inscription in a contemporary hand: " . . . Book Newyork. . . . Anno Domini . . . 1789 Atatis [sic] Suae." (See plate 5.)

---

[15] Fielding, 3:7. The item referred to is no. 1656, an engraving of Moses for an American edition of Brown's Family Bible.

[16] I am grateful to Barbara Lambert, Keeper of the Musical Instrument Collection in the Boston Museum of Fine Arts, for calling my attention to this important advertisement, which is reproduced in Rita Susswein Gottesman's *The Arts and Crafts in New York* (New York: Printed for the New-York Historical Society, 1954; reprint, New York: Da Capo, 1970), as entry 887.

[17] McKay, 15.

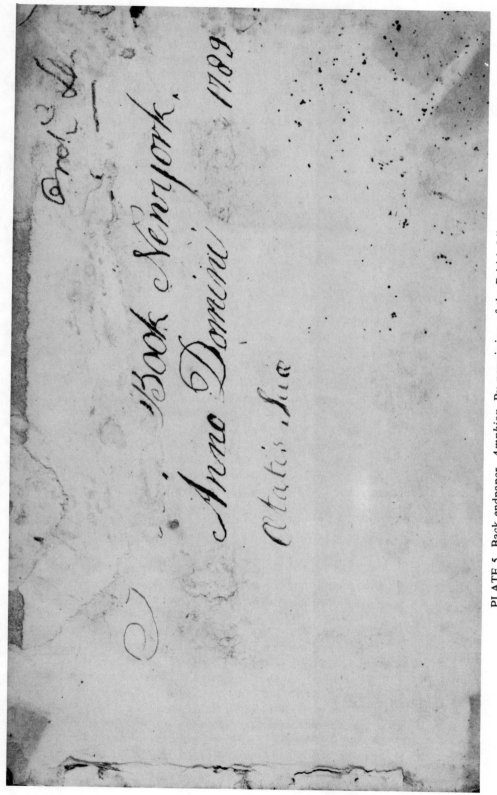

PLATE 5. Back endpaper, *Amphion*. By permission of the British Library.

Thus the tune book must have been published no later than 1789, and there is clear internal evidence that the British Library's dating of "ca. 1780" is much too early.

When, then, did *Amphion* actually appear? It is reasonable to assume that the British Library cataloger based his conclusion on the fact that the *Amphion* title-page was a copy of that which appears on the 1779 edition of Andrew Law's *Select Harmony*. The "ca. 1780" date seems logical enough—until you learn that the engraved "rudiments of music" on pages 1-4 of *Amphion* were, in fact, copied almost verbatim from the preliminaries in the 2nd (1786?) edition of Law's *Rudiments of Music,* which puts a somewhat different complexion on matters. It is plain that Burger and Tiebout must have known at least the two tune books by Andrew Law, but were the *Select Harmony* (1779) and the *Rudiments of Music* (ca. 1786) their sole printed sources, or even their major printed sources for *Amphion?* The evidence does not point in that direction.

Several of the 33 items reprinted in *Amphion* were comparatively scarce. The following were printed in four or fewer previous sources: (a) ANTHEM, "If the Lord himself," appeared in Law's *Select Harmony* of 1779 and 1782, the *Worcester Collection* of 1786 and 1788, and Andrew Adgate's *Philadelphia Harmony* of 1789; (b) DENMARK appeared in Law's *Select Harmony* of 1782, the *Massachusetts Harmony* of 1784, the *Worcester Collection* of 1786 and 1788, and the Adgate *Philadelphia Harmony* of 1789; (c) DENBIGH appeared in Law's *Select Harmony* of 1782, the *Massachusetts Harmony* of 1784, and the *Worcester Collection* of 1786 and 1788; (d) LEEDS appeared in Law's *Select Harmony* of 1782 and Adgate's *Philadelphia Harmony* of 1789; (e) PSALM 57 appeared in Lyon's *Urania* of 1761 and Jocelin's *Chorister's Companion* of 1782; (f) SOPHRONIA appeared in Law's *Hymns and Tunes* of 1783, Adgate's *Philadelphia Harmony* of 1789, and the *Selection of Sacred Harmony,* 1788; (g) WILLIAMSTOWN appeared in Law's *Rudiments of Music,* ca. 1786 and Chauncey Langdon's *The Beauties of Psalmody* of 1786; and (h) Law's own BUNKER-HILL appeared in Law's *Select Number* of 1781 and the *Massachusetts Harmony* of 1784.

Based on these eight tunes alone, the compilers could have copied these tunes from not only the 1779 *Select Harmony* and the ca. 1786 *Rudiments of Music,* but also from Law's *Select Number* (1781), Law's *Select Harmony* (1782), Jocelin's *Chorister's Companion* (1782), Law's *Hymns and Tunes* (1783), the *Massachusetts Harmony* (1784), Langdon's *The Beauties of Psalmody* (1786), the *Worcester Collection,* 1st ed. (1786), the *Worcester Collection,* 2nd ed. (1788), *A Selection of Sacred Harmony* (1788), Adgate's *Philadelphia Harmony* (1789)—and even Lyon's earlier *Urania* (1761).

If the tunes OLD 100TH and WINDSOR are eliminated from the content analysis since they were universally reprinted in almost all collections of tunes, 17 of the 31 *Amphion* tunes may be found in either the 1779 *Select Harmony* or the ca. 1796 *Rudiments of Music,* but some of the other tunes are troublesome. Take PSALM 57, for instance. If (as seems probable) it was borrowed from Jocelin's

Chorister's Companion, the *Amphion* compilers could have found 10 additional *Amphion* tunes there—but only 4 of the 10 are not in the *Select Harmony* and the *Rudiments of Music* from which they definitely borrowed, which means there are still nine tunes unaccounted for. Or take Law's own BUNKER-HILL, which could have been borrowed from the 1781 *Select Number,* but was more likely borrowed from the 1784 *Massachusetts Harmony,* where the *Amphion* compilers could have also found 10 additional *Amphion* tunes. Only one of the 10 is found in neither the *Select Harmony,* the *Rudiments of Music* or the *Chorister's Companion.* The chances are that they took BUNKER-HILL from the *Select Number,* from which they could have picked up two additional tunes, thus cutting down the total number untraced to seven, even though only five of the 31 *Amphion* tunes may be found there. All these seven unaccounted tunes may be found in either the 1st (1786) or 2nd (1788) edition of the *Worcester Collection,* each of which contains 20 of the 31 tunes found in *Amphion,* in the anonymously compiled Philadelphia tune book, *A Selection of Sacred Harmony,* which contains 15 of the 31 *Amphion* tunes, or the 1789 edition of Adgate's *Philadelphia Harmony,* which contains no less than 23 of the 31. There is also some reason to believe that Burger and Tiebout had access to the 1782 as well as the 1779 edition of Law's *Select Harmony,* which included 12 of the 31 *Amphion* tunes. If they had access only to the tune books mentioned in this paragraph in addition to the 1779 *Select Harmony* and the ca. 1782 *Rudiments of Music,* the provenance of all 31 *Amphion* tunes could be accounted for.[18]

Another little problem having to do with *Amphion* is intriguing—did John Burger, Jr. or Cornelius Tiebout do the music engraving? We know that Tiebout engraved the title-page, but did he also engrave the music plates? This seems very doubtful. For one thing, we find, at the bottom right of page 23 in *Amphion,* the legend: "I. Burger & C. Tiebout Sc."; for another, there seem to be two distinct hands evident in the book. Fortunately, we do have the music plate from the May 1790 issue of the *New York Magazine* signed "Burger J[unr] Sc[t]" in a very distinctive hand which seems to be similar to that on pages 5, 6, 7, 20, 22, 26, 27, 31, and 32 of *Amphion* while the engraving of the tunes on the other pages seems to be the work of a recognizably different engraver. From this, one must conclude that *Amphion* was indeed a joint undertaking on the part of the two young men.

Again, attention must be drawn to the illuminating preface in which Tiebout and Burger point out that "in selecting the tunes, they have depended but little on their own judgment, nor on the judgment

---

[18] I have found the appendices in Richard A. Crawford, *Andrew Law, American Psalmodist* (Evanston: Northwestern University Press, 1968; reprint, New York: Da Capo, 1981) and especially Appendix IV ("Index of Tunes in Andrew Law's Tunebooks") invaluable in checking the provenance of the *Amphion* tunes and in helping me to determine, to my own satisfaction, that it cannot really be considered a piracy of any individual tune book by Law.

of any particular person; this they have submitted to the taste of a number of approved Musicians." The procedure, if not the wording, is reminiscent of that followed by Isaiah Thomas when he brought out his very successful *Worcester Collection*.

The conclusion seems inevitable. Tiebout and Burger did use quite a bit of material from Law, but they also drew freely from Thomas, Adgate, Jocelin, and probably others in putting together their modest little tune book. Is *Amphion* another piracy from Andrew Law? Well, partly so, but not in the same sense that Daniel Bayley's *Select Harmony* was a piracy from Law's *Select Harmony*. According to the standards of the age in which they lived, our enterprising teen-aged tune-book compilers did nothing dreadfully unethical, and they deserve more praise for their initiative than blame for their reliance upon wiser and more experienced tunesmiths of their time.

Music Publishing in New England

by

H. Earle Johnson

We properly think of music as "sound." Yet supporting every performer, whether artist of the concert hall or amateur in the home, is an army of contributing agencies, each responsive to changing sociological, economic, and cultural rhythms of the time. Invention, transportation, immigration, fashion—each plays its part in the manufacture of instruments, in concert management, teaching, leisure, and retailing. These, increasing in number and diversity with the years, influence the conditions under which we perform. Important to them, without which we could not function, are publishers of music from the greatest unto the least. We judge them by their success in business, but many rank high in solicitude for the artistic well-being of their communities. American musicologists now deem them silent partners of our music-making.

New England's music publishers were fertile in ideas and vigorous in leadership. Yankee initiative paralleled and sometimes, but not always, led that of Philadelphia, Baltimore, and New York. *The Whole Book of Psalms* ("The Bay Psalm Book") of 1640 stands foremost, the earliest existing volume of American imprint, issued in Cambridge by the Stephen Day Press, "an appendage of Harvard College." Twelve tunes in two-part harmony with diamond-shaped notes cut on wood were added for an edition of 1698. There were 27 editions to 1762 in America and about 22 in England and Scotland by 1756.

Then came John Tufts, a clergyman of Newburyport, with *A Very Plain and Easy Introduction to the Singing of Psalm Tunes,* perhaps issued as early as 1714, although no copy prior to 1721 survives.[1] A modest pamphlet of twelve pages, Tufts' contains 37 tunes set in three parts with instructions for "using the voice." Thomas Walter, minister at Roxbury, compiled *The Grounds and Rules of Music Explained, or An Introduction to the Art of Singing*

---

[1] An edition of Tate and Brady, Boston 1713, was "the second known American imprint to contain musical notation." See Richard J. Wolfe, *Early American Music Engraving and Printing* (Urbana: University of Illinois Press, 1980), 16, n. 9. Wolfe gives a thorough discussion of advances in printing during these eventful days.

by Note in 1721, printed by J. Franklin, whose fifteen-year-old brother, Benjamin, was his apprentice. Both of these were reissued, Tufts' to 1733, Walter's to 1764. Walter's was the first music to be printed with bar lines in the Colonies. Josiah Flagg's *A Collection of the Best Psalms Tunes, in Two, Three, and Four Parts* (1764) was the largest collection printed in New England by that date. Engraved by Paul Revere and printed on paper made in the Colonies, it was a small, oblong volume comprising secular and sacred music. Then, in the year of Beethoven's birth, came William Billings' *The New England Psalm Singer,* the first hymn-book of all-American composition.

These five establish New England's primacy in the publishing of music, and as a focal point of psalmody, locally printed, for itinerant masters of singing schools. Newburyport (Mass.) and Exeter (New Hampshire), Charlestown, Northampton and Watertown (Mass.), New Haven and Cheshire (Conn.) for Andrew Law, shared the field with Boston. Their editing and publication are an oft-told story.

Narrower concepts of psalmody gave way to works such as *The Worcester Collection,* published by Isaiah Thomas in 1786 (not, as has been supposed, the first to be printed from moveable type). This and *Bridgewater* (1802), Belknap's *Middlesex* (1807), *Norfolk* (1805), *Old Colony* (1818/19, 1823), and an overabundance of similar collections served an eager, churchly public. Boston firms retained and extended their leadership with the partnership of Isaiah Thomas and Ebenezer Andrews leading the way until 1807, followed by Manning and Loring for a decade, and that of Richardson with various partners, emerging for the 1820s.[2] The successful *Handel and Haydn Collection of Church Music* (Richardson and Lord, 1820) led hundreds of similar works in the public's esteem for the period generally following 1815, but the popularity of psalmody continued until after 1850 in remote communities.

*   *   *   *   *

Secular music emerged without organizational support. Edward Enstone of Boston was among America's earliest known music merchants, "master of music and dancing master,"[3] but there is no record of him as a publisher. Mein and Fleming (or Fleeming), booksellers, advertised "The Liberty Song" ("In Freedom We're Born" sung to "Hearts of Oak") in July 1766. Engraved on copper plates, it is cited as the first separately-printed music in the Colonies,

---

[2] A list of Massachusetts copyrights may be found in the author's *Musical Interludes in Boston 1795-1830* (New York: Columbia University Press, 1943; reprint, New York: AMS Press, 1960). See also *Grove's Dictionary of Music and Musicians,* American Supplement, 2nd ed., s.v. "Tune-books."

[3] Oscar G. Sonneck, *Early Concert-Life in America (1731-1800)* (Leipzig: Breitkopf & Härtel, 1907; reprint, New York: Musurgia, 1949), 9 note, which cites the *Boston News-Letter,* 16-23 April 1716.

but we can not be certain that Mein and Fleming were the printers; no
copy survives. John Boyles published *An Abstract of Geminiani's
Art of Playing on the Violin, German Flute, Violoncello, Thorough
Bass, and the Harpsichord with some Additions* (title abbreviated!)
in 1769, surely the first instrumental tutor printed in America. There
is a copy in the John Carter Brown Library.

The American Revolution released progressive forces in all areas
of productivity, including music, at the very time great publishing
houses were flourishing in Europe. Philadelphia led with at least
ten publishers before 1800; Boston's fifteen were smaller in size.

* * * * *

Early New England periodicals included music in their pages.
The first to appear was "The Hill Tops, a New Hunting Song," in
the *Royal American Magazine,* vol. 1, 1771, Boston. Isaiah Thomas
and Ebenezer Andrews included twenty-eight musical selections in
the *Massachusetts Magazine* from 1789, notably Hans Gram's "The
Death Song of an Indian Chief" (in part) in 1791, the first orchestral
score printed in America. Of broadsides, the most notable was "The
American Hero" (ca. 1775), later set to "Bunker Hill," a "Select Tune"
of Andrew Law which had appeared in Boston the year before; this
and Billings' hymn "Chester" (1778) became popular war hymns of
the Revolutionary period.

The popularity of broadsides comprises a separate category.[4]
Thomas (later known as Robert Treat) Paine's "The Boston Patriotic
Song," better known as "Adams and Liberty," was published in 1798
by Thomas and Andrews, by Linley and Moore, and by Van Hagen
in 1800 (not to be confused with Dickinson's "Liberty Song" of 1768
or "A New Massachusetts Liberty Song" attributed to Joseph Warren
of 1774). The theme of "Adams and Liberty" made it popular in
New England, but not entirely in Philadelphia where enthusiasm for
"Liberty" did not always extend to "Adams." There were many
others, leading to a vast output of one and two-page popular songs.[5]

Joseph Tinker Buckingham printed twenty-one selections of
music in *Polyanthus* from 1812 to 1814 and John Rowe Parker
nineteen in *The Euterpeiad,* America's second musical periodical,
between 1820 and 1822.[6] Parker also issued what is probably the
first dealer's catalog in the States. (There are copies in Harvard's

---

[4] See Carleton Sprague Smith, "Broadsides and Their Music in Colonial America"
in *Music in Colonial Massachusetts 1630-1820* (Boston: The Colonial Society of
Massachusetts, 1980), 157-367. See also Arthur F. Schrader, "Songs to Cultivate the
Sensations of Freedom," 105-56 in the same volume.

[5] Harry Dichter and Elliott Shapiro, *Handbook of Early American Sheet Music* (New
York: R. R. Bowker Co., 1941; reprint, New York: Dover, 1977).

[6] H. Earle Johnson, "The John Rowe Parker Letters," *Musical Quarterly* 62 (1976):
72-86. For an account of America's first music periodical, see the same author's "Henry
C. Lewis's Musical Magazine," *Notes* 32 (1977): 7-12.

Houghton Library and the American Antiquarian Society.)

We cannot be more intimately concerned with music than by songsters. These small, portable volumes comprised the layman's musical companion until the advent of the harmonica, or mouth organ (patented in Germany in 1822 but coming into use somewhat later in America). A songster is defined by Irving Lowens as "a collection of three or more secular pieces intended to be sung." These are often only lyrics, citing appropriate tunes as in early books of psalmody. Philadelphia led in the production of songsters and New York followed, but Lowens lists 108 issued in Massachusetts between 1775 and 1800.[7]

Prosperity in the New World attracted both the able and the unable from Europe to a social climate encouraging — yea impelling — development of every latent ability. Some disappeared into the woodlands. Others turned to more stable occupations, as instrument manufacture (Maretzek and Strakosch), retailing (Hillegas, Carr, Hewitt, Van Hagen, and Graupner), and teaching — these or a combination thereof, as "musician and umbrella maker."[8]

Peregrinations of the Van Hagen family — father, mother, and juvenilia — from South Carolina in 1774 to Boston, where Peter Sr. directed music at the Haymarket Theater, led to his role as publisher. Van Hagen was the first in Boston to list ballads and keyboard works in quantity, e.g., *A New Federal Overture to be played at the Haymarket Theater* on 3 July 1799. I have located 81 titles by this firm, and twenty are advertised which do not survive in major collections. Except for "Adams and Liberty," "Rise Columbia," "New Yankee Doodle" and those by Steibelt, Paisiello, Storace, Pleyel from ballad operas, they are a sorry lot with Peter too often the tunesmith. All were one-page and crudely printed, although quality paper has assured their survival.

Little secular music was printed in Boston before the Revolution. Music type, first available in 1767, was not satisfactorily used until 1786 when Isaiah Thomas set up the first enduring typographic music press at Worcester. Music publishing was strongly influenced by improvements in printing, however, particularly by new methods of lithography after 1825.[9] We are often led to think of music publishing as "sheet music," a narrow view, perhaps owing to its runaway success during the 19th century.

There were few pianos, harpsichords, or organs in Boston, but Van Hagen had a brief association with Benjamin Crehore of Milton, better known as an instrument maker. When the senior Van Hagen died in 1803, Gottlieb Graupner took over the stock, such as it was. Peter Van Hagen Jr., only twenty-one, was disinclined to business.

---

[7] Irving Lowens, *A Bibliography of American Songers* (Worcester: American Antiquarian Society, 1976).

[8] In New London, Conn., 1984, there is an "Ice Cream and Sewing Machine" store.

[9] See Wolfe, *Early American Music Engraving and Printing,* 12, 241.

Graupner was a man for his time. Born 1767 in Hannover, Germany, he emigrated to England, played oboe in Haydn's orchestra when the "Salomon" symphonies were brought out, and arrived in Boston, via Prince Edward Island and Charleston, S.C., at the age of thirty. After a period as theater musician, he formed a "Conservatorio or Musical Academy" with Francis Mallet, a Frenchman, and Filipo Traetta, son of an illustrious father. Ere long Graupner found his calling as music dealer, publisher, and conductor. He led the first continuing orchestra in America — the Philo Harmonic, ca. 1807-ca. 1827 — was co-founder of the Handel and Haydn Society (1815) and published the first work by J. S. Bach in America (1806), a "Polonoise" from the Sixth French Suite. He withdrew it from the next edition of *Rudiments of the Art of Playing on the Piano Forte* as "too difficult."[10]

I have identified 520 Graupner publications, Richard Wolfe a few more. These include three each by Haydn and Handel; and five by Mozart, each increasingly known through performance; then Clementi, Cramer, Gluck, Grétry, Martini, Pleyel, Rossini, Stamitz, and Weber — surely a worthy lot — and Arnold, Bishop, Braham, Dibdin, Hook, Kelly, Reeve, and Shield, each known for ballad operas. Graupner also deserves credit for a series of instrumental preceptors for piano, German flute, clarinet (arr. from flute), and several collections of "admired melodies." Owing to his British experience, Graupner dealt with Clementi & Co. to import pianos and "all the latest and most fashionable Glees, Duetts, Songs, Xc Xc." while continuing his association with Benjamin Crehore (d. 1819) of Milton.

Although all publications marked "Copyright" are not listed by the Clerk of the District Court, 168 copyrights for music were issued between 1791 and 1827. Of these, 147 were sacred compilations. There were three of dances (sets of cotillions), two instructors each for voice and fife, one each for drums and violin. John Rowe Parker's *A Musical Biography* was copyright 18 December 1824; Pilkington and Greenwood's *A Musical Dictionary,* an abridgement of Busby and Arnold (1776),[11] on 6 June 1812. Other works were songs and piano solos, often waltzes and marches. Graupner copyrighted only three or four of his own works; others were either not published or do not survive. The fact that only eighteen of the 168 were issued before 1800 confirms the slow growth of publishing in Boston; of these, three were patriotic songs to words by Americans with music by Arne, Bray, and Shield.

---

[10] For a full discussion of Graupner's publications, see the author's *Musical Interludes in Boston*.

[11] Thomas Busby [with the assistance of Samuel Arnold], *A Complete Dictionary of Music* (London: Printed for R. Phillips, 1786). Other editions: 1801, 1806, and 1811.

Boston was center of the New England publishing industry. From Providence, R.I. and Northampton, Mass., from Brattleboro and Fairhaven, Vermont, occasional volumes were issued, both sacred and secular, usually the work of amateurs. Authorized denominational hymnals were not yet frequent. Francis Hopkinson had compiled a hymnal for the Lutheran Church in New York (1767) and Samuel Holyoke for the Baptist Churches of the United States, copyright Boston 1803. Other than these the only denomination mentioned is the Universalist (1807, 2nd ed. 1810) and the *Universalist Hymn Book* in 1821. There was a further edition in 1823.

A small edition of Handel's *Messiah* was printed in New York by Sage and Clough (1803), probably too early to find acceptance by existing choruses. James Loring's edition of *Messiah* (Boston 1817) "published under the patronage and inspection of the Handel and Haydn Society" was also complete with fifty-five numbers in 144 pages, and sold widely.

* * * * *

Publishing, not publishers, is the main objective of this essay, though the two are at times inseparable. Fortunes of selected firms as they moved from place to place; of renumberings which, on Washington Street in Boston, give wrong impressions of removal; accounts of the weak as they are consumed by the strong — these comprise more of a distraction than worthwhile exercise for the scholar. Distribution of merchandise was difficult, explaining in part why branches were established in distant cities and sheet music was reprinted at more than one location. The Post Office was not established until 1825; shipping by water was safer and surer. As for importation, the American market did not often warrant publication of full scores, scores in parts, contemporary music, or certain large works until past the turn of the 20th century. World War I turned the tide when European sources were not available and American firms were propelled into a leadership which they have sustained.

A new era began with Jacksonian democracy (1829-37). Realignment of business structures came with improved transportation and communication, dispelling much of the nation's sectionalism and impelling a rising middle class toward increasing cultural involvement. Agencies were established in the Midwest by Eastern firms, notably by Ditson.

* * * * *

Oliver Ditson & Co. can be traced to Ebenezer Batelle in 1783, apparently the second music publisher in Boston. Oliver H. Ditson, born 1811, worked for several firms until 1835. Thereafter, in full stride with four stalwart sons, he bought out more than fifty small firms in the next half-century. Firth-Pond & Co. (1867), William Hall & Son, J. L. Peters (1877) of New York; Lee & Walker (1875), G. André & Co. (1879), F. A. North & Co. (1890) of Philadelphia; and G. D. Russell (1877) of Boston were among them. In Boston,

Ditson, in the words of Dena J. Epstein, was "the normal graveyard" for similar enterprises.[12] G. P. Reed, Nathan Richardson, and others were taken over by Bradlee, who with Prentiss had long since lost its identity. Henry Tolman & Co., likewise a predator for the weak and unwary, was the fish that got away, succumbing not to Ditson but to Root and Cady of Chicago, a firm with Boston origins. Through annexation and growth, Ditson increased its prestige and marketing skills, acquiring a catalog of 100,000 works by 1890, the largest in the nation. Every item was available through branches in Philadelphia, New York, Cincinnati (1860), or from agencies such as Lyon and Healy of Chicago, established 1864 by Ditson.

Ditson, alert to the times, reprinted great works from the German romanticists as they became basic to America's musical experience. An insatiable household market, plus needs of the emerging public schools, libraries, choral societies, and choirs built up a demand for music from the least meritorious to the great masterworks except, perhaps, for full scores. Ditson brought out the first American edition of Beethoven's complete piano sonatas in 1856, and of *The Well-Tempered Clavier* (Czerny edition). Mendelssohn's *Songs without Words* followed and, in 1869, Dwight's translation of *The Passion According to St. Matthew*. Haydn and Mozart sonatas were in the 1870 catalog, but not those of Schubert or Schumann. There were standard biographical works and *Letters of Beethoven* and of *Mendelssohn*. By 1870 Ditson was virtually the only publisher in America of complete oratorios by Handel, Beethoven, Rossini, Neukomm, Mendelssohn, and Costa, as well as cantatas and oratorios by leading Americans such as George Bristow and Dudley Buck.

Buck, Paine, Parker, W. E. Thayer, and Chadwick were men of the new age and of a new ethic, overtaking long-time leaders Baker, Emerson, Mason, Hastings, Sharland, Southard, Elam Ives, Woodbury, G. F. Root, and Bradbury, whose enormous production of hymn and anthem books sold into the millions. Americans in every instance, these men were dedicated compilers and tunesmiths whose music entered every home and house of worship, ranking them only slightly below the saints.

The new day saw two new categories of music come to the fore, one as an enduring success, the other for a limited time. With Novello's introduction in England of the anthem, glee, and choral octavo, unbound and cheap, the long hegemony of the psalm-tune and choir volume lost its primacy.[13] (And let us not forget the male glee-club!) Publishers could venture works by lesser-known Americans at slight cost. Anthems are a very Protestant form, and American churches took them up with fervor. (Few "classical" composers

---

[12] Dena J. Epstein, *Music Publishing in Chicago before 1871: The Firm of Root & Cady 1858-1871,* Detroit Studies in Music Bibliography, 14 (Detroit: Information Coordinators, 1969). Epstein also gives dated plate numbers for Reed, Richardson, and others of Boston.

[13] *Short History of Cheap Music* (London and New York: Novello, Ewer, 1887).

wrote anthems—Mendelssohn, for example, only two.) Hence Dudley Buck (b. 1839), P. A. Schnecker (b. 1850), John Hyatt Brewer (b. 1856), James H. Rogers (b. 1857), Harry Rowe Shelley (b. 1858) and William H. Neidlinger (b. 1863) were but a few of those whose leafy branches overshadowed the choirlofts of every denominational edifice. And henceforth the firms of Oliver Ditson and G. Schirmer (originally Beer and Schirmer) assumed leadership, joined as an equal by Arthur P. Schmidt after 1876.

A more temporary innovation, that of the melodeon, harmonium, or reed-organ, came to maturity in America in the 'sixties. Albums of music for a limited keyboard and expressive range were actively promoted, particularly by White, Smith & Co.[14] Theirs was a success lasting not much beyond the turn of the century, doomed by the progress of invention: the player-piano, phonograph, and, eventually, the electronic organ.

The band played a vigorous part in American life. Band music was available from Michael Hillegas of Philadelphia in 1759,[15] and George Washington was actively concerned with the excellence of all corps under his command.[16] A declared band supplier in Boston from 1867 to 1908 was the Jean White Publishing Co., on Washington Street.[17] We await a study of this firm's career in a period when every Village Green had its bandstand and local ensemble.

*   *   *   *   *

Magazines expressly devoted to articles and information on music come under the umbrella of music publishing. We have mentioned John Rowe Parker's *The Euterpeiad* (1820-22). Hach's *Journal of Music* (1838-40) was too early to have much to say. Except for a minuet, no orchestral work by Beethoven was produced in Boston until 3 April 1841. "From this dates the history of Beethoven in Boston," Dwight wrote in *The Harbinger* of 1841. J. S. Dwight's *Journal of Music* (1852-81), initially sponsored by Ditson, was the finest of its kind. *The Folio,* published by White, Smith & Co. (1869-95), was a house organ mainly useful for gossip and White's ephemeral compositions. Thirty-four music journals were published in the 1850-98 era, most of them as advertising media for Boston firms.[18]

---

[14] See H. Earle Johnson, *"The Folio* of White, Smith & Co.," *American Music* 2 (1984): 88-104.

[15] *Pennsylvania Gazette,* 5 June 1764 and earlier.

[16] Raoul Camus, *Military Music of the American Revolution* (Chapel Hill: University of North Carolina Press, 1976), 129-30.

[17] White, Smith & Perry, founded 1867, was also on Washington Street, but there was no relationship between the two.

[18] Notable dissertations and theses concerning American periodicals during the 19th century include Sister Mary Veronica Davison, "American Music Periodicals 1853-1899" (Ph.D., University of Minnesota, 1973); William J. Weichlein, *A Checklist of American Music Periodicals, 1850-1900,* Detroit Studies in Music Bibliography, 16

Literary magazines throughout America printed articles on music as well as songs. Lowens finds 183 articles on music in periodicals of American Transcendentalism between 1835 and 1850. *The North American Review* (1815) carried music and articles from 1822, and *The Atlantic Monthly* from its beginning in 1857.[19]

It is said that Arthur Paul Schmidt (1846-1921) was grateful for the opportunities afforded him in the United States. He had worked for G. D. Russell before that firm merged with Ditson in 1877. Native composers of larger forms were in need of an advocate; in the years after 1876 Schmidt's own firm brought out important works such as John Knowles Paine's "Spring" Symphony (1880), the first symphonic score issued by an American publisher.

Schmidt concentrated on Americans, on anthems and glees, on the parlor song and on piano pieces.[20] His larger publications included Mrs. H. H. A. Beach's "Gaelic" Symphony; one hundred works of Arthur Foote[21] and many by George Chadwick; eighteen by Edward MacDowell and by those of his alias, Edgar Thorne; by Frederick Converse and Henry Hadley; songs and pianoforte pieces by Margaret Ruthven Lang; and hundreds, literally hundreds, of miscellaneous selections by composers who entered the American home and church but have never entered an American musical dictionary, to wit: 64 pieces by G. F. Ritter, 70 anthems by A. W. Lansing, 72 by George W. Marston — who will say they are worthless? (The number of meritable American musicians from all periods of our musical life who are *not* in dictionaries far exceeds those who are.) The list of popular and profitable publications by this firm is a long one, as Ayars states. Notable for his support of Americans, A. P. Schmidt was also alert to new trends in Europe.

Other than anthems and organ works by T. Tertius Noble, little of comparable worth was issued after Schmidt's withdrawal from the firm in 1916. Times were changing, phonograph and radio were at hand, and the parlor song became a waning commodity. The firm was managed by Henry Austin until its purchase in the spring of 1960 by Summy-Birchard of Evanston, Illinois.[22]

(Detroit: Information Coordinators, 1970); Charles Edward Wunderlich, "A History and Bibliography of Early American Musical Periodicals, 1782-1852" (Ph.D., University of Michigan, 1962); Vera S. Flandorf, "Music Periodicals in the United States: A Survey of Their History and Content" (M.A., University of Chicago, 1952); Irene Millen, "American Musical Magazines, 1786-1865" (M.L.S., Carnegie Institute of Technology, 1949).

[19] Joseph Mussulman, *Music in the Cultured Generation* (Evanston: Northwestern University Press, 1971).

[20] Christine Merrick Ayars, *Contributions to the Art of Music in America by Music Industries of Boston 1640-1936* (New York: H. W. Wilson, 1937; reprint, New York: Johnson Reprint Corp., 1969).

[21] Wilma Reid Cipolla, *A Catalog of the Works of Arthur Foote, 1853-1937,* Bibliographies in American Music, 6 (Detroit: Information Coordinators, 1980).

[22] I knew Henry Austin slightly, a septagenerian fuddy-duddy, straight out of Dickens, who maintained the quarters until Honeywell (I believe) bought the building, doubled the rent, and scared the wits out of Mr. Austin who retired to Princeton, New Jersey.

How did the records of this pioneer firm survive? By the quick action of Richard S. Hill of the Library of Congress whose inspired, timely appearance at 120 Boylston Street and subsequent negotiations saved them from the trash can. We can share Richard Hill's excitement on receipt of a letter to the Library of Congress dated 3 May 1960, shortly after the move, which reads in part:

> Knowing of your interest in the Arthur P. Schmidt Co. materials, I want to let you know that we have come across ten large bound volumes (plate books). This is a listing by plate number of everything the Arthur P. Schmidt Co. ever published. . . . We would be happy to send them to you.
>
> [signed] Robert Dahnert, Copyright Dept.
> Summy-Birchard Publishing Co.

No other American publisher's history is so well documented, and we are indebted to Richard S. Hill for saving this collection for the Library of Congress. There, in due course, its parts were organized into the present archive by Donald W. Krummel, Wayne Shirley, and others. Housed in the Music Division, the archive comprises 100,000 items of correspondence (mostly after 1889) and 51,000 manuscripts in 114 sturdy boxes. Wilma Reid Cipolla is presently engaged in preparing a history of the firm.

The Oliver Ditson firm was sold to Theodore Presser of Philadelphia in 1937 with a catalog listing 3,500 vocal, 5,000 pianoforte, 6,000 octavo, 4,800 instrumental works, and 3,000 miscellaneous titles. No records prior to 1900 survive, according to Arnold Broido, general manager of Presser, now located in Bryn Mawr. Would we had a Ditson chronicle equal to that of Root and Cady,[23] or an inventory to parallel that of Arthur P. Schmidt!

*   *   *   *   *

Two branches of music publishing remain to be discussed, however briefly. First, the volumes of miscellaneous pieces begun in days following the Revolution as exemplified by Gottlieb Graupner's *The Musical Magazine* of 1803 (3 vols.). G. P. Reed issued *Gems of German Song* in the 1830s containing works by Schubert. Ditson, in its turn, fathered the *Wreath Series, The Musician's Library* of 100 volumes, and *The Music Student's Piano Course,* all standard for many years. In 1909 Chapple of Boston, a firm not otherwise associated with music, brought out *Heart Songs,* an all-time bestseller.[24] This type of volume was basic furnishing for every American home, a self-educative force for good music.

---

[23] Epstein, *Music Publishing,* 8.

[24] *Heart Songs* was reissued (New York: Da Capo, 1982) with an introduction by Charles Hamm.

For the public school, Ginn and Company (1867), book publishers, led the way. Thereafter Silver, Burdett (1884), D. C. Heath (1885), and C. C. Birchard (1901) ardently cultivated the expanding educational market.[25] Boston Music Co. (1885) continues as a retail store independent of G. Schirmer; however the names of Carrie Jacobs-Bond and Ethelbert Nevin are still invoked there on occasion, as was the name of Charles Wakefield Cadman for many years at White, Smith & Co. C. C. Birchard became Summy-Birchard in 1956/57. B. F. Wood (1893 Maine, 1917 Mass.), with its "Edition Wood" was mindful of the church organist, but was purchased by Belwin, Mills in 1956/60. McLaughlin, Reilly (1904) specialized in music for the Catholic Church.

Ernst C. Schirmer (d. 1958), a nephew of G. Schirmer (b. 1865), was manager of Boston Music Company in 1891. In 1917 he established his own firm, owing much to Thomas Whitney Surette, head of a music teacher's summer school in Concord, and to Prof. Archibald T. Davison of Harvard. The latter was transforming the Glee Club from maudlin praise of dear Old Siwash into an ensemble featuring works of the Renaissance, English madrigals, folk songs, and choruses by Mendelssohn and Brahms. These, unavailable in America or in octavo editions, were issued by E. C. Schirmer for an expanding college and university clientele. Under the editorship of Surette and Davison, *The Home and Community Songbook* became an outstanding work, still in demand.[26] A series of graded preceptors contributed to the firm's reputation, while choral works of Randall Thompson and Daniel Pinkham sell widely, the former's *Alleluia* (1940) three million or more copies. Since the death of E. C. Schirmer's two sons Ernest and Carl, the firm has remained, first under the presidency of Robert MacWilliams (d. 1985) and since 1986 under Robert Schuneman, the major music publishing house in Boston.

*   *   *   *   *

After World War II a young man from the armed forces, William Schwann, purchased a phonograph-record shop in Cambridge, opposite the Massachusetts Institute of Technology. When the long-playing record made its debut the number of issuing companies increased and Schwann mimeographed lists of new recordings for his customers and friends. As demand increased, a more substantial tabulation was in order; hence, in 1946, *The Schwann Record Catalog,* now known as *Schwann Compact Disc Catalog* (monthly) and *Schwann* (quarterly). "Schwann" maintains its high standard as a scholarly periodical.

---

[25] Silver, Burdett had branches in New York, Chicago, and San Francisco. Its headquarters are now in Morristown, N.J. Ginn & Co. and D. C. Heath are in Lexington, Mass.

[26] Archibald Thompson Davison and T. W. Surette, *The Home and Community Song Book* (Boston: E. C. Schirmer, 1921).

For books about music, New England's record is modest yet substantial. The publishers Ditson, Alfred Mudge, and the Page Company printed books readily accepted in their day. Page, for example, issued a series of popular works *Grand Opera in America, Annals of Music in America,* and *The Orchestra* from 1898 to 1912. As would be expected, volumes issued by the Harvard and Yale University presses are of high-ranking scholarship. Little, Brown & Co. and Houghton Mifflin issue meritable works on occasion. The American Antiquarian Society in Worcester sponsored Irving Lowens' *A Bibliography of American Songsters* (1976); *American Sacred Music Imprints, 1698-1810: A Bibliography* by Allen Perdue Britton and Irving Lowens, completed by Richard Crawford, is (1987) about to appear.

Certain works mentioned above, by nature of their subject matter, take us back to the earliest times discussed on the first page of this essay. American publishers and dealers are sometimes hard to disjoin, but firms without retail outlets have a higher ratio of survival. The retail "music store" is in a sorry state; witness Siegling Music Co. of Charleston, S.C., which closed in 1971 after 150 years of continuous service. Theodore Presser is no longer in Philadelphia, and G. Schirmer of New York is now "conglomerated." No publishing house formed before 1860 survives under its original name. Today we equate recording companies with music publishers. Northeastern University in Boston has begun a promising career with a selective list of LPs.

The careers of Van Hagen, Graupner, Ditson, G. Schirmer, E. C. Schirmer, and their fellowship derived largely from the strengths of their leadership. Poor Peter Van Hagen, wife at elbow, never quite made it, nor was his time propitious. Gottlieb Graupner, the quiet, natural leader, was typical of millions of emigrating Germans. Charles H. Ditson, a several-generation Yankee, was in the right place at the right time. These firms — these men — scanned America's broadening musical horizon with vision; each was zealous in the cause of good music. They are too often an underprized species to the scholar, but their dedication and skills comprise a record of vast consequence to the impelling growth of music in America.

CHAPTER 5

From Sherburne, N.Y., to the Library of Congress: The Progress of a Musical American Family

by

Dena J. Epstein

In March 1970, L. Quincy Mumford, the Librarian of Congress, announced a new endowment for music at the Library of Congress, the McKim Fund, to support the "composition and performance of violin and piano duos as well as other related activities."[1] The Fund was the bequest of Mrs. W. Duncan McKim, who, as Leonora Jackson, had been a well-known concert violinist around the turn of the century, playing with "the Berlin Philharmonic and the Gewandhaus Orchestra in Leipzig under Nikisch, as well as the New York Philharmonic, the Boston Symphony, and many others in the United States."[2] The press release did not mention the long association of her family with American music in the successive stages of its development. The musical activities of Mrs. McKim, her mother, and her uncles provide a capsule history of music in the United States from its simple rural beginnings to the flowering of chamber music in our national library.

In another bequest, Mrs. McKim's estate presented twenty-one volumes and three boxes of scrapbooks, diaries, programs, and reviews to the Maryland Historical Society in Baltimore. From these materials, together with a variety of other sources, it is possible to outline the story of her family, a tale that would have delighted Dick Hill.

The story as far as it is now known begins about 1796 with the birth of Seth Higgins "(ancestry undetermined)" in Sherburne, New York, a town due west of Albany on the Chenango River between Binghamton and Utica. Seth Higgins was the father of twelve children, of whom at least four are known to have been musical— the second, Hiram Murray, born at Warsaw, N.Y., and the 5th-7th, Thomas Metcalf, Adoniram Judson, and Elizabeth, all born at Laona, N.Y. (The genealogist of the Higgins family reports "The name of the wife is unknown. Informant could not furnish dates.")

---

[1] Library of Congress Press Release no. 70-27, dated 26 March 1970.

[2] Ibid.

Sometime later the family moved west to Palmyra, Wisconsin, a hamlet about 25 miles southwest of Milwaukee.[3]

Elizabeth, the seventh child, was the central link in this family chain, for she was to be the mother of Leonora Jackson McKim. In an interview many years later, Elizabeth Higgins described her childhood: "There was a family of twelve boys and girls, all musically inclined, in my father's home. He was passionately devoted to music, and had a big organ built in the parlor, around which we gathered night after night, singing the great choruses of the classics."[4] No contemporary account of the organ or the classics has been found; Elizabeth's recollection is our only glimpse of the family's musical activities at home.

The first contemporary report refers to 1843, when "H. M. Higgins was a music teacher, and in that capacity traveled over the prairies, holding here and there his singing classes."[5] By 1850 a family concert troupe had been formed called the "Columbians" or the Higgins Family, two brothers and two sisters. The Lexington, Ky., *Statesman* for 28 January praised their "style of music and manner of execution," and the Louisville *Courier* for 31 January called them "one of the most delightful bands of songsters that ever visited the West. . . . They are thorough musicians. The harmony and melody of the several voices are unequaled. . . ."[6]

How long the concert troupe survived is not known. In March 1852 Elizabeth Higgins (Miss Libbie) was in Athens, Georgia, where admiring friends wrote poems in her *Forget-Me-Not Album* in praise of her singing,[7] but there is no indication of the presence of the other members of the troupe. In 1854 the *New York Musical Review and Choral Advocate* (vol. 5, 2 February 1854, p. 44), reported that A. J. Higgins had "several large music classes in the vicinity of Harrodsburg, Ky. He is enterprising and capable." This news may have been out-of-date when it was printed, for on 10 April a dispatch from Lacon, Illinois reported that he "came here about a year ago, and taught one course of twenty lessons, which resulted in the organization of the 'Lacon Harmonic Society.'" The report added: "Some of our Western teachers are now on their way to New-York to attend the Musical Institute. . . . Messrs. A. J. and H. M. Higgins [are included]. . . . T. M. Higgins is already there."[8]

---

[3] Katharine Chapin Higgins, *Richard Higgins . . . and His Descendants* (Worcester, Mass.: Printed for the Author, 1918), 591-92.

[4] Katherine Graham, "An American Girl and Her Violin," *Metropolitan Magazine* 11 (1900): 282-83.

[5] *Chicago Tribune*, 2 April 1863, p. 4, col. 2, quoting "H. M. Higgins' Quarterly Circular."

[6] Quoted in the *American Monthly Musical Review and Choir Singers' Companion* 1 (1 July 1850): 70; 1 (1 September 1850): 103; and 2 (1 March 1851): 41.

[7] This autograph album is part of the Leonora Jackson McKim Papers, Ms. 1780, at the Maryland Historical Society. All sources not otherwise identified come from this collection. My grateful thanks to the Society for permission to quote from them.

[8] *New-York Musical Review and Choral Advocate* 5 (27 April 1854): 139.

Libbie Higgins did not accompany her brothers. Her history is now known only in bits and pieces, some of them contradictory, but enough has been found to outline the story of a woman dedicated to music in a world with limited opportunities. Her *Forget-Me-Not Album* offers tantalizing hints of her personality and character. On 19 August 1853, Mary A. Higgins wrote in Palmyra, Wisconsin "To Sister Libbie":

> Careless, lighthearted and gay,
> Thoughtful, romantic and wild,
> Joyous as sweet birds in May,
> Unaffected, as nature's own child.

"Mother" wrote in Palmyra on 29 April 1854: "Dark and thorny has been thy pathway, clouds have often obscured thy horizon. . . . May the *desire* of thy heart be given thee, and mayest thou ascend the Hill of Science." We do not know what the thorns and clouds may have been, but the "science" must have been music.

While her brothers were studying with Lowell Mason and George F. Root in New York, Miss Libbie Higgins, "recently one of the popular troupe called 'Columbians,'" was married on 20 July 1854 in Milwaukee to James E. Browne, Esq., of Quincy, Illinois.[9]

In 1855 Adoniram Judson and Hiram Murray Higgins settled in Chicago and opened a music store at 54 Randolph Street.[10] Before the end of the year the firm began to publish music, depositing for copyright *I Have No Mother Now,* by Franz Staab, a local bandmaster, on 29 October.[11] Thus far each successive stage of the family's musical activities was typical of the musical development of pioneer America—moving westward, organizing a family concert troupe, progressing from itinerant singing teacher who settled temporarily wherever a class could be formed to the more settled occupation of running a small music store, selling instruments, concert tickets, and sheet music, and then publishing music for a local market.

Before the end of the year, Higgins Brothers had deposited for copyright two songs by Joseph Philbrick Webster, the clergyman from Elkhorn, Wisconsin, who was to write some of their most successful songs. (Webster's *Lorena* became the most popular song of the Confederacy during the Civil War.[12]) The firm grew with

---

[9] Ibid., 5 (3 August 1854): 277.

[10] *Daily Democratic Press* (Chicago), 28 July 1855, p. 2, col. 6. The *Daily Chicago Times* for 1 January 1856 ran an advertisement (3:8) for the firm as "dealers in all kinds of musical instruments, sole agents for Light [*sic,* i.e., Lighte], Newton & Bradbury's piano fortes . . . Instruction Books for all kinds of musical instruments; also, Guitar and Violin Strings . . . Melodeons, Guitars, Violins, Accordeons, Flutinas, Flutes, and Brass Instruments . . . wholesale or retail, at the lowest prices. Piano Stools in great variety. . . ."

[11] Deposit date from the copy in the Library of Congress.

[12] Richard Barksdale Harwell, *Confederate Music* (Chapel Hill: University of North Carolina Press, 1950), 86, and Mary Boykin Chesnut, *A Diary from Dixie,* ed. Ben Ames Williams (Boston: Houghton Mifflin Company, 1949), 304.

Chicago, expanding from a small store to a four-story building.[13]

In 1858 Higgins Brothers published *The Valentine; or, The Spirit of Song* "by Miss Libbie Higgins." Whether she was still married to James Browne is not known. The partnership of Higgins Brothers was dissolved early in 1859, and the brothers continued to publish separately. A. J. Higgins left the field in 1861, but H. M. Higgins continued to publish until 1867, when he sold his plates to J. L. Peters, of St. Louis, who in turn sold them a year later to DeMotte Brothers, of Chicago.[14] By 28 September 1867, Libbie Higgins was married to Charles Pringle Jackson,[15] and it was as Mrs. E. H. Jackson, i.e., Elizabeth Higgins Jackson, that she published at her own expense the first four of a series of six *Songs of Affection* with a DeMotte Brothers imprint. After that firm's demise, the last two songs in the series were published "for the composer" by Root & Cady in 1869 and were deposited for copyright by C. P. Jackson.[16] As her series of songs was appearing, her first child Ernest was born about 1868.[17]

October 1874 found her in Ohio

> . . . spending a few days in . . . [Cleveland], resting, preparatory to commencing her fall and winter work. As a vocal teacher, she ranks among the first in the land, and is perhaps the only lady who holds musical conventions and is teaching large classes. Her ability as a teacher is remarkable . . . if you want some one to teach your young people or adults, to read music *'at sight,'* or to drill, organize and systematize your choirs, or to instruct the more advanced in voice culture, thorough bass and harmony, you will indeed be fortunate if you can secure her services. She purposes spending the coming winter in this State. . . . Mrs. Jackson is a sister of our old friend and contemporary, H. M. Higgins, of Chicago.[18]

Up to this time, the activities of the Higgins family were well within the school of native American music led by Lowell Mason and George F. Root. But what had been acceptable through the Civil

---

[13] *Daily Chicago Times,* 31 March 1858, p. 2, col. 3, adv.

[14] *Chicago Tribune,* 1 February 1859, p. 1, col. 7, adv.; 29 May 1867, p. 1, col. 7, adv.; *The Presto* 12 (19 September 1895): 23. Further details about the publishing career of the firm can be found in Dena J. Epstein, *Music Publishing in Chicago before 1871: The Firm of Root & Cady, 1858-1871,* Detroit Studies in Music Bibliography, no. 14 (Detroit: Information Coordinators, 1969), 7-11.

[15] *The Forget-Me-Not-Album* has a "Tableau" dated Chicago, 29 September 1867, signed "Husband, Chas. P. Jackson."

[16] Epstein, *Music Publishing,* 119.

[17] In a manuscript "Life and Career of Leonora Jackson, Written by Her Brother, Ernest H. Jackson," in the Leonora Jackson McKim Papers, he wrote "Ten years older than she I was." A certificate signed by her father states that she was born in Boston, 20 February 1878. Most of the accounts give her birthdate as 1879.

[18] *Brainard's Musical World* 11 (October 1874): 150.

War was becoming provincial and old-fashioned in the 1870s. As the taste for European music grew in the United States, Libbie Jackson grew dissatisfied with her training and skill. Three years after the birth of Leonora on 20 February 1878 in Boston,[19] Mrs. Jackson went to Italy to study singing with Madame Marchesi.[20] Ernest accompanied his mother and studied piano in Vienna, but there is nothing in the McKim Papers to suggest that Leonora was in Europe as a small child. She may have remained in Chicago with her father.

How long Mrs. Jackson stayed in Europe is not known. Ernest's piano studies proved unsatisfactory, and he returned to the United States and about 1888 entered Harvard.

Mrs. Jackson had already turned her attention to Leonora. "I am proud to think," she said, "that my daughter inherits her musical temperament from our side of the family. . . . Even as a baby the sound of a violin would send her into ectasies of joy. . . . We bought her a little violin, and I gave her her first lessons in the nursery. . . ."[21] At six Leonora began serious lessons, first with Albert Ruff, then Carl Becker, who was in turn succeeded by Simon Jacobsohn, a fine Russian violinist, one-time concertmaster in the Theodore Thomas Orchestra, and later teacher successively at the Cincinnati College of Music and the Chicago Musical College.[22]

By 1891, when Leonora was about twelve, Theodore Thomas had settled in Chicago. Perhaps it was through his old colleague Jacobsohn that he heard of the girl violinist and recommended that she be taken to Paris for further study. In the examination for admission to the Conservatoire, she passed second in a field of 165.[23] In a manuscript biography of his sister, Ernest Jackson wrote:

> Our parents were with Leonora that year in Paris, while I . . . was having my senior year at Harvard. Madam Marchesi with whom mother had studied ten years before . . . in Vienna, was then living in Paris . . . [and] took a special interest in sister. . . . Unhappily [in June 1892] our parents suffered severe financial losses, and but for the generosity of several American patrons of art, we could have gone no further. . . .

A masterful public relations campaign must have been mounted to assemble that group of generous patrons, "leading citizens in nearly every city of the United States. The Vanderbilts, Sears, the Pullmans,

[19] "Life and Career of Leonora Jackson. . . ."

[20] Ibid.

[21] Graham, "An American Girl," 283.

[22] Ibid. "Jacobsohn, Simon E., 1839-1902; Fine Russian violinist, pupil of Weller and David, from 1860 concertmaster at Bremen, in 1872-78 concertmaster in the Thomas Orchestra in New York . . . "—Waldo Selden Pratt, *New Encyclopedia of Music and Musicians,* new and rev. ed. (New York: Macmillan Company, 1943), 467.

[23] Clipping from *Washington Evening News,* 8 February 1894, in Jackson scrapbook.

the Ditsons, Mrs. Senator Brice of Washington, and the McDonalds of Cincinnati are among her patrons. . . ."[24] The determination that fueled the drive for patrons was not the young violinist's. In 1940 she wrote to her brother of her mother:

> She has been disappointed in her own career due to domestic reasons, also in her ambition for you to become a pianist when she gave you the opportunity in Vienna, so she just naturally had to fall back on me. You know, and I know wild horses could not have stopped her, her ambition was simply immense. Of course I never cease to marvel at her fortitude and perseverance and all credit is certainly hers.[25]

The donated funds took Leonora to Berlin for study with Joseph Joachim, the most eminent violinist of his day. The father returned to the States, but the mother accompanied Leonora and Ernest to Berlin, the musical Athens of the 1890s. Summers were spent in the United States where Leonora gave concerts both to raise money and to enable the patrons to observe her progress. An item in the Chicago *Sunday Inter Ocean* for 10 December 1893 (p. [26], col. 6) gives a hint of the heady company in which she traveled:

> Mr. and Mrs. George M. Pullman left for New York Thursday in their private car, taking with them Mrs. Jackson, Miss Leonora Jackson, and Ernest H. Jackson.

In the fall of 1894, Leonora began a diary that recorded the musical and social activities that filled their days in Berlin — frequent concerts, receptions, soirées, and of course (for her) many hours of practice, rehearsals, and lessons. Mother must have loved every minute of it. What a contrast to Palmyra, Wisconsin! The diary mentions many friends who became eminent — Bronislaw Hubermann, for example — but the central figure was Joachim. He grew very fond of her and permitted her to be described as his "favorite pupil." The breadth of her training was hinted at in the diary entry for 20 October 1894: "I had a lesson with Prof. Joachim, played the 1. sonate of Bach. . . . My E string broke and he gave me his Strad to play on. . . ." She was then sixteen years old.

In 1895, the *Musical Courier*'s Berlin correspondent Otto Floersheim wrote of her:

> When she came to Berlin some two years ago, Joachim received her at once into his class at the Hoch Schule, and I have it on high authority that he deems her the most promising pupil in the institution. He had her play in two of his orchestral concerts last winter — a mark of unusual preference. During the winter but four violin solos were

---

[24] *Musical Courier* 23 (4 December 1895): 15.

[25] Letter (typescript) from Leonora Jackson McKim to Ernest H. Jackson, 7 September 1940.

rendered at these concerts; of these Miss Jackson played two . . . as she possesses, in addition to her rare gifts, extreme youth and a pleasing personality, if given due time for study, she should have a distinguished career.

Earlier in the same report:

> Saturday evening, the 9th inst., as soloist of the first orchestra concert of this season at the Hoch Schule, she played the adagio of the sixth concerto of Spohr, and the second concerto of Wieniawski under the master's personal leadership, and with notable success. Joachim honored her by applauding heartily from the conductor's stand.[26]

She made her debut with the Berlin Philharmonic playing the Brahms Concerto with Joachim himself leading the orchestra.[27] The concerto, written in 1879, was less than 20 years old, still a rather controversial work. That she chose it for her debut under the direction of the man for whom it was written was quite an accomplishment for an American girl, still in her teens. (The exact date of this concert has not been determined. Ernest Jackson cites 17 October 1895, but no contemporary verification of that date has been found.) After her debut, she made "a very successful tour of Germany and Scandinavia."[28] In 1897 she was awarded the Berlin Mendelssohn prize, 1500 marks, from a field of twenty-two competitors.[29] She then returned to the United States, "where she played 160 concerts in her first season of 1900-1901; since then she has played with the foremost mus. organizations in Europe and America."[30]

Her first appearance with the New York Philharmonic, a public rehearsal, was described in detail in the *New York Times:*

> An audience of unusual size. This was to be attributed only to one cause, the reappearance in the land of her birth of Miss Leonora Jackson. . . . Those who sit in high places in the social circles of this city are concerned in the making of a career for this girl. She was sent abroad by a syndicate of well-disposed women. . . .
>   Yesterday . . . most of those who had contributed to the fund for her education . . . were on hand to see what had been the outcome of their good deed. That they were to

---

[26] *Musical Courier,* ibid.

[27] Henry C. Lahee, *Famous Violinists of Today and Yesterday* (Boston: L. C. Page & Company, 1899), 342. Lahee commented on p. 300 ". . . until recently few women played the violin."

[28] Theodore Baker, *Baker's Biographical Dictionary of Musicians,* 3d ed., rev. and enl. by Alfred Remy (New York: G. Schirmer, 1919), 431.

[29] *Musical Times* 38 (1 November 1897): 766. Lahee, *Famous Violinists,* 343, describes command performances before the Empress of Germany and Queen Victoria at Windsor Castle and Osborne House, in the Isle of Wight.

[30] *Baker's Biographical Dictionary,* 431.

be pleased was a foregone conclusion. Given a pretty girl, and a difficult piece of music [the Brahms concerto], the applause was sure to be of an extravagant nature. . . . Miss Jackson might have achieved an easier success with her audience if she had played the Mendelssohn or the Bruch concerto. That she elected to play the sublime and difficult music of Brahms spoke volumes for her courage. . . .

Miss Jackson has a sound and healthy talent. It was worthwhile for the beneficent ladies to cultivate it. She has a splendid bow arm, one whose masculine freedom and strength promise much for her future as a virtuoso. Her stopping is not quite perfect, but it is generally correct. Her style is in the main characterized by musicianly taste rather than by deep emotional power. . . . She plays smoothly, clearly, and with an approach to finish. Her tone is good and round, and her cantabile is distinguished by much smoothness and grace. She plays with a good deal of authority for one so young, but her lack of emotional force deprives her work of inspiring influence. . . .[31]

The review of the concert itself on 7 January 1900 (p. 18, cols. 1-3) was entirely devoted to that controversial figure, Johannes Brahms!

Other contemporary reviews were equally favorable, all commenting on her youth. (At the time of this concert she was not yet 22.) *The Musical Times* of London for 1 December 1896 (37:830) praised her "great technical mastery and artistic feeling"; Henry C. Lahee wrote of her "fine tone, natural musical feeling, and complete technique. Few violinists can play with such quiet, intense sentiment. . . . Of the three hundred or more pupils of Joachim . . . Maud Powell and Leonora Jackson are among the brightest lights from the United States. . . ."[32]

But there were unfavorable reviews as well, especially in Chicago, where professional jealousy may have played a role:

Jackson is advertised as a "great" artist, but she does not at present justify her claim to such distinction. There are two girls in Chicago today who are far superior in . . . talent . . . but who have not been fortunate enough to possess pushing relatives or to obtain beneficent contributors. Miss Jackson is a mechanical player with a moderate amount of technic, very little style, correctly cold and coldly correct. Her frigidity communicated itself to the audience who applauded with chilling reserve.[33]

After such a promising beginning, why is Leonora Jackson forgotten today while Maude Powell, with whom contemporaries

---

[31] *New York Times,* 6 January 1900, p. 6, col. 7.

[32] Lahee, *Famous Violinists,* 326.

[33] *Musical Leader* 1 (19 December 1900): 3-4. This journal wrote many nasty reviews, once describing the young Frederick Stock as a "fifth-rate conductor . . . a nuisance to be abated by injunction without notice." Ibid., 4 (7 August 1902): 8.

paired her, is still remembered as a much loved American artist? The answer may lie in Leonora's decision to retire, at least temporarily, in 1910 from concert life. *Musical America* for 25 March 1911 (13:25) broke the story with the headline: "Prefers Farm to Concert Honors":

> Leonora Jackson, the violin virtuoso, who has dropped completely out of sight musically for the past year or so, has been "discovered." She has bought a country house not far from Albany, and is farming. . . . Although she has her Stradivarius with her and has been doing considerable composition this winter, . . . she makes butter and superintends a farm of fifty acres as if she enjoyed it.
>
> Miss Jackson is taking her long vacation under protest from her family, who have no sympathy with her "back-to-the-soil" aspirations, and are a little in trepidation of what this independent young person is likely to do next. Miss Jackson, interviewed for *Musical America,* said frankly, " . . . I think I deserve a little private life of my own if I want it, and I do. I am just living here on the farm quietly, and I have no intention of leaving it — that is, not now." . . .
>
> The violinist . . . is still no more than a girl . . . a little boyish in her independent air. . . . She has a gun and a dog . . . works in the garden in Summer, and traps rabbits in Winter. . . .
>
> "I've spent more years of my public life in Europe than in America," she said, "though I have toured all through the United States. . . . I have played in nearly every country in Europe, except Italy and Russia. My life has been a series of railroad journeys, hotel rooms, and concert halls, a succession of cities and audiences. And I have worked very hard. Now I am taking a vacation."

The family's disapproval was a foregone conclusion. A glimpse of what must have been a complex relationship was provided in Leonora's letter to her brother of 7 September 1940:

> Mother and I were never on such easy terms. You were her confidant, your privilege to be her favorite, that is as it should be considering the difference in our ages.

Ernest saw things somewhat differently:

> We have our sainted mother to thank for her fine philosophy of life, and her example of facing all problems with courage and confidence, knowing no fear. She knew no fear, and from our childhood took pains to allow no talk in our presence of fear or nervousness.[34]

---

[34] E. H. Jackson, "Life and Career of Leonora Jackson."

It is not known whether Leonora resumed her career before her marriage on 12 October 1915 to W. Duncan McKim, a wealthy physician and writer from Baltimore, 23 years her senior.[35] Libbie Higgins Jackson died in Brooklyn in June 1916.[36] From all accounts, the McKim's marriage was a happy one, with much private music. In 1930, when the McKims spent the winter in Hawaii, she gave a complimentary concert for the students of the Punahou School in Honolulu, playing the Franck sonata, among other works.[37] W. Duncan McKim died on 16 April 1935, aged 80,[38] while Mrs. McKim lived on for thirty-four years, dying on 7 January 1969. Her love for the violin was expressed in her bequest, establishing the McKim Fund to provide concerts that "feature sonata recitals for violin and piano and will include . . . works especially commissioned by the Fund" — an appropriate, meaningful conclusion to a life devoted to music.

---

[35] *Who Was Who in America,* vol. 1, 1897-1942 (Chicago: A. N. Marquis Company, 1942), 816.

[36] Higgins, *Richard Higgins and his Descendents,* 592.

[37] Clipping from the *Honolulu Star Bulletin,* 8 March 1930, in Jackson scrapbook.

[38] *Who Was Who. . . .*

Part III

The Music Trade

The Dispersal of Engraved Music Plates and Copyrights in British Auctions, 1831-1931

by

James B. Coover

Music, printed and manuscript, books about music, and musical instruments have been consigned for sale at auction since the end of the sixteenth century. Not so engraved music plates and copyrights! Sales of these took place principally between 1831 and the First World War, almost exclusively in England,[1] and the great majority of them were conducted in the sales rooms of a single London auctioneer, Puttick & Simpson. A few sales are known before 1831, only three after 1920; between those dates there were nearly two hundred. By the last quarter of the nineteeth century, Puttick's was staging an average of six a year entirely devoted to plates and copyrights. Whether this flurry of activity was prompted by the great changes in British life wrought by events of the Victorian Era, or by Puttick & Simpson's pre-eminence as auctioneers of music, is difficult to say. And probably not necessary. Whatever the promptings, this was an unusual period in the history of the music trade.

Charles Humphries and William C. Smith examined most of the sources containing information about plate and copyright sales prior to 1831 in preparing their *Music Publishing in the British Isles . . . to the Middle of the Nineteenth Century.*[2] Here and there they note the transfer of such properties among music publishers—the earliest, Robert Bremner's purchase of some plates belonging to John Cox at a sale in 1764 (he bought others from Mrs. John Johnson in 1777 and from Mrs. Welcker in 1779). The authors also note Longman & Broderip's acquisition of John Johnson's stock and plates around 1778; the sale of "several thousand engraved plates"

This study, as well as a forthcoming monograph on Puttick & Simpson to be published in the series Detroit Studies in Music Bibliography, was greatly assisted by grants-in-aid from the American Council of Learned Societies and the Research Foundation of the State University of New York.

[1] The notable exception was M. Thomas & Sons' sale of George E. Blake's plates and printing tools in Philadelphia in 1871. See an account of the sale and facsimiles of several pages of the catalog in Richard J. Wolfe's *Early American Music Engraving and Printing* (Urbana: University of Illinois Press, 1980), 267-70.

[2] 2d ed. (New York: Barnes & Noble, 1970).

belonging to John Welcker advertised for 6 July 1789; another advertisement for a sale in 1797 of a stock of 12,000 engraved plates taken over from John Bland in 1795 by Lewis, Houston & Hyde; and the purchase by Thomas Preston of the plates belonging to H. Wright (some previously the properties of the Walshes and of Elizabeth Randall), as well as those belonging to Thomas Skillern, probably in 1803. Whether these transfers were effected by private sales or at auctions, Humphries and Smith do not say, though they do note that the Bremner sale in 1789 was advertised as an auction.

Copyrights of musical compositions, usually accompanied by the plates from which to print further copies, have, of course, been transferred from owner to owner in untold numbers over the years through private treaty. It was and is a common practice, but most of the records of such transactions are not readily available to us. Those in the files of publishers no longer active were probably destroyed or lost when their operations ceased.[3] Those in the files of firms still active are not open to view. Changes of copyright ownership and the negotiations surrounding those changes, therefore, are nearly impossible to document — except between 1831 and 1931, the principal period covered in this list. The public nature of plate and copyright auctions during these years (they were not by invitation; any passerby could step in and bid), the availability of printed catalogs from these sales (most of which show, in manuscript, names of the buyers and the prices they paid), and the extensive reports on these events carried in contemporary periodicals all combine to open a window on the trade in music copyrights — at least for one brief moment in time.

Most of the titles sold were "popular" works. The era of the largest and most frequent sales coincided with the ascendancy of the British music hall and a dramatic increase in the availability of cheap pianos for making music in the home. The sales were laden, consequently, with music-hall repertory, including royalty ballads, along with relatively easy, romantic works for solo piano, harp, or flute, and with part songs by the hundreds. There was also an abundance of lightweight chamber music put on the block, much of it obviously churned out in response to the immediate yearnings of the populace. And for this burgeoning group of amateurs, there were also tutors of every kind, for every level of proficiency. Some whose copyrights fetched astonishingly high prices at auction then remain in the catalogs of the publisher who bought them and still reap profits today.

Not everything consigned for sale was ephemeral. Good, classical works — a few titles, at least — were part of most publishers' catalogs, and a small number of publishers whose stock was dispersed at auction actually specialized in the works of the better composers.

---

[3] When they were not, they can yield remarkable information. See, for example, the use of documents found by Jeffrey Kallberg in the files of the defunct publisher Ashdown in his article "Chopin in the Marketplace: Aspects of the International Publishing Industry in the First Half of the Nineteenth Century: Part I — France and England," *Notes* 39 (1982-83): 535-69.

Puttick's sale in 1860 of some 63,000 plates consigned by Wessel & Co., for example, comprised hundreds of titles by Beethoven, Liszt, Mendelssohn, Mozart, and others and included, in one lot alone, the complete, authorized, English edition of Chopin's piano works.[4] Not surprisingly, the "popular" ditties fetched better prices, sometimes astronomical prices. Mascheroni's unbelievably popular *For All Eternity* was the pinnacle, bringing £2240 at a Puttick's sale on 7 November 1898.[5] Other examples include Watson's song "Anchored," bought by the publisher Blockley in 1894 for £1212; Arditi's "Il bacio" by B. Williams in 1871 for £716; Albrecht's "Der Rheinfall" by Blockley in 1883 for £407. Coote's piano solos were in great demand and usually commanded enormous prices; his "Prince Imperial Galop" and "Snow-Drift Galop" were knocked down in a 1875 sale for £900 and £561, respectively. Some sales liquidating the complete stock of a publisher's plates and copyrights brought far less than these single items; for example, the 267 lots comprising the business of George Emery & Co., sold on 18 February 1874, made only £370. Many unprofitable popular works went unsold (the plates were probably melted down by their disappointed owners to be re-used) or brought very small amounts. Compared to the prices fetched by Coote's galops and Mascheroni's ballads, the £177-11s which the publisher Ashdown paid for the seventy-one Chopin piano compositions in the Wessel sale stands forth as a transcendent bargain. They stayed in Ashdown's catalogs throughout the life of the firm.

Sales at auction of the copyright in printed *books* began in the earliest years of the eighteenth century. To bid for, or to consign, small parts of the ownership of a "good seller" was a routine matter in the book trade. Booksellers (most of whom in the eighteenth and early nineteenth centuries were also publishers) might well own fractional portions such as 3/52, 21/1500, or 7/60, etc., of a number of books. Lengthy lists of publishers'/booksellers' names in imprints from this period signal such "share books," as they are called.[6] The plates from which "share books" were printed, however, did not often enter into the sales; they appeared in few sales of copyrights except those for musical works. From 1807 to 1901, the well-known firm of Hodgson & Co. — to which Puttick's is sometimes thought analogous — auctioned off the copyrights to books, maps, journals, and the like, and on occasion the plates from which they were printed, but these sales hardly compare with Puttick's. The items were usually long

---

[4] Chopin's dealings with Wessel have been described recently by Jeffrey Kallberg in his excellent essay "Chopin in the Marketplace."

[5] This sum is more than half the amount which the dealer Quaritch paid for a Gutenberg Bible, on vellum, in its original binding, at the sale of the famous Ashburnham Library the same year!

[6] Terry Belanger offers a fascinating description of these practices in his classic dissertation, "Booksellers' Sales of Copyright: Aspects of the London Book Trade, 1718-1768" (Columbia University, 1970). See also his "From Bookseller to Publisher: Changes in the London Book Trade, 1750-1850," in *Bookselling and Book Buying,* ed. Richard G. Landon (Chicago: American Library Association, 1978), 7-16.

runs of periodicals, large series of books, and multi-volume sets, all vast in size and requiring prodigious numbers of plates. Sales of music copyrights and plates, conversely, involved hundreds of titles, mostly short pieces, each requiring as few as a half dozen to a dozen plates, some even less.

Auctions of music plates and copyrights were different from the usual auctions for other reasons. For one thing, the "collecting bug" was largely absent. No bidders sought items to add to their admired library at home or for later sale to other collectors. There was sharp competition in the sale room, but it lacked the character or romance of one masterful collector shrewdly bidding against another for a manuscript, an incunabulum, or a prime Shakespeare folio—described as the "most perfect known." It was business. Items on the block were simply merchandise, from which the fortunate buyer expected to realize a profit by re-publishing the work under his own style (imprint), or whose pewter plates, acquired cheaply, he would melt down for future re-use.

Publishers came and publishers went. Donajowski, for example, bought plates and copyrights steadily at Puttick's sales from 1875 until 1917. His own plates and copyrights were consigned to Puttick's in that year, after which the firm dropped from the list of active London publishers. Others, notably Ashdown, Augener, Chappell, Boosey, Cramer, and Schott, bought methodically throughout the years, adding—with perhaps more prudence than some other, now nearly-forgotten, firms—to already established successful catalogs. Their increasing dominance of the bidding at Puttick's sales can be traced in the sale catalogs, a marked set of which is in the British Library.[7] Even a casual study of Ashdown's purchases over a period of years reveals careful selection, mostly of durable works, to complement the copyrights the firm was buying directly from composers. Many of the titles patiently acquired in Puttick's rooms appear in Ashdown's famous *General Catalogue* of 1896, consisting of seven parts, divided by medium, with an *Addenda,* the whole totalling 593 densely-packed pages. The *Trois Petites Pièces* by Bachmann, purchased by Ashdown for £4-13s in the Cox sale 15 June 1890, is there priced at 6s, or separately at 2s apiece. Two immensely popular pieces, Warren's *To the Woods* and Pridham's *Battle March,* which were bought at the Brewer sale in December of the same year for £683 and £1022 respectively, are priced at 4s each.

Legal ownership of copyrights was apparently transferred entirely through the documentation of the auction. The registers at Stationers' Hall seem never to have been annotated to reflect a transfer of

---

[7] Puttick's earliest predecessor, Mr. Stewart, began business in 1794. The Puttick & Simpson name appeared on catalogs for 125 years—1846 to 1971. During that time it conducted over 10,500 sales of a wide range of materials. The set at the British Library fills 72 shelves, 14 full presses, and all contain the names of buyers and prices fetched in manuscript. Over 10 percent of the sales, some 1,650, was devoted exclusively to music materials (unlike most auctioneers, Puttick's almost never included music in sales with other kinds of properties—in "mixed" sales).

property. It is unlikely that "titles" or "deeds" on paper ever changed hands at a sale—at least no such documents are known to exist. Puttick's "Conditions of Sale," printed in each catalog, clearly imply that possession of the plates, receipts for their purchase, and the public nature of the sales made for sufficient entitlement.

The peak of activity in Puttick's rooms came during the last twenty-five years of the century. Coincident with it was the efflorescence of piracy which, the publishers cried, shrank dramatically the profits they were anticipating from best-sellers, such as Coote's many galops or tunes like Lane's hugely successful *Tatters*. Daily reports of "piratical copies seized" in raids on the "pirates' lairs" appeared in newspapers for many years leading up to the passage of the Copyright Act of 1906, which effectively put an end to the nefarious business. There seems no reason to doubt that the brazen entrepreneurs ground out hundreds of thousands of cheap lithographic reprints which were then marketed aggressively by a swarm of hawkers in the streets and marketplaces all over Britain. By the 1890s, the situation was chaotic, and getting worse. American piracies were being imported. Some British pirates grew bold enough to print catalogs.[8] Others offered to print any piece on customer's demand if more than 500 copies were ordered. Yet Parliament dallied. Despite this, however—and notwithstanding their loud public anguish over their impending doom—publishers continued to pay extraordinarily high prices at Puttick's auctions for the legal rights to pieces which were among the most frequently pirated.[9]

During any given ten-year period these sales attracted largely the same group of buyers. The "regulars" around 1890, for example, included the firms Agate, Beal, the two Jefferys, Hutchings, B. and J. Williams, Tuckwood, Donajowski, Hart, Ransford, Evans, Mathias & Strickland, Cannon, Beresford, Mocatta, and others. An atmosphere of collegiality must have prevailed, for they were old, and perhaps friendly, adversaries from previous bidding wars. An account of a visit to one of Puttick's plate sales printed in the *Musical*

---

[8] I have not been able to locate any original copies of these, but such lists are mentioned occasionally in the journals and newspapers of the day. For example, the *Musical Opinion & Music Trade Review* in March 1903 (p. 479) reprints an article from the *Daily Telegraph* which says, in part, "Piracy is so profitable that its agents draw up catalogues and send them broadcast." Again, in August of 1905 (pp. 829-30), the same journal reprints a letter from the Leeds Musicsellers' Association to the *Yorkshire Post* about a pirate whose premises were recently raided and stock destroyed but who "resumed operations almost immediately and now issues a catalogue offering 500 different piracies for sale." The *London & Provincial Music Trades Review* for 15 February 1903 reprinted a "List of Pirated Works . . . left by hawkers at houses in the Shepherd's Bush district." The titles number over a hundred and include such astonishly popular works as *The Toilers, Ora pro nobis, The Holy City, A Bird in a Gilded Cage, Tell Me, Pretty Maiden, Whisper and I Shall Hear,* and *The Stars and Stripes Forever* (Sousa's marches were popular with the pirates).

[9] This prolonged and acrimonious, but now curiously entertaining, "war" between the pirates and the publishers is documented and chronicled in the author's *Music Publishing, Copyright and Piracy in Victorian England* (London: Mansell, 1985).

Opinion and Music Trade Review in June of 1904 supports that notion. A publisher's "Traveller," whose normal occupation was representing his firm to music sellers in the provinces, wrote to say that he

this day, wandered out of his usual track and, lo and behold, found himself in Eldorado, — on the veritable Tom Tiddler's ground.

I regarded up to this occasion the assertion that £100 notes actually existed . . . as a sort of after-dinner jest by those funny people who delight you with truthful anecdotes of mermaids, sea-serpents, and disinterested friends. . . . I profess my belief now that sundry and several persons actually do possess a hundred pounds; moreover that there exists more than one person who can and did spend that sum and more.

I found myself in Leicester Square and in Messrs. Puttick & Simpson's sale-rooms one day while the copyrights of Messrs. Hutchings & Romer were being sold and formed one of a very select group then and there assembled to assist in the programme, part of which was to quaff good old sherry and smoke some very decent cigars, and bid some very extraordinary prices per plate for aforesaid copyrights. Your wandering and eccentric Traveller entered very cordially into the arrangement, and did his best to oblige the company with the cigars and sherry, and smiled his benignest smile on both the bidder and bidded at, the latter being Mr. Simpson, who rather seemed to be enjoying the occasion. The first sensation of the sale was when Blumenthal's song, "The Requital," was offered and knocked down to Mr. Hutchings for 42s per plate, making its cost £67 4s.

Recovering a little from the "Requital" flutter, shadows crossed our path. "Shadows" is a song by Gibbs, which is so popular that I did not know of its existence; but somebody knew something of it for it was knocked down for £6 10s per plate (total £39).

After a page or two of the catalogue was disposed of at comparatively mild prices came the big thing, "The Choristers' Album" (720 ½ plates) a series of part songs, be it remembered, which sell to the public for a few pence per copy. After a spirited competition, Mr. Littleton (Novello & Co.) came off victor with £2 per plate (£1440). Who would not be a music publisher. "Lurline" — bright sparkling "Lurline" — to my surprise only fetched 8s per plate, the number of plates possibly being the cause; 1658 plates at 8s however telling up to the respectable figure of £763 given by Mr. Hutchings.

I only waited for one more sensation, and that was brought about by Mattei's Grand Waltz, comprising, with arrangements, 46 plates. This brought £9 10s per plate (£437)! This went to Mr. B. Williams, of Paternoster Row. . . . It was amusing to take note of the individualities of the bidders. Mr. Hutchings simply looked straight in his catalogue, and gently murmured his bid. Mr. Romer, also [his previous partner], was intent on his catalogue but spoke loudly. Mr. Littleton merely nodded; his were expressive nods, worth a hundred pounds apiece. The Brothers Mullen (who bought for the B. Williams business) were vigorous and enthusiastic. Mr. Tuckwood made his bids in a hurry. Friend Donajowski was in an exalted frame of mind. Paxton bid against himself, and bought the piece he was bidding for. Mr. Smallwood, acting for J. Williams, nodded his head sideways and most emphatically; while Mr. Ashdown frequently took up the running when the bids slackened, and it was all odds that he meant having the lot at any price when he once began to bid. . . .

We are fortunate to have "Traveller's" description of such sales—the kind of music up for sale and the extraordinary prices some of it fetched (many incunabula in book auctions of the time were bringing far less than "bright sparkling *Lurline*"), the company present and its manners, and—what is sorely missing from today's sale rooms—"good old sherry" and "very decent cigars."

*   *   *   *   *

When the fashions of the Victorians changed—the traditional British music hall, for example, was gone by about 1918—the sales of plates and copyrights ebbed. Only twelve were staged after 1910, and the number of plates unsold and the low prices for the others betoken waning interest. Musical tastes were improved—the middle-class was increasingly better-educated—but there were probably more tangible reasons. Gramophones (some of which began to show up in Puttick's musical instrument sales by the 1920s), an incipient movie industry, and radio broadcasting brought the populace potent new modes of entertainment. The dance hall and the "revue" diluted, then captured, the music hall audiences, and after 1910 American ragtime was the rage. The public sale of plates and copyrights stopped in 1931, but we can suppose that the principals, the buyers and sellers, merely stepped off stage, out of view, and continued transactions. The era of privately negotiated sales of copyrights by hustling literary and musical agents had dawned, and with it was swept away this short-lived phenomenon, their sale in public.

*   *   *   *   *

The list of sales is arranged chronologically by sale date and is followed by two alphabetically ordered indexes. The first sets out auctioneers other than Puttick's, whose sales are documented. The second is by consignor so that, for example, the several sales of Duff & Stewart's plates and copyrights can be located.

Citations in the list describe seven numbered elements. No. 1 names the consignor (they are all music publishers) with their addresses at the time of the sale. No. 2 identifies the auctioneer. Catalogs exist for all but a few of the sales listed, and no. 3 gives locations—and in many cases provides libraries' pressmarks—for those I have seen.[10] The Puttick & Simpson catalogs in the British Library are, of course, the most important and informative copies of those catalogs available because they are interleaved with sheets bearing buyers' names and prices fetched. If any catalogs elsewhere furnish the same information, I have so indicated. Still in no. 3, following the location of existing copies, I have transcribed a brief portion of the title page statement. These are occasionally enlightening, in most cases useful, and in a few entertaining. The number of lots in the sale is recorded after this title.

Sales of plates and copyrights were considered newsworthy by several contemporary journals, and no. 4 includes citations of this literature. The *Musical Opinion and Music Trade Review* and the *London and Provincial Music Trades Review* are indicated by the abbreviations *MO&MTR* and *L&PMTR*. The titles of any other journals mentioned are spelled out in full.

The buyers listed in no. 5 for some sales is not complete but a selection of those most active in the bidding. (It is worth noting how many of these names turn up, also, in the index to consignors!) For some sales buyers are not given, even though their names were recorded in the catalog cited. Following the buyers' names is usually the total amount realized by the plates in a sale, when such information was available and seemed pertinent.[11]

Selling the properties of some firms required more than one sale—sometimes by more than a single auction house—and when that was the case, readers are referred to the dates of other sales in no. 6. If the printed stock derived from the plates was sold in a separate sale, this too has been noted with its date and auctioneer.

No. 7, in some entries, contains occasional comments about the astonishing prices made by a number of compositions. In a number of entries there is no need for points 6 and 7, and they are omitted. Two other abbreviations are used frequently:

n&p   identifies a catalog in which buyers' names and prices fetched are recorded;

b.i.   means "bought in" by the consignor or auctioneer, either to prevent the lot going to another bidder for less than the consignor considered fair, or because the bids did not reach a "reserve" price placed on the lot.

---

[10] Sigla are those used in the *Répertoire internationale des sources musicales.*

[11] Lengthy lists of titles sold, their purchasers' names, and the prices they fetched at most of Puttick & Simpson's plate sales are included in my complete bibliography of the firm's music sales, forthcoming in the series Detroit Studies in Music Bibliography (Detroit: Information Coordinators).

1803 May 24-27

1. Consignor: DR. ARNOLD.

2. Auction by Mr. White.

3. Catalog, US-R and US-Wc: *Catalogue of the Extensive and Entire Musical Library of the late . . . also many Thousands of Engraved Plates, Copyrights. . . .* Plates, day 4, lot 153: "All the plates of Dr. Arnold's edition of Handel's work, in Numbers of upwards eight Thousand, a particular account of which will be produced at the Sale"; lots 107-32: "Plates and Copies of Dr. Arnold's Works."

4. Lit.: not found.

5. Buyers of plates not recorded in either catalog cited.

1812 December 18

1. Consignor unnamed.

2. Auction by Mr. Stewart, at his Great Room, 194 Piccadilly.

3. Catalog, compiler, with some Ms. annotations but without n&p: *Catalogue of the Works of Handel . . . together with the Plates of all Handel's Celebrated Oratorios. . . .* Total of 3130 plates, lots 81-103.

4. Lit.: not found.

5. Buyers not recorded in catalog cited.

1824 September 20-21

1. Consignor: WHITAKER & CO., MESSRS.

2. Auction by Mr. Musgrave.

3. Catalog, GB-Ob, pressmark 7897.d.13(7): *Catalogue of the Genuine Stock in Trade of . . . Engraved Music Plates with the Very Valuable Copyrights Attached Thereto, Comprising all the Favorite Compositions of Messrs. Whitaker and Reeve. . . .* 656 lots (plates of W's works, lots 45-81, many more items; of R's works, lots 82-107).

4. Lit.: not found.

5. Buyers not recorded in catalog cited.

1826 December 13-15

1. Consignor unnamed.

2. Auction by Mr. Musgrave.

3. Catalog, GB-Ob, pressmark 7897.d.13(11): *Catalogue of a Choice Collection of Vocal and Instrumental Music . . . Many Hundred Engraved Plates of Favorite Modern Composers. . . .* 290 lots.

4. Lit.: not found.

5. Buyers not recorded in catalog cited.

1831 June 21-22

1. Consignor: VERNON, CHARLES.

2. Auction by Mr. Watson.

3. Catalog, US-NYp: *Valuable and Genuine Stock in Trade of . . . Engraved Music Plates, Violins* [etc.]. Plates, lots 167-77.

4. Lit.: not found.

5. Buyers not recorded in catalog cited.

1831 July 1-5

1. Consignor: COGGINS, J., late of Piccadilly.

2. Auction by Mr. Wheatley.

3. Catalog, GB-Lbl, pressmark S.C.W.17.(10) with n&p: *Collection of Books in History, Biography* [etc.]: *A Small Collection of Books on Music, and the Copyrights and Copper Plates. . . .* Plates, lots 1033-70.

4. Lit.: not found.

5. Buyers: Green, and several others.

1832 January 24-25

1. Consignor: BARNETT AND CO. — A DEALER, REMOVED FROM DEAN STREET.

2. Auction by Mr. Watson.

3. Catalog, compiler: *Choice Collection of Modern Music, including the Printed Stock of the Late Barnett and Co. The Engraved Music Plates, with Copyrights, and Stock in Trade of a Dealer, Removed from Dean Street. . . .* Plates, lots 148-52 only.

4. Lit.: not found.

5. Buyers not recorded in catalog cited.

1. Consignor unnamed.

2. Auction by Mr. Watson.

3. Catalog, compiler and US-NYp: *Stock in Trade of Engraved Music Plates, Printed Music, and Musical Instruments.* . . . 200 lots.

4. Lit.: not found.

5. Buyers not recorded in catalog cited.

1832 September 19-21

1. Consignor unnamed.

2. Auction by Mr. Watson.

3. Catalog, US-NYp: *Musical Library of the Late Sanderson . . . and the Valuable Plates and Copyrights of the Late Mr. Jacob's National Psalmody and Selection of Classical Compositions.* . . . 397 lots.

4. Lit.: not found.

5. Buyers not recorded in catalog cited.

1832 October 10-11

1. Consignor: MR. FARN.

2. Auction by Mr. Watson.

3. Catalog, compiler and US-NYp, no n or p: *Genuine Stock in Trade of the Late . . . Quantity of Printed Music . . . Plates and Copyrights.* Plates, lots 143-58.

4. Lit.: not found.

5. Buyers not recorded in catalog cited.

1834 February 19-22

1. Consignor: KNAPTON, PHILIP (?).

2. Auction by Mr. Watson.

3. Catalog, compiler: *Assemblage of Music, including the Library of Music of . . . the Compositions of the Most Eminent Masters . . . the Remaining Stock in Trade, including the Engraved Music Plates with Copyrights Attached to a Portion of Them.* . . . Plates, lots 526-42 (mainly works by Knapton).

4. Lit.: not found.

5. Buyers not recorded in catalog cited.

1834 March 4

1. Consignor unnamed [T. LINDSAY?].

2. Auction by Mr. Watson (at Town's Room).

3. Catalog, compiler, without n or p: *Valuable Stock in Trade of Engraved Music Plates, Principally Copyrights, Printed Music . . . by Direction of Mr. T. Lindsay. . . .* Plates, lots 1-54C.

4. Lit.: not found.

5. Buyers not recorded in catalog cited.

1835 January 13-17

1. Consignor: CLEMENTI, MUZIO, & CO.

2. Auction by Mr. Watson.

3. Catalog, compiler, with some n&p: *Very Valuable Stock in Trade of the Late Firm of . . . Upwards of 40,000 Engraved Music Plates, a Great Portion of Which are Copyright . . . Unpublished Mss. . . .* Plates, lots 1-712.

4. Lit.: not found.

5. Buyers: Purday, Keith, Paine, Chappell, Metzler, Green, Monro & May, Cocks, D'Almaine, et al.

6. Watson conducted sales of Clementi's printed stock 12 January 1836, 26 April 1836, 12 July 1836, and 25 October 1836.

1836 June 17-18, 21-22

1. Consignor: PAINE & HOPKINS, MESSRS.

2. Auction by Mr. Watson.

3. Catalog, compiler without n or p: *Valuable Stock in Trade . . . 12,000 Engraved Music Plates, with the Valuable Copyrights Attached Thereto, Printed Music . . . Instruments. . . .* Plates.

4. Lit.: not found.

5. Buyers: Humphries & Smith note that some of Paine & Hopkins' plates and copyrights were purchased by Robt. Cocks & Co. in 1836. This sale?

6. Watson also sold the printed stock and instruments of the firm, 21 June 1836 and 6 July 1836.

A CATALOGUE

OF THE VERY

VALUABLE STOCK IN TRADE

OF THE LATE FIRM OF

MUZIO CLEMENTI & CO.

COMPRISING UPWARDS OF

40,000

Engraved Music Plates,

A great Portion of which are Copyright.

In the Catalogue will be found among other highly popular Works, CLEMENTI'S INTRODUCTION TO THE ART OF PLAYING ON THE PIANO FORTE; APPENDIX TO DITTO; GRADUS AD PARNASSUM, 3 vols.; PRACTICAL HARMONY, 4 vols.; HAYDN'S CREATION, SEASONS, 12 SYMPHONIES, and MOZART'S DITTO, ADAPTED BY CLEMENTI; VOCAL HARMONY, EDITED BY HORSLEY, 6 vols.; WRAGG'S FLUTE PRECEPTOR; COOKE'S SINGING TUTOR; AND OTHER TREATISES; NICHOLSON'S LE BOUQUET, 24 Nos.; SELECT AIRS, 12 Nos.; FANTASIAS, 13 Nos.; SOCIAL PIECES, 6 Nos.; MOZART'S MELODIES, 3 vols.; MELODIES OF DIFFERENT NATIONS, &c. &c. and

UNPUBLISHED MANUSCRIPTS.

THE INSTRUMENTS,

CONSIST OF

Clarinets, Flutes, by Nicholson, &c. Fifes, Flageolets, Drums, Tambourines,

Royal Kent Bugles, Harper's Improved; Captain Rigge's Bugles; Cavalry Bugles and Trumpets,

Violins (one by ROGERIUS), *Tenors, and Violoncellos, Canterburies, What Nots; Flute, Violin, Guitar, and other Cases,*

ONE HUNDRED & TWENTY REAMS OF PRINTING DEMY,

Reeds, Mouth Pieces, Bags, Tuning Hammers, and all other articles connected with the Trade,

Which will be Sold by Auction, by

MR. WATSON,

AT MR. TOWN'S ROOM, 26, CONDUIT STREET,

BOND STREET,

On TUESDAY, JANUARY 13, 1835, & following Days,

AT ELEVEN FOR TWELVE O'CLOCK PRECISELY,

May be Viewed on the Monday preceding and Mornings of Sale, Catalogues, price 1s. 6d. each, at the place of Sale, the Auction Mart, and at the Offices of

MR. WATSON,

Auctioneer, House Agent, and Appraiser,

79, CHEAPSIDE.

The printed music stock of Clementi
—much of it probably struck from these plates—
was auctioned by Mr. Watson 12 January 1836.

1. Consignor unnamed.

2. Auction by Mr. Watson.

3. Catalog, compiler without n or p: *New Vocal and Instrumental Music, a Number of Engraved Music Plates, Together with Two Libraries* [and Instruments]. . . . 200 lots.

4. Lit.: not found.

5. Buyers not recorded in catalog cited.

1844 November 1-2

1. Consignor unnamed (G. H. AND J. C. WHITE?).

2. Auction by Mr. Fletcher.

3. Catalog at GB-Ob, pressmark 2591.d.3*(46), no n or p: *Stock in Trade of Messrs. G. H. and J. C. White . . . Also Musical Instruments . . . Together with the Engraved Music Plates, and the Usual Miscellaneous Items of a Music Seller's Stock.* . . . Plates, lots 430-42.

4. Lit.: not found.

5. Buyers not recorded in catalog cited.

1847 April 1

1. Consignor: CHALLONER, NEVILLE BUTLER (Prof. of the Harp).

2. Auction by Puttick & Simpson.

3. Catalog, GB-Lbl, pressmark S.C.P.2(8), with n&p: *Collection of Music . . . Also Above 500 Engraved Music Plates* [principally works for the harp].

4. Lit.: not found.

5. Buyers: most lots to Watts.

1848 date unknown

1. Consignor: WALKER & SON.

2. Auctioneer unknown.

3. Catalog, GB-Lbl, pressmark 7807.d.9.(23), but lost during World War II: *Catalogue of the Valuable Music Plates and . . . Copyrights, Belonging to the Firm of. . . .*

4. Lit.: not found.

5. Buyers unknown.

6. Puttick's conducted two sales of the printed stock of George Walker (the same firm?), 3 July 1851 and 18 July 1851.

1848 April 14

1. Consignor: GREEN, JOHN (33, Soho Square).

2. Auction by Puttick & Simpson.

3. Catalog, GB-Lbl, pressmark S.C.P.6(8): *Portion of the Stock of* [Part II] *Engraved Music Plates, Many Thousand in Number.*

4. Lit.: not found.

5. Buyers: none, the sale was "withdrawn"; see 6 June 1848.

1848 June 6

1. Consignor: GREEN, JOHN (33, Soho Square).

2. Auction by Puttick & Simpson.

3. Catalog, GB-Lbl, pressmark S.C.P.6(14): *Portion of the Stock of* [Part III] *Many Thousand Engraved Music Plates.*

4. Lit.: not found.

5. Buyers: none, for again the sale apparently did not take place. Cf. 21 March 1849.

1849 March 21-22

1. Consignor: GREEN, JOHN (33, Soho Square).

2. Auction by Puttick & Simpson.

3. Catalog, GB-Lbl, pressmark S.C.P.9(11), with n&p: *Stock of* [Part IV], *6,000 Engraved Music Plates. . . .* Plates, lots 1-103, 168-264.

4. Lit.: not found.

5. Buyers: Williams, Walden, Watts, Pedder. Total, £259-47d.

6. Puttick's conducted sales of the printed stock 27 March 1848, 9 June 1848, and another of plates and copyrights 7 January 1852.

1. Consignor: MR. PRESTON (of Dean Street) — [COVENTRY & CO.].

2. Auction by Puttick & Simpson.

3. Catalog, GB-Lbl, pressmark S.C.P.13(3), with n&p: *Nearly 2,000 Engraved Music Plates and Copyrights, a Portion of the Stock of the Late Preston. . . .* 406 lots.

4. Lit.: may be the sale referred to by Humphries & Smith in their *Music Publishing in the British Isles* in which, they say, Novello bought some plates from the stock of Coventry & Hellier.[1]

5. Buyers: B. Williams, Cocks, Lonsdale, Novello, et al. Total, £230-5s.

1849 December 22

1. Consignor: CHAULIEU, CHARLES, et al.

2. Auction by Puttick & Simpson.

3. Catalog, GB-Lbl, pressmark S.C.P.13(5), with n&p: *The Remaining Printed Stock, the Original Mss. with the Copyrights, and the Engraved Plates of the Late Eminent Pianist's Works. . . .* Plates, lots 231-42.

4. Lit.: not found.

5. Buyers: plates unsold; offered again, 9 August 1850, q.v.

1850 August 9-10

1. Consignor: CHAULIEU, CHARLES, et al.

2. Auction by Puttick & Simpson.

3. Catalog, GB-Lbl, pressmark S.C.P.16(6), with n&p: . . . *The Remaining Printed Stock, the Unpublished Mss. with the Copyrights Thereto, and the Engraved Music Plates of the Unpublished Works of the Late. . . .* Plates, lots 382-417.

4. Lit.: not found.

5. Buyers: White, Purday, Etherington, et al.

---

[1] Charles Humphries and William C. Smith, *Music Publishing in the British Isles . . . to the Middle of the Nineteenth Century,* 2d ed. (New York: Barnes & Noble, 1970).

1. Consignor: A WEST END MUSIC PUBLISHER.

2. Auction by Puttick & Simpson.

3. Catalog, GB-Lbl, pressmark S.C.P.20(7), with n&p: *First Portion of the Stock of the Late George Walker . . . 500 Engraved Music Plates with the Copyrights Therein from the Catalogue of a West End Music Publisher. . . .*

4. Lit.: Humphries & Smith, *Music Publishing in the British Isles,* note a sale in 1851 at which Novello bought 4780 plates of sacred works from the stock of Charles Coventry — perhaps this sale.

5. Buyers: Andrews, Holloway, Carey, Hopkins, Dean, Duncombe, et al. Total, £176-15s.

1852 January 7

1. Consignor: GREEN, JOHN (33, Soho Square).

2. Auction by Puttick & Simpson.

3. Catalog, GB-Lbl, pressmark S.C.P.23(2), with n&p: *2,500 Engraved Music Plates, with Copyrights* [Part V] *of the Stock of.* . . . Plates, lots 1-187.

4. Lit.: not found.

5. Buyers: Webb, B. Williams, Watts, Deacon, et al. Total, £162-16s.

6. Other sales by Puttick's, 14 April 1848, 6 June 1848, and 21 March 1849, q.v.

1852 March 5

1. Consignor: KEEGAN, JOHN, et al.

2. Auction by Puttick & Simpson.

3. Catalog, GB-Lbl, pressmark S.C.P.23(12), with n&p: *Collection of Music, including the Stock in Trade of . . . Comprising the Engraved Music Plates of his Copyright Publications.* . . . Plates, lots 1-523.

4. Lit.: not found.

5. Buyers: Broome, Cocks, Tansley, Lonsdale, et al.

1852 June 23

1. Consignor: [MR PEACHEY], et al.

2. Auction by Puttick & Simpson.

3. Catalog, GB-Lbl, pressmark S.C.P.26(3), with n&p: *Catalogue of the Stock of the Late Mr. Phillips; also 2,500 Plates from the Catalogue of a London Publisher.* . . . Plates, lots 1-111.

4. Lit.: not found.

5. Buyers: Cocks, B. Williams. Realized £148-2s-11d.

1852 December 7-8

1. Consignor: JOHANNIG & CO., et al.

2. Auction by Puttick & Simpson.

3. Catalog, GB-Lbl, pressmark S.C.P.28(6), with n&p: *Valuable Modern Stock, 3000 Engraved Music Plates, Stock of Printed Music.* Plates, lots 1-132.

4. Lit.: not found.

5. Buyers: Watts and Webb, but most bought by Broome. Total, £143.

1853 January 19-21

1. Consignor: OLLIVIER, CHARLES.

2. Auction by Mr. J. Fuller.

3. Catalog, compiler, without n&p: *Whole of the Valuable Stock of Printed Music, Plates, Copyrights, etc., by all the Modern Composers.* . . . Plates, lots 82-226, 277-327.

4. Lit.: not found.

5. Buyers not recorded in catalog cited.

1853 August 17-18

1. Consignor: "A LONDON PUBLISHER" (CALKIN & BUDD?).

2. Auction by Puttick & Simpson.

3. Catalog, GB-Lbl, pressmark S.C.P.32(9): *1,900 Engraved Music Plates from the Catalogue of a London Publisher.* . . . Plates, lots 138-218.

4. Lit.: not found.

5. Buyers of plates: Duncombe, et al. Total, £112.

1853 December 20-22

1. Consignor: DUNCOMBE, JOHN (17, Holborn Hill).

2. Auction by Puttick & Simpson.

3. Catalog, GB-Lbl, pressmark S.C.P.33(10), with n&p: *Valuable and Extensive Stock of the Late . . . Plates, Engravings, Copyrights, Stock. . . .* Plates, lots 555-661.

4. Lit.: not found.

5. Buyers: White, B. Williams, Jefferys, Deacon, Watts, et al.

1855 November 16-17

1. Consignor not identified.

2. Auction by Puttick & Simpson.

3. Catalog, GB-Lbl, pressmark S.C.P.43(2), with n&p: *Valuable Collection of Music . . . Engraved Plates and Copyrights of Several Modern Compositions.* . . . Plates, lots 425-71, with some lithographic stones.

4. Lit.: not found.

5. Buyers: Cocks, "P," et al. Plates realized £100.

1858 March 17

1. Consignor unidentified.

2. Auction by Puttick & Simpson.

3. Catalog, GB-Lbl, pressmark S.C.P.53(4), with n&p: *Valuable Miscellaneous Music . . . a Small Collection of Engraved Plates with Copyrights.* . . . Plates, lots 331-55.

4. Lit.: not found.

5. Buyers: Roberts, et al. Plates realized small amounts.

1859 September 1

1. Consignor: EWER & CO. (Oxford Street).

2. Auction by Puttick & Simpson.

3. Catalog, GB-Lbl, pressmark S.C.P.62(9), with n&p: *Considerable Portion of the Stock of . . . 12,000 Engraved Music Plates of Important Copyright works* [with some lithographic stones and titles]. . . . Plates, lots 1-681.

4. Lit.: not found.

5. Buyers: Ollivier, Augener, Metzler, J. Williams, Novello, Addison, Schott, et al. Realized £1414-19s.

283.18.8

Lot.	Title.	Author.	No. of Plates.	
160	*Pirate's Bride ...	Gould ...	6	
	*Queen of the starry night	Jolly ...	6—12	— 18. —
161	*Roses bloom in summer only	S. Glover ...	6	
	*Ditto, Guitar accompaniment	Luigi	3	
	*Ditto, Cornet Solo ...		1—10	7.10.—
162	*Over the dancing billows	J. W. Cherry .	6	
	*Read that sacred Book	S. Glover ...	6—12	
163	*Reindeer (no title plate)	J. Smith ...	4	
	*Rose had been wash'd ...	Webbe ...	5	
	*Red cross Knight, as a Song	Arnold ...	7—16	
164	*Rejoice greatly	Handel ...	7	
	*Rose sweetly blooming	Spohr ...	6	
	*Ditto, Guitar accompaniment	Luigi	3—16	2.10.6
165	Recollection ...	Haydn ...	5	
	*Rule Britannia ...	Arne ...	2	
	Remember, Love, remember	Parke ...	5	
	*Sapling Oak ...	Storace ...	8—15	1.1.3
166	Scots wha hae ...	Scotch ...	2	
	Sympathy	Haydn ...	3	
	She never told her love	Ditto ...	2	
	Sprig of Shillelah ...	Irish ...	2	
	Slighted Love ...	Horn ...	6—15	
167	*Stars of the Garden (Illustrated)	S. Glover ...	6	
	*Ditto, Guitar accompaniment	Luigi	3	
	*Ditto, for two voices	Wilson ...	6	
	*Ditto, Piano	C. Muller ...	6—21	6.16.6
	(250 Title Sheets at 20s. per 100.)			
168	*Say not love is like a rose	J. W. Hobbs ...	6	
	*Ditto, Guitar accompaniment	Dipple ...	3—9	2.2.9
169	*Sailor's Home ...	E. J. Westrop.	6	
	*Say not this heart is a rover	Linda ...	4	
	*Sing with me (Song of the lute)	Keller ...	5—15	1.2.6
170	*Sing the old song again	G. Barker ...	7	
	*Story of the heart ...	Ditto ...	6—13	2.12.—
171	*Still his image ...	Weber ...	3	
	*Starry eyes (Il Balen) ...	Verdi ...	4	
	*Sweet home fare thee well	W. Ball ...	5—12	— 16.—
172	*Summer Dew, in E ...	G. Barker ...	6	
	*Ditto in D	Ditto ...	5	
	*Summer Dreams ...	J. E. Loder ...	6—17	6.7.6
173	*Swiss Peasant ...	G. T. May ...	6	
	*Sunbeam and the Wave	Shrivall ...	6	
	*Summer Moon ...	Arnold ...	6—18	1.4.—

316.19.10

158

315.19.10

Lot.	Title.	Author.	No. of Plates.	
174	*Sing me the songs you used to sing.	S. Glover ...	6	
	*Ditto, Guitar accompaniment	Luigi	3	
	*Sing no more that song of gladness..	S. Glover ...	6—15	2.4.6
175	*Summer Friends ...	J. W. Cherry .	6	
	*Ditto, Guitar accompaniment	Luigi	3—9	2.5.—
176	*Speak not lightly ...	J. W. Cherry .	6	
	*Ditto, Guitar accompaniment	Luigi	3—9	1.19.6
177	*Sea Nymph's call, in A flat	J. W. Cherry.	7	
	*Ditto in G	Ditto ...	6—13	3.5.—
178	*Sunny Smiles ...	S. Glover ...	6	
	*This bright world of our's	Ditto ...	6—12	6.18.—
178A	*Three favourite Songs ...	Kucken		
	No. 1. Those bright black eyes	...	7	
	„ 2. Thou lovely Maid	...	3	
	„ 3. We meet by chance	...	4	
	Title	...	1—15	
179	*That dreadful Piano next door, words by	J. Stonehouse .	7	
	*Then Love come to me	A. Lee ...	7—14	
180	*Thy gentle voice ...	J. Wittenberg .	6	
	*Ditto, Guitar accompaniment	Dipple ...	3	
	*Trumpet's Voice (Mrs. Hemans)	A. D. Roche...	12—21	1.8.—
181	*Total Eclipse ...	Handel ...	3	
	*Thou that tellest glad	Ditto ...	7	
	*Tears such as tender	Ditto ...	3	
	*Thou soft flowing Avon	Arne ...	5—18	1.7.—
182	*The holy Sabbath Morn	F. Wallerstein.	5	
	*Sweet Sabbath Eve	Ditto ...	6	
	*Flowers amid the corn	Ditto ...	5	
	*Peace be still	T. Arnold ...	5—21	4.19.9
183	*Visions of happy days	G. Barker ...	6	
	*Ditto, two Voices		6	
	*Ditto, Guitar accompaniment	Dipple ...	3	
	*Ditto, Concertina and Piano	Bertini ...	4—19	4.19.9
184	*What's become of all the money	W. Ball ...	6	
	*Thou whose tuneful Voice	Ditto ...	5	
	*Why Mamma should I not love	Miss Single ...	6—17	.19.8
185	*'Tis home where the heart is (Air le Desir) words by	J. Young ...	3	
	*'Twas a sweet voice ...	S. Nelson ...	5	
	*Tho' with ease thou say'st forget	T. H. Bayly...	6—14	1.8.—
186	*'Twas within a mile ...	Scotch ...	5	
	*Wanderer, in E flat	Schubert ...	6	
	*Way to be happy	Verdi ...	5—16	1.16.

350.10.0

174

Pages from the catalog of Messrs. Foster's auction of 6,000 plates and copyrights 30 April 1860.

7. Heller's *24 Preludes,* op. 81 made £15 (Witt); Attwood's *Cathedral Music,* 243 plates, £24-6s (Novello); Spohr's *Jessonda,* 210 plates, £31-19s (Novello).

1860 April 30

1. Consignor: HOLLOWAY, THOMAS (5, Hanway Street).

2. Auction by Messrs. Foster.

3. Catalog, compiler, with n&p: *A Catalogue of Musical Copyrights and Plates (about 6,000).* . . . 284 lots.

4. Lit.: not found.

5. Buyers: Blockley, J. Williams, D'Alcorn, Lonsdale, B. Williams, Brewer, Metzler, Chappell, Purday.

6. Other sales: Puttick's of plates, 6 July 1864, and of printed stock, 30 March 1868, q.v.

1860 June 19-22

1. Consignor: MAY, HARRY (11, Holborn Bars).

2. Auction by Mr. Hatch (Old Bond St.).

3. Catalog, compiler (Z. T. Purday's unmarked copy): *The Stock-In Trade, about 14,000 Music Plates, Valuable Copyrights and Printed Music of.* . . . 900 lots.

4. Lit.: not found.

5. Buyers not recorded in catalog cited.

1860 July 2-3

1. Consignor: PURDAY, ZENAS TRIVETT (45, High Holborn).

2. Auction by Puttick & Simpson.

3. Catalog, GB-Lbl, pressmark S.C.P.67(6), with n&p: *Stock of Purday . . . Engraved Music Plates, Copyrights, Printed Stock.* . . . 416 lots.

4. Lit.: not found.

5. Buyers: G. Williams, Brewer, J. Williams, Metzler, Jefferys, Blockley, et al.

1860 July 23

1. Consignor: WESSEL & CO. (Hanover Square).

2. Auction by Puttick & Simpson.

3. Catalog, GB-Lbl, pressmark S.C.P.68(2), with n&p: *Entire, Very Extensive, Important and Valuable Stock of Plates and Copyrights of . . . (retiring), including about 63,000 Engraved Music Plates of Standard Writers. . . .* 2370 lots.

4. Lit.: not found.

5. Buyers: Ashdown, Augener, Brewer, Ewer, Metzler, Wheatstone, J. Williams, et al. Ashdown was principal buyer. Realized £7634-10s.

7. See here text and footnote 3, p. 224.

1861 March 26

1. Consignor: EMINENT MUSIC PUBLISHER [i.e., COCKS & CO.]

2. Auction by Puttick & Simpson.

3. Catalog, GB-Lbl, pressmark S.C.P.73(4), with n&p: *Some Surplus Stock of . . . including 2,000 Engraved Music Plates and 100 Original Mss. of Valuable Copyright Works. . . .* Plates, lots 1-274.

4. Lit.: not found.

5. Principal buyers: Ashdown and Ollivier. Many "passed" plates and very low prices throughout.

1862 May 21

1. Consignor: TOLKIEN, MR. (of 28, King William Street).

2. Auction by Mr. C. Kelly (Charles St., Berners St.).

3. Catalog, compiler, without n&p: *Sale of 5000 Music Plates, by Order of . . . Valuable Copyrights and Non Copyright Works. . . .* 187 lots.

4. Lit.: not found.

5. Buyers not recorded in catalog cited.

1862 June 24

1. Consignor: CAMPBELL, JOHN (53, New Bond Street).

2. Auction by Puttick & Simpson.

3. Catalog, GB-Lbl, pressmark S.C.P.81(8), with n&p: *Valuable Stock of . . . above 6,000 Engraved Music Plates of Copyright Works.*

4. Lit.: not found.

5. Buyers: Augener, Blockley, Brewer, Ashdown, Metzler, J. Williams, et al. Many lots b.i. Realized £926-7s.

7. Shelton's *Oh, Dear, What Can the Matter Be?* made £1-16s (Blockley); *The Mother's Assistant at the Pianoforte,* £9-15s (Ashdown).

1863 January 28

1. Consignor: HEDGLEY, JOHN (Ebury Street, Pimlico).

2. Auction by Puttick & Simpson.

3. Catalog, GB-Lbl, pressmark S.C.P.85(2), with n&p: *Stock of Music . . . Engraved Music Plates, Together with Instruments. . . .* Plates, lots 928-65.

4. Lit.: not found.

5. Buyers: Novello, Broome, Lonsdale, et al.

1863 August 31

1. Consignor: PURDAY, THOMAS E. (Oxford Street).

2. Auction by Puttick & Simpson.

3. Catalog, GB-Lbl, pressmark S.C.P.89(7), with n&p: *Engraved Music Plates of Valuable Copyright Works, the Stock of. . . .* 402 lots.

4. Lit.: not found.

5. Buyers: Ashdown, Augener, Emery, Brewer, Novello, Ollivier, Metzler, Ollivier, et al. Total, £665-15s.

7. Hobb's *Captive Greek Girl* fetched £260 (J. Williams).

1863 December 3-5

1. Consignor unidentified.

2. Auction by Puttick & Simpson.

3. Catalog, GB-Lbl, pressmark S.C.P.90(6), with n&p: *Musical Library of the Late Edward Taylor . . . Rare Madrigals . . . also about 2,000 Engraved Music Plates* [lots 1105-48] *including Copyrights of Dr. Spohr.*

4. Lit.: not found.

5. Buyers are recorded in catalog cited.

1864 May 18

1. Consignor unidentified.

2. Auction by Puttick & Simpson.

3. Catalog, GB-Lbl, pressmark S.C.P.94(4), with n&p: *Library of the Late Walmisley . . . 1,000 Engraved Music Plates with Copyrights of Popular Works. . . .* Plates, lots 369-411.

4. Lit.: not found.

5. Buyers: most plates went unsold.

1864 July 6

1. Consignor: HOLLOWAY, THOMAS (Hanway Street).

2. Auction by Puttick & Simpson.

3. Catalog, GB-Lbl, pressmark S.C.P.94(7), with n&p: *About 2,000 Engraved Music Plates Embracing Valuable Copyright Works . . . also about 500 Plates, the Copyright Works of Thomas Attwood Walmisley. . . .* Holloway's plates, lots 1-211.

4. Lit.: not found.

5. Buyers: Ashdown, Augener, Blockley, Broome, Lonsdale, J. Williams, et al. Many lots unsold.

6. Another sale by Messrs. Foster, 30 April 1860, q.v.

1864 July 27

1. Consignor: "A MUSIC SELLER."

2. Auction by Mr. C. Kelly.

3. Catalog, US-Cu.

[Note: This is in the inventory of a large group of valuable auction sale catalogs of music plates and copyrights sold en bloc to the University of Chicago a number of years ago by the First Edition Bookshop. This catalog could not be found in 1984.]

1. Consignor: COCK, HUTCHINGS & CO. (62-63 New Bond
   Street).

2. Auction by Puttick & Simpson.

3. Catalog, GB-Lbl, pressmark S.C.P.96(4), with n&p:
   *. . . about 35,000 Plates and Copyrights of Messrs.
   Lamborn Cock, Hutchings & Co. (formerly Leader &
   Cock) Who are Dissolving Partnership. . . .* 1,977 lots.

4. Lit.: not found.

5. Buyers: Ashdown, Augener, Cock, Ollivier, et al. Total,
   £10,932-16s.

6. Sale of printed stock by Puttick's, 6 February 1865.

7. Plates and copyrights of many works by Sterndale Bennett,
   including pianoforte solos and duets, 273 plates, which
   made £409-10s (Cock); *6 Songs,* op. 35, £99-4s (Cock);
   May Queen, arrs., parts, etc., 662 plates, £554-8s (Cock).

1865 May 3

1. Consignor: FOSTER & KING, MESSRS. (Regent Street).

2. Auction by Puttick & Simpson.

3. Catalog, GB-Lbl, pressmark S.C.P.99(2), with n&p: *Stock of
   3,000 Engraved Music Plates with Copyrights.* 362 lots.

4. Lit.: not found.

5. Buyers included Metzler and Turner. Total, £479-10s
   (many lots unsold).

1865 September 14

1. Consignor: ADDISON & LUCAS (Regent Street).

2. Auction by Puttick & Simpson.

3. Catalog, GB-Lbl, pressmark S.C.P.102(3), with n&p: *Stock
   of 60,000 Engraved Music Plates and Copyrights of. . . .*
   3,858 lots.

4. Lit.: *Musical Standard* 4 (1865): 120-21, with list of some
   items purchased, buyers' names and prices fetched.

5. Buyers: Cocks, Oliphant, J. Williams, Ashdown, Augener,
   et al. Total, £13,581.

6. Another sale of plates and copyrights, Puttick's, 17 December 1866, q.v.

7. Donizetti's *Lucia di Lammermoor* made £157 (Cock); Costa's *Eli,* £112, and *Naaman,* £567 (both Cock).

1866 May 7-12

1. Consignor: METZLER, G., MESSRS. (Great Marlborough Street).

2. Auction by Puttick & Simpson.

3. Catalog, GB-Lbl, pressmark S.C.P.107(5), with n&p: *. . . Stock of 50,000 Engraved Music Plates and Copyrights. . . .* 2,702 lots.

4. Lit.: not found.

5. Buyers: Ashdown, Augener, Blockley, Brewer, D'Alcorn, Hutchings, Wilcock, J. Williams. Many lots b.i. Total, £7,441-10s.

6. Another sale by Puttick's, 30 March 1868, q.v.

7. Many lots not part of Metzler's stock but introduced "by permission" of R. Andrews.

1866 August 8

1. Consignor: JEWELL, J. H. (104, Great Russell Street) et al.

2. Auction by Puttick & Simpson.

3. Catalog, GB-Lbl, pressmark S.C.P.110(4), with n&p: *Stock of 5,000 Engraved Music Plates and Copyrights of Jewell; Plates from Another Stock* [consignor unidentified]. . . . Jewell's plates, lots 1-634; other stock, lots 635-90.

4. Lit.: not found.

5. Buyers: Cramer, Hutchings, J. Williams, et al. Total, £1039-6s.

7. Included were three Balfe operas, *Maid of Artois,* £53-12s (Cramer; sold in Cramer sale of 27 March 1881, q.v., for £168); *Joan of Arc,* £74-10s (Hutchings); *Siege of Rochelle,* £73-17s (Cramer).

1866 December 17-18

1. Consignor: ADDISON, LUCAS & CO. (210, Regent Street).

2. Auction by Puttick & Simpson.

3. Catalog, GB-Lbl, pressmark S.C.P.112(1), with n&p:
   Upwards of 20,000 Engraved Music Plates of Valuable
   Copyright Works, Chiefly from the Stock of. . . . 1,234
   lots.

4. Lit.: not found.

5. Buyers: an unsuccessful sale; few items sold, prices low.
   Total, £111-4s.

1867 May 20-31

1. Consignor: D'ALMAINE & CO., MESSRS.

2. Auction by Mr. Robins (Waterloo-Place).

3. Catalog not found.

4. Lit.: *Musical Standard* 6 (18 May 1867) notes receipt of a 335-
   page catalog, containing autographs, unpublished manuscripts, portraits, vocal and instrumental music, a "vast
   stock of ninety thousand music plates and copyrights."

5. Buyers: Humphries and Smith (op. cit.) say the name and
   goodwill were purchased by Joseph Emery, who continued the business. The *L&PMTR* in 1877 reported "the
   business of the late D'Almaine, the pianoforte manu-
   facturer . . . about to pass into the hands of Messrs.
   Grover & Grove." The following appeared in the *Musical
   Times,* 1 June 1867:

   The Stock of Messrs. D'Almaine and Co., the sale of
   which whilst we write is still progressing, is so extensive,
   and the date of the publications cover so long a period,
   that the catalogue embraces almost a history of the rise
   and progress of music in this country, at least from the
   time when the general public began to take a real
   interest in the art. The prices paid for some of the
   works at this sale may perhaps surprise some of our
   readers; and may serve as a proof that good songs,
   even, once stamped with the public approval are not
   allowed to die out, in spite of the crushing effect of the
   "Royalty" system, whilst the sacred music of the established church writers is always certain to be in steady
   demand. We subjoin the names of some of the works,
   with the prices which they fetched: —Montgomery's
   song, "Aladdin's Lamp" (Brewer), £57. Rodwell's
   song, "Banks of the Blue Moselle" (Brewer), £15.
   Rodwell's ballad, "Beautiful blue violets" (Brewer),
   £42. Bishop's ballad, "The bloom is on the rye"
   (Hutchings and Romer), £282. S. Glover's song, "The
   bloom upon the cherry tree" (Brewer), £33. S.
   Glover's duet, "The Fairy Queen" (R. Cocks and Co.),
   £38. Parry's Scotch Melodies (B. Williams), £27 16s.
   Hemy's Pianoforte Tutor (Metzler and Co.), £502 10s.
   Crouch's song, "Dermot Astore" (Hutchings and

Romer), £168. Alexander Lee's song, "Down where the blue bells grow" (R. Cocks and Co.), £75. Rodwell's song, "Draw the sword, Scotland" (Brewer), £22 10s. Hatton's Songs (Brewer), £159 10s. Flood's "Heaven is my home" (R. Cocks and Co.), £65. Ditto, a duet (B. Williams), £52. Alexander Lee's song, "He wipes the tear from every eye" (Brewer), £348. Ditto, duet (B. Williams), £42. Mrs. Mackinlay's song, "Jesus wept" (Brewer), £15 12s. Crouch's song, "Kathleen Mavourneen" (Hutchings and Romer), £532. And Loder's Instruction for the Violin (Hutchings and Romer), £59 10s. Arnold's Cathedral Music was bought by Messrs. Novello, Ewer, and Co., for £91 11s, which firm also purchased nearly the whole of the sacred music in the catalogue.

1867 date unknown

1. Consignor: EWER & CO.

2. Sold by private treaty.

3. No catalog found.

4. Lit: *Musical Standard* 6 (1 June 1867): 349, notes that Novello & Co. have purchased the business, "thus acquiring the exclusive right of publishing the entire compositions of Mendelssohn. . . ."

5. Buyer: Novello & Co.

6. Other copyrights and plates sold by Puttick's, 1 September 1859, q.v.

1867 August 8-10

1. Consignor: MR. BRETELL, et al.

2. Auction by Puttick & Simpson.

3. Catalog, GB-Lbl, pressmark S.C.P.117(3), with n&p: *Antiquarian and Modern Music . . . the Late Mr. Bretell's Copyrights and Printed Stock of Opera Libretti; Stereotype Plates; also 1,000 Engraved Music Plates* [consignor not identified]. . . . Bretell's plates, lots 1222-67; stereos, lots 1268-73; the 1,000 lots 1274-1313.

4. Lit.: not found.

5. Buyers: Lacy, Mitchell, J. Williams, et al.

7. Stereos included Auber's *Fra Diavolo*, 95 plates, £4 (Lacy); Flotow's *Martha*, 75 plates, £4-8s (Mitchell); Rossini's *Barber*, 71 plates, £5-10s (Mitchell); Verdi's *Il Trovatore*, 70 plates, £6-10s (Lacy).

1. Consignor: PROWSE, THOMAS (Hanway Street).

2. Auction by Puttick & Simpson.

3. Catalog, GB-Lbl, pressmark S.C.P.119(11), with n&p:
   . . . *Music and Instrument Stock of the Late Prowse,
   Comprising 6,000 Engraved Music Plates of Copyright
   Works. . . .* Plates, lots 525-765, 2,415 plates.

4. Lit.: not found.

5. Buyers: Blockley, Brewer, Smyth, B. Williams, J. Williams,
   et al.

1868 March 30

1. Consignors: METZLER, GEORGE, MESSRS. (Great
   Marlborough Street) — PROWSE, THOMAS (Hanway
   Street) — HOLLOWAY, THOMAS (Hanway Street).

2. Auction by Puttick & Simpson.

3. Catalog, GB-Lbl, pressmark S.C.P.121(1), with n&p: *Several
   Thousand Music Plates, including Many Valuable Copyright Works, viz. — I. Nearly 4,000 Plates from the Stock of
   the Late Metzler; II. The Stock of the Late Mr. Holloway;
   III. The Remaining Stock of the Late Prowse.* Plates,
   Metzler's, lots 1-187?; Prowse's, 199-317; Holloways',
   318-79.

4. Lit.: not found.

5. Buyers: Hutchings, McDowell, B. Williams, J. Williams,
   et al. Realized £584.

6. Other sales: Metzler plates and copyrights, by Puttick's, 5
   May 1866; Prowse plates, 30 January 1868 and printed
   stock, 1 September 1868, by Puttick's; another Holloway
   sale by Messrs. Foster, 30 April 1860, q.v.; Holloways'
   printed stock, by Puttick's, 2 May 1868.

7. Highest hammer price was £22-8s by Hutchings for Glover's
   Come to the Sunset Tree, duet. Most items went unsold.

1868 June 22

1. Consignor: MUSIC PUBLISHING CO. (Great Newport
   Street).

2. Auction by Puttick & Simpson.

3. Catalog, GB-Lbl, pressmark S.C.P.122(9), with n&p: *Music
   Copyrights and Plates (Except the Opera Libretti). . . .*
   493 lots.

4. Lit.: not found.

5. Buyers: Bell, Brewer, Hutchings, B. Williams, J. Williams, et al.

6. Sales of printed stock by Puttick's, 23 June and 3 November 1868.

7. Sale included pewter plates and titles, woodcuts, and stone titles.

1869 August 28

1. Consignor unnamed.

2. Auction by Puttick & Simpson.

3. Catalog, GB-Lbl, pressmark S.C.P.131(7), with n&p: *Ancient and Modern Music . . . Musical Instruments . . . Music Plates, Mss. and Copyrights. . . .* Plates, lots 501-23.

4. Lit.: not found.

5. Buyers: lots 501-15 were "sold privately to J. Duffin" for £98.

7. Duffin's purchase included *Five Songs on Uncle Tom's Cabin.*

1869 November 29

1. Consignors: ADDISON, ROBERT, & CO. (Little Marlborough Street?) — HIME & ADDISON (of Manchester).

2. Auction by Puttick & Simpson.

3. Catalog, GB-Lbl, pressmark S.C.P.133(1), with n&p: *. . . Stock of Engraved Music Plates and Copyrights of the Late Addison; also Engraved Plates and Copyrights of Hime & Addison, and Others; and Other Highly Valuable Unpublished Copyright Mss. . . .* Addison's plates, lots 1-1087; the others, 1140-1257.

4. Lit.: *Musical Times* 14 (January 1870): 333, with a list of items sold, some buyers' names and prices fetched.

5. Buyers: Ashdown, Augener, Blockley, Chappell, L. Cock, Hutchings, Metzler, Ollivier, J. Williams, et al. Realized £4842-15s.

6. Another sale, of Addison's printed stock, by Puttick's, 1 April 1867.

7. An important sale; high prices fetched, e.g.: Costa's *Eli* made £1,462 (J. Williams); Thomas's *Welsh Melodies,* £946 (L. Cock); Costa's *Namaan,* £33 (Cock) [made £567 in sale of 14 September 1865, q.v., and £463 in sale of 15 October 1872, q.v.].

1. Consignor unnamed.

2. Auction by Puttick & Simpson.

3. Catalog, GB-Lbl, pressmark S.C.P.138(8), with n&p: *Miscellaneous Music; Copyrights and Engraved Music Plates . . . also Musical Instruments. . . .* Plates, lots 286-385.

4. Lit.: not found.

5. Buyers: plates principally to Hayes and Bell; most unsold. Total, £66-3s for whole sale.

1870 October 17

1. Consignor: OLLIVIER, ROBERT WILBY (Old Bond Street).

2. Auction by Puttick & Simpson.

3. Catalog, GB-Lbl, pressmark S.C.P.139(1), with n&p: *Large and Important Stock of Engraved Music Plates and Copyrights . . . Together with the Entire Stock of Printed Music; also Instruments. . . .* 2068 lots.

4. Lit.: not found.

5. Buyers: Ashdown, Hutchings, Purday, Robinson, B. Williams, et al.

7. Wrightson's *Sweet Home,* in several arrs., with stone titles, fetched £433-10s.

1870 November 23

1. Consignor: WHITTINGHAM, ALFRED (Oxford Street).

2. Auction by Puttick & Simpson.

3. Catalog, GB-Lbl, pressmark S.C.P.140(1), with n&p: *Ancient and Modern Music, and Important Musical Copyrights and Engraved Plates; Music Library of a Gentleman. . . .* Plates, lots 1283-1552.

4. Lit.: not found.

5. Buyers: Augener, Novello, Jenkins, et al. Total, £1130.

6. Another sale of Whittingham's plates by Puttick's, 29 March 1877, q.v.

1871 March 27

1. Consignor: CRAMER & CO., LTD (201, Regent Street).

2. Auction by Puttick & Simpson.

3. Catalog, GB-Lbl, pressmark S.C.P.142(1), with n&p: *Part I, the Entire, Extensive and Important Stock of Engraved Music Plates and Copyrights.* 2-612 lots.

4. Lit.: not found.

5. Buyers: Ashdown, Augener, Brewer, Cock, Novello, Weippert, et al. Total, £34,518.

6. Another Puttick's sale of the firm's plates, 8 February 1875, q.v.

7. Arditi's *Il bacio,* several versions, arrs. and keys, 147 plates, made £716-12s (B. Williams); Wallace's *Maritana,* 738 plates, £2232-9s (Hutchings).

1871 May 22

1. Consignor: BLAKE, G. E. (Philadelphia, Pa.).

2. Auction by M. Thomas & Sons.

3. Catalog, US-NYp: *Large and Valuable Stock of Music Plates, Sheet Music, Musical Instruments . . . Stock of. . . .*

4. Lit.: Wolfe, *Early American Music Engraving,* 267-70.

5. Buyers unknown. Wolfe transcribes only that portion of the sale catalog listing printer's tools, not plates.

1872 August 21

1. Consignor: DEARLE & CO. (42, Maddox?).

2. Auction by Puttick & Simpson.

3. Catalog, GB-Lbl, pressmark S.C.P.151(10), with n&p: *Engraved Music Plates and Copyrights . . . Seceding from the Publishing Business.* 403 lots.

4. Lit.: not found.

5. Buyers: Ashdown, McDowell, Morley, Purday, Rudall, et al. Total, £191.

1872 October 15-17

1. Consignor: LAMBORN COCK & CO. (New Bond Street).

2. Auction by Puttick & Simpson.

3. Catalog, GB-Lbl, pressmark S.C.P.152(1), with n&p: *Stock of Engraved Music Plates and Copyrights, in Consequence of Dissolution of Partnership.* 941 lots.

4. Lit.: *Monthly Musical Record* (1 November 1872): 159-60, notes some of the valuable lots sold, buyers' names, and prices fetched.

5. Buyers: Ashdown, Case, Cramer, Cocks, Hutchings, J. Williams. Total, £14,625.

6. Other sales by Puttick's: printed stock, 20 January 1873; plates 20 February 1877, 26 January 1881, and 14 December 1887, q.v.

7. Sterndale Bennett's *May-Queen,* op. 39 made £1,837; Costa's *Namaan,* complete, 1357 plates, made £463 (b.i.) [sold in sales of 14 September 1865, 29 November 1869, and 20 February 1877, q.v.].

1872 December 20

1. Consignor: DAVIDSON, FRANCES A.

2. Auction by Puttick & Simpson.

3. Catalog, GB-Lbl, pressmark S.C.P.153(8), with n&p: *Stereotype Plates, Stock and Copyrights of the Opera Libretti Known as Davidson's Musical Opera-Books, Printing Office, Lease.* 4,351 plates, 80,000 books.

4. Lit.: not found.

5. Buyers are recorded in catalog cited.

1873 April 26

1. Consignor: OLIPHANT, THOMAS.

2. Auction by Puttick & Simpson.

3. Catalog, GB-Lbl, pressmark S.C.P.155(9), with n&p: *Valuable Music Copyrights and Plates of the Late . . . Songs and Ballads. . . .*

4. Lit.: not found.

5. Buyers: Ashdown, Augener, Lucas, Novello, Purday, J. Williams, et al. Total, £2358.

1874 February 18

1. Consignor: EMERY, GEORGE & CO. (Oxford Street).

2. Auction by Puttick & Simpson.

3. Catalog, GB-Lbl, pressmark S.C.P.160(4), with n&p: *Valuable Stock of Engraved Music Plates and Copyrights.* 267 lots.

4. Lit.: not found.

5. Buyers: Ashdown, Blockley, Broome, Brewer, D'Alcorn, Chappell, Cramer, Pitman, B. Williams, J. Williams, et al. Total, £1,695.

7. Beyer's *Modern Pianoforte Tutor* made £5-4s (Jefferys).

1874 February 20

1. Consignor: SHEPHERD, JOHN (20, Warwick Lane).

2. Auction by Puttick & Simpson.

3. Catalog, GB-Lbl, pressmark S.C.P.160(6), with n&p: *Whole of the Stock of Engraved Music Plates of the Late. . . .* 236 lots.

4. Lit.: not found.

5. Buyers: see those listed for sale of 18 February 1874. Total, £1,695.

7. Nutter's *Mendelssohn's Wedding March,* for organ, brought £51 (Emery) [see 18 February 1874!].

1874 August 17

1. Consignor: WEIPPERT, A. N. (Regent St.) — STEAD, HENRY & CO. (Piccadilly).

2. Auction by Puttick & Simpson.

3. Catalog, GB-Lbl, pressmark S.C.P.163(12), with n&p: *Assemblage of Music Plates and Copyrights.*

4. Lit.: not found.

5. Buyers: see those listed for sale of 18 February 1874.

7. Plumpton's *Only To Know* fetched £87 (Morley).

1875 February 8

1. Consignor: HOPWOOD & CREW, MESSRS. (42, New Bond Street).

2. Auction by Puttick & Simpson.

3. Catalog, GB-Lbl, pressmark S.C.P.165(11), with n&p: *Whole of the Stock of Engraved Music Plates and Copyrights.* 1,380 lots.

4. Lit.: *Monthly Musical Record* (March 1875): 43, provides a list of some items sold, buyers' names and prices fetched.

5. Buyers: Ashdown, Bath, Brewer, Chappell, Metzler, J.
Williams, et al. Realized £16,779.

6. Other sales: printed stock by Puttick's, 24 March 1875.

7. Coote's *Prince Imperial Galop* made £990 ("to applause from the audience"); his *Snow-Drift Galop,* £561 (b.i.). Tinney's *Fizz Galop,* £76 (Chappell).

1875 March 18

1. Consignor: CRAMER & CO. (201, Regent Street).

2. Auction by Puttick & Simpson.

3. Catalog, GB-Lbl, pressmark S.C.P.166(8), with n&p: *. . . Stock of Engraved Music Plates and Copyrights.* 1,739 lots.

4. Lit.: *Monthly Musical Record* (May 1875): 76, with a list of more important items sold, buyers' names, and prices fetched.

5. Buyers: Ashdown, L. Cock, Hutchings, Metzler, Mills, Purday, Scrutton, J. Williams, et al. Realized £13,000.

6. Another sale of the firm's plates by Puttick's, 27 March 1871, q.v.

7. Cramer's Chamber *Trios for Female Voices* made £1,040; Sullivan's *O ma charmante,* £525; McFarren's *Harmony,* £159; Richter's *Harmony and Counterpoint,* £333.

1875 June 30

1. Consignor: OETZMANN & CO. (27, Baker Street).

2. Auction by Puttick & Simpson.

3. Catalog, GB-Lbl, pressmark S.C.P.168(11), with n&p: *Collection of Music . . . Full and Vocal Scores . . . Stock of Music Plates and Copyrights; also Instruments.* 434 lots.

4. Lit.: not found.

5. Buyers of plates: Blockley, Broome, Bell, Donajowski, Mills, Pettit, White.

1875 August 16

1. Consignor: DAVIS, ALFRED J. (218, Kentish Town Rd.).

2. Auction by Puttick & Simpson.

3. Catalog, GB-Lbl, pressmark S.C.P.169(10), with n&p: *Miscellaneous Music, including the Library of Sampson Moore; 40 Sets of Engraved Music Plates and Stock. . . .* Plates, lots 318-88.

4. Lit.: not found.

5. Buyers of plates: Broome, Davis, Pitman, Pettit.

1875 November 22

1. Consignor: DUFF & STEWART (147, Oxford Street).

2. Auction by Puttick & Simpson.

3. Catalog, GB-Lbl, pressmark S.C.P.170(7), with n&p: *Valuable Copyrights and Engraved Music Plates.* 1,631 lots.

4. Lit.: *Monthly Musical Record* (December 1875): 179, provides a list of some items sold, buyers' names, and the extraordinary prices fetched.

5. Buyers: Augener, Bath, Bell, Blockley, Broome, Hime, Metzler, Pitman, J. Williams. Realized £10,000.

6. Other sales of the firm's plates were conducted by Brown, Swinburne & Morrell, 9 December 1878, and by Brown & Tooth, 15 November and 26 November 1884, q.v.

7. Gabriel's *Only* brought £516 (Metzler), Levey's *Esmaralda*, £546 (Hime), Balfe's *Il Talismano*, £418 (Hime).

1876 February 28

1. Consignors: CARD, E. J. (St. James Street) — AMOS & SON, MESSRS. (of Norwood) — MARTIN, G. W.

2. Auction by Puttick & Simpson.

3. Catalog, GB-Lbl, pressmark S.C.P.172(10), with n&p: *Collection of Music, including* [a library]; *also about Two Hundred Lots of Valuable Music Plates and Copyrights, the Publications of. . . .* Plates, lots 689-871.

4. Lit.: not found.

5. Buyers: principally Blockley and Morley.

1877 February 20

1. Consignor: LAMBORN COCK & CO. (New Bond Street).

2. Auction by Puttick & Simpson.

3. Catalog, GB-Lbl, pressmark S.C.P.178(4), with n&p: *Stock of Engraved Music Plates and Copyrights.* 379 lots.

4. Lit.: *Monthly Musical Record* (1877): 50, provides a list of some items sold, buyers' names, and prices fetched.

5. Buyers: Ashdown, Augener, Cock, Cox, Metzler, Novello, Mills, J. Williams.   Realized £8,254.

6. Other sales by Puttick's: printed stock 20 January 1873; plates 15 October 1872, 26 January 1881, and 14 December 1887, q.v.

7. Sterndale Bennett's *May Queen* made £1,875; his *Six Songs,* op. 23 and 35, £536 [bought by Cock in November 1869 for £260]; Costa's *Namaan,* £710 [cf. 29 November 1869 and 5 October 1872].

1877 July 11

1. Consignor: SIMPSON & CO. (33, Argyll Street).

2. Auction by Puttick & Simpson.

3. Catalog, GB-Lbl, pressmark S.C.P.181(2), with n&p: *Stock of Engraved Music Plates and Copyrights . . . in Consequence of Dissolution of Partnership.* 173 lots.

4. Lit.: *MO&MTR,* 1 April 1879—a note about the sale.

5. Buyers are recorded in catalog cited. Sale total, only £213-3s.

6. The *MO&MTR* announced that the business was for sale by private treaty, and that a month later its copyrights would be auctioned by Brown, Swinburne & Morrell, 18 May 1879.

1877 November 26

1. Consignor: SPRAKE & PALMER CO. (122, Upper Street, Islington).

2. Auction by Puttick & Simpson.

3. Catalog, GB-Lbl, pressmark S.C.P.182(13), with n&p: *Small but Valuable Stock of Music Plates and Copyrights.* 32 lots.

4. Lit.: not found.

5. Buyers: Broome, D'Alcorn, Donajowski, et al.   Total, £313.

1878 March 4

1. Consignor: DAVISON, HENRY (17, Market Place, Oxford Circus).

2. Auction by Puttick & Simpson.

3. Catalog: GB-Lbl, pressmark S.C.P.184(2), with n&p: *Music Plates and Copyrights of the Stock of Popular Publications.* 324 lots.

4. Lit.: not found.

5. Buyers: Ashdown, Hutchings, Tebby, White, et al. 1103 plates realized £313.

1878 March 18

1. Consignors: WILCOCKE, S. H. (103, Newington Causeway) — HIME & SON (Liverpool).

2. Auction by Puttick & Simpson.

3. Catalog, GB-Lbl, pressmark S.C.P.184(4), with n&p: *Music Plates and Copyrights of Wilcocke; Selections from Hime & Son Stock* [i.e., plates]. 292 lots.

4. Lit.: not found.

5. Buyers: Bell, Broome, Crampton, Mills, Pitman, Patey, White, et al. Total, £581-1s.

1878 May 21-23

1. Consignor: LONSDALE, CHRISTOPHER (26, Old Bond Street).

2. Auction by Puttick & Simpson.

3. Catalog, GB-Lbl, pressmark S.C.P.185(3), with n&p: *Engraved Music Plates and Copyrights, also Stock in Trade.* 716+ lots.

4. Lit.: not found.

5. Buyers: Brewer, Mill, Morley, Jr., J. Williams, et al. Realized £3,048.

6. Other sales: More of the printed stock sold by Puttick's 25 April 1878; stock of LONSDALE & CO. sold 18 October 1880.

7. Gabriel's *The Forsaken* fetched £203 (Mills), Loder's *The Diver,* £113 (Morley, Jr.).

1878 December 9-12

1. Consignor: DUFF & STEWART, MESSRS. (2, Hanover Street).

2. Auction by Brown, Swinburne & Morrell.

3. Catalog: US-Cu and US-Wc, pressmark ML145.D9, without n&p: *Valuable Copyrights and Engraved Music Plates of. . . .*

4. Lit.: *L&PMTR* 14 (15 December 1878): 15 and *MO&MTR* 2 (January 1879): 23, 28, each with a list of some items sold, buyers' names, and prices fetched.

5. Buyers: Ashdown, Bath, Blockley, Hime, Jefferys, Metzler, Lonsdale, Willey, J. Williams (as reported in the literature).

6. Other sale: Puttick's sale of plates, 22 November 1875, q.v.

1879 April 22-23

1. Consignors: SCRUTTON & CO., MESSRS. (Little Marlborough Street) — PILLOW, J. W., MR. (of Liverpool).

2. Auction by Browne, Swinburne & Morrell (at Oxenham's Salesrooms).

3. Catalog not found.

4. Lit.: Sale announced in *MO&MTR* 2 (May 1879): 27, and in *L&PMTR* 18 (15 April 1879): 18, which notes a catalog available.

5. Buyers: Blockley, Cox, Cramer, Lonsdale, J. Williams, et al. (as reported in the literature).

1879 May 15

1. Consignor: SIMPSON & CO. (Argyll Street).

2. Auction by Brown, Swinburne & Morrell.

3. Catalog not found.

4. Lit.: Business for sale by private treaty announced in *MO&MTR* April 1879; a month later, ibid., this auction is noted.

5. Buyers are not reported in the literature.

6. Other sales: plates sold by Puttick's, 11 July 1877, q.v.

1879 November 20

1. Consignor: BELL, GEORGE (Covered Market, Leeds).

2. Auction by Puttick & Simpson.

3. Catalog, GB-Lbl, pressmark S.C.P.193(1), with n&p: *Stock of 4,000 Engraved and Stereotyped Plates, Copyrights, and Unpublished Mss. of George Bell.* 421 lots.

4. Lit.: not found.

5. Buyers: most lots unsold. Realized £65.

6. Another sale of plates and copyrights by Puttick's, 19 November 1886, q.v.

1879 November 22

1. Consignor: D'ALCORN (HENRI) (Poland Street, Oxford Street?).

2. Auction by?

3. Catalog not found.

4. Lit.: *MO&MTR* 23 (January 1900): 287, notes that the plates and copyrights of the firm were offered at public auction on this date, bought by Hart & Co. for £405. Not verified; see following entry.

1879 December 2-5

1. Consignor: D'ALCORN (HENRI).

2. Auction by Brown, Swinburne & Morrell.

3. Catalog not found.

4. Lit.: Announced in *MO&MTR* 3 (December 1879): 33, and noted as past in January 1900 issue. Mentioned in *L&PMTR* 25 (November 1879): 21, and 26 (December 1879): 19-20. *Monthly Musical Record* 10 (1880): 15, provides a list of some items sold, buyers' names, and prices fetched.

5. Buyers: Ashdown, Jefferys, Lonsdale, Palmer, Willey, J. Williams, et al.

6. See other sale announced for 22 November 1879.

7. *MO&MTR* 5 (July 1882): 450 reports that D'Alcorn, seeking "fresh fields and pastures new," has sold the business to W. W. Hastings and gone to farming. The company, under the style of D'Alcorn was bankrupt in 1899.

1880 May 31-June 5

1. Consignor: METZLER & CO. (Great Marlborough Street).

2. Auction by Puttick & Simpson.

3. Catalog, GB-Lbl, pressmark S.C.P.196(14), with n&p: . . . *Stock of 50,000 Engraved and Stereo Music Plates and Copyrights* [including that for *H. M. S. Pinafore*]. . . . 2,261 lots.

4. Lit.: Announced in June 1880 *MO&MTR* as "no doubt the largest stock of copyrights and plates that has ever been brought to the hammer at one time." *L&PMTR* 32 (15 June 1880): 11, and the *Monthly Musical Record* 10 (1880): 99-100, provide almost identical lists of items fetching large sums, with buyers' names and those prices.

5. Buyers: Ashdown, Trimnell, B. Williams, and J. Williams, but the majority of lots b.i. by Metzler. £16,509 realized for 17,642 plates.

6. Others sales of plates by Puttick's, 7 May 1866 and 30 March 1868, q.v.

7. Hemy's *Royal Modern Tutor for the Piano* was b.i. for £3,010; Raff's *Suite in B-flat for Piano,* £246; Gounod's *Irene,* £196; Sullivan's *The Chorister,* £556. Gabriel's *Only,* bought by Metzler for £516, 22 November 1875, brought £193 here from Ashdown.

1881 [s.d.]

1. Consignor: NEUMEYER & CO. (of Neumeyer Hall).

2. By private treaty?

3. Catalog not found.

4. Lit.: *MO&MTR* 4 (May 1881): 301, reports that the plates and copyrights have been purchased by Novello, Ewer & Co. The catalog includes "the whole of the valuable copyrights of Heinrich Hofmann."

1881 January 26

1. Consignor: COCK, MR. LAMBORN (63, New Bond Street).

2. Auction by Puttick & Simpson.

3. Catalog, GB-Lbl, pressmark S.C.P.200(16), with n&p: *Engraved Music Plates and Copyrights, the Residue of the Stock of. . . .*

4. Lit.: *Monthly Musical Record* (1881): 60, and *L&PMTR* 40 (15 February 1881): 13, each provide a short list of items sold, buyers' names, and prices fetched.

5. Buyers: Ashdown, Augener, Cusins, J. Wood, Cramer, B. Williams. Realized £2,186 for 4,456 plates.

6. Other sales: printed stock by Puttick's, 20 January 1873; plates and copyrights 15 October 1872, 20 February 1877, and 14 December 1887, q.v.

7. Bennett's edition of Bach's *Preludes and Fugues* made £41 (Ashdown); Pinsuti's *Minster Windows,* £81 (Wood).

1. Consignor unidentified.

2. Auction by Puttick & Simpson.

3. Catalog, GB-Lbl, pressmark S.C.P.206(7), with n&p: *Musical Instruments . . . also Music.* Separate catalog tipped in at end, 3 pages, 13 lots of *Copyright Music Plates and Valuable Copyright Compositions of Ed. Reyloff, Henri Latour, Harry Dale, and Geo. Lee.*

4. Lit.: not found.

5. Buyers of plates included Ashdown.

7. Latour's *Air de danse* made £82 (Ashdown). Reyloff's *Bourrée* made £38.

1882 April 19

1. Consignor: TURNER, JOHN ALVEY (of Bishopsgate Street).

2. Auction by Messrs. Oxenham.

3. Catalog not found.

4. Lit.: Noted in *MO&MTR* 5 (May 1882): 326.

5. Buyers unknown.

1883 April 16-24

1. Consignor: WILLIAMS, BENJAMIN (60, Paternoster Row).

2. Auction by Puttick & Simpson.

3. Catalog, GB-Lbl, pressmark S.C.P.213(1), with n&p: *Immense Stock of Music Plates and Copyrights, Furniture, Lease, Trade Stock, Goodwill,* etc. 2,829 lots.

4. Lit.: *MO&MTR* 6 (1883): 348-49, and *L&PMTR* 68 (15 May 1883): 25, each provide a list of some items sold, buyers' names, and prices fetched.

5. Buyers: Ashdown, Hadley, Hart, Jefferys, Metzler, et al. Hadley bought heavily at the sale but by June had sold his purchases to Ashdown. Sale realized £24,800 (book debts, £5,333).

6. Other sales of plates by Puttick's, 3 November 1890, 25 April 1894, 28 April 1894, and 23 May 1913, q.v.

7. Smallwood's *Youthful Pleasures* brought £277 (Hadley), his *Sea Shells,* £336 (Mullen), Haydn's *Twelve Symphonies,* ed. Clementi, £11 (Ashdown).

1. Consignor: BLOCKLEY, JOHN (3, Argyll Street).

2. Auction by Puttick & Simpson.

3. Catalog, GB-Lbl, pressmark S.C.P.214(3), with n&p: *Stock of Engraved Music Plates with the Important Copyrights Attaching Thereto . . . Unpublished Mss. of the Late Mr. . . .* 1,407 lots.

4. Lit.: *MO&MTR* 6 (1883): 438, and *L&PMTR* 69 (15 June 1883): 30, each provide a long list of items sold, buyers' names, and prices fetched.

5. Buyers: Ashdown, R. Cocks, T. Blockley, Mills, Purday, et al. Many of the lots were bought by Blockley's sons, Thomas and Theodore. Realized £21,907.

6. Many items re-sold at the sale of THEODORE BLOCKLEY properties at Puttick's, 7 June 1886, q.v.

7. Blockley's own *Arab's Farewell to His Favourite Steed* brought £640, his *Jessie's Dream,* £589 from one of his sons (see later sale of *Arab's Farewell,* 28 April 1897!).

1883 [s.d.]

1. Consignor: EWALD & CO. (Argyll Street).

2. Private treaty?

3. Catalog not found.

4. Lit.: Sale noted in *Musical Times,* June 1883, p. 338 — whole of the copyrights bought by C. Jefferys.

5. Buyers unknown.

1884 January 10

1. Consignor: SHEPHERD & KILNER (16, Southampton Street).

2. Auction by Puttick & Simpson.

3. Catalog, GB-Lbl, pressmark S.C.P.217(7), with n&p: *. . . Goodwill, Stock, Plates and Copyrights of . . . also Instruments.* 362 lots.

4. Lit.: not found.

5. Buyers: an unimportant sale; no lot made over £2.

6. Another sale of plates by Puttick's, 24 February 1885, q.v.

1. Consignor: HUTCHINGS & ROMER (9, Conduit Street, Regent Street, and 10-11 Little Marlborough Street).

2. Auction by Puttick & Simpson.

3. Catalog, GB-Lbl, pressmark S.C.P.219(6), with n&p: *Stock of Engraved Music Plates, with the Important Copyrights and Publishing Rights Attaching Thereto; Unpublished Mss., Goodwill, Lease, Machinery.* . . . 2,333 lots.

4. Lit.: *MO&MTR* 7 (1884): 424, 472, and the *Musical Times,* 1 June 1884, p. 351, each provide a list of some items sold, buyers' names, and prices fetched. A long article in *L&PMTR* 80 (15 May 1884) provides another and comments, " . . . a more important sale has not been held for many years," and in a later article, after the sale, furnishes a list of items sold, buyers' names, and prices.

5. Buyers: Ashdown, Hutchings, Novello, B. Williams, Romer, and many others. 21,143 plates made £23,145.

6. Surplus stock and plates sold by Messrs. Kelly & Co., 23-24 September 1884; six more sales were conducted by Puttick's — 7 May 1889, 6 November 1889, 4 October 1892, 1 March 1894, 22 March 1901, and 5 May 1908, q.v.

7. Barnett's *Ancient Mariner* went for £1,209 to Novello. Wallace's *Maritana* was b.i. for £1,064. Crouch's *Kathleen Mavourneen* brought £504 (Romer). See "Traveller's Tale" about the sale, reprinted above, pp. 240-41 in the Introduction.

1884 May 28

1. Consignor: DONALDSON, ROBERT (Glasgow).

2. Auction by Puttick & Simpson.

3. Catalog at end of that for sale described above (May 19-28), 2 pages, 31 lots of unexceptional material.

1884 September 23-24

1. Consignor: HUTCHINGS & ROMER.

2. Auction by Messrs. Kelly & Co. (of Martin St.).

3. Catalog not found.

4. Lit.: sale announced in *MO&MTR* — "surplus stock of sheet music and plates . . . immense stock," and in *L&PMTR* — "Surplus stock of sheet music, stereotype plates, copyrights, &c."

5. Buyers unknown.

1. Consignors: CZERNY, WILLIAM (211, Oxford Street) —
   SPRAGUE & CO. (7, Oxford Mansion).

2. Auction by Puttick & Simpson.

3. Catalog, GB-Lbl, pressmark S.C.P.221(3), with n&p:
   *Engraved Music Plates, Copyrights and Publishing
   Rights, Unpublished Mss.* [in a separate section] *Copy-
   right Music Plates and Unpublished Mss. of Sprague &
   Co.* 428 and 37 lots.

4. Lit.: not found.

5. Buyers [both properties]: Ashdown, Augener, McDowell,
   Ransford, J. Williams, et al. Totals: Czerny's, £4326;
   Sprague's, £184.

6. Another Czerny sale by Puttick's, 15 November 1887, q.v.
   Sales of Sprague & Co.'s, 25 November 1884 and 24
   February 1885, q.v.

7. Many lots unsold, many prices low.

1884 November 15

1. Consignor: DUFF & STEWART.

2. Auction by Brown & Tooth.

3. Catalog not found.

4. Lit.: not found.

5. Buyers unknown.

6. Other sale of plates conducted by Puttick's, 22 November
   1875; by Brown, Swinburne & Morrell, 9 December 1878;
   and by Brown & Tooth, 26 November 1884, q.v.

1884 November 26

1. Consignor: DUFF & STEWART.

2. Auction by Brown & Tooth.

3. Catalog at US-Cu, without n&p.

4. Lit.: *L&PMTR* 87 (15 December 1884): 30, provides a list
   of some items sold, buyers' names, and prices fetched.

5. Buyers: Ashdown, Blockley, Enoch, Orsborn & Tuckwood,
   et al (as reported in the literature).

6. Other sales: see preceding entry, 15 November 1884.

1884 November 25

1. Consignors: SPRAGUE & CO. (7, Oxford Mansion) —
   ROBERTS, H. S. (of Folkestone).

2. Auction by Puttick & Simpson.

3. Catalog, GB-Lbl, pressmark S.C.P.221(10), with n&p:
   *Valuable Library of the Late George Benson . . .
   Remainder of the Stock of Sprague & Co.; Plates and
   Copyrights of Roberts* [his own works]. . . . Sprague
   plates, lots 467-92; Roberts', lots 493-99.

4. Lit.: not found.

5. Buyers: Blockley, Pettit, Reeves, Robinson, et al.

6. Other sales of Sprague & Co. plates by Puttick's, 21 October
   1884 and 24 February 1885, q.v.

1885 February 24

1. Consignors: SHEPHERD & KILNER (16, Southampton
   Street) — SPRAGUE & CO. (7, Oxford Mansion) —
   BENSON, GEORGE.

2. Auction by Puttick & Simpson.

3. Catalog, GB-Lbl, pressmark S.C.P.222(16), with n&p:
   *Musical Property, including Instruments; Plates and
   Copyrights . . . Residue of Shepherd & Kilner Stock;
   Remaining Stock of Sprague & Co.; Plates and Copy-
   rights of the Late Benson.* Plates, lots 1-54.

4. Lit.: not found.

5. Buyers: Blockley, Hammond, Hart, Pettit, McDowell, et al.
   Total, £644.

6. Other sales by Puttick's of Shepherd & Kilner plates, 10
   January 1884; of Sprague & Co.'s, 21 October and 25
   November 1884, q.v.

7. Lots 1 and 2, copyrights and plates of C. V. Stanford's
   Canterbury Pilgrims and *Savanorola* went unsold.

1885 June 23-24

1. Consignors: UNIDENTIFIED — PURDAY, CHARLES
   HENRY — COOPER, JOHN WILBYE.

2. Auction by Puttick & Simpson.

3. Catalog, GB-Lbl, pressmark S.C.P.224(11), with n&p:
   *Small but Valuable Stock of Engraved Music Plates and
   Copyrights . . . also the Plates and Copyrights of the Late
   Cooper, and those of the Late Purday; also Instruments.*
   70 lots (partly thematic).

4. Lit.: not found.

5. Buyers: a poor sale, making only £165-6s-8d.

1886 April 14

1. Consignor: WILLIAMS, W., & CO. (221, Tottenham Court
   Road).

2. Auction by Puttick & Simpson.

3. Catalog, GB-Lbl, pressmark S.C.P.228(6), with n&p: *Stock
   of Engraved Music Plates of.* . . . 545 lots.

4. Lit.: not found.

5. Buyers: many lots unsold; remainder bought by Ashdown,
   Blockley, Donajowski, Hart, Hutchings, Guest, Littleton,
   Ransford, J. Williams. Total, £898-9s.

1886 June 7

1. Consignor: BLOCKLEY, THEODORE (72, Berners Street).

2. Auction by Puttick & Simpson.

3. Catalog, GB-Lbl, pressmark S.C.P.228(19), with n&p:
   *Engraved Music Plates, Printed Stock, Copyrights and
   Unpublished Manuscripts . . . Purchased at the Sale of
   the Late John Blockley* [see 11 June 1883] *with Others
   Recently Acquired.* 742 lots.

4. Lit.: *MO&MTR* 9 (July 1886): 493, provides a list of some
   items sold, buyers' names, and prices fetched.

5. Buyers: Ascherberg, Ashdown, Donajowski, Hart, Romer,
   et al. Total, £2,955-8s. Goodwill purchased by Agate.

6. Another sale at Puttick's, 11 June 1883 (John Blockley).

1886 August 20

1. Consignor: CUBITT, W. D., SONS & CO. (124, High
   Holborn).

2. Auction by Puttick & Simpson.

3. Catalog, GB-Lbl, pressmark S.C.P.229(20), with n&p:
   *Assemblage of Musical Instruments; Engraved Copyright
   Plates of Various Publications.* . . . Plates and printed
   stock, lots 186-225.

4. Lit.: not found.

5. Buyers are recorded in catalog cited.

1. Consignor: BELL, GEORGE (Covered Market, Leeds).

2. Auction by Puttick & Simpson.

3. Catalog, GB-Lbl, pressmark S.C.P.230(12), with n&p:
   Plates, Copyrights and Unpublished Manuscripts of. . . .
   235 lots.

4. Lit.: not found.

5. Buyers: Ashdown and Hart dominated the bidding. Total,
   £80-3s.

6. Another sale of Bell's plates by Puttick's, 20 November 1879.

7. Mostly novelties. Leigh's *Say Mamma if He Pops,* 2
   versions, made £15 (Hart), Badarzewska's *Faith, Hope,
   and Charity* (3 pieces), £15 — the highest prices fetched
   by any lots.

1886 November 24

1. Consignors: POHLMANN, MESSRS., & SONS (London and
   Halifax) — LYON & HALL, MESSRS. (Brighton) —
   SWAN, DAVID (Glasgow).

2. Auction by Puttick & Simpson.

3. Catalog, GB-Lbl, pressmark S.C.P.230(14), with n&p:
   *Engraved and Stereotyped Music Plates, Copyrights, and
   Unpublished Manuscripts of.* . . . Pohlmann's plates,
   lots 1-66; L & H's, 67-123; Swan's, 124-46.

4. Lit.: *MO&MTR* 10 (1887): 182, with list, buyers' names,
   and prices fetched.

5. Buyers: Ashdown, Blockley, Allen, Donajowski, Francis &
   Day, Jefferys, Wilcock, et al. Total, £812-8s.

7. *MO&MTR* 16 (June 1893): 563 notes that the catalog of
   POHLMANN & CO. of Dublin has been sold to Mathias
   & Strickland!

1887 May 2-3

1. Consignor: WILLEY & CO. (14A, Great Marlborough
   Street).

2. Auction by Puttick & Simpson.

3. Catalog, GB-Lbl, pressmark S.C.P.232(12), with n&p:
   Engraved Music Plates and Copyrights. 773 lots.

4. Lit.: *MO&MTR* 10 (July 1887): 470-71, and *L&PMTR* (15 May 1887): 25, each provide a list of some items sold, buyers' names, and prices fetched.

5. Buyers: Ashdown, Augener, Agate, Donajowski, Evans, Hart, Howard, Hutchings, Jefferys, Morley, Peck, Romer, Reynolds, et al.   Total, £3262-11s.

1887 November 15

1. Consignor: CZERNY, WILLIAM (Berners Street).

2. Auction by Puttick & Simpson.

3. Catalog, GB-Lbl, pressmark S.C.P.236(12), with n&p: *Engraved Music Plates and Copyrights, Lease, Goodwill,* etc.   Plates, lots 1-241.

4. Lit.: *MO&MTR* 11 (December 1887): 133-34, and *L&PMTR* (15 January 1887): 29 and 31, each provide a list of items sold, buyers' names, and prices fetched.

5. Buyers: Agate, Ashdown, Cramer, Evans, Hart, Hutchings, Orsborn & Tuckwood, Romer, J. Williams, et al.   Total, £1584-8s.

6. Another sale of Czerny's plates, by Puttick's, 21 October 1884, q.v.

7. Lease and goodwill went unsold.   Mendelssohn's *L'Ange qui chante* brought £15, Tours' *Huit Morceaux de salon,* vln-pf., £110-14s.

1887 December 14

1. Consignor: COCK, J. LAMBORN (New Bond Street).

2. Auction by Puttick & Simpson.

3. Catalog, GB-Lbl, pressmark S.C.P.236(19), with n&p: *Remainder of Engraved Music Plates and Copyrights, Former Stock of. . . .* 269 lots.

4. Lit.: not found.

5. Buyers are recorded in catalog cited.

6. Puttick's sales of plates, 15 October 1872, 20 February 1877, 26 January 1881; of printed stock, 20 January 1873.

1888 July 2

1. Consignor: RANSFORD & BEAL (trading as RANSFORD & SON) (2, Princes Street).

2. Auction by Brown & Tooth (at Messrs. Oxenham's).

3. Catalog not found.

4. Lit.: *MO&MTR* 11 (August 1888): 519, notes the sale.

5. Buyers included Ransford and Beal (see note 7).

6. Puttick's conducted other sales of the plates, 25 June 1891 and 17 July 1894, q.v.

7. Ransford & Beal dissolved partnership; both bought at sale and continued business separately.

1889 May 7-9

1. Consignor: HUTCHINGS & CO. (Blenheim Street).

2. Auction by Puttick & Simpson.

3. Catalog not found.

4. Lit.: The sale is noted in both *MO&MTR* 12 (June 1889): 454, and *L&PMTR* (May 1889) with lists of items sold, buyers' names, and prices fetched.

5. Buyers: Ashdown, Chappell, Hayes, Phillips, Page, Schott, Whittingham. Total, £6619.

6. Other Puttick's sales of the firm's plates: 19 May 1884, 6 November 1889, 4 October 1892, 1 March 1894, 22 March 1901, and 5 May 1908, q.v.

7. Gabriel's *Cleansing Fires* went for £300 (b.i.). Mattei's *Odi tu,* and in English as *Oh Hear the Wild Winds Blow,* was b.i. for £427.

1888 [s.d.]

1. Consignor: unidentified.

2. Auction by Brown & Tooth (at Oxenham's Salesrooms).

3. Catalog not found.

4. Lit.: *MO&MTR* 11 (1888): 561, reports on this sale of copyrights without identifying consignor, but provides a list of items sold and prices fetched.

5. Buyers unknown.

1889 June 25-26

1. Consignor: ASCHERBERG, E., & CO. (DUNCAN DAVISON & CO.) (211, Regent Street).

2. Auction by Puttick & Simpson.

3. Catalog, not at GB-Lbl; at US-Cu, without n&p: *12,000 Engraved Music Plates, Copyrights, Mss. etc. of. . . .* 437 lots.

4. Lit.: *MO&MTR* 12 (August 1889): 550, and *L&PMTR* (15 July 1889): 25, each provide a list of some items sold, buyers' names, and prices fetched.

5. Buyers: Ashdown, Augener, Beal, Blockley, Donajowski, Jefferys, Orsborn & Tuckwood, Paxton, Ransford, Whittingham (as reported in the literature). Many lots b.i.

1889 November 6-8

1. Consignor: HUTCHINGS & ROMER (9, Conduit Street).

2. Auction by Puttick & Simpson.

3. Catalog not found.

4. Lit.: *MO&MTR* (December 1889): 145, and *L&PMTR* (15 November 1889) each include a lengthy report on this sale with a list of some items sold, buyers' names, and prices fetched.

5. Buyers: Ashdown, Augener, Beresford, Blockley, Evans, Hayes, Hart, Hopkinson, Patey, J. Williams, et al. Realized £6,733-13s.

6. Other Puttick's sales: 19 May 1884, 7 May 1889, 4 October 1892, 1 March 1894, 22 March 1901, and 5 May 1908.

7. Mattei's *Odi tu* made £611 "amidst applause" [b.i. at previous Hutchings & Romer sale, 7 May 1889, for £427]. Lady Arthur Hill's *In the Gloaming* made £286, Crouch's *Kathleen Mavourneen,* £409 [cf. sale, 19 May 1884].

1890 January 15

1. Consignor: COX, ALFRED (29, King Street).

2. Auction by Puttick & Simpson.

3. Catalog, at US-Cu, without n&p: *Stock of 2,600 Engraved Music Plates and Valuable Copyrights of. . . .* 243 lots.

4. Lit.: *MO&MTR* 13 (February 1890): 245, provides a list of items sold, buyers' names, and prices fetched.

5. Buyers: Ashdown, Orsborn & Tuckwood, Schott, et al. (as reported in the literature).

1890 April 21

1. Consignor: KEPPEL, MESSRS. (Regent Street).

2. Auction by Puttick & Simpson.

3. Catalog not found.

4. Lit.: *MO&MTR* 13 (June 1890): 405, provides a brief list of items sold, buyers' names and prices fetched.

5. Buyers: Chappell, Mocatta, Whittingham, et al. (recorded in the literature).

7. Roeckel's *Lord Mayor Whittington* fetched £156 (Chappell); Blumenthal's *When the House Is Still* made £63-5s (Chappell).

1890 April 24

1. Consignor: WOOD, MESSRS., & CO. (Great Marlborough Street).

2. Auction by Puttick & Simpson.

3. Catalog not found.

4. Lit.: *MO&MTR* 13 (June 1890): 405, provides a brief list of items sold, buyers' names and prices fetched.

5. Buyers: Augener, Beal, Beresford, Hart, Orsborn & Tuckwood, Ransford, et al (recorded in the literature).

7. Waldstein's *Giant Note Method for Piano, Voice and Organ* fetched £550 (Hart), while Smallwood's *Twilight Starts* made £4-4s (Augener).

1890 November 3

1. Consignor: WILLIAMS, B., MESSRS. (19, Paternoster Row).

2. Auction by Puttick & Simpson.

3. Catalog not found.

4. Lit.: *MO&MTR* 14 (December 1890): 113, provides a brief list of items sold, buyers' names, and prices fetched.

5. Buyers: Ashdown, Agate, Beal, Grice, Paxton, Hutchings, et al (recorded in the literature).

6. Other Puttick's sales of plates: 16 April 1883, 25 April 1894, 28 April 1897, and 22 May 1913, q.v.

1890 December 8-13

1. Consignor: BREWER, S. J., & CO. (Bishopsgate Street).

2. Auction by Puttick & Simpson.

3. Catalog, GB-Lbl, P&S#2775,[1] with n&p: *Very Valuable Stock of Engraved Music Plates, Copyright Works, Printed Music, Unpublished Manuscripts.* . . . 1,359 lots.

---

[1] After August 1888, the Puttick & Simpson catalogs in the British Library no longer bear the pressmark (S.C.P.), only the serial number.

4. Lit.: *MO&MTR* 14 (January 1891): 155, and *L&PMTR* (December 1890): 19, each provide a list of some items sold, buyers' names, and prices fetched.

5. Buyers: Agate, Ashdown, Blockley, Cramer, Hart, Jefferys, McDowell, Orsborn & Tuckwood, Ransford, B. Williams, J. Williams, et al. Total, £22,300.

6. Other Puttick sales: of printed stock, 13 February 1891; of plates, 15 December 1890 and 28 May 1891.

7. Smallwood's *Fairy Barque* brought £1008 (McDowell), Pridham's *Battle March,* £1022 (Ashdown), Farmer's *Violin Tutor,* £1752 (J. Williams), Wallace's opera *Amber Witch,* £74-10s (Cramer).

1890 December 15

1. Consignor: BREWER, S. J., & CO. (Bishopsgate Street).

2. Auction by Puttick & Simpson.

3. Catalog, GB-Lbl, P&S#2776, with n&p: *Part II: Stock of Upwards of 90,000 Engraved and Stereotyped Music Plates.* 2,969 lots.

4. See notes for sale of 8-13 December 1890.

5. See notes for sale of 8-13 December 1890.

6. See notes for sale of 8-13 December 1890.

1891 May 28

1. Consignor: BREWER, S. J., & CO. (Bishopsgate Street) — VIADUCT CO. (Newman Street, Oxford Street).

2. Auction by Puttick & Simpson.

3. Catalog, GB-Lbl, P&S#2813, with n&p: *Residue of the Stock of Engraved Music Plates, Copyrights, Mss. of . . . Together with Properties Purchased by the Viaduct Co. at Brewer's First Sale.* 420 lots.

4. Lit.: not found.

5. Buyers: Ashdown, Beal, Hart, Pass, Hutchings, Schott, B. Williams, et al.

6. Other sales of Brewer's properties: printed stock, 13 February 1891; plates, 8 December 1890, 15 December 1890, and 28 May 1891, q.v. Another sale of Viaduct's plates, by Puttick's, 14 July 1898, q.v.

7. The only high-priced lot was Smallwood's *Sylvan Echoes* which brought £42 (Beale).

1. Consignor: RANSFORD & SON, MESSRS. (2, Princes Street).

2. Auction by Puttick & Simpson.

3. Catalog, GB-Lbl, P&S#2820, with n&p: *Stock of Engraved Music Plates and Copyright Works, Printed Music, Unpublished Manuscripts.* 328 lots.

4. Lit.: *MO&MTR* 14 (1890/91): 432, provides a list of items sold, buyers' names, and prices fetched.

5. Buyers: Ashdown, Blockley, Hopkinson, Howard, Music Publ. Co., Orsborn, Tuckwood, et al.

6. Other sales of plates: by Brown & Tooth, 2 July 1888 (reported in the *MO&MTR* 11 [August 1888]: 519), and by Puttick's, 17 July 1894.

1891 December 2-4

1. Consignors: MARSHALL'S LTD. (70, Berners Street) — BERTINI, ALPHONSE (Berners Street).

2. Auction by Puttick & Simpson.

3. Catalog, GB-Lbl, P&S#2843, with n&p: *Stock of Engraved Music Plates and Copyrights of. . . .* Marshall's plates, lots 1-446; Bertini's, 447-691.

4. Lit.: *L&PMTR* (15 December 1891): 29, and the *Magazine of Music* (January 1892): 17-18, provide lists of items sold, buyers' names, and prices fetched.

5. Buyers: Agate, Ashdown, Cocks, Donajowski, Enoch, Francis Bros. & Day, Hart, Orsborn, B. Williams, Wood, et al. Realized £4025-7s.

6. The printed stock of both publishers was auctioned by Puttick's, 26 January 1892; a small group of Bertini's, 22 December 1891.

7. Bonheur's *Standard Pianoforte Tutor* sold for £424 (Quentin), Hutchinson's opera *Glamour,* for the same, and Pontet's *Last Milestone* fetched £225 (Beresford).

1892 April 28

1. Consignor: MOUTRIE & SON (55, Baker Street).

2. Auction by Puttick & Simpson.

3. Catalog at US-Cu only, without n&p: *3,000 Engraved Music Plates and Copyrights of . . . and other Properties.* 165 lots.

4. Lit.: *MO&MTR* 15 (June 1892): 426, provides a short list of items sold with buyers' names and prices fetched.

5. Buyers: Ashdown, Beresford, Blockley, Evans, Mocatta, Pattison, Ransford, J. Williams, et al.   Realized £889.

1892 May 9-11

1. Consignor: HOME, R., & SON (Music Engraver).

2. Auction by Lyon & Turnbull, Edinburgh.

3. Catalog at US-Cu only [Sale of Engraved Music Plates, Stereos, Type, and Plant].   61 p.

4. Lit.: not found.

5. Buyers are not recorded in the catalog cited.

1892 October 4-6

1. Consignor: HUTCHINGS & ROMER (Great Marlborough Street).

2. Auction by Puttick & Simpson.

3. Catalog, GB-Lbl, P&S#2895.

4. Lit.: *MO&MTR* 16 (November 1892): 106-07, and *L&PMTR* (October 1892): 27 and 29, each provide a list of items sold, buyers' names, and prices fetched.

5. Buyers: Ashdown, Beresford, Blockley, Cocks, Doremi, Cannon, Hart, McDowell, Mathias & Strickland, Phillips & Page, Sheard, Wilcock, et al.   Realized £6,225-15s.

6. Other Puttick's sales of H & R plates: 19 May 1884, 6 November 1889, 1 March 1894, 22 March 1901, and 5 May 1908, q.v.

7. Gabriel's *Cleansing Fires* made £330 [cf. sales of 5 February 1895 and 5 October 1904], Piccolomini's *True Is My Heart*, £3-3s (Sheard), Balfe's opera *Rose of Castille* £123 (Cannon).

1893 May 1-7

1. Consignor: JEFFERYS, C., & SON (67, Berners Street).

2. Auction by Puttick & Simpson.

3. Catalog, GB-Lbl, P&S#2936, with n&p: *Plates, Copyrights, and Stock in Trade.*   1,906 + 58 lots (4,588 plates).

4. Lit.: *MO&MTR* 16 (June and July 1893): 562 and 621, provides a list of items sold, buyers' names, and prices fetched.

5. Buyers: Ascherberg, Ashdown, Bath, Beal, Beresford, Donajowski, Doremi, Hart, F. Jefferys, G. Jefferys, Sheard, et al. Realized £11,793.

7. Vandervell's *Immer Wieder Gavotte,* with arrs., knocked down to F. Jefferys for £930. 22 numbers from Verdi's *Il Trovatore* made £502 (*G.* Jefferys). As the *Musical News* 5 (July 1893): 30, commented, "Enormous prices for trifles!"

1893 May 4

1. Consignor: WOOD & CO. (Great Marlborough Street).

2. Auction by Puttick & Simpson.

3. Catalog, GB-Lbl, P&S#2937, with n&p: *Plates and Copyrights Belonging to.* . . . 45 lots.

4. Lit.: not found.

5. Buyers: principally Ashdown.

7. Note that this small sale occurred halfway through the Jefferys & Son sale of May 1-7.

1893 November 9

1. Consignor: WHITE, HENRY, CO. (237, Oxford Street) — WHITE, S. (38, Booksellers' Row).

2. Auction by Puttick & Simpson.

3. Catalog, GB-Lbl, P&S#2964, with n&p: *Engraved Music Plates (Copyright and Non-Copyright) of* . . . *Select Collection of Engraved Plates of S. White.* 329 lots.

4. Lit.: not found.

5. Buyers: Ashdown, Avant, Barnett, Blockley, Hart, Howard, Turner, et al. Realized £316 (with 1,862 passed plates).

7. Many lots unsold or b.i.

1894 March 1

1. Consignor: HUTCHINGS & ROMER (Great Marlborough Street).

2. Auction by Puttick & Simpson.

3. Catalog, GB-Lbl, P&S#2986, with n&p: *Remainder . . . of Engraved Music Plates, Copyrights and Publishing Rights.* . . . 476 lots.

4. Lit.: not found.

5. Buyers: principally Ashdown and Cannon.   Total, £1739-11s.

6. Other Puttick's sales of the firm's properties: 19 May 1884, 7 May 1889, 6 November 1889, 4 October 1892, 1 March 1894, 22 March 1901, and 5 May 1908, q.v.

1894 April 25

1. Consignor: WILLIAMS, B. (Paternoster Row).

2. Auction by Puttick & Simpson.

3. Catalog, GB-Lbl, P&S#2997, with n&p: *Engraved Music Plates and Copyrights of . . . Together with the Goodwill.* 319 lots.

4. Lit.: *MO&MTR* 17 (June 1894): 589, provides a long list of items sold, buyers' names, and prices fetched; shorter list in *L&PMTR* (15 May 1894): 29.

5. Buyers: Ashdown, Blockley, Cramer, Hart, Mocatta, Mullen, Orpheus, Dowding, Donajowski, Phillips & Page, B. Williams, Whittingham, et al.   Realized £9,103-10s.

6. Other Puttick's sales of plates: 16 April 1883, 3 November 1890, 28 April 1897, and 22 May 1913, q.v.

7. Watson's famous *Anchored* went to Blockley for £1212-15s, Pinsuti's *Bugler* to Ashdown for £189-3s, *J. Hile's Catechism* to Hart for £550, and Pridham's *Yorkshire Bells,* with duet, vln., &c., to Ashdown for £715-10s.

1894 April 27

1. Consignor: CUSINS, SIR WILLIAM G.

2. Auction by Puttick & Simpson.

3. Catalog, GB-Lbl, P&S#2998, with n&p: *Engraved Music Plates, Property of the Late . . . and other Private Properties . . . also a Large Collection of Unpublished Manuscripts with the Copyrights* [owners not identified]. Cusins' plates, lots 146-70; copyrights, lots 1-145.

4. Lit.: not found.

5. Buyers: Ashdown, Bland, Donajowski, McLaughlin, Tuckwood, Turner, J. Williams.   Total, £126-13s.

1894 April 27

1. Consignor: INTERNATIONAL MUSIC PUBLISHING SYNDICATE, LTD. (Chiswell).

2. Auction by Puttick & Simpson.

3. Catalog, GB-Lbl, P&S#2998A, with n&p: *Engraved Music Plates, the Property of . . . with Copyrights and Publishing Rights.* 206 lots.

4. Lit.: not found.

5. Buyers: Cocks, D'Alcorn, Honingsberg, Pass, Turner, et al. Realized £174-3s.

1894 July 17

1. Consignor: RANSFORD, MESSRS., & SON (31, Conduit Street).

2. Auction by Puttick & Simpson.

3. Catalog, GB-Lbl, P&S#3019, with n&p: *Engraved Music Plates and Copyright Works, Unpublished Mss.* . . . 171 lots.

4. Lit.: not found.

5. Buyers: Ashdown, F. Jefferys, Pass, Rossini, St. Cecilia, B. Williams, et al. Realized £171.

6. Other sales of plates by Puttick's: 25 June 1891 and 27 March 1895, q.v.

7. Many lots unsold.

1894 July 26

1. Consignor: JEFFERYS, G. F., & CO. (78, Newman Street).

2. Auction by Puttick & Simpson.

3. Catalog, GB-Lbl, P&S#3022, with n&p: *Stock of Engraved Music Plates.* . . . 319 lots.

4. Lit.: not found.

5. Buyers: Ashdown, D'Alcorn, G. Jefferys, Lyric, St. Cecilia, Turner, Wilcock, et al. Total, £2100.

7. Many lots went to either F. Jefferys or G. Jefferys. To the latter, Owens' *Melodious Melodies,* for organ, 315 plates, £235-5s.

1894 December 10

1. Consignor: MARRIOTT & WILLIAMS, LTD. (295, Oxford Street).

2. Auction by Puttick & Simpson.

3. Catalog, GB-Lbl, P&S#3038, with n&p: *Stock of Engraved Music Plates and Copyrights.* 285 lots.

4. Lit.: not found.

5. Buyers: Ashdown, Marriott, Pass, Prowse, St. Cecilia, Tuckwood, Thornton, et al. Realized £283.

6. Another sale of plates by Puttick's, 4 December 1895, q.v.

1. Consignor: MATHIAS & STRICKLAND, MESSRS. (Oxford Street) — TRIMNELL, W. F. (Bristol).

2. Auction by Puttick & Simpson.

3. Catalog, GB-Lbl, P&S#3049, with n&p: *Copyrights and Engraved Music Plates from the Catalogue of . . . also Copyrights with the Engraved Plates, the Property of W. F. Trimnell. . . .* 238 lots.

4. Lit.: *MO&MTR* 18 (March 1895): 393, provides a list of items sold, buyers' names, and prices fetched.

5. Buyers: Ashdown, Augener, Carey, R. Cocks, McDowell, Pass, Simrock, Vaughan, Whittingham, Trimnell, J. Williams.   Realized £3,382.

6. Other sale of Mathias & Strickland's plates by Puttick's: 25 March 1896 and 14 October 1903; of Trimnell's, 24 September 1902, q.v.

7. Gabriel's *Cleansing Fires* purchased by Whittingham for £300 [cf. sales of 4 October 1892 and 5 October 1904]. Pontet's *Nea* brought £104-10s from Ashdown.

1895 March 27

1. Consignor: JEFFERYS, G. F., & CO. (78, Newman Street).

2. Auction by Puttick & Simpson.

3. Catalog, GB-Lbl, P&S#3060, with n&p: *Stock of Engraved Music Plates.* 160 lots.

4. Lit.: not found.

5. Buyers: Ashdown, Chapman, Tuckwood, Turner, B. Williams, et al. Total, £123 (many lots unsold).

6. Other sales of plates by Puttick's: 25 June 1891 and 17 July 1894.

7. Sale included a number of copyrights of works by S. Glover.

1894 June 5

1. Consignor: LONDON MUSIC PUBLISHING CO., LTD. (7, Great Marlborough).

2. Auction by Puttick & Simpson.

3. Catalog, GB-Lbl, P&S#3080, with n&p: *Engraved Music Plates, with the Copyrights and Publishing Rights.* 883 lots.

4. Lit.: not found.

5. Buyers: Ashdown, Mathias & Strickland, et al. Realized £3,893.

7. The firm had acquired the catalog of KLEIN & CO. in 1891, including Piccolomini's *The Toilers* which here brought £610 from Ashdown. McFarren's ed. of *Messiah* went to Witt for £77.

1895 September 4

1. Consignor: WILLIS MUSIC CO. (8, Newman Street).

2. Auction by Tooth & Tooth.

3. Catalog not found.

4. Lit.: sale is reported in *MO&MTR* 18 (1894/95): 801.

5. Buyers unknown.

6. Another Tooth & Tooth auction of the firm's plates, 10 June 1896. Other sales by Puttick's, 31 October 1906 and (probably) 8 June 1931, q.v.

1895 December 14

1. Consignor: MARRIOTT & WILLIAMS, LTD. (295, Oxford Street).

2. Auction by Puttick & Simpson.

3. Catalog, GB-Lbl, P&S#3110, with n&p: *Valuable Copyrights, Publishing Rights, Engraved Music Plates of. . . .* 250 lots.

4. Lit.: not found.

5. Buyers: G. Jefferys, Orsborn, Prowse, et al. Realized £184.

6. Another Puttick's sale of the firm's plates: 10 December 1894, q.v.

1896 February 11

1. Consignors: McDOWELL, J., & CO. (13, Little Marlborough Street) — WHITTINGHAM & McDOWELL.

2. Auction by Puttick & Simpson.

3. Catalog, GB-Lbl, P&S#3127, with n&p: *Stock of Copyrights and Engraved Music Plates of. . . .* 481 lots.

4. Lit.: *MO&MTR* 19 (March 1896): 409 and *L&PMTR* (April 1896): 29, each provide a list of some items sold, buyers' names, and prices fetched.

5. Buyers: Ashdown, Augener, Beal, Blockley, Bowerman, Carnett, Donajowski, Hammond, Hart, Orsborn, Tuckwood, J. Williams, Whittingham, et al. Realized £3,307.

7. Smallwood's teaching piece *Fairy Barque* was b.i. for £1810-10s [cf. sale of 8 December 1890]. Loder's *Violin Tutor* was worth £133 (Whittingham).

1896 March 25

1. Consignor: MATHIAS & STRICKLAND, LTD. (Princes Street).

2. Auction by Puttick & Simpson.

3. Catalog, GB-Lbl, P&S#3139, with n&p: *Stock of Copyrights and Engraved Music Plates, Goodwill and Book Debts of.* . . . 373 + 60A lots.

4. Lit.: *MO&MTR* 19 (May 1896): 556, in a long article, provides a list of items sold, buyers' names, and prices fetched.

5. Buyers: Ashdown, Augener, Beal, Blockley, Donajowski, Doremi, Novello, Orpheus, Orsborn, Phillips & Page, Schott, et al. Realized £4,389.

6. Other sales of plates by Puttick's: 5 February 1895 and 14 October 1903, q.v.

7. Lane's *Carmencita* brought £137-14s (Strickland), Bonheur's *Standard Pianoforte Tutor,* £795-12s (Whittingham) [cf. sale of 4 December 1891], Piccolomini's *Saved by a Child* £310-10s (Ashdown).

1896 May 20

1. Consignor: MOCATTA, B., & CO. (Berners Street).

2. Auction by Puttick & Simpson.

3. Catalog, GB-Lbl, P&S#3154, with n&p: *Portion of the Valuable Stock of Copyrights and Engraved Music Plates.* 295 lots.

4. Lit.: *MO&MTR* 19 (June 1896): 630, provides a short list of items sold, buyers' names, and prices fetched.

5. Buyers: Ashdown, Cocks, Enoch, Mocatta, Prowse, Reeder & Walsh, et al. Realized £733-18s.

7. Mattei's *Carita* fetched £201-17s, Wilson's *Carmera* £79-16s.

1896 June 10

1. Consignor: WILLIS MUSIC CO. (High House, Upminster).

2. Auction by Tooth & Tooth.

3. Catalog at US-Cu, without n&p.

4. Lit.: Noted in *MO&MTR* 19 (1895/96): 702.

5. Buyers unknown.

6. Another sale of the firm's plates by Tooth & Tooth, 4 September 1895; Puttick's, 31 October 1906; and (probably) 8 June 1931, q.v.

1896 November 3

1. Consignor: PATEY & WILLIS (44, Great Marlborough Street).

2. Auction by Puttick & Simpson.

3. Catalog, GB-Lbl, P&S#3182, with n&p: *Portion of Copyrights and Engraved Music Plates.* 420 lots.

4. Lit.: *MO&MTR* 20 (January 1897): 269, provides a list of some items sold, buyers' names, and prices fetched.

5. Buyers: Ashdown, Boosey, Curwen, Bowerman, Lingey, Larway, Lucas, Novello, Tuckwood, et al. Realized £1,813-12s.

6. Another sale of plates by Puttick's, 24 September 1902.

7. Gatty's *True till Death,* with pfte. and band parts, made £640.

1896 November 16

1. Consignor: REID BROS. (436, Oxford Street).

2. Auction by Puttick & Simpson.

3. Catalog, GB-Lbl, P&S#3185, with n&p: *Copyrights, Engraved Music Plates and Goodwill of . . .* [owing to death of surviving partner]. 292 + lots.

4. Lit.: *MO&MTR* 20 (December 1896): 201, provides a list of some items sold, buyers' names, and prices fetched.

5. Buyers: Ashdown, Beresford, Curwen, Dowding, Hart, Hammond, Leadbeater, Newsam, Orpheus, Swan, Turner, Tuckwood, et al. Realized £2,000.

6. Another sale of Reid's printed stock by Puttick's, 15 December 1896.

7. Wadham's *Come to Me* sold for £362-5s (Orpheus), Jude's *Skipper* for £275-10s (Beresford). Ashdown bought 1,180 passed plates @ 6.25d.

1. Consignor: WILLIAMS, B., & CO. (19, Ivy Lane).

2. Auction by Puttick & Simpson.

3. Catalog, GB-Lbl, P&S#3230, with n&p: *Whole of the Valuable Stock of Copyrights, Engraved Music Plates, Unpublished Mss., Goodwill and Right to Use the Name.* 671 lots.

4. Lit.: *MO&MTR* 20 (June 1897): 633-34, provides a list of some items sold, buyers' names, and prices fetched.

5. Buyers: Agate, Ashdown, Beresford, Hart, Doremi, Prowse, Schott, Swan, Donajowski, Willcocks, et al. Realized £1,134-12s.

6. Other Puttick's sales of Williams' plates: 16 April 1883, 3 November 1890, 25 April 1894, and 22 May 1913.

7. Blockley's *Arab's Farewell to His Favourite Steed,* which was b.i. for £640 at the sale of 11 June 1883 (q.v.), made only £4-5s here!

1898 July 11

1. Consignor: AUGENER & CO., LTD. (Regent Street and Newgate Street).

2. Auction by Puttick & Simpson.

3. Catalog, GB-Lbl, P&S#3321, with n&p: *Valuable Copyrights and Plates, Being a Portion of the Stock of. . . .* 937 lots.

4. Lit.: not found.

5. Buyers: Surprisingly few lots were sold; of those, most went to Augener. Other buyers included Beal, Curwen, Paxton, Reid, et al. Realized £2,385.

1898 July 14

1. Consignors: WILCOCK, DAVID (Imperial Arcade, Ludgate Hill) — THE VIADUCT PUBLISHING CO. (Newman Street).

2. Auction by Puttick & Simpson.

3. Catalog, GB-Lbl, P&S#3322, with n&p: *Copyrights and Engraved Music Plates . . . also Copyrights Originally Belonging to the Viaduct Publishing Co.* 229 lots.

4. Lit.: not found.

5. Buyers: Blockley, Curwen, Hart, Morley, Pass, Reid, et al. Realized £593.

6. Another sale of Wilcock's plates by Puttick's, 8 December 1903; another of Viaduct's, 28 May 1891, q.v.

1898 November 7-16, 23-30

1. Consignor: COCKS, ROBERT, & CO. (Burlington Street).

2. Auction by Puttick & Simpson.

3. Catalog, GB-Lbl, P&S#3338, with n&p: *Extensive Stock of Copyrights, Engraved Music Plates, Stereos, and Mss. of. . .* [plus goodwill, use of name, and premises]. First sale 2,096 lots; second, lots 2,097-3,568.

4. Lit.: *MO&MTR* 21 (December 1898): 200-01, provides a lengthy list of items sold, buyers' names, and prices fetched. A later article, "Profits of Music Publishing," 22 (February 1899): 344-45, refers to the sale.

5. Buyers: Dean, Hart, Gould, Leonard, Larway, Leadbeater, J. Williams, et al. The new firm, Gould, dominated. Realized over £40,000.

6. Another sale of Cocks' instrument stock by Puttick's, 13 December 1898.

7. Extraordinary prices were paid for many items, e.g.: Pridham's *Sailor's Dream* went to Leadbeater for £1,178; Mascheroni's *For All Eternity* brought £2,240 from Gould; Smallwood's *Home Treasures* was b.i. for £1,381-16s.

1899 September 12

1. Consignor: AGATE & CO. (15, Newman Street).

2. Auction by Puttick & Simpson.

3. Catalog, GB-Lbl, P&S#3399, with n&p: *Copyrights, Engraved Music Plates and Stereos.* 313 lots.

4. Lit.: *MO&MTR* 23 (December 1899): 207, provides a short list of items sold, buyers' names, and prices fetched.

5. Buyers: Ashdown, Beresford, Blockley, Gould, Hammond, Hart, Leonard, Orpheus, Paxton, Leadbeater, Turner, Tidmarsh, et al. Realized £1,144.

7. McFarren's *Beating of My Own Heart,* which was bought by Brewer for £360-5s at the sale on 27 March 1881 (q.v.) fetched only £9 here.

1. Consignor: DOREMI & CO., LTD. (Argyll Place).

2. Auction by Puttick & Simpson.

3. Catalog, GB-Lbl, P&S#3404, with n&p: [Liquidation] *of the Valuable Copyrights, Engraved Music Plates and Stereos of. . . .* 836 lots.

4. Lit.: *MO&MTR* 23 (December 1899): 207-08, provides a list of some items sold, buyers' names, and prices fetched.

5. Buyers: Ashdown, Donajowski, Gould, Hammond, Hart, Leadbeater, Leonard, Nichol, Reeves, Reid, Rossini, Schott, et al. Realized £1,490 (with 9141 passed plates).

6. Another sale of Doremi's plate by Puttick's, 31 January 1907, q.v.

7. Lennox's *Love's Golden Dream* made £308 (Smith), Beethoven's *Piano Sonatas,* op. 17 and 18, made £1-16s (Hammond).

1899 November 27

1. Consignor: MORLEY, W. & CO. (14, Maddox Street).

2. Auction by Puttick & Simpson.

3. Catalog, GB-Lbl, P&S#3414, with n&p: *Valuable Copyrights, Engraved Music Plates and Stereos of. . . .* 558 lots.

4. Lit.: *MO&MTR* 23 (January 1900): 280-81, provides a list of some items sold, buyers' names, and prices fetched.

5. Buyers: Agate, Beal, Curwen, Dean, Cary, Leonard, Reynolds, Turner, Schott, et al. Realized £3,498.

6. Another Puttick's sale of Morley's plates, 20 May 1915, q.v.

7. Tours' *New Kingdom,* and duet, brought £247-10s (Reynolds), Roeckel's popular *Stormfiend,* with orch. parts, £263-10s.

1899 December 4-8

1. Consignor: STANLEY LUCAS, WEBER, PITT & HATZFELD, LTD. (84, New Bond Street).

2. Auction by Puttick & Simpson.

3. Catalog, GB-Lbl, P&S#3416, with n&p: *Copyrights, Engraved Music Plates and Stereos, Goodwill and the House.* 1,474 lots.

4. Lit.: *MO&MTR* 23 (January 1900): 282-83, provides a list of some items sold, buyers' names, and prices fetched.

5. Buyers: Agate, Ashdown, Augener, Bosworth, Cary, Donajowski, Bumpus, Hatzfeld, Hammond, Lucas, Reid, Schlesinger, et al. Realized £3,949.

6. Another sale of the firm's plates by Puttick's, 26 April 1901.

7. Berlioz' *Te Deum,* vocal score, brought £4-7s (Schlesinger), Clutsam's *Ma Curlyheaded Babby,* £660 (Hatzfeld), Kjerulf's *Album of Songs* £610-13s (Lucas), Beringer's *Daily Technical Studies,* £2209-3s (Bosworth—and still in Bosworth's catalog!).

1900 March 19

1. Consignors: ELTON & CO. (Dean Street) — MILLS, J. A. (Moorgate Street) — SLATER & SON (Camden Road) — WAUD, W. W. — MORLEY, S.

2. Auction by Puttick & Simpson.

3. Catalog, GB-Lbl, P&S#3434, with n&p: *Copyrights, Engraved Music Plates and Stereos, Properties of.* . . . Plates of Elton, lots 1-199; Mills, 200-24; Salter, 225-77; Waud, 278-92; Morley, 293-302. 311 lots.

4. Lit.: *MO&MTR* 23 (April 1900): 502, provides a list of some items sold, buyers' names, and prices fetched.

5. Buyers: Blockley, Broome, Donajowski, Green, Hammond, Gould, Leadbeater, Mathias, Orpheus, Rossini, Turner, et al. Realized £380.

7. Kotzwara's *Battle of Prague* sold for 10s!

1900 April 9

1. Consignors: WILLIS & HALL (32, Castle Street) — [KLENE & CO. (83, New Oxford Street) — TAUBE & CO. (Berners Street)].

2. Auction by Puttick & Simpson.

3. Catalog, GB-Lbl, P&S#3442, with n&p: *Copyrights and Engraved Music Plates of.* . . . Willis & Hall's plates, lots 1-257; Klene's, 258-91; Taube's, 293-99.

4. Lit.: *MO&MTR* 23 (May 1900): 572, provides a list of some items sold, buyers' names, and prices fetched.

5. Buyers: Agate, Beresford, Curwen, Dean, Broome, Hart, Harvey, Orpheus, Reeves, Reid, Wilcock, et al.

7. Badarzewska's *Maiden's Prayer* brought £1-5s-6d (Orpheus).

1. Consignor: PHILLIPS & OLIVER (41, Great Portland Street).

2. Auction by Puttick & Simpson.

3. Catalog, GB-Lbl, P&S#3481, with n&p: *Valuable Copyrights, Engraved Music Plates and Stereos.* 167 lots.

4. Lit.: *MO&MTR* 24 (December 1900): 212, provides a list of some items sold, buyers' names, and prices fetched.

5. Buyers: Ashdown, Bowerman, Cramer, Gould, Reeves, Reid, Richards, Sindall, Wilcock, et al. Realized £3,085.

6. Other Puttick's sales of the firm's plates: 14 October 1903 and 26 June 1906, q.v.

7. Gounod's *Divine Redeemer,* and arrs., made £616-10s. Sindall, the firm's manager, bought many lots, the lease and goodwill, and continued the business as Phillips & Oliver.

1901 March 22

1. Consignors: HUTCHINGS & ROMER (39, Great Marlborough Street) — CANNON & MITCHELL.

2. Auction by Puttick & Simpson.

3. Catalog, GB-Lbl, P&S#3519, with n&p: *Engraved Music Plates, with the Important Copyrights and Publishing Rights . . . of Messrs. Cannon & Mitchell . . . Trading as Hutchings & Romer.* 490 lots.

4. Lit.: not found.

5. Buyers: Leadbeater, Leonard, Pass, Reeves, Whittingham, et al. Realized £636.

6. Other sales of the firm's plates by Puttick's: 19 May 1884, 7 May 1889, 6 November 1889, 4 October 1892, 1 March 1894, and 5 May 1908, q.v.

1901 April 26

1. Consignor: STANLEY LUCAS, WEBER, PITT & HATZFELD, LTD. (84, New Bond Street).

2. Auction by Puttick & Simpson.

3. Catalog, GB-Lbl, P&S#3531, with n&p: *Valuable Copyrights, Engraved Music Plates and Stereos, from the Catalogue of. . . .* 197 lots.

4. Lit.: *MO&MTR* 24 (June 1901): 645, provides a list of some items sold, buyers' names, and prices fetched.

5. Buyers: Agate, Ashdown, Bosworth, Cary, Hammond, Curwen, Lyric, Moore, Novello, Paxton, Schott, et al. Realized £2,571.

6. Another sale of the firm's plates by Puttick's, 4 December 1899, q.v.

7. A series of 18 songs by Jensen fetched £211-4s (Wood), Meyer-Helmud's *Album of Songs* £130-18s (Laudy).

1901 November 6

1. Consignor: BATH, J. (Berners Street).

2. Auction by Puttick & Simpson.

3. Catalog, GB-Lbl, P&S#3568, with n&p: *Music Copyrights and Engraved Music Plates of.* . . . 524 lots.

4. Lit.: *MO&MTR* 25 (December 1901): 22, provides a list of some items sold, buyers' names, and prices fetched.

5. Buyers: Gardiner, Bowerman, Leadbeater, Phillips, Maynard, Reid, Reeves, Reynolds, Phillips & Oliver, Wickins, et al.

1902 September 24-25

1. Consignors: PATEY & WILLIS (Berners Street) — [HOUGHTON & CO. (39, Great Marlborough Street) — SINCLAIR, J. — MR. TRIMNELL (i.e., W. F. TRIMNELL, of Bristol)].

2. Auction by Puttick & Simpson.

3. Catalog, GB-Lbl, P&S#3659, with n&p: *Entire Stock of Music with the Valuable Copyrights Attaching Thereto, Lease, Goodwill, Stock in Trade of Patey & Willis; also other Properties.* . . . 851 lots.

4. Lit.: *MO&MTR* 26 (1903): 143, provides a list of some items sold, buyers' names, and prices fetched.

5. Buyers: Dean, Evans, Blockley, Larway, Leonard, Reid, H. White, et al. Realized, for P & W's plates, £5,427-16s; Houghton's, £35-6s; Sinclair's, £74-8s; Trimnell's, £214-6s.

6. Another sale of Patey & Willis plates by Puttick's, 3 November 1896, q.v.

7. Rubinstein's *Voices of the Woods* made £137-10s (Dean), N. Johnson's *Two Lyrics* £378 (Blockley).

1. Consignors: PHILLIPS & OLIVER (Great Portland Street) — MATHIAS & STRICKLAND (231, Oxford Street).

2. Auction by Puttick & Simpson.

3. Catalog, GB-Lbl, P&S#3763, with n&p: *Engraved Music Plates and Copyrights of.* . . . 187 lots.

4. Lit.: *MO&MTR* 27 (1903): 145, provides a list of some items sold, buyers' names, and prices fetched.

5. Buyers: Ashdown, Cary, Curwen, Leonard, Morley, Paxton, Pewtress, Orpheus, Reeves, Swan, Stevens, et al. Realized £309.

6. Other sales of Phillips & Oliver's plates, by Puttick's: 13 November 1900 and 26 June 1906; of Mathias & Strickland's plates: 5 February 1895 and 25 March 1896, q.v.

1903 December 8

1. Consignors: WILCOCK, DAVID (8, St. Anne's Chambers) — LYRIC MUSIC PUBLISHING CO. (112, Clarence Road) — [ADAMS, ALBERT (Birmingham)].

2. Auction by Puttick & Simpson.

3. Catalog, GB-Lbl, P&S#3782, with n&p: *Engraved Music Plates and Copyrights of.* . . . Wilcock's plates, lots 1-133; Lyric's, 134-224; Adams 225-36.

4. Lit.: not found.

5. Buyers: Adams, Ashdown, Benjamin, Blockley, Curwen, Reeves, Willcocks, B. Williams, et al. Realized £224; Wilcock's, £146; Lyric's, £26; Adams', £52.

6. Another Puttick's sale of Wilcock's plates, 14 July 1898; of Adams', 5 May 1904, q.v.

1904 May 5

1. Consignors: MOORE, SMITH & CO. (Poland Street, Oxford Street) — ADAMS, ALBERT (Birmingham) — ET AL.

2. Auction by Puttick & Simpson.

3. Catalog, GB-Lbl, P&S#3829, with n&p: *Copyrights and Music Plates of.* . . . Moore's, lots 1-258; Adams', 259-85.

4. Lit.: not found.

5. There were no bids for the Moore, Smith properties; Adams' copyrights made only £91.

6. Other Puttick's sales of Moore, Smith's plates, 1 November 1917; of Adams', 8 December 1903.

1904 May 11

1. Consignor: HATZFELD & CO.

2. Auction by Robinson & Fischer.

3. Catalog, reportedly at US-Cu, but could not be found in 1984.

4. Lit.: *L&PMTR,* 15 June 1904, with a short list of items purchased by Messrs. Metzler in the sale, with prices.

1904 May 30-31

1. Consignor: BEAL, C. W., & CO. (Oxford Circus Avenue).

2. Auction by Puttick & Simpson.

3. Catalog, GB-Lbl, P&S#3836, with n&p: *Copyrights and Engraved Music Plates of . . . also Lease of the Premises.* 693 lots [at the conclusion of 1st day's sale, 9 lots of ARROWSMITH & MARTIN copyrights].

4. Lit.: not found.

5. A bill of sale tipped into GB-Lbl copy indicates the lease, goodwill, and stock in trade of Beal was sold for £1,900.

1904 October 5

1. Consignor: WHITTINGHAM, WALTER (13, Little Marlborough Street).

2. Auction by Puttick & Simpson.

3. Catalog, GB-Lbl, P&S#3859, with n&p: *Copyrights, Engraved and Stereotyped Music Plates and Stock of Printed Music.* 325 lots.

4. Lit.: *MO&MTR* 28 (1904): 138, provides a list of some items sold, buyers' names, and prices fetched.

5. Buyers: Ashdown, Beal, Chester, Donajowski, Dowding, Larway, Leonard, Phillips & Page, Reeves, Swan, Vincent, et al. Realized £3,781-13s.

6. No other sales.

7. Smallwood's immensely popular *Fairy Barque,* with arrs., was sold to Phillips & Page (who immediately resold it to Swan) for £1,424-10s. *MO&MTR* notes that of the piece "ten thousand copies for a long time have been sold annually." Bonheur's *Standard Pianoforte Tutor* brought £780 (Larway). Sold earlier in sales on 25 March 1896 for £795-12s, and on 4 December 1891 for £424. Gabriel's *Cleansing Fires* sold in earlier sales of 4 October 1892 for £330 and 5 February 1895 for £300.

1904 October 27

1. Consignor: JEFFERYS, LTD. (67, Wells Street).

2. Auction by Puttick & Simpson.

3. Catalog, GB-Lbl, P&S#3866, with n&p: *Valuable Copyrights, Music Plates and Stock of Printed Music . . . and Goodwill.* 407 lots.

4. Lit.: *MO&MTR* notes with a list of some items sold, buyers' names and prices fetched.

5. Buyers: Ashdown, Augener, Banks, Bayley & Ferguson, Hart, Leadbeater, Leonard, Metzler, Pitman, et al. Realized £2,353.

6. No other sales.

7. Vandervell's *Immer wieder Gavotte,* in numerous arrs. (143 plates), made £929. At Puttick's sales of 1 May 1893, it made £930.

1905 May 18-19

1. Consignor: BERESFORD, HARRY (25, Soho Square).

2. Auction by Puttick & Simpson.

3. Catalog, GB-Lbl, P&S#3927, with n&p: *Copyrights, Music Plates, Stock of Printed Music and the Tito Mattei Royalties . . . of the Late Beresford.* 400 lots.

4. Lit.: *MO&MTR* 28 (June 1905): 690, provides a list of some items sold, buyers' names, and prices fetched.

5. Buyers: Ashdown, Donajowski, Dowding, Chanot, Evans, Leadbeater, Maynard, Morley, Pitman, Roder, Tuckwood, et al. Realized £3,959.

7. Jude's *Skipper* made £570 (Ashdown), Pontet's *Last Milestone,* £531 (Tuckwood).

_____

1. Consignor: DEAN, FRANK & CO. (Berners Street).

2. Auction by Puttick & Simpson.

3. Catalog, GB-Lbl, P&S#3965, with n&p: _Copyrights, Performing and other Rights, Together with the Stock of Printed Music._ 260 lots.

4. Lit.: brief notice in _MO&MTR_ 29 (December 1905): 220, with a list of some items sold, buyers' names, and prices fetched.

5. Buyers: Ashdown, Crowest, Feldman, Hammond, Leadbeater, Harris, Price & Reynolds, Reid, Swan, et al. Realized £1,256-14s.

1906 June 26

1. Consignor: PHILLIPS & OLIVER (Great Portland Street) — ET AL.

2. Auction by Puttick & Simpson.

3. Catalog, GB-Lbl, P&S#4031, with n&p: _Musical Instruments . . . a Few Lots of Copyrights and Music Plates, the Remaining Stock of. . . ._ Plates, lots 215-54.

4. Lit.: not found.

1906 October 31

1. Consignors: ORPHEUS MUSIC PUBLISHING CO. (Moorgate Station Arcade) — WILLIS MUSIC CO., LTD. (8, Newman Street).

2. Auction by Puttick & Simpson.

3. Catalog, GB-Lbl, P&S#4056, with n&p: _Copyrights, Engraved and Stereotyped Music Plates of Orpheus . . . and the Full-Priced Editions of the Important Publications of Willis_ [in order to concentrate on cheaper publications]. 310 lots.

4. Lit.: not found.

5. Buyers: Ashdown, Beal, Crowest, Dowding, Leonard, Maynard, Pass, Reeves, Reid, Sorrel, Willcocks, et al. Realized £1,549-9s.

6. Earlier sales of Willis plates were conducted by Tooth & Tooth, 4 September 1895 and 10 June 1896, q.v.

7. Mascheroni's _Soldier's Song_ brought £285-15s (Harris), his _Eternal City,_ b.i., £22-16s.

1. Consignor: HELLER, A. M., & CO. (18, Wells Street).

2. Auction by Puttick & Simpson.

3. Catalog, GB-Lbl, P&S#4076, with n&p: *Copyrights, Engraved and Stereotyped Music Plates, Stock, Goodwill, Book Debts.* 131 lots.

4. Lit.: not found.

5. Buyers: Ashdown, Beal, Chester, Hutchings, Pitman, Reeves, Reid, et al. Realized £875.

7. Needham's *Complete Scales and Arpeggi Manual* made £365 (Reid).

1907 January 31

1. Consignor: DOREMI & CO. (9, Argyll Street).

2. Auction by Puttick & Simpson.

3. Catalog, GB-Lbl, P&S#4083, with n&p: *Copyrights, Engraved and Stereotyped Music Plates and Stock of. . . .* 155 lots.

4. Lit.: *MO&MTR* 30 (February 1907), provides a list of some items sold, buyers' names and prices fetched.

5. Buyers: Ashdown, Crowest, Fortescue, Dowding, Hawkes, Harris, Maynard, Oxford, Phillips, Reeves, J. Williams, et al. Realized £325.

6. Another sale of Doremi's plates by Puttick's, 18 October 1899, q.v.

1908 May 5

1. Consignor: HUTCHINGS & ROMER (39, Great Marlborough Street).

2. Auction by Puttick & Simpson.

3. Catalog, GB-Lbl, P&S#4207, with n&p: *Copyrights, Plates, Stock and Goodwill of. . . .* 405 lots.

4. Lit.: *MO&MTR* 31 (June 1908): 717, provides a brief list of some items sold, buyers' names, and prices fetched.

5. Buyers: Ashdown, Beal, Cannon, Enoch, Hatzfeld, Crowest, Leonard, Novello, Pass, Reeves, Revell, Schott, Woolhouse, et al. Realized £681.

6. Other plate sales by Puttick's: 19 May 1884, 7 May 1889, 6 November 1889, 4 October 1892, 1 March 1894, 22 March 1901, q.v.

7. Many lots b.i. Wallace's opera *Maritana,* which made £2232-9s at a sale 27 March 1871, made £59-8s here.

1909 June 15

1. Consignor: LUBLIN & CO., LTD. (83, Mortimer Street).

2. Auction by Puttick & Simpson.

3. Catalog, GB-Lbl, P&S#4323, with n&p: *Schedule of Musical Copyrights and Non-Copyrights, Together with the Engraved and Stereotyped Plates, Stock* [and the lease] *Offered in One Lot.* 7 pp. of compositions, 114 copyrights, plates, and some mss.

4. Lit.: not found.

5. Buyers are recorded in catalog cited.   Total realized £1000.

1911 May 25

1. Consignor: PECK, FELIX (47, South Molton Street).

2. Auction by Puttick & Simpson.

3. Catalog, GB-Lbl, P&S#4540, with n&p: *Stock of Copyrights and Engraved Music Plates, including the Whole of the "Grosvenor Edition," and Unpublished Mss.* 166 lots.

4. Lit.: not found.

5. Buyers: Maynard, Pass, Reeves.   Realized only £10-9s-6d.

1912 June 27

1. Consignor: BARNARD, GEORGE J. (Great Marlborough Street).

2. Auction by Puttick & Simpson.

3. Catalog, GB-Lbl, P&S#4660, with n&p: *Copyrights, Engraved Plates, Stock and Goodwill of the Late Mr. Barnard, Trading Under the Style of SWAN & CO.* 400 lots.

4. Lit.: not found.

5. Buyers: Ashdown, Agate, Donajowski, Hammond, Oliver, Orpheus, Pass, Pitman, Reeves, et al.   Realized £2,159. Many lots unsold.

7. Smallwood's *Fairy Barque,* sold in earlier sales, here, in 10 versions, made £703-5s. It went again in sale of 8 June 1931, for £494.

1. Consignor: WILLIAMS, B., & CO., LTD. (26, Goodge Street).

2. Auction by Puttick & Simpson.

3. Catalog, GB-Lbl, P&S#4795, with n&p: *Copyrights, Engraved Music Plates, Stock, Goodwill and Book Debts of.* . . . 169 lots.

4. Lit.: not found.

5. Buyers: Agate, Beal, Mullens, Oliver, Pitman, Reeves, Reid, et al. Realized £674.

6. Other Puttick's sales of Williams' plates: 16 April 1883, 3 November 1890, 25 April 1894, and 28 April 1897, q.v.

1913 December 1-2

1. Consignor: WICKINS & CO. (10, Lancashire Court, New Bond Street).

2. Auction by Puttick & Simpson.

3. Catalog, GB-Lbl, P&S#4795, with n&p: *Copyrights, Engraved Music Plates, Stock, Goodwill and the Lease of.* . . . 710 lots.

4. Lit.: not found.

5. Buyers: Beal, Linwood, Maynard, Oliver, Reeves, Reid, Pitman, Warren, et al. Realized £4,210.

7. Florence Wickins' *Rapid Pianoforte Tutor* was b.i. for £1495.

1914 June 4

1. Consignor: HALL & CO. (31, Castle Street, Berners Street).

2. Auction by Puttick & Simpson.

3. Catalog, GB-Lbl, P&S#4857, with n&p: *Copyrights, Engraved Music Plates and Stock.* 156 lots.

4. Lit.: not found.

5. Buyers: Agate, Beal, Brooks, Linwood, Mathias, Maynard, Metzler, Pitman, Warren, et al. Realized £469, with 613 passed plates.

1915 May 20

1. Consignor: MORLEY, W., & CO. (25, Great Marlborough Street).

2. Auction by Puttick & Simpson.

3. Catalog, GB-Lbl, P&S#4942, with n&p: *Copyrights, Engraved Music Plates and Stereos*. 258A lots.

4. Lit.: not found.

5. Buyers: Brooks, Leonard, Oliver, Warren, et al. Realized £2,405, with 1180 passed plates.

6. Another sale of Morley's plates by Puttick's, 27 November 1899.

7. Roeckel's popular *Stormfiend* (b.i. at an earlier Morley sale for £263) here made £103.

1917 May 14-17

1. Consignor: DONAJOWSKI, ERNEST (24, Castle Street).

2. Auction by Puttick & Simpson.

3. Catalog, GB-Lbl, P&S#5128, with n&p: *Music Copyrights, Engraved Plates and Stock*. 1,698 lots.

4. Lit.: not found.

5. Buyers: Beal, Paxton, Pitman, Reid, Schott, Warren, et al. Total, £4321-5s (Schott bought 13,462 passed plates).

1917 November 1

1. Consignor: MOORE, SMITH & CO. (19, Hanover Square).

2. Auction by Puttick & Simpson.

3. Catalog, GB-Lbl, P&S#5167, with n&p: *Copyrights, Engraved Music Plates, Stereos, Stock*. 262 lots.

4. Lit.: not found.

5. Buyers: Ashdown, Beal, Brooks, Dowding, Linwood, Pass, Reid, Oliver, Warren, et al. Realized £1,097.

6. Another Puttick's sale of the firm's plates, 5 May 1904.

1918 January 3

1. Consignor: EVANS & CO. (Castle Street, E.).

2. Auction by Puttick & Simpson.

3. Catalog, GB-Lbl, P&S#5190, with n&p: *Music Copyrights, Engraved Music Plates and Stock of*. . . . 277 lots.

4. Lit.: not found.

5. Buyers: Beal, Reid, Leonard, et al. An undistinguished group of properties.

1. Consignor: CANNON & CO. (16, Market Place, Oxford Circus, late of Great Marlborough Street).

2. Auction by Puttick & Simpson.

3. Catalog, GB-Lbl, P&S#5653, with n&p: *Stock of Engraved Music Plates, with the Important Copyrights, and Publishing Rights.* . . . 263 lots.

4. Lit.: not found.

5. Buyers: Beal, Cannon, Hammond, Oliver, Phillips & Page, Reeves, Warren, et al. Many lots unsold. Realized £384-6s.

1923 May 10

1. Consignor: NEWMAN MUSIC CO.

2. Auction by Robins, Gore & Mercer.

3. Catalog, US-Cu, with names of buyers only: *Valuable Copyrights, Engraved Music Plates, and Stereos.* . . . 208 lots.

4. Lit.: not found.

5. Buyers: Beal, Buck, Marsh [i.e., Duff & Stewart], Adams [Ascherberg?], Phillips & Page, et al.

7. Many lots unsold. Catalog pages unusually arranged in 5 columns: Title, Composer, No. of Plates, No. of Keys, and "Royalties" (almost all 1d to 3d).

1931 June 8

1. Consignor: PHILLIPS & PAGE (Oxford Circus).

2. Auction by Puttick & Simpson.

3. Catalog, GB-Lbl, P&S#6875, with n&p: *Music Copyrights, Engraved Music Plates, Stock and Goodwill of.* . . . 301 lots. Lot 269, "The Willis Catalogue," occupies pages 49-55.

4. Lit.: not found.

5. Buyers: Cramer, Dowding, Evans, et al.

6. No other sales of Phillips & Page properties. For others of Willis Music Co., see 4 September 1895, 10 June 1896, and 31 October 1906.

7. Many lots unsold, including all of the "Willis Catalogue." Gounod's *Divine Redeemer,* 4 keys, several arrs., brought £270 (Cramer); Smallwood's *Fairy Barque,* 10 arrs., brought £494 [see earlier sales: 28 May 1891, 11 February 1896, 5 October 1904, and 27 June 1912].

Index to Auctioneers
other than Puttick & Simpson

Brown, Swinburne & Morrell
22 Apr 1879
2 Dec 1879

Brown & Tooth
5 Nov 1884
26 Nov 1884
? ? 1888

Fletcher, Mr.
1 Nov 1844

Foster, Messrs.
30 Apr 1860

Hatch, Mr.
18 Jun 1860

Kelly, C., Mr.
21 May 1862
27 Jul 1864
23 Sep 1884

Lyon & Turnbull
9 May 1892

Musgrave, Mr.
20 Sep 1824
13 Dec 1826

Oxenham, Messrs.
19 Apr 1882

Robins, Mr.
20 May 1867

Robins, Gore & Mercer
10 May 1923

Robinson & Fischer
11 May 1904

Stewart, Mr.
18 Dec 1812

Thomas, M., & Sons (USA)
22 May 187_

Tooth & Tooth
3 Sep 1895
10 Jun 1896

Watson, Mr.
21 Jun 1831
24 Jan 1832
27 Jul 1832
19 Sep 1832
10 Oct 1832
19 Feb 1834
4 Mar 1834
13 Jan 1835
17 Jun 1836
17 Nov 1837

Wheatley, Mr.
1 Jul 1831

White, Mr.
24 May 1803

Unknown
? ? 1848

CONSIGNORS **Unnamed**
8 Dec 1812
27 Jul 1832
19 Sep 1832
17 Nov 1837
1 Nov 1844
16 Nov 1855
17 Mar 1858
18 May 1864
28 Aug 1869

24 Aug 1870
? ? 1888

Adams, Albert
8 Dec 1903
5 May 1904

Addison & Lucas
14 Sep 1865

Addison, Lucas, & Co.
17 Dec 1866

Addison, Robert, & Co.
29 Nov 1869

Agate & Co.
12 Sep 1899

Amos & Son
28 Feb 1876

Andrews, R.
7 May 1866

Arrowsmith & Martin
30 May 1904

Ascherberg, E., & Co.
25 Jun 1889

Augener & Co.
11 Jul 1898

Barnard, George J.
27 Jun 1912

Barnett & Co.
24 Jan 1832

Bath, J. (printer)
6 Nov 1901

Beal, C. W., & Co.
30 May 1904

Bell, George
20 Nov 1879
19 Nov 1886

Benson, George
24 Feb 1885

Beresford, Harry
18 May 1905

Bertini & Co.
2 Dec 1891

Blake, G. E. (of Phila.)
22 May 1871

Blockley, John
11 Jun 1883

Blockley, Theodore
7 Jun 1886

Bretell, Mr.
8 Aug 1867

Brewer & Co.
8 Dec 1890
15 Dec 1890
28 May 1891

Campbell, J.
24 Jun 1862

Cannon & Co.
4 Oct 1921

Cannon & Mitchell
22 Mar 1901

Card, E. J.
28 Feb 1876

Challoner, Neville Butler
1 Apr 1847

Chaulieu, Charles
22 Dec 1849

Clementi, Muzio, & Co.
13 Jan 1835

Cock, Hutchings, & Co.
14 Nov 1864

Cock, Lamborn, & Co.
15 Oct 1872
20 Feb 1877
26 Jan 1881
14 Dec 1887

Cocks & Co.
26 Mar 1861

Cocks, Robert, & Co.
7 Nov 1898

Coggins, J.
    1   Jul   1831

Cooper, John Wilbye
    23   Jun   1885

Coventry, Charles ?
    3   Jul   1851

Coventry & Co.
    19   Dec   1849

Cox, Alfred
    15   Jan   1890

Cramer & Co.
    27   Mar   1871
    18   Mar   1875

Cubitt, W. D., Sons & Co.
    20   Aug   1886

Cusins, Sir William G.
    27   Apr   1894

Czerny, William
    21   Oct   1884
    15   Nov   1887

D'Alcorn, Henri
    22   Nov   1879
    2   Dec   1879

D'Almaine & Co.
    20   May   1867

Davidson, Frances A.
    20   Dec   1872

Davis, Alfred J.
    16   Aug   1875

Davison, Duncan, Co.
    25   Jun   1889

Davison, Henry
    4   Mar   1878

Dean, Frank, & Co.
    14   Nov   1905

Dearle & Co.
    21   Aug   1872

Donajowski, Ernest
    14   May   1917

Donaldson, Robert
    28   May   1884

Doremi & Co., Ltd.
    18   Oct   1899
    31   Jan   1907

Duff & Stewart
    22   Nov   1875
    9   Dec   1878
    15   Nov   1884
    26   Nov   1884

Duncombe, John
    20   Dec   1853

Elton & Co.
    19   Mar   1900

Emery, George, & Co.
    18   Feb   1874

Evans & Co.
    3   Jan   1918

Ewald & Co.
    ?   ?   1883

Ewer & Co.
    ?   ?   1867
    1   Sep   1859

Farn, Mr.
    10   Oct   1832

Foster & King
    3   May   1865

Green, John
    14   Apr   1848
     6   Jun   1848
    21   Mar   1849
     7   Jan   1852

Hall & Co.
     4   Jun   1914

Hatzfeld & Co.
    11   May   1904

Hedgley, John
    28   Jan   1863

Heller, A. M., & Co.
     8   Jan   1907

Hime & Son
    18   Mar   1878

Hime & Addison
    29   Nov   1869

Holloway, Thomas
    30   Apr   1860
    30   Mar   1868
     6   Jul   1864

Home, R., & Sons
     9   May   1892

Hopwood & Crew
     8   Feb   1875

Houghton & Co.
    24   Sep   1902

Hutchings & Romer
    19   May   1884
     7   May   1889
     6   Nov   1889
     4   Oct   1892
     1   Mar   1894
    22   Mar   1901
     5   May   1908

International Music Publishing Syndicate, Ltd.
    27   Apr   1894

Jefferys, C., & Son
     1   May   1893

Jefferys, G. F., & Co.
    26   Jul   1894
    27   Mar   1895

Jefferys, Ltd.
    27   Oct   1904

Jewell, J. H.
     8   Aug   1866

Johannig & Co.
     7   Dec   1852

Keegan, J.
     5   Mar   1852

Keppel
    21   Apr   1890

Klene & Co.
     9   Apr   1900

Knapton, Philip
    19   Feb   1834

Leader & Cock
    14   Nov   1864

Lindsay, T.?
     4   Mar   1834

London Music Publishing Co., Ltd.
     5   Jun   1895

Lonsdale, Christopher
    21   May   1878

Lublin & Co., Ltd.
15   Jun   1909

**Lucas, Stanley, Weber, Pitt &
Hatzfeld, Ltd.**
4   Dec   1899
26   Apr   1901

Lyon & Hall
24   Nov   1886

Lyric Music Publishing Co.
8   Dec   1903

MacDowell, J., & Co.
11   Feb   1896

Marriott & Williams, Ltd.
10   Dec   1894
4   Dec   1895

Marshall's, Ltd.
2   Dec   1891

Martin, G. W.
28   Feb   1876

Mathias & Strickland
5   Feb   1895
25   Mar   1896
14   Oct   1903

May, Harry
18   Jun   1860

Metzler, G.
7   May   1866
30   Mar   1868
31   May   1880

Mills, J. A.
19   Mar   1900

Mocatta, B., & Co.
20   May   1896

Moore, Smith, & Co.
5   May   1904
1   Nov   1917

Morley, S.
19   Mar   1900

Morley, W., & Co.
27   Nov   1899
20   May   1915

Moutrie & Son
28   Apr   1892

Music Publishing Co.
22   Jun   1868

"A Music Seller"
27   Jul   1864

Neumeyer & Co.
?   ?   1881

Newman Music Co.
10   May   1923

Oetzmann & Co.
30   Jun   1875

Oliphant, Thomas
26   Apr   1873

Ollivier, Charles
19   Jan   1853

Ollivier, Robert Wilby
17   Oct   1870

Orpheus Music Publishing Co.
31   Oct   1906

Paine & Hopkins
17   Jun   1836

Patey & Willis Co.
3   Nov   1896
24   Sep   1902

Peachey, Mr.
23 Jun 1852
17 Aug 1853

Peck, Felix
25 May 1911

Phillips & Oliver
13 Nov 1900
14 Oct 1903
26 Jun 1906

Phillips & Page
8 Jun 1931

Pohlmann & Sons
24 Nov 1886

Preston, Mr.
19 Dec 1849

Prowse, Thomas
30 Jan 1868
30 Mar 1868

Purday, Charles Henry
23 Jun 1885

Purday, Thomas E.
31 Aug 1863

Purday, Zenas Trivett
2 Jul 1860

Ransford & Son
2 Jul 1888
25 Jun 1891
17 Jul 1894

Reid Bros.
16 Nov 1896

Roberts, H. S.
25 Nov 1884

Salter, Mr.
19 Mar 1900

Scrutton & Co.
22 Apr 1879

Shepherd, John
20 Feb 1874

Shepherd & Kilner
10 Jan 1884
24 Feb 1885

Simpson & Co.
11 Jul 1877
15 May 1879

Sprague & Co.
21 Oct 1884
25 Nov 1884
24 Feb 1885

Sprake & Palmer
26 Nov 1877

Swan, David
24 Nov 1886

Swan & Co.
27 Jun 1912

Taube & Co.
9 Apr 1900

Tolkien, Mr.
21 May 1862

Trimnell, W. F.
5 Feb 1895
24 Sep 1902

Turner, John Alvey
19 Apr 1882

Vernon, Charles
21 Jun 1831

Viaduct Co.
28 May 1891

Walker, George
    ?   ?   1848
    3   Jul 1851

Walker & Son
    ?   ?   1848

Weippert, A. N.
   17 Aug 1874

Wessel & Co.
   23 Jul 1860

A West End Music Publisher
    3   Jul 1851

White, Henry
    9 Nov 1893

White, S.
    9 Nov 1893

Whittingham, Alfred
   23 Nov 1870

Whittingham, Walter
    5 Oct 1904

Whittingham & MacDowell
   11 Feb 1896

Wickins & Co.
    1 Dec 1913

Wilcock, David
   14 Jul 1898
    8 Dec 1903

Wilcocke, S. H.
   18 Mar 1878

Willey & Co.
    2 May 1887

Williams, Benjamin
   16 Apr 1883
    3 Nov 1890
   25 Apr 1894
   28 Apr 1897
   22 May 1913

Williams, W., & Co.
   14 Apr 1886

Willis & Hall
    9 Apr 1900

Willis Music Co.
    4 Sep 1895
   31 Oct 1906
    8 Jun 1931

Wood, Messrs., & Co.
   24 Apr 1890
    4 May 1893

CHAPTER 7

The Beginnings of Current National Bibliography for German Music

by

D. W. Krummel

The last half of the eighteenth century and the first decades of the nineteenth comprise a particularly rich period, both for German music and for German music bibliography. The well-known monuments may be the great compilations of Forkel, Gerber, and Becker; but no less important were the early periodical listings of newly published music, which are the subject of this essay.[1] Richard S. Hill, of course, viewed this period and topic as one of his specialities. His Hoffmeister investigations began in the 1930s. His activities in the Library of Congress mission just after the war brought him in further touch with the Leipzig music publishers. My own interest in this subject was stimulated by his uncompleted group project for a transcript of the entries of the *Messkataloge*. The present study may serve to recall his instincts for uncovering significant events in the history of music and its documents.

A classic dichotomy separates musical *theoretica*—primarily with a literary text, and intended to be read and studied—from *practica*—with a musical text, intended for use in performance, and often given in German as *Noten* or *Musikalien*. The distinction makes broad and general sense, notwithstanding such vast and awkward gray areas as libretti and other books of texts, or pedagogical methods and instructional exercises. Moreover, the distinction changes over the course of history, as it is affected by the characteristics of the materials being described.

The eighteenth century began by preferring its *practica* in manuscript rather than printed copies, thanks to the collapse of typographic music printing during the seventeenth century. In the German-speaking world, instrumental and secular music were affected more than sacred. Engraved music re-emerged slowly through the last decades of the eighteenth century, as entrepreneur publishers rose out of the world of manuscript music copyists more

---

[1] The major previous survey of this topic is Hans-Martin Plesske, "Zur Geschichte der deutschen Musikbibliographie: Die periodische Verzeichnung der praktischen Musik," *Beiträge zur Musikwissenschaft* 5 (1963): 97-111.

often than that of the typographic printers of *theoretica*. The new music publishers were also necessarily more flexible and more evasive, as their audiences came successively to change from the court orchestras of mid-century, to the performers at subscription and other public concerts (which were often arranged by the entrepreneur-publishers themselves), to the personal *Kenner und Liebhaber* and the practitioners of *Hausmusik* at the end of the century. The history is further complicated by the powerful figure of J. G. I. Breitkopf, whose large special corner of the market involved both *theoretica* and *practica* set in type, as well as his rental service in manuscript and printed *practica*.

This survey of the changing bibliographical record is a story of two long-term changes: (1) the bias toward *theoretica* in 1750, critical and scholarly in character, becomes a bias toward *practica* in 1800, commercial and promotional in character; and (2) the irregular and unstable auspices typical even as late as 1780 were supplanted by periodic, effective, and solidly established auspices by the 1830s. The first change is suggested in the first two sections of this essay, which contrast the earliest serial listings of *theoretica* and *practica;* the second is suggested in the last three sections, which describe successively the Leipzig book-fair lists or *Messkataloge,* 1775-1820; the *Intelligenzblätter* for Rochlitz's *Allgemeine musikalische Zeitung* (AmZ), 1798-1838; and the Whistling-Hofmeister lists, which began in 1817.

* * * * *

Scholars of the Enlightenment. We begin with those well-known figures of German music journalism, whose imagination was attracted more to the philosophy and criticism than to the practice of music. One finds nearly two hundred titles of new music, for instance, cited during the first three years of Lorenz Mizler's *Neu-eröffnete musikalische Bibliothek* (Leipzig: Im Verlag der Verfassers, 1739-54). Just over half of these are the subject of fairly extensive reviews, while the rest are at least listed as "Musikalische Neuigkeiten," often with brief commentary.[2] Friedrich Wilhelm Marpurg also cited new music in his *Historisch-kritische Beyträge* (Berlin: J. J. Schützens sel. Witwe; G. A. Lange, 1754-62, with a sixth issue to vol. 5 dated 1778). In all, some 88 titles are cited as "Neuigkeiten" or among the "Vermischte Sachen," while several dozen more are the subject of major reviews.[3] Mention should also be made of Marpurg's

---

[2] These appear for vol. 1 in no. 2, pp. 75-77; no. 3, pp. 76-78; no. 4, pp. 82-88; no. 5, pp. 75-78; and no. 6, pp. 97-101. For vol. 2, see no. 1, pp. 148-58; no. 2, pp. 291-96; no. 3, pp. 169-86; and no. 4, pp. 122-24. In vol. 3 (with the pages now successive), pp. 168-70, 364-73, 577-604, and 765-78, etc.

[3] The listings, variously headed, appear for instance in vol. 1 (1754-55), pp. 70-75, 145-48, 475-78, and 514; in vol. 2 (1756), pp. 570-76; in vol. 3 (1757), pp. 163-67, 367-70, and 554-60; in vol. 4 (1758), pp. 187-88, 333-36, 393-407, and 559-64; and in vol. 5 (1760-62), pp. 1-19, 221-28, 246-52, and 347-55.

"Verzeichnis deutscher Odensammlungen mit Melodien," spread over nine issues of his *Kritische Briefe* (Berlin: F. W. Birnstiel, 1759-63). Some 43 titles are cited in admirable bibliographical detail and with critical comments, so as to make this an important if little recognized milestone in the history of specialized music bibliography.[4] The tradition continues with Johann Adam Hiller's *Wöchentliche Nachrichten* (Leipzig: Im Verlag der Zeitungs-Expedition, 1766-71). The four volumes in the series include nearly 75 reviews of considerable importance and insight that cover new music. Also of interest to bibliographers are Hiller's musical reports from France for 1767, which include a listing of four *theoretica* and 62 *practica* published in Paris.[5]

In addition to these specifically musical magazines, several other general journals also mention new music. While a full survey of this genre must lie beyond the scope of this essay, several examples can illustrate the point. The single extant copy of the *Freye Urtheile und Nachrichten zur Aufnehmen der Wissenschaften und der Historie Überhaupt* from 1750, for instance, includes several reviews of both *theoretica* and *practica*.[6] From Hiller's years also comes Christian Adolp Klotz's *Deutsche Bibliothek der schönen Wissenschaften* (Halle: J. J. Gebreuer, 1767-71). Roughly a dozen music books are reviewed in its 24 quarterly issues, their length running from 33 pages for C. G. Neander's *Lieder der Deutschen* (Berlin: Winter, 1766), to this couplet that says all that needs to be said about the same author's *Geistliche Lieder* (Riga: Hartknoch, 1766):[7]

> Hübsch gedruckt und schlecht gemacht,
> auf dass sie singe, wer Lust hat!

Between 1776 and 1784 the Leipzig publisher Siegfried Lebrecht Crusius issued an *Allgemeines Verzeichniss neuer Bücher mit kurzen Anmerkungen*. A supplementary "Gelehrten Anzeiger" clearly establishes Crusius among our erudite bibliographers. His lists are supplemented by annual classified indexes, in which class VI. is for the fine arts and sub-class VI.4 for music. The eight annual indexes include 124 music entries in all, while other entries like "Oden und Lieder" and "Operetten" pick up at least 25 more identifiable music works. As usual the emphasis is on *theoretica* and type-set music, although a number of engravings are cited, usually with some mention of the term *Stich* and with the collation given in terms of

---

[4] Vol. 1, pp. 160-64, 170-72, 240-47, 250-53, 355-57, 497-99; and vol. 2, pp. 46-48, 49-52, and 427-38.

[5] Vol. 2 (1767-68), pp. 205ff., esp. pp. 215-16, 221-24, and 229-32.

[6] I have not been able to learn more about this journal in the main sources on German periodical bibliography. The single copy of the *37. Stück*, in the Bibliothèque Royale in Brussels (Fétis 4618), comprises pp. 289-96 and is dated 12 May 1750. The British Library also has a pamphlet responding to an article in the journal, but apparently nothing of the journal itself.

[7] Vol. 1 (1768), pp. 108ff, and 181.

Bogen. Here one finds reference to major literary works like Forkel's *Musikalische Bibliothek* and Hiller's amplification of Adelung's *Anleitung,* as well as an array of clavier sonatas, Benda dramatic works, and Reichardt songs. The annotations are informative, whether descriptive or evaluative. Scheibe, for instance, is exposed as the compiler of the 1776 Masonic song book. Suggestions in its title notwithstanding, Hässler's sonatas are much too difficult for amateurs, and much to their loss. Reichardt's *Oden und Lieder* makes it clear that his complete Singspiel, *Liebe nur beglückt,* ought to be published as well. As for Vierling's six sonatas dedicated to Kirnberger, the reviewer observed, "Fourteen years ago these sonatas would have been more acceptable than today; ah, what might Kirnberger have said to this?"[8]

Crusius's final year also saw the brief appearance of the *Musicalische Bibliothek* of Hans Adolf, Freiherr von Eschstruth. Page 116 in the first and only volume announces sixteen new titles.[9] Several later music journals follow a similar plan. Between February 1793 and January 1794, Carl Spazier issued 51 weekly numbers of his *Berlinische musikalische Zeitung.* Each number runs to four pages, at first with new music listed among the "Nachrichten" at the end of the third page. Toward the end of the year the music moves over to page 4, where it often receives short critical reviews. In all, upwards of a hundred titles are cited, many of them in French. As befits a journal devoted substantially to printed music itself, the works cited are *practica* more often than *theoretica.* A similar recognition for *practica* is seen in the two numbers of Heinrich Christoph Koch's *Journal der Tonkunst* (Erfurt: Keyser, 1795). Ten pages in the first number are devoted to "Recenzionen und Anzeigen," while the second devotes nineteen, the last four of them comprising a "Verzeichniss neuer Musikalien" of some 39 items.[10] These journals may increasingly be concerned with *practica,* but their conception remains one that culminates in the famous retrospective lists of Johann Sigmund Gruber (1783, 1785, and 1790) and Johann Nikolaus Forkel (1792). All four titles in question, it should be remembered, specify the phrase "Litteratur der Musik." While Forkel admittedly found it useful to include a 20-page list of early

---

[8] Crusius's music references are in vol. 1, p. 747; vol. 2, pp. 1003-04; vol. 3, p. 1018; vol. 4, pp. 992-93, and see also 994-96; vol. 5, pp. 992-93; vol. 6, pp. 983-84, and see also 997-99; vol. 7, p. 971, also p. 967; and vol. 8, p. 975. The Scheibe attribution and the Hässler reference are in vol. 1, p. 514 (items 1084 and 1086); the Reichardt in vol. 6, p. 526 (item 796); and the Vierling in vol. 6, p. 525 (item 793).

[9] Further bibliographical references are buried in other entries. Vol. 1, pp. 35-37, for instance, includes an index to sixteen new editions reviewed in Forkel's *Musikalischer Almanach für Deutschland* (Leipzig: Schwickert, 1782); pp. 41-64 presents a "Verzeichnis jetztlebender Componisten in Deutschland" with lists of their music, including a reference to Beethoven, "Erst siben Jare alt, drei *Sonaten* fürs Clavir, fol. Speier 1783. Auch *Lider* in Speierischen Blumenlese." On pp. 113-16 is found a discussion of music in Charleston, South Carolina.

[10] Part VI, pp. 258-61.

music manuscript sources, one can still sense his strong concern for orderliness, a concern that would encourage him to find some way to exclude the vast and burgeoning contemporary literature of engraved and manuscript *musica practica*.

One single journal stands out above the rest as a bibliographical record: Carl Friedrich Cramer's *Magazin der Musik* (Hamburg: In der musicalischen Niederlage, 1783-89). Here, over a six-year period, nearly a hundred musical editions were reviewed, and over a thousand more listed. Cramer's numbering scheme for bibliographical entries (see Table 1, pp. 312-13) may be messy and confusing, but what is more important is the fact that he apparently intended to make some point of, and take some pride in, the quantitative count in its own right. His journal's imprint will be seen again shortly. If the other journals mentioned so far seem to culminate in Forkel, here is the one that leads to a point closer to Ernst Ludwig Gerber's *Historisch-biographisches Lexikon der Tonkünstler* (Leipzig: Breitkopf, 1790-92; extended, Leipzig: Kühnel, 1812-14).

These nine journals — Cramer among them excepted here — cite no more than 800 new musical works altogether. For all their significance in the history of musical thought, they must be conceded to record a very small portion of the total output of the music press, strongly biased toward typeset editions, especially in their early years. A more important source, but one limited in a different way, involves the music catalogues issued by retailers and entrepreneurs.

* * * * *

The Commercial Music Lists. A tradition of commercial, as distinguished from scholarly, music bibliography — if we may use the word tradition at all in such a necessarily opportunistic and experimental world — properly begins with the adventuresome and opportunistic J. G. I. Breitkopf. His fascination with music publishing and the resulting development of his music type date from the 1750s. The next decade saw the advent of his copying business, and along with it a concern for bibliographical access to his musical repertory. As we shall see, his heirs would continue to recognize the value of promotional efforts through bibliography, even as their approach to music printing came to change from the speculative to the conservative.

Breitkopf's thematic catalogues, issued between 1762 and 1787, are well known.[11] Less famous but somewhat more extensive in their coverage are the non-thematic catalogues, which fall into three sequences. The first is devoted to printed music and bears the title *Verzeichniss musikalischer Bücher*. The first edition appeared in 1760 in 32 pages; the second through sixth editions appeared a few years apart to 1780, and continue the pagination consecutively

---

[11] These are reproduced, and discussed in Barry S. Brook's introduction to *The Breitkopf Thematic Catalogue: The Six Parts and Sixteen Supplements* (New York: Dover Publications, 1965).

TABLE 1

NUMBERED BIBLIOGRAPHICAL REFERENCES IN CRAMER'S *Magazin*

Pages	Nos.	Bibliographical References
		Jahrgang 1, 1. Hälfte (1783)
29-57	1	extended review (of Reichardt *Kunstmagazin*)
57-67	2-7	reviews (i.e., averaging about one page each)
68-93	8-51	brief reviews (i.e., averaging considerably less)
93-103	52	extended review
103-04	53	review
104-30	54-325	list of 272 new titles
131-37	326-29	reviews
137-47	330	extended review, followed by several bibliographical notices, unnumbered
239-73	331-32	other extended reviews
273-95	333-584	". . . ein Verzeichnis der geschriebenen Musicalien, die seit der Herausgabe des grossen vollständigen musicalischen Catalogus bey Herrn Westphal eingekommen sind" with 252 citations
296-317	585-610	reviews
400-10	611	extended review (of Sarti, *Giulio Sabino*)
410-13	612-16	reviews
413-42	617	extended review (of *Le Brigandage de la musique italienne*)
442-60	618-36	reviews
460-78	637	extended review (of E. W. Wolf, *Ostercantate*)
478-520	638-81	brief reviews
520-53	682-703	"Verzeichnis der merkwürdigen in December voriges und Januar dieses Jahrs zu Paris herausgekommenen Musicalien"
523-29	704-867	"Neu eingekommene gedruckte und in der Westphalische Niederlage zu haben Musicalien"
		Jahrgang 1, 2. Hälfte (1783)
800-24		"Ankündigungen" 1-12, with identification of some reviews
912-21	868-916	brief reviews

TABLE 1

NUMBERED BIBLIOGRAPHICAL REFERENCES—*Continued*

313

Pages	Bibliographical References
1115-36	"Ankündigungen" 1-16, listing new publications
1238-1358	"Recensionen, Ankündigungen" 1-31
1359-64	"Folgendes sind noch einige Titel von musicalischen Producten, die in diesem Jahre das Licht der Welt erblickt haben, und in den Messcatalogen von 1783 und änderwärts angeführt stehen," 29 titles in all, with a commentary on pp. 1364-71
1371-72	five titles of "Neu fertige gewordene Werke sind bey mir zu haben . . . Speyer, d. 14. Weinmund. Bossler"

Jahrgang 2, [1. Hälfte] (title page dated 1784)

243	"Ankündigungen" 1-14
503-24	review of Cramer's *Oden und Lieder*
535-51	other reviews, numbered 2-8
595-629	"Recensionen" 1-3, "aus dem Mercure de France von diesem Jahre . . ."
677-99	"Ankündigungen" 1-9

Jahrgang 2, 2. Hälfte (title page dated 1786)

847-890	"Recensionen" 1-28
891-902	"Ankündigungen" 1-9
1035-80	"Recensionen" 1-22
1080-84	"Ankündigungen" 1-4
1179-84	"Ankündigungen" 1-4
1209-61	"Recensionen" 1-5
1262-71	"Ankündigungen" 1-6
1281-1337	"Recensionen" 1-35
1338-77	"Ankündigungen" 1-3

"Erstes Vierteljahr," 1789

includes reviews, i.e., pp. 270-80, nos. "3-8"

through page 172. In all, roughly 2000 titles are listed. The second series, devoted to unpublished music, is entitled *Verzeichniss musikalischer Werke . . . welche nicht durch den Druck bekannt gemacht worden.* Its four editions, which appeared between 1761 and 1780, include about 4000 titles. Completing the set is a separate *Verzeichniss lateinischer und italienischer Kirchen-Musiken,* which appeared in 1769 and contains about 500 more titles. The systematic arrangement follows a simple classed scheme similar to that in the thematic catalogues, with a few revisions but very little expansion. A correlation of the non-thematic with the thematic catalogues will be valuable.[12] Both need also to be correlated against the massive 1802 Breitkopf & Härtel *Hauptkatalog.*[13] Its 684 pages include roughly 10,000 entries, also in a classified arrangement but with no index. This huge list further constitutes a backdrop against which the later *AmZ* lists will form something of a continuation.

In 1770 the Hamburg dealer Johann Christoph Westphal began issuing promotional lists of the holdings in his "Musikalische Niederlage" — the same institution that in 1783 was to be associated with Cramer's journal discussed above. Westphal's propensity for cataloguing is seen in the total of over 40 lists that he issued over the next 26 years, as summarized in Table II (see pp. 316-17). While about 25,000 citations are listed, there are in fact probably no more than 10,000 different editions involved, or at most 15,000. Even so, we are now considering ten to fifteen times as much music as in all the various learned music journals together. Forkel speaks of Westphal's efforts in arranging subscription concerts: it is plausible to see his activities extending widely through the music world, the bibliographies forming one promotional aspect of the plan.[14]

---

[12] See Brook, x-xii.

[13] The work can be dated quite exactly through its references, mostly to the *Allgemeine musikalische Zeitung.* The basic set (pp. viii, [1]-276) mentions the 1802 volume of this periodical on p. 274. Part II (pp. [277]-359) mentions the October 1803 issue on p. 359. Part III (pp. [362]-[432]) mentions the October 1804 issue on p. 432. Part IV (pp. [4332]-[508]; lacking 0o2 in the Brussels copy, Fétis 5200) mentions the November 1806 issue on p. 508. Part V (pp. [509]-90; gathering Yy misbound in the Brussels copy) has so far proven hard to date with any conclusiveness because of contradictory information. Part VI (pp. [591]-624) mentions Beethoven's op. 73 piano concerto, which Kinsky-Halm dated from February 1811. Other Breitkopf catalogues include a series of special *Messkataloge,* as cited by Brook, as well as still others collected in the RISM files now in Paris.

Several of the books discussed here are signed continuously from the original set through their supplements, and include some curious anomalies, for instance a new supplement beginning on the third or fourth leaf of a gathering. Detailed collations need to be done, and preferably using copies bound less snugly than those in Brussels. It is by working with the signatures in the Brussels copy of this Breitkopf catalogue (a duodecimo in half-sheets), for instance, that one can determine that four leaves from the sixth supplement (3F1-4) are mis-bound in the midst of the fifth supplement (between 2Y6 and 2Z1).

[14] In working with the Westphal catalogue it is important to know about Miriam Terry, "C. P. E. Bach and J. J. H. Westphal — a Clarification," *Journal of the American Musicological Society* 22 (1969): 106-15. Johann Jacob Heinrich Westphal (1756-

The relationship between Westphal and Böhme is not clear. Both worked in Hamburg; and Westphal's last extant list is from 1796, just four years after Böhme's first list and the same year as Böhme's second and more important list. Nor is it clear what the relationship is between the lists that mention Böhme alone and those that fall into an entirely separate sequence and mention Günther & Böhme.[15] A close reading of the title page statements raises more questions than it clarifies. In all, the catalogues list perhaps 30,000 entries, many of which are probably duplicated in several other lists although the classified arrangement and absence of indexes frustrates a comparison. The contents of the two sets are summarized in Table III (see pp. 318-19).

While the Breitkopf, Westphal, and Böhme lists are apparently the most extensive ones of their time, other entrepreneurs can also be identified from their catalogues. The 1773 list prepared by Christian Ulrich Ringmacher, a Berlin music dealer and publisher, is of special interest for its thematic incipits.[16] While the manuscripts of Christian Gottfried Thomas's *Der grosse thematische Catalogus,* as well as *Der erste Nachtrag* and *Summarisches Verzeichnis,* are all lost, other published writings document the extravagant and admirable aspirations of a true master entrepreneur, 170 years too soon for UNESCO.[17] The Leuckart catalogues of 1787-92 have been recognized as

---

1852), the Mecklenburg organist and friend of C. P. E. Bach, part of whose extensive collection is now in Brussels (and was used extensively in the present study), is not to be confused with the Hamburg music dealer discussed here.

[15] The firm of Günther and Böhme is an evasive one, cited in passing in the major works on early music publishing (Gerber, Fétis, Eitner's *Buch- und Musikalienhändler*), but not in any of the main sources on German publishing in general (the Kapp and Goldfriedrich history, the Kirschner lexica, or the indexes to the massive *Geschichte der deutschen Buchhandels*), nor in Hans-Martin Plesske's valuable "Bibliographie der Schrifttums zur Geschichte deutscher und österreichischer Musikverlage," *Beiträge zur Geschichte des Buchwesens* 3 (1968): 135-222. The fair catalogues themselves give us a few of the particulars through several entries in 1795 (four for the Ostermesse, all of them identifying the Leipzig agency of Leo, which presumably handled copies for the fair itself) and 1796 (eleven for the Ostermesse and eight more for the Michaelismesse, all of them naming the Leipzig agency of Kleefeld). For the most part the composers named are an obscure lot. Seven of the 23 titles cannot be found in RISM, by composers C. F. Ebers, A. C. Heyse, "von Lackner," and Franz Lauske. From these and other composer entries we are led to further imprints in RISM, a few of them naming Günther and Böhme but most of them naming Johann August Böhme alone, one of them (RISM M 7803-04) extant in variant issues from both. From these additional entries—two for J. K. Ambrosch, eight for Antonio Bianchi, 27 for Friedrich Kirmair, six for August Eberhard Müller—we may estimate that the firm issued perhaps upwards of a hundred titles in the 1790s, apart from its music rental activity. The best-known works would appear to be the first editions of four early Mozart symphonies (K. 161b = 199, 162, 173dB = 183, and 186b = 202), Müller's vocal scores for *Figaro* and *La clemenza di Tito,* and several Mozart spuriosities done by Müller himself (RISM M 7800-04).

[16] Cited in Barry S. Brook, *Thematic Catalogues in Music: An Annotated Bibliography* (Hillsdale, N.Y.: Pendragon Press, 1972), entry 1065; the title page is reproduced by Brook on p. 226.

[17] See Barry S. Brook, "Piracy and Panacea: On the Dissemination of Music in the Late Eighteenth Century," *Proceedings of the Royal Musical Association* 102 (1975-76): 13-36.

TABLE 2

SYNOPSIS OF THE WESTPHAL CATALOGUES (Fétis 5205 in B-Br)

Item	Date	Title (Contents) and Pagination
1	1770	*Verzeichnis von Musicalien* . . . (The first basic list, with 500 entries), 37 pp.
2	1772	*Verzeichnis von Musicalien* . . . (The second basic list, with 1200 entries), 64 pp.
3	n.d.	[Untitled list, beginning 'Sinfonien'] (Presumably a supplement to 2), pp. 3-15
4	1774	*Verzeichnis von Musicalien* . . . (The third basic list, with 1600 entries), 92 pp. + [2] pp. of index
5	1776	*Beilage zum zweyten Anhang* . . . (A supplement to two major supplements no longer extant, with 200 entries), pp. [147]-162
6	1777	*Verzeichnis von Musicalien* . . . (The fourth basic list, with 3000 entries), 152 pp. + 2 pp. of addenda and an index
7	1777	*Anhang zum Verzeichnis* . . . (A supplement to 6, with 500 entries), pp. 153-82
8	1777	*Vorläufige Anzeige* . . . *ausser dem grossen Verzeichniss und Anhang* (Another supplement to 6, with 300 entries), 20 pp.
9	1778	*Verzeichnis von Musicalien* . . . (The fifth basic list, with 3200 entries), 152 pp.
10	1778	*Anhang zum Verzeichnis* . . . (A supplement to 9, with 1500 entries, suggesting a sudden considerable expansion of the holdings), 72 pp.
11	n.d.	*Folgende Werke werden ehestens erwartet und hiermit vorläuffig angezeiget* (Another informal supplement), 4 pp.
12	July 1778	*An neuen Sachen sind noch ferner eingekommen.* . . , 3 pp.
13	October 1778	*Erster Beytrag zum Verzeichniss,* 20 pp.
14	February 1779	*Zweyter Beytrag zum Verzeichniss* . . . ; *Zweyter Auflage des ersten Beytrags,* 29 pp.
15	March 1779	*Folgende neue Musikalien sind eingekommen* . . . , 4 pp.
16	August 1779	*Zweyter Anhang des grossen Verzeichnisses* (continuing 10 above), pp. [73]-108
17	December 1779	*Neue eingekommene Werke,* 12 pp.

TABLE 2

317

SYNOPSIS OF THE WESTPHAL CATALOGUES — *Continued*

Item	Date	Title (Contents) and Pagination
18	February 1780	*Neue eingekommene Werke*, 8 pp.
19	May 1780	*Eingekommene neue Werke*, 16 pp.
20	July 1780	*In der musicalische Niederlage . . . eingekommen . . .* , 8 pp.
21	December 1780	*In der musikalischen Niederlage . . . eingekommen . . .* , 8 pp.
22	July 1781	*In der musicalischen Niederlage . . . eingekommen . . .* , 8 pp.
23	December 1781	*Folgende neue Musicalien . . . angekommen . . .* , 8 pp.
24	July 1782	*Anhang des Verzeichnisses* (mis-dated 1772, another supplement to 10 *opposite*), 12 pp.
25	1782	*Verzeichniss derer Musicalien* (A major list of 5000 entries superseding 10 *opposite*), 287, [9] pp. Other copies in the Gemeente Museum (Charbon 1:158) and in Bologna (Gaspari 1:153)
26	1783	*Anhang zum Verzeichniss*, 52 pp.
27	1784	*Anhang zum Verzeichniss*, 20 pp.
28	1785	*Anhang zum Verzeichniss*, 16 pp.
29	1785	*Verzeichnisz einiger neuen Werke*, 4 pp.
30	July 1785	*Verzeichnisz einiger neuen Werke*, 8 pp.
31	July 1786	*Verzeichniss einiger neuen Werke*, 16 pp.
32	March 1787	*Anhang zum Verzeichniss*, 8 pp.
33	October 1787	*Anhang zum Verzeichniss*, 23 pp.
34	June 1788	*Anhang zum Verzeichniss*, 32 pp.
35	February 1789	*Neue eingekommene Musicalien*, 16 pp.
36	April 1790	*Neue eingekommene Musikalien*, 12 pp.
37	October 1792	*Eingekommene neue Musikalien*, 16 pp.
38	March 1793	*Eingekommene neue Musikalien*, 12 pp.
39	February 1794	*Eingekommene neue Musikalien*, 8 pp.
40	August 1794	*Eingekommene neue Musikalien*, 8 pp.
41	January 1795	*Eingekommene neue Musikalien*, 12 pp.
42	June 1795	*Eingekommene Musikalien*, 8 pp.
43	September 1795	*Eingekommene Musikalien*, 16 pp.
44	April 1796	*Eingekommene Musikalien*, 20 pp.

TABLE 3

SYNOPSIS OF THE BÖHME CATALOGUES (Fétis 5206 in B-Br)

Date	Title and Contents	Vol./Item
1796	Günther u. Böhme, *Verzeichnis der neuesten Musikalien . . . zu haben sind . . . , 3. Fortsetzung* (39 pp., classified), with a *Nachtrag* (pp. 40-45), and another list of works "auch in Commission in der Kleefeldtschen Buchhandlung in Leipzig zu bekommen sind" (pp. 46-47), and a page of "Inhalt" (p. 48)	2/1
1796	--, ---, *4. Fortsetzung* (35 pp. classified), with a *Nachtrag* (pp. 35-43) and a *2. Nachtrag* (pp. 43-48)	2/2
1796	--, ---, *5. Fortsetzung* (35 pp. [pp. 1-16 misbound above], classified), with a *Nachtrag* (pp. 35-40)	2/3
1797	--, ---, *6. Fortsetzung* (28 pp., classified), with a *Nachtrag* (pp. 29-37) and an added *Verzeichnis* (pp. 38-40)	2/4
1797	--, ---, *7. Fortsetzung* (30 pp., classified), with a *Nachtrag* (pp. 30-40)	2/5
n.d.	--, ---, *8. Fortsetzung* (24 pp., alphabetical), with a *Nachtrag* (pp. 25-32), and a *2. Nachtrag* (pp. 33-40)	2/6
1799	Böhme [alone], *Verzeichnis der neuesten Musikalien . . . zu haben sind, 4. Fortsetzung* (63 pp., alphabetical)	1/1
1799	--, ---, *5. Fortsetzung* (48 pp., classified)	1/2
1799	--, ---, *9. Fortsetzung* (33 pp., alphabetical), with a *Nachtrag* (pp. 34-44) and *2. Nachtrag* (pp. 45-48)	1/3
n.d.	--, ---, *10. Fortsetzung* (29 pp., alphabetical), with a *Nachtrag* (pp. 30-40)	1/4

TABLE 3

SYNOPSIS OF THE BÖHME CATALOGUES – *Continued*

Date	Title and Contents	Vol./Item
1800	--, ---, *11. Fortsetzung* (40 pp., alphabetical), with a *Nachtrag* (pp. 41-48)	w.f.
1800	--, *Verzeichnis von Musikalien . . . verlegt* (10 pp., alphabetical), with a *2. Nachtrag* (pp. 23-29; the lacking first *Nachtrag* presumably covered pp. 11-22)	2/7
1801	--, *Verzeichnis der neuesten Musikalien . . . zu haben sind . . . , 12. Fortsetzung* (46 pp., alphabetical), with a *Nachtrag* (pp. 46-48)	1/6
1802	--, ---, *13. Fortsetzung* (79 pp., classified)	1/7
1802	--, *Verzeichnis der neuesten Musikalien . . . zu haben sind* (19 pp., alphabetical), with an *Anhang* (pp. 20-22)	2/8
1802	--, *Verlagsverzeichnis* (47 pp., classified), with an added p. of "Inhalt" (p. 48), *1. Nachtrag* (pp. 49-55), and a *2. Nachtrag* (also pp. 50-55, but with mostly new listings!)	2/9
1803	--, *Verzeichnis der neuesten Musikalien . . . , 14. Fortsetzung* (80 pp., classified), with a *Nachtrag* (pp. 81-88)	1/8
1804	--, ---, *15. Fortsetzung* (43 pp., classified), with a *Nachtrag* (pp. 44-48)	1/9
1805	--, ---, *16. Fortsetzung* (34 pp., classified), with a *Nachtrag* (pp. 35-38)	1/10
1806	--, ---, *17. Fortsetzung* (52 pp., classified)	1/11
1809	--, *Verlagsverzeichnis* (102 pp., classified), with "Inhalt" added (pp. [103-04]) and *1. Nachtrag* (pp. [1]-8)	2/10

documenting the changing needs of the performer's repertory.[18]
Other catalogues exhibit the stock of particular publishers. Some are
thematic, among them those by Bossler in Speyer (1790-94),[19] while
others, mostly yet to be described and studied, are "plate catalogues"
of the variety associated with Cari Johansson.[20] Occasionally we
will need to distinguish between the list of publications issued by
a publisher who also served as a dealer, and the list of sale or rental
stock of a dealer who also served as a publisher.[21] For now, the
main importance of the commercial lists must be recognized, since
here we have a far more extensive record of the music of the time,
tied to contemporary performance tastes much as the listings of the
learned bibliographers discussed earlier were tied to contemporary
intellectual thought.

* * * * *

The Leipzig Fair Catalogues. In 1775 the *Messkataloge* re-enter
the picture. The semi-annual Easter and Michaelmas fairs, held since
the late middle ages in Frankfurt and Leipzig, are recognized as a
major force in the establishment of a German book trade, while the
catalogues of these fairs, issued beginning in 1564, provide an
invaluable source for the study of early German publishing in general.
Albert Göhler's index of the early music entries covers about 1140
titles for the last 36 years of the sixteenth century and about 1900
more for the seventeenth.[22] Both *theoretica* and *practica* are
included. As German music publishing declined during the early
eighteenth century, the music sections of the fair catalogues came
to be abandoned, those from Frankfurt in 1750 and those from
Leipzig in 1759. For the early part of the century Göhler cites about
625 entries, most of them *theoretica*.

In 1775 a separate "Musikalien" section reappears for the Leipzig
fairs, with 46 titles for the Easter fair and 11 more for Michaelmas.
The coverage increases during the 1780s and 1790s, and (apart from
lean years from 1799 to 1801) burgeons over the next decades, reaching

---

[18] Described in Jan LaRue, "Ten Rediscovered Sale Catalogues: Leuckart's
Supplements, Breslau 1787-1792," in *Musik und Verlag: Festschrift K. G. Vötterle*
(Kassel: Bärenreiter, 1968), 424-31.

[19] The catalogues are mentioned in Otto Erich Deutsch, "Thematische Kataloge,"
Fontes artis musicae 5 (1958): 75. No specific location is given, and later references
all seem to trace back to Deutsch.

[20] Cari Johansson, *French Music Publishers' Catalogues of the Second Half of the
Eighteenth Century* (Stockholm: Almqvist & Wiksell, 1955).

[21] Rellstab's catalogues (i.e., Brussels, Bibliothèque Royale, Fétis 5204) come to mind,
as described in Rudolf Elvers, "Die bei J. K. F. Rellstab in Berlin bis 1800 erschienenen
Mozart-Drucke," *Mozart Jahrbuch* (1957), 153-57.

[22] Albert Göhler, *Die Messkataloge im Dienste der musikalischen Geschichtsforschung*
(Leipzig: C. F. Kahnt, 1901); also his *Verzeichnis der in den Frankfurter und Leipziger
Messkatalogen der Jahre 1564 bis 1759 angezeigten Musikalien* (Leipzig: C. F. Kahnt,
1902).

a high point of 595 titles in 1812. As the statistical totals in Table 4 (see pp. 322-23) will suggest, the Easter fairs are always the more extensive. With the Michaelmas fair of 1819 the sharp decline begins, and after the 1820 fairs the music sections terminate, presumably in deference to the Whistling-Hofmeister lists discussed below. In all, over the 46-year period, a total of 9328 music titles are included.

This period also saw the rise of German music engraving, documented in the fair catalogues through the names of the four most prolific firms for these years:

1775: Ringmacher, Hartknoch, Löffler, Breitkopf—all of them using movable type

1790: Breitkopf, Hilscher, Rellstab, Bossler—the first and third of whom used type, the other two engraving

1806: Breitkopf, Kühnel, Polt, Vollmer—the first of whom used all forms, the second engravings, the last two mostly movable type

1816: Breitkopf, Schlesinger, Hofmeister, Peters—all of them by now using engravings primarily

This overriding trend apart, mention should be made of the fact that some major publishers who used engravings—all of them located in cities other than Leipzig, incidentally—are little represented in the fair lists: Simrock with a mere 21 entries, Schott with 20, Böhme with 18, Hoffmeister in Vienna with 13, Artaria with 11, Falter with 3, André with 2, and Götz and Gombart with none at all. Most Viennese firms—Cappi, Mollo, Mechetti, Steiner, and Traeg among them—are also missing entirely, although their editions may in fact on closer examination prove to be present but listed under another agency, as was the case with Weigl, whose editions bear the imprint of Weigel in Leipzig. It is also of some interest to note that several citations specify the use of the new method of printing music, lithography.[23] Equally surprising is the evidence of decentralization of German music publishing that these catalogues so conclusively demonstrate: the 9328 titles come from roughly 400 different publishers, who were located in no fewer than 150 different cities![24]

* * * * *

Rochlitz's Intelligenzblätter. A separate section of this survey must also be devoted to Johann Friedrich Rochlitz's *Allgemeine*

---

[23] For instance, the *Ouvertüre und Gesänge* to an unidentified setting of *Wilhelm Tell* in the 1805 *Ostermesse* catalogue ("auf Steinplatten gedruckt"); Joseph Baader's *Der baiersche Krieger* in the 1806 *Ostermesse* catalogue ("auf Stein gezeichn. u. abgedruckt"); and a *Choralbuch* for Bavarian Protestants in the 1819 *Ostermesse* catalogue ("in Stein lithographirt").

[24] A facsimile reprint of these catalogues, with indexes by composer, publisher, and place of publication, is now in the planning stages.

TABLE 4

MUSIC IN THE LEIPZIG *MESSKATALOGE*

Year	Ostermesse		Michaelismesse		Annual Total
	Pages	Total Items	Pages	Total Items	
1775	878-80	46	945	11	57
1776	90-92	33	168-69	21	54
1777	282-83	23	363-64	16	39
1778	492-94	34	575-76	22	56
1779	696-97	31	779-81	23	54
1780	910-12	34	1009-10	25	59
1781	114-17	39	216-17	23	62
1782	358-60	44	464-65	27	71
1783	631-34	47	733-34	31	78
1784	894-98	64	1000-01	31	95
1785	110-14	77	212-14	33	110
1786	375-80	83	479-80	16	99
1787	629-33	68	742-44	31	99
1788	136-41	74	284-87	43	117
1789	141-46	89	264-65	24	113
1790	150-54	78	269-71	39	127
1791	157-62	84	268-70	39	133
1792	148-52	70	262-66	65	135
1793	157-63	95	281-82[4]	59	154
1794	163-67	75	269-70	34	109
1795	155-62[1]	114	297-300	45	159
1796	170-75	89	318-23	67	156
1797	214-21	104	367-69	38	142

[1] Beginning of octavo format; previous volumes are in quarto.

TABLE 4
MUSIC IN THE LEIPZIG *MESSKATALOGE— Continued*

| Year | Ostermesse | | Michaelismesse | | Annual |
	Pages	Total items	Pages	Total Items	Total
1798	214-22	111	381-82	18	129
1799	199-201	29	371	8	37
1800	222-27	86	403-05	25	111
1801	212-16	57	384-85	12	69
1802	269-75	89	463-68	66	155
1803	258-70	184	440-43	55	239
1804	239-53	223	467-80	179	402
1805	274-89	244	457-62	68	312
1806	224-36	212	384-89	76	288
1807	143-54	171	195-301	96	267
1808	211-27	265	386-93	128	393
1809	188-200	209	341-48	120	329
1810	205-23	292	391-96	92	384
1811	203-20	276	386-94	126	402
1812	176-98	338	354-70	257	595
1813	147-64	273	262-72	148	421
1814	151-63	173	324-32	101	274
1815	180-201	292	384-91	109	401
1816	202-26	370	405-12	108	478
1817	243-69	377	477-85	114	491
1818	227-48	315	473-83	154	469
1819	261-83	323	502-05	59	382
1820	257-58	9	488-89	12	21

musikalische Zeitung (Leipzig: Breitkopf & Härtel, 1798-1848).   The contents of this landmark music journal are well known, the reviews of Beethoven in particular.   Entirely separate from the critical notices of new musical editions—upwards of a thousand of them over the 50 years of the journal—are the brief citations of perhaps 20,000 new editions of music that appeared between 1798 and 1838 in supplementary *Intelligenzblätter*.   These supplements run from two to eight pages apiece, and appear at irregular intervals with as few as nine or as many as 26 a year, each with the month and year specified.   The history is summarized in Table 5 (see pp. 326-27).   Included are short announcements and comments directed mostly to music dealers, as well as the "Neue Musikalien" that could be obtained from Breitkopf (and presumably from other dealers as well).   Here by all odds is the most extensive bibliographical record of new music published during this period, both in its size and in the frequency of its appearance for dating purposes, if not in the detail or demonstrably in the accuracy of its citations.

Admittedly the value of the precise dates of listing, down to the particular month and year, is somewhat offset on closer examination by the practice of grouping according to publisher.   A new list seems to have been put together whenever enough material had come in to justify one, and often the contents of a whole list are devoted to new editions from a single publisher.   Of the ten lists from 1813, for instance, only nos. 4 and 9 are "von verschiedenen Verlegern"; list 1 is entirely from Simrock, list 2 from Schlesinger, list 7 from Breitkopf; lists 3 and 6 contain mostly Kühnel and Breitkopf, list 5 Hofmeister and more Simrock, list 8 mostly Zulehner, and list 10 all Hofmeister and Breitkopf.   These lists were obviously assembled from what was received rather than through any systematic search for new titles.   The compilers being at the mercy of the publishers, it is always possible that works were listed that were never published, or for which plates were engraved but no copies run off in the absence of any orders or other expression of interest from purchasers.

Over its 40-year history, the *Intelligenzblätter* averaged 70 columns of copy a year, or 500 entries for new music per year.   The first six years exceed this average, while the years 1814-26 fall somewhat short, for whatever reason.   Successors in the *AmZ* to the *Intelligenzblätter* include the special "Ankundigüngen" sections that appear after 1838, most often in the individual issues of the journal itself.   In 1836 there is also seen a special "Ostermesse Bericht" from the Vienna firm of Diabelli which continued for several years.   This later history of Rochlitz's journal, however, belongs to another chapter in the account of the rise of modern German current music bibliography.   The relationship of these lists to the Whistling-Hofmeister lists is an essential part of our story, of course; for now, it is sufficient to recall that the modern German music publishing trade, which scarcely existed in 1785, was by the 1830s obviously a flourishing industry.   To fill in the picture, however, it is useful to introduce the function and coverage of the Whistling-Hofmeister lists themselves.

The Whistling-Hofmeister Series. The studies by Ratliff[25] and by Hopkinson and Elvers[26] — pursued independently and simultaneously — between them say most of what needs to be said about the set, and in the absence of any opportunity to compare the specific coverage of the various component parts — or to contrast it with the last of the fair catalogues and the *Intelligenzblätter* — this report can add only a few relevant details. For instance, the set may be monumental, but it is not unprecedented as the oldest of the present-day current music bibliographies, since the music section in the *Bibliographie de la France* dates continuously from 1811. Ratliff's publisher index shows us that foreign publishers were far better represented here than in the *Messkataloge.* (A comparison with the *Intelligenzblätter* is impossible, since so many of its "verschiedene Verleger" are yet to be fully identified.) While Ratliff's introduction emphasizes the internal coverage of the set through 1827, Elvers and Hopkinson clarify the complicated bibliographical history of the set. Based on their presentation, the *coup d'oeil* in Table VI (see p. 328) will be useful.

Several matters are conspicuously unclear about the great series. Over 35 years it obviously changed in its basic purpose, in a way quite similar to the transformation of the 1876 *U.S. Catalogue* into the *Cumulative Book Index.* In 1817 the set was first conceived as a listing of all music then in print; by 1852 it was a listing only of new publications. The transition from a function of availability to one of announcement was obviously necessary considering the vast proliferation of music publishing. It further reflects the rising interest in music copyright protection, since newly protected titles needed to be identified so as to warn off aspirant pirates. How precisely the transition in function took place has yet to be determined, but it will be done, in part, through a study of the patterns of deletion. Legend has it that items in the various *Monatsberichte* do not always show up in their appropriate *Handbücher* cumulations later on; the specifics are yet to be laid forth, and would be worth knowing about. For dating purposes, the standard practice — for the scholar fortunate enough to work in the library that has everything — would be to locate a title first in one of the *Handbücher,* then (at least after 1851) to identify it in its *Jahresverzeichnis,* and finally, if the inquiry called for an even more specific date, to look through the contributory *Monatsberichte* for the particular citation.

A direct comparison of this set with the *Messkataloge* and with the *Intelligenzblätter* is a vast chore in the absence of indexes to any of them, further complicated by the systematic classification found in

---

[25] Carl Friedrich Whistling and Friedrich Hofmeister, *Handbuch der musikalischen Litteratur: A Reprint of the 1817 Edition and the Ten Supplements, 1817-1827,* with a new introduction by Neil Ratliff (New York: Garland Publishing Co., 1975).

[26] Rudolf Elvers and Cecil Hopkinson, "A Survey of the Music Catalogues of Whistling and Hofmeister," *Fontes artis musicae* 19 (1972): 1-7.

TABLE 5

AmZ INTELLIGENZBLÄTTER TOTALS

Vol.	Date	Total Number of Issues	Total Number of Columns[1]
1	1798-99	20	106
2	1799-1800	20	86
3	1800-01	14	56
4	1801-02	19	76
5	1802-03	26[2]	112
6	1803-04	21	92
7	1804-05	14	60
8	1805-06	12	48
9	1806-07	12	52
10	1807-08	12	52
11	1808-09	12	48
12	1809-10	14	60
13	1811	18	86
14	1812	18	80
15	1813	10	48
16	1814	9	40
17	1815	8	32
18	1816	11	48
19	1817	9	36
20	1818	12	52

[1] Each column will average from 8 to 15 citations.

[2] The Table of Contents mentions 27 issues, but only 26 are extant and accountable in the page numbering sequence.

TABLE 5
AmZ INTELLIGENZBLÄTTER TOTALS— Continued

Vol.	Date	Total number of Issues	Total Number of Columns
21	1819	7	28
22	1820	10	40
23	1821	10	44
24	1822	9	44
25	1823	12	52
26	1824	10	44
27	1825	12	52
28	1826	18	84
29	1827	14	56
30	1828	21	80
31	1829	19	72
32	1830	16	64
33	1831	9	40
34	1832	17	72
35	1833	17	68
36	1834	17	72
37	1835	13	52
38	1836	18	88[3]
39	1837	13	56[3]
40	1838	16	68

[3] Includes a special Ostermesse catalog from the Vienna firm of Diabelli.

N.B. The Schnase reprint includes the *Intelligenzblätter* interfiled in vols. 1-12 and 14-16, and bound together at the end in vols. 13 and 17-40. Lacking from the reprint are vol. 2, no. 5; vol. 3, no. 8; and vol. 14, no. 1.

TABLE 6

SUMMARY OF THE HOFMEISTER-WHISTLING SERIES

No.	Year	Series
1	1817	The first *Handbuch,* covering ca. 1780-1815[1]
2	1818-27	The ten annual *Nachträge,* correcting and updating 1[1]
3	1828	A "2. Auflage" of the *Handbuch,* cumulating 1 and 2, but with many deletions
4	1829	An *Ergänzungsband* for 3, comprising a supplement for 1828 along with indexes to creators and publishers
5	1829-33	*Monatsberichte* [1. Folge], listing new publications
6	1834	*Ergänzungsband 2* for the *Handbuch,* cumulating 3, 4, and 5
7	1834-38	*Monatsberichte,* neue Folge
8	1839	*3. Ergänzungband* for the *Handbuch,* cumulating 6 and 7
9	1839-43	*Monatsberichte,* 3. Folge
10	1844-45	A "3. Auflage" of the *Handbuch,* cumulating 8 and 9
11	1844-51	*Monatsberichte,* 4. Folge. [The series number will now be seen to be coordinated with the volume number of the *Handbuch*.]
12	1854	*Handbuch,* Band 4
13	1852	The *Verzeichnis* series begins, consisting of annual interim cumulations between the *Monatsberichte* and the quinquennial or sometimes even less frequent *Handbücher*—this practice to continue forward into the present century

[1] Reprinted in Ratliff.

Whistling-Hofmeister. Even so, the 1700 estimated entries in the first *Handbuch,* announced as covering only through 1815, are a small portion of the 8000 entries in the *Messkataloge* up to this date, or the equal figure for the *Intelligenzblätter,* of which perhaps no more than 40 per cent are also in the *Messkataloge.* In other words, the first *Handbuch* is obviously a very selective list—at most it contains one title in eight found in the other two—although the specifics for inclusion remain to be investigated. The importance of the set cannot be questioned, although its contribution to the declining fortunes of the *Intelligenzblätter* would seem more plausible than demonstrable. Nevertheless, the termination of the music section in the *Messkataloge* has to be seen as almost certainly attributable to the rising fortunes of the first *Handbuch* and its early *Nachträge.*

*   *   *   *   *

Other lists exist, to be incorporated into the picture.[27] The work of several scholars studying particular publishers, for instance, and of Dan Fog most notably in studying early music loan collections, should add titles to the record and provide further insight into the story of how music merchants actually made a living and influenced musical tastes at the same time—if indeed they actually did either. For now, the present overview should be useful as we consider the changing relationships and attitudes of composers and performers toward the music publishers who brought them together in the course of one of the most brilliant periods in music history.

---

[27] Out of the scope of this study but still highly relevant to the topic, for instance, is Christian Gottlob Kayser's *Vollständiges Bücherlexikon,* the *Sachregister* (Leipzig: Schumann, 1838), which indexes 1500 music titles, in section II.A., pp. 96-101, for the period 1750-1832.

Part IV

Recordings

CHAPTER 8

Records as Documents

by

Philip Lieson Miller

As one who grew up with the phonograph and has lived to experience the "ultimate" in sound reproduction time after time, I wonder what is left to develop in the years ahead. I know that the disc will soon be a thing of the past, that sound and picture will come together on laser beams, but how will the *sound* be improved? By amplification (Lord save us!), by somehow enhancing the tone qualities, by the use of electronic instruments? Perhaps it is as well not to live too long into the future.

The first music I knew, aside from a few family friends who sang or played the piano, was via a small-sized Victor with a morning-glory horn. My father was not musical in the sense of making music, but he was fond of opera, and as a young man in New York he had done his full share of concert going. Having moved to the country, really isolated in the winter, he not only enjoyed hearing his old favorites, but he wanted his children to grow up knowing them. At the same time we became familiar with the recording artists. It wasn't long before the original tin horn was replaced with a wooden one, which gave a more mellow sound. In the course of a few years we invested in a table model Victrola (i.e., a machine with the horn enclosed — more beautiful to look at and supposedly superior in sound, but this is questionable). By that time I had been bitten, and our record collection grew largely according to my developing tastes.

I remember a preview of the Orthophonic Victrola in the auditorium of the Engineering Society in 1925 which really swept me off my feet. A few electrical recordings had already been sneaking into the monthly lists without announcement. They were identifiable by the letters V. E. etched in the wax, but I don't remember having heard anyone remarking on the new sound. The big sensation, once the secret was out, was hearing the Associated Glee Clubs of America singing *The Bells of Saint Mary's*. One thousand voices (count 'em) on one ten-inch record side! As a matter of fact Columbia had even gotten ahead of Victor with those thousand voices singing *John Peel* and *Adeste fideles* (Victor's second side was also *John Peel*). Remarkably, those early attempts to catch a live concert sound realistic even today. But before electrical recording could be appreciated it was necessary to have the proper

333

playing equipment. The Orthophonic Victrola was the answer. But in 1926 the Brunswick Company produced their Panatrope, with electrical reproduction, and Victor had to try to cap it with the Electrola.

Those of us who bought these wonderful new phonographs were satisfied that now nothing could be added. Although some attempts were made in the 1930s to develop a longplaying disc and even stereophonic recording—and somewhere along the line the expression High Fidelity was coined—those were bad days for the industry (and all industry). They were good days for the recorded repertory, however, as a continuous stream of fabulous things was coming from abroad. In 1949 Columbia threw its bombshell with LP by which the record's greatest shortcoming (excuse it, please) was overcome. But the next advance in recording technique was Stereo, and now we are getting used to Digital Recordings (without, as yet, the benefit of the proper equipment for playing them).

But what does all this mean in the quality of reproduction? In the acoustical period the sound may not have always been faithful, but it was honest. I well remember Eva Gauthier declaring as much when some of her records were played. In her day it was not possible to fake, she said, though of course there were problems. The man we would now call the producer had to see to it that the singer was properly placed in relation to the horn—this would naturally vary according to the size and characteristics of the voice—and that he or she would step backward with the climactic notes that might blast. But there was no such thing as editing or patching performances. If anything went wrong the performer had to start over. With electrical recording many things were made possible: a singer could sing duets with himself, or if a note was out of singer's range, a colleague's voice could be dubbed in. But the concept of a recording with all the blemishes edited out is a fairly recent one.

Record collecting is a house of many mansions. Some nowadays will be satisfied with nothing less than the last word in fidelity—whether that means fidelity to the producer's dreams or to the sound as we would hear it in a hall. Many collectors of vocal records are interested only in tonal beauty (a very personal reaction, I may add), some in the musicianship and artistry of the performer and some in the rarity of the recording, or indeed of the label. Among collectors artistry has little to do with monetary values. But to the archivist—in the increasing numbers of library archives or in private collections—the record is a document, the preservation of a performance, perhaps a moment in history. And records are now accepted as musicological tools. Discography is a part of musicological dissertations, and critics today do not hestiate to compare contemporary performances with recordings made by artists they never have heard.

It was my misfortune to miss Caruso. Just by a hair. My first opera was *Carmen,* with Farrar and Martinelli, Thanksgiving Day 1919. Caruso was something to look forward to, but alas, he died before this was fulfilled. Yet I feel I know Caruso well so familiar are his records. It is oft-told history that the industry hit its stride in

1904 when Caruso made his first Victor Red Seal Records. Today, 66 years after his death, Caruso's records are repeatedly being remastered for an enduring market. And granting the improvements in at least some of the digitally revitalized recordings, the best of them can still sound more than acceptable from good 78 pressings. Tenors come and tenors go — even Gigli and Tauber — but Caruso is eternal.

Of course there was only one Caruso. Some others in the acoustical era were successful, some were not. McCormack was both a warm friend and an almost equally popular recording artist, as was the soprano Alma Gluck. Some great artists came late to recording — Patti and Lilli Lehmann were approaching 60, Sembrich began when she was 45. Sembrich made no secret of her terror before the recording horn; the remarkable thing is that some of her records are so good. But Emma Albani, only 52 in 1904, gives little evidence of the greatness that must have been hers. McCormack, so successful on acoustic recordings, did not take quite so well to the microphone. (He was 41 when electrical recording came in 1925.) On the other hand, Sir George Henschel, recorded acoustically at 64 in 1914, is little different from his electrical discs made in 1928 at age 78! Fritz Kreisler was another artist whose tone was mellower, more melting, in acoustic recordings.

Another aspect of historical recordings that has not been fully explored is the effect of conductors on performances. For many years, as we remember, the conductor was anonymous. Since about 1928, as singers came to be recorded in larger halls with full orchestras, it has been customary to give the conductor's name on the labels, and increasingly these are important names. Does the conductor on the record exert the kind of control he has over the singers in the opera? Going back to the anonymous acoustic days, it would surely be possible to detect many influences. For example, while Toscanini was at the Metropolitan, Victor issued recordings by the stars of some of his notable productions. In the big ensembles from *Un ballo in maschera* (1913) — Hempel, Duchène, Caruso, Rothier, and de Segurola — certainly we may recognize the hand of the Maestro. And from his famous 1909 *Orfeo* we have the duet of Gadski and Homer. It is a particularly fine bit of teamwork which surely bears his stamp. Similarly, the première of Wolf-Ferrari's *Le donne curiose* in 1912 featured Farrar and Jadlowker, whose duet recording must owe something to the great conductor. And I have often wondered about the well-known Sembrich-Eames Letter Duet from *Le nozze di Figaro* which, at the time of recording, they were singing with Mahler at the Met.

It is rarely possible to judge the size of a voice or instrumental tone in recordings. In the early days it is very likely that the difficulty in catching a big tone was responsible for mediocre results; on the other hand, with electrical recording a very small voice could be made to sound huge. This is still true of the latest digital discs. In popular music, of course, these realities have been basic. Without the microphone the careers of singers like Crosby and Sinatra would have been impossible. All sorts of electronic effects are part and parcel of pop recording. If recordings in that field are documents, they simply document themselves. But what of the latest techniques applied to opera singers? One gets the impression that our greatest tenors are incapable of anything less than a double F, that shading and nuance are a lost art. What will our grandchildren make of them? Or will opera, like popular music, in that day be dependent on tricks?

Happily, interest in singers of the "Golden Age" still runs high. Particularly in England this interest is catered to by the large record companies. Retrospectives have been issued surveying the art of some of the greats—Patti, Melba, Chaliapin, Teyte—or of whole periods as in Michael Scott's *The Record of Singing*. Live performances in Covent Garden from the earliest days of electrical recording have been reissued (in this country even the "echoes" Mapleson was able to catch in the Metropolitan from 1901 to 1903 are available for study). And for a survey of various performing styles we now have 64 singers represented on an 8-disc set of Schubert songs (1898-1952). The value of composers performing their own works hardly needs stressing.

Fortunately the greatest care has been taken with the retrospectives, every effort extended to find the true voice sometimes hidden among extraneous noises. To determine at what speed an early recording was made the producer must consider the key in which the selection was probably sung, often on the basis of the singer's tone as we know it from other recordings. (Recording tempo was often speeded up to get the song or aria within time limits which could affect the phrasing and style of the performance.)

But of what documentary value is a patchwork of multiple performances? For the future, is musical performance undergoing a process of depersonalization? If every voice is to be brought to the same decibel count, how will our descendents know Carreras from Pavarotti? Are we archivists wasting our time? As the golden voices pour out from the speakers one is tempted to exclaim with Dr. Johnson: "Wonderful! Wonderful! I wish it weren't possible!"

Part V

"Popular" Music

CHAPTER 9

Slouching Toward IASPM:
An Odyssey[1]

by

Frank C. Campbell

For approximately the last twenty years, the study of American music and musical life has been generally accepted as a worthwhile endeavor for American historians. Although it grew more slowly, the study of American jazz and other popular music has reached a similar status. The founding of the Sonneck Society in 1975 and the founding of the International Association for the Study of Popular Music (IASPM) in 1981 brought these two fields forcefully to the attention of students, scholars, and educators. Now that they have reached firm ground, it seems appropriate to chronicle the journeys, which encountered many prejudices and obstacles and even seemed, at times, in danger of being stigmatized for good.

In the 1960s a series of events focused attention on the conflicting opinions that existed among American as well as European scholars over the historical significance of the American musical scene vis-à-vis our musical heritage from Western Europe. Frank Lloyd Harrison stated one side of the case:

> American musicologists are in a special and perhaps unique position in relation to the musical history of their own country. This is partly, but not entirely, explained by the fact that American musical scholarship developed in close contact with the "official" musicological outlook of Europe, but without real involvement in the musical culture of either Europe or America. It has meant that the attention of American musical historians has been turned almost wholly away from the music of their own country and society. As a consequence some aspects of music in America during the past half century that are now seen to be important for American music as a whole, and for the understanding of the American arts abroad, have failed to be recorded, and none has been thoroughly studied by those most competent to do so. It has justly been held that the artistic expressions

---

[1] IASPM is the acronym for the International Association for the Study of Popular Music. The word "slouching" is used here in the sense of meanings given in *Roget's International Thesaurus,* 4th edition, p. 171: "slouch, shuffle, plod, shamble, limp, hobble. . . ."

of a society need the closest study during the thirty years or so after they have taken place. After that time firsthand contacts with the artists and observations of their immediate and wider relations with the social millieu become increasingly difficult. Records become less precise and more scattered, until eventually reconstruction becomes a major historical and imaginative enterprise. A symptom rather than necessarily the most cogent case of this is the lack of serious study of the technical and social aspects of American jazz.[2]

Harrison was only one among a number of musicologists from abroad whose views of American music and its history showed more objectivity than had been widely prevalent among our own scholars. One could twit Harrison for his claim that no competent Americans had studied their own heritage. True, American studies were outside our scholarly mainstream, but there had been a number of competent chroniclers of American music including John Tasker Howard, William Treat Upton, Dena Epstein, Richard S. Hill, Irving Lowens, and Gilbert Chase. Perhaps most important of all was Oscar Sonneck, whose labors on behalf of American music had begun in 1899 when he returned from his studies abroad. For the next two and one-half years, Sonneck traveled from New England to South Carolina gathering references to musical life in America before 1800, largely from newspapers. Many of these were in the Library of Congress, where he was appointed Chief of the Music Division in 1902.

Oscar George Theodore Sonneck in a relatively short time set standards of scope and scholarship in his studies of American music that may never be surpassed. With the advantages of a superb education and an unusual objectivity, he perceived that the American music scene and American music itself were worthy of scholarly study without risking chauvinism on the part of American music historians. Except for a few figures, however, our musical heritage was regarded with suspicion for decades after Sonneck's death. As the study limped (or "slouched") along, it gradually accumulated credit through the efforts of an increasing number of historians until the founding of the Sonneck Society in 1975. The Society was focused on the study of American music in all its aspects. It was particularly appropriate that the Society be named after Sonneck, for he had set an example for Americans, beginning three-quarters of a century before.

The listings in Appendix I (see pp. 362-64), which should definitely be consulted at this point, provide a highly selective overview of events and publications that slowly chronicled and revealed our own history to us and brought about an informed point of view. This helped to establish American studies as a bona fide field of study within American musicology.

---

[2] Frank Ll. Harrison, Mantle Hood, and Claude V. Palisca, *Musicology* (Englewood Cliffs, N.J.: Prentice-Hall, 1963), 60-61.

Among the important publications, Gilbert Chase's *America's Music* (1955) occupies a landmark position. Chase was then, at age forty-nine, a mature and distinguished scholar who seems to have escaped the blocs that often limited his American peers when judging their own music. In his "foreword" to the Chase book, Douglas Moore wrote:

> . . . Gilbert Chase, a musician and scholar who understands and enjoys all kinds of music, has collected all the strands that have gone into the fabric of our musical speech—and a fascinating web of incompatibles they turn out to be. Who could imagine a pattern which would include Billings, Foster, Gottschalk, Chadwick and Gershwin? Each of them contributed substantially to our musical tradition, and when we can grasp their interrelationship we perceive that there is indeed an American music and a hardy one just beginning to feel its strength and destined to stand beside our other contributions to world culture.[3]

Other influential voices were raised, including those of Joseph Kerman, Donald McCorkle, and Wiley Hitchcock. Kerman's views were expressed in "A Profile for American Musicology," a paper read at the thirtieth annual meeting of the American Musicological Society, 27 December 1964. Kerman made a number of well-reasoned observations about the nature of American musical scholarship as contrasted with that in western Europe, which had developed on the foundations of its own musical heritage. It seems almost incredible, however, that nine years after Gilbert Chase, Douglas Moore, and others expressed enlightened attitudes toward American music, and more than half a century after Sonneck's work, Joseph Kerman revealed the same blind spot, as he wrote:

> . . . our identity as scholars depends on growth away from an older alien tradition into something recognizably our own. European observers have a very simple recipe for national integrity: study your own American music, they say, as we have built our musicology around *Stamm* and *Liederbuch,* Risorgimento opera and Elizabethan madrigal, Bulgar folksong, and the like. The critically-inclined scholar has a very simple answer: unfortunately, American music has not been interesting enough, artistically, to merit from us that commitment. Even so experienced a visitor as Harrison fails to see the extent to which the American mind dwells in the present, and how little in the past; and the critical attitude is exactly that which takes the past up *into the present,* rather than admiring it as an antiquity. The student of Beethoven feels concerned with the present because the music is (as we say) "alive"; the student of Marenzio or Louis Couperin is concerned with music that can be brought to life; but Francis Hopkinson or Lowell

---

[3] Gilbert Chase, *America's Music: From the Pilgrims to the Present* (New York: McGraw-Hill, 1955), ix.

Mason or Theodore Chanler—surely they would defy all efforts at resuscitation. Man, they are dead. About jazz, Harrison has a real point, but such an extremely complex one that I ask leave to pass over it in the present discussion. It does not appear to me that a characteristically American musicology can be built on native repertory. It can be built only with a native point of view.[4]

The conflicts that were being aired set some of the best of the pro-American studies minds to work searching their own motivations and bringing out their rationales for all others to witness. In 1966, Donald McCorkle's article "Finding a Place for American Studies in American Musicology" provided a thoroughgoing overview of the reverse chauvinism that had been prevalent for so many years. McCorkle's concluding paragraphs on "The Role of the American Musicological Society" summarized the position of the AMS which had ranged from hesitance shifting frequently to a downright hostile attitude toward the musical creativity of the American musician.

> . . . one wonders if we as a society do not have a responsibility to give more leadership for the cause of American studies, without in any sense emphasizing American studies in our purpose, by virtue of our designation as the American Musicological Society.
>
> We have come far toward fulfilling Professor Kinkeldey's desire expressed to me a decade ago, when he said he wished that each meeting of the Society could have one good paper on an American subject. We have not achieved this goal, but we have seen a substantial increase in the number of superior papers read and published. The American specialists abhor chauvinism and inverse chauvinism equally; they wish only to have American studies accorded the dignity of full musicological status, already accorded by the Society to all other studies in historical musicology.
>
> We have smiled long enough over the inclusion of American fine-art and popular music within exotica and curiosa; the repertoire and the historical, descriptive, critical, and comparative methods needed to study it are well within the realm of musicologica. The European-oriented musicologist may well be at a loss for some time to come to contend with, and find hierarchical concepts in, what seems at a superficial glance to be a complex but ungratifying heritage. But I am convinced that we have been much too concerned with making ultimate appraisals on the basis of an infinitesimal amount of documentation. The specious prejudgment of unknown American music history has had a pernicious effect on the recovery of a large and perhaps intrinsically important heritage. It is time to search instead for the heritage and to apply the attributes of humanistic scholarship to it.[5]

---

[4] Joseph Kerman, "A Profile for American Musicology," *Journal of the American Musicological Society* 18 (1965): 67-68.

[5] Donald McCorkle, "Finding a Place for American Studies in American Musicology," *Journal of the American Musicological Society* 19 (1966): 83-84.

In 1971, H. Wiley Hitchcock[6] established the Institute for Studies in American Music at Brooklyn College. The Institute, a division of the Department of Music in the School of Performing Arts, was to constitute one of the most significant events in the rapidly developing field of scholarship in American music studies. The purpose of the Institute was to function primarily as a research and information center, but not to offer courses or award degrees. Since that time the Institute has issued the *I.S.A.M. Newsletter,* a series of musical editions (*Recent Researches in American Music,* one of the series published by A-R Editions, Madison, Wisconsin), and *I.S.A.M. Monographs* (scholarly studies and basic reference works); it has also sponsored fellowships, colloquia, and conferences.

The first of the Institute's monograph series is Richard Jackson's *United States Music: Sources of Bibliography and Collective Biography* (1973), in which thoughtful annotations reflect the compiler's broad experience. The third is Rita Mead's checklist of *Doctoral Dissertations in American Music* (1974). In his foreword to Mead's compilation, Hitchcock wrote:

> At the 1964 annual meetings of the American Musicological Society, in a paper called "A Profile for American Musicology," Joseph Kerman dismissed scholarly studies of American music as a futile exercise. . . .
>
> In the decade since that remark was made, trends in our concert life, in the recording industry, in radio programming and musical journalism have run counter to Professor Kerman's view. And Ms. Mead's bibliography forcefully documents the fact that for many young scholars American music has been anything but dead. Anyone who scans the 1226 entries of the present monograph must realize that, despite the general transatlantic bias of scholarly studies in music in the universities of the U.S.A., work in American music has been done on a surprisingly large and broad scale. Most surprised will be those whose notion of what has been going on in American-music studies in our universities is based on the annual lists of dissertations in musicology published by the American Musicological Society. For by no means have dissertations on American music been written only within the discipline of musicology; on the contrary, other disciplines — sociology, theater, anthropology, history, American Studies, theology, literature, education, and still others — have been almost more hospitable.

Richard Crawford, under a grant from the Rockefeller Foundation, was named a Senior Research Fellow of the Institute for Studies in American Music for 1973-74. He gave Fellowship Lectures on

---

[6] Hitchcock's *Music in the United States: A Historical Introduction* (Englewood Cliffs, N.J.: Prentice-Hall, 1969) emphasized and expanded on the attitude shown by Gilbert Chase in his *America's Music* (1955) as he wrote "I have . . . attempted to view it [i.e., American music] in the round, believing that pop songs as well as art songs, player-pianos as well as piano players, are important parts of the American musical experience."

March 4 and 14, 1974, entitled "American Studies and American Musicology" and "A Hardening of the Categories." The first lecture began:

> The signs are plain that the study of American music is coming of age. The 1974 Winter Meetings of the Music Library Association in Champaign-Urbana can be taken as a symptom of this new condition. Afternoon sessions were devoted entirely to American music topics, and the evenings were given over to excellent performances of American music: a concert of new music, a jazz-band performance, a concert of gospel music, and a performance of the opera *Rip Van Winkle,* by the 19th-century American composer George Frederick Bristow. One meeting was devoted entirely to reports from various "centers" for the study of American music. Six different centers, including the Institute sponsoring this lecture, reported, and others could have been called upon. The American Musicological Society has U.S. Bicentennial plans which include an emphasis on American music unusual for the Society until very recent years.[7]

These two lectures presented a brilliant state of the art of American studies in music. It is interesting to note also that eight years later Crawford's stature and his main field of interest were further recognized:

> The discipline of musicology in this country is kept in focus by its professional organization, the American Musicological Society. In 1982 the Presidency of the AMS passed from the hands of Howard Smither (University of North Carolina) to Richard Crawford (University of Michigan). It is not without significance that for the first time the AMS presidency is entrusted to a distinguished Americanist, a scholar who has devoted his career to the history of music in the United States. This would seem to indicate that American scholarship and the AMS — which in 1984 reaches its fiftieth anniversary during President Crawford's term — have finally embraced American studies as a major emphasis of musicology in the United States.[8]

The halting (or "slouching") journey toward general acceptance of studies of American jazz and other popular music was almost that of the proverbial rake, whose progress would lead the unsuspecting to Bedlam if not even to Hades. The roots in Africa, Storyville, Tin Pan Alley, Broadway, and other exotic milieux branded this music unworthy of the kind of respect and serious study that had grown up around the classics from our European heritage.

---

[7] Richard Crawford, *American Studies and American Musicology: A Point of View and a Case in Point,* I.S.A.M. Monographs, no. 4 (Brooklyn: Institute for Studies in American Music, 1975), 1.

[8] George J. Buelow, "Musicology in the United States in 1981-1982," *Acta Musicologica* 15 (1983): 253-54.

In print, despite evidence to the contrary demonstrated in Appendix II,[9] negative reactions toward American jazz and other popular music began to diminish in the 1920s and 30s when acceptance and even enthusiasm were shown by writers in magazines and books appearing largely in Europe. More and more this was shown in writing in the 1940s and 50s; in the 1960s and 70s widespread attention and serious consideration became common.

Wiley Hitchcock, writing about Gilbert Chase's *America's Music* in the *New Grove Dictionary* (1980), described it as "the first historical study of music in the USA to treat folk and popular music as seriously as art and religious music."[10] Douglas Moore's foreword to the Chase book chronicled America's attitude toward its European musical heritage and its gradual realization and appreciation of its own creativity as a cultural phenomenon to be cherished:

There have been many problems, but apparently lack of public appreciation has not been one of them. . . . There were, however, no European courts for the cultivation of art music and opportunities were rare for the training and development of individual talents. . . . Our emerging talent was packed off to Europe to learn civilized ways. Our wealthy patrons, as they invariably do in a frontier society, regarded the European label as the only sure means of achieving cultural prestige. . . .

Small wonder, then, that a serious dichotomy developed in the field of American composition. Our educated young people, fresh from German or French influences, did their loyal best to write good German or French music. For subject matter they turned to "remote legends and misty myths" guaranteed to keep them from thinking about the crudities of the land which they found so excruciating upon their return from abroad. They did, however, bring back with them a professional competence which was to be their significant contribution to the American scene.

Meanwhile the uneducated creator, finding good stuff about him, carried on a rapidly developing music speech which was a blend of European folk music, African rhythm, and regional color, and discovered that the public liked his music and was ready to pay for it handsomely. As a result via the minstrel ballad, through ragtime into jazz, a genuine popular American music made its appearance and was given every encouragement by the entertainment industry. European musicians were quick to recognize the originality and value of this music and, beginning with Debussy, accepted it as a new resource.

The American serious group, however, anxious to preserve their new-found dignity, nervously dismissed this music as purely commercial (a lot of it was and is), and until it

---

[9] Appendix II, pp. 365-70.

[10] *New Grove Dictionary of Music and Musicians* (1980), s.v. "Chase, Gilbert."

was made respectable by the attention paid to it by Ravel and Stravinsky there were only occasional attempts to borrow from its rhythms and melodies.[11]

Irving Lowens, unusually sensitive to cultural history, eloquently put into perspective some of the knotty conflicts that had plagued us. His *Music and Musicians in Early America* (1964) includes a chapter entitled "American Democracy and American Music (1830-1914)," in which he says:

> For well over a century now, it has been argued that the "youth" of the American nation both explains and excuses our supposed lack of a noteworthy musical culture. This, I submit, is sheer nonsense. First of all, national maturity is no precondition for the creation of memorable art. Furthermore, there was no musical vacuum here. Even during the very years of this country's birth, noteworthy musical developments were in progress. It is surely more accurate to say, along with the distinguished student of American democracy, James Bryce, that the arts have flourished in almost every environment, and quite without relation to the age of the political state. . . .
>
> After the Civil War, the greatest single controlling influence in American intellectual life came to be that exerted by a powerful small group, the big-business class. Ultimately, the ante-bellum tyranny of the majority was superseded by a new tyranny of the minority, a libertarianism much different in its crass materialism from the idealistic libertarianism of the first years of the American republic. The "almighty dollar" became the standard of value, infecting the country with contempt for things of the spirit.
>
> At the same time, a gradual decline in the vitality of American popular music was evident, a development which coincided with a burst of creative activity from our fine-art composers. The 1880s saw the advent of the first consequential American school since the days of the 18th-century singing-masters. Four men in particular towered over their contemporaries: John Knowles Paine, George Whitefield Chadwick, Horatio W. Parker, and Edward MacDowell. . . . It is natural that they composed, for the most part, in the then current late-romantic European idiom. But they all returned home and achieved considerable status as teachers and composers of fine-art music in a wealth-oriented libertarian society.
>
> The 20th century ushered in a reaction against the rampant individualism of the previous decades. Responsible individuals attempted to restate equalitarian values in the face of an irresponsible libertarianism. . . .
>
> As the equalitarian drive gathered impetus, popular music took on new life. The generative vigor of the marches of John Philip Sousa, the operettas of Victor Herbert, and the rags of Scott Joplin is manifest even in their lineal

---

[11] Chase, *America's Music,* vii-viii.

descendants of today—band music, musical comedy, and jazz. But we must turn to Charles Ives for an extraordinary reflection in music of the delicate balance between libertarianism and equalitarianism of those years. Ives was a composer of sonatas and symphonies, but he deliberately quoted extensively from such popular music as gospel songs, patriotic ditties, and marches. His curious synthesis of fine-art music and popular music, a purely musical resolution of the American social duality, seems to mirror the dynamics of the age with startling verisimilitude.[12]

Many Americans, especially those with strong academic backgrounds and the other accouterments of the sophisticated, find themselves uncomfortable in facing up to a liking for popular music—or, for that matter, any taste favored by the hoi polloi. Richard Crawford, in a lecture referred to above, points out some relevant phenomena as recognized by Marcel Proust in *The Past Recaptured:*

> This brings us to the question of the individual historian as a member of a culture, as a participant in its musical life. In *The Past Recaptured,* the last volume of *Remembrance of Things Past,* Marcel Proust writes of the artistic insights that came to him when, after years of isolation, he went out again into society. Thinking himself a failed, sterile writer, Proust experienced in society flashes of insight which signalled to him that all of the material he would ever need to write about was lodged in his own memory. One comment in particular is relevant to our discussion. It is, in fact, the basic text for the rest of this lecture. Proust here evaluates the relative significance of what we are here calling vernacular and cultivated experience. He writes:
>
>> The truths which the intellect apprehends directly in the world of full and unimpeded light have something less profound, less necessary then those which life communicates to us against our will in an impression which is material because it enters us through the senses but yet has a spiritual meaning which it is possible for us to extract.
>
> Historians of music deal with both sense experience and intellectual experience, and they are sometimes confused about just how to do it. Virtually all musicologists are practicing musicians, or were at some time. Before that they were players, listeners, whistlers, singers. Had their own vernacular background not been intense, they would hardly have chosen music as a profession. Like most musicians, historians are born with some special aural aptitude, and they have worked to train this faculty. Moreover, they are not satisfied to remain ignorant of the structure, techniques, and general workings of the music they admire. They

[12] Irving Lowens, *Music and Musicians in Early America* (New York: Norton, 1964), 264, 269-71.

submit the evidence of their disciplined ears and memories to the disciplined inquiry of their minds. This is standard musicological procedure. So far, so good. However, the only music that musicologists are likely to scrutinize closely is music brought forward by conscious decision — music, in Proust's phrase, "which the intellect apprehends directly in the world of full and unimpeded light." What about music "communicated to us against our will"? What about our own musical vernacular — the musical baggage we carry around with us but never give much attention to: scraps of operas and quartets, alma maters, hymns, nursery rhymes, commercials, pop-tunes from our past? Proust's statement suggests that these are not merely random leavings. He suggests that powerful sense impulses chose them — impulses almost surely now forgotten — and he also implies that we will be enlightened if we can discover what these impulses were, and why our senses chose certain pieces and not others "against our will." Every music historian has his own professional "cultivated" repertories; every music historian also has his own "inner book of unknown symbols": his own internal musical vernacular.[13]

I did come to understand that popular art was not inferior to high art, and decided that popular art achieved a vitality of both integrity and outreach that high art had unfortunately abandoned. Popular art dealt with common realities and fantasies in forms that provided immediate pleasure — it was vital aesthetically, as work. And because it moved and was moved by the great audience, it was also vital culturally, as relationship.[14]

In June 1981, popular music achieved significant status with the first international meeting in Amsterdam of IASPM. Within approximately fifteen months many chapters were formed, so that when the second international meeting was held in Reggio Emilia, Italy, in September 1982, there were national chapters in twenty-three countries. An American chapter was formed in May 1983 (at Dartmouth College in Hanover, New Hampshire), with Charles Hamm as president.

When I saw the program of the meeting in Italy, the overriding impression for me was the incredible scope of subjects listed, which was strong evidence that IASPM was long overdue. During the meeting in Italy the IASPM officers announced that the meetings would address the group's chief problem by devoting its six-day conference to the question "What Is Popular Music?" The question will probably remain with us ad infinitum, for it is not likely to be answered to everyone's satisfaction. The excerpts below are two approaches to an answer. Charles Hamm has attempted a precise definition:

---

[13] Crawford, *American Studies and American Musicology,* 7-8.

[14] Robert Christgau, *Any Old Way You Choose It* (New York: Penguin Books, 1973), 3.

I define *popular song* as a piece of music that is
written for, and most often performed by, a single voice
or a small group of singers, accompanied by either a single
chord-playing instrument or some sort of band, ensemble,
or small orchestra;

usually first performed and popularized in some form
of secular stage entertainment, and afterward consumed
(performed or listened to) in the home;

composed and marketed with the goal of financial gain;

designed to be performed by and listened to by persons
of limited musical training and ability; and

produced and disseminated in physical form — as sheet
music in its early history, and in various forms of mechanical
reproduction in the twentieth century.

This definition was arrived at after the fact, after I had
grasped that popular song had a character and history
distinct from that of any other kind of music. The definition
embraces the songs of such figures as James Hook, Oliver
Shaw, John Hill Hewitt, Henry Russell, Thomas Moore,
Dan Emmett, Stephen Foster, Septimus Winner, Charles K.
Harris, James Bland, Harry von Tilzer, Paul Dresser,
George M. Cohan, Irving Berlin, Jerome Kern, Cole Porter,
George Gershwin, Chuck Berry, Bob Dylan, Paul Simon,
the Beatles, Elton John, the Rolling Stones, Dolly Parton,
Patti Smith, and Bruce Springsteen. It excludes the music
of William Billings, which is for vocal ensemble; Child
ballads and other traditional Anglo-American songs, which
were transmitted in oral tradition; the band music of John
Philip Sousa and the ragtime music of Scott Joplin and
others, which is instrumental; all church music, even that
for solo voice; most jazz, which is instrumental. [15]

Arnold Shaw has written a somewhat impressionistic character-
ization, which is equally valid on its own terms:

The history of popular music from the death in obscurity
of Stephen Foster to the widely lamented passing of Oscar
Hammerstein II is a tale of creative aspiration and doctrinaire
neglect, of condescension and prejudice, of dedication and
payola, of talent, trash, and many turns of taste, but in an
over-all view, of the development of an amazingly varied
and appealing body of song that has gradually moved away
from the cliché towards a more realistic and artistic
expression of human values. It is a more vulgar, but also
a more vital, body of song than the genteel arbiters of taste
would have it — and its influence abroad is so great precisely
because it has been so spontaneous and unashamed in
embodying the romantic dreams, the anxieties, the fulfillment
and the frustrations, as well as the crazy fads and playful

---

[15]   Charles Hamm, *Yesterdays: Popular Song in America* (New York:
Norton, 1979), xvii-xviii.

moments, of the American people, or, more specifically, of each courting and dancing generation of the American people.[16]

From the beginning of IASPM, the label "popular music" has provided an umbrella for many styles of musical expression, each with its own widely different characteristics. The aficionados of "cool" jazz would probably disdain linkage with the fans of ragtime, Dixieland, or heavy metal rock. But since labels are a practical and necessary, if imprecise, device, I am using "popular music" in this discussion just as IASPM has done in its meetings up to now. This can be demonstrated by citing titles of papers given in Reggio Emilia, Italy, and Las Vegas, Nevada. They have included: "Black Political Songs in South Africa"; "There's No Such Thing as 'Folksong' or 'Fakesong' in England"; "Country Music: How a Popular Form Became 'Real Popular'"; "From Tango to 'Rock Nacional' — A Case Study of Changing Popular Taste in Buenos Aires"; "Rock Around the Veld: African Responses to Early Rock 'n' Roll"; "Randy Newman's Americans."

Writings about these musics have proliferated since the twenties, with each category of literature differing from the other almost as drastically as the music itself. However the music and the writing have differed, they hold in common the power to attract zealous disciples. For example, the jazz aficionados have an understandable pride deriving largely from the brilliantly creative activities of their performers and composer-performers. The enormous influence of a Dizzy Gillespie, a Satchmo Armstrong, a Billie Holiday, a Duke Ellington, and many others has spearheaded a music which has spread worldwide and influenced three-quarters of a century of powerful musical and cultural development. Along with this has grown a large body of writing on the subject. Pop music has a smaller bibliography, but those strongly drawn to it are just as zealous as the devotees of jazz. I am fully aware of the divergencies of these groups. Nevertheless, in this study, I have taken the liberty of considering them together, for I am chronicling the rise and the decline of a train of prejudiced feeling and thought that for too long a time considered the two as music from "the wrong side of the tracks."

A publication intended to honor Richard S. Hill and to reflect his interests must cover many subjects, including popular music. Although I worked for Dick for sixteen years and saw him almost daily, I am still in awe of the breadth and depth of his knowledge, his expertise, his scholarly approach to all subjects, but most of all his indefatigable energy which he used with the abandon of a spendthrift, almost to the day he died. Whatever subject attracted Dick benefitted from his skill in perceiving quickly the very core of the matter and treating it with intense scrutiny and a disciplined method

---

[16] Arnold Shaw, "Popular Music from Minstrel Songs to Rock 'n' Roll," in *One Hundred Years of Music in America,* ed. Paul Henry Lang (New York: G. Schirmer, 1961), 140.

of study. His style of writing was one of excited discovery rather than dull, self-conscious gravity. If there was any other outstanding characteristic it was his freedom from the kind of intellectual *hauteur* that still often blocks the study of American music.

The breadth and multifarious nature of Dick's interests were always remarkable, but the subject of American music and especially American popular music were often on his mind. James Maher's words would have pleased him for their freshness and candor:

> Intellectual pieties, like their religious counterparts, live long and die hard, acquiring while they endure the votive glow of received truth. This book gladly risks offending that among them which looks upon music of the daily ordinary as being beyond academic redemption. To put the matter briefly, the author takes American popular song and its creators seriously. Furthermore, he feels that the best work of the American song writers in the recent past provided an important, as well as delightful, contribution to our native arts.[17]

In the United States the Classics from our European heritage were for many the predominant focus of musicological study—a focus maintained by the refugee scholars who sought asylum here before and during the second World War. As early as the post-war years, in the mid-forties, however, several scholars from abroad had shown interest in our vernacular music by studying and writing about some of it. These included Otto Gombosi and Hans Nathan.

Two of Dick Hill's exhaustive investigations of popular American songs were published in *Notes*—"Not So Far Away in a Manger" in 1945 and "Getting Kathleen Home Again" in 1948. Although "Away in a Manger" is not exactly an American pop tune, its popularity as a traditional Christmas song almost places it there. Dick was able to lay to rest the widespread myth that the words (and even one of the musical settings) were by Martin Luther, but he was not able to pinpoint the author of the text. The most popular musical setting turned out to be but one of over forty.

Thomas Paine Westendorf's "I'll Take You Home Again, Kathleen" was truly a pop tune. Dick's study provides a valuable insight into the circumstances surrounding the typical development of a popular "hit" in the United States. First published by John Church and Company in 1876, its popularity quickly became a nationwide phenomenon. Including the various copyrighted arrangements that followed, the song did not reach clear public domain status until 18 July 1932. Even though Westendorf wrote about three hundred other vocal and instrumental works (many of which were published also by Church and sold well) none ever achieved the broad success that "Kathleen" enjoyed. Apart from other fees Westendorf may have earned from Church, he was paid $50 per month by them for many years, probably largely for the continuing sales of his first "hit."

---

[17] James T. Maher, "Introduction," *American Popular Song* by Alec Wilder (New York: Oxford Univ. Press, 1977), xxiii.

In my search for evidence of the growing interest in popular music, I was agreeably surprised to find Otto Gombosi's 1946 article "The Pedigree of the Blues." Gombosi was particularly broad in his interests, as is demonstrated by this essay, but he had first become known for his doctoral dissertation — a stylistic study of the works of Jacob Obrecht. The quotation below shows an admirable attempt at objectivity in judging the blues, as well as the credit due to two men far removed from the scholarly community, i.e., W. C. Handy and Abbe Niles.

> I do not propose to make any attempt at an esthetic evaluation of blues and boogey-woogey. It is not the historian's task to take sides either for or against any of the phenomena of our musical life.
>
> Before entering the sterile vacuum of historical investigation let me make a confession. I do not know much about the finer distinctions of popular music. I have not had the patience so justly required from the scholar to delve to the very bottom of the quicksands of popular music. I am afraid I even have neglected to read most of the writings about our subject because a few samples seemed to justify my prejudice. I have read, however, some of the best recommended and most praised books, among them those by Winthrop Sargeant and Hughues Panassié, and, of course, Abbe Niles's enlightening introduction to the Blues *Anthology* of the man who is the recognized "father of the blues," W. C. Handy.[18]

As Dick Hill did in studying Kathleen's career, Gombosi worked with meticulous scholarly discipline to seek the origins of the blues as a musical form with the kind of observations which might have mystified many blues composers, including Handy himself, the so-called "father" of the blues.

On 28 December 1943, Richard A. Waterman, an anthropologist with training in music, read a paper before the ninth annual meeting of the American Musicological Society in New York, entitled "'Hot' Rhythm in Negro Music," which was later published in the first issue of the *Journal of the American Musicological Society* (Spring 1948).[19] Waterman's analyses, although musically detailed, emphasized the anthropological approach; he considered anthropology a respectable parallel field through which developing interests could be channeled. Publication of essays on such topics was apparently not yet a wholly approved policy in the AMS, for no other comparable article was published in its journal until 1974, when Frank Tirro's "Constructive Elements in Jazz Improvisation"[20] appeared.

---

[18] Otto Gombosi, "The Pedigree of the Blues," Music Teachers National Association, *Volume of Proceedings . . . 40th Series,* ed. Theodore M. Finney (Pittsburgh: The Association, 1946), 382.

[19] Waterman, "'Hot' Rhythm," 24-37.

[20] Tirro, "Constructive Elements," 27 (1974): 285-305.

AMS members' attention to jazz and other popular music in the 1950s and 1960s was sporadic, at best, and confined to papers given at local chapter meetings. They included:

Hans Nathan, "Early Banjo Tunes and the American Syncopation," Midwest Chapter, Chicago, 14 November 1954

Bruno Nettl, "Preliminary Notes on Urban Folk Music," Midwest Chapter, Indianapolis, 28 April 1956

Irving Lowens, "The Unpublished Popular Song: Added Grist for the Social Historian's Mill," Greater Washington Chapter, College Park, Maryland, 15 May 1958

Albert Angstadt, "Demonstration of Jazz Techniques," Gulf States Chapter, Hattiesburg, Miss., 14-15 March 1961

Richard Allen, "Some Unusual Aspects of New Orleans Jazz," Gulf States Chapter, New Orleans, 9 November 1963

Robert Taylor, Lazarus Ekwueme, Lawrence Gushee, "Symposium: Metamorphoses of African Rhythm in the Americas," New England Chapter, New Haven, 15 April 1967

Bruno Nettl, "Examples of Folk and Popular Music From Khorosan," Midwest Chapter, Chicago, 11 November 1967

Ira Lieberman, "Rock Music: A Survey," Texas Chapter, Austin, 9 November 1968

Nathan Davis, "The European Scene in Jazz," Allegheny Chapter, Morgantown, West Virginia, 1 November 1969

Jazz was not given a close examination of its musical characteristics until 1938, when Winthrop Sargeant's *Jazz: Hot and Hybrid* first came out. In the preface to the third edition (1975) Sargeant wrote:

When *Jazz: Hot and Hybrid* first appeared in 1938 . . . it was the only serious musicological study of its type in existence. There had, of course, been a great deal of previous writing about Jazz. . . . But practically all of this writing was concerned with the personalities of Jazz artists, the history of their migration from the Old South, the discography of the subject and the opinions — mostly ecstatic — of various devotees of the art. An analysis of Jazz considered as a form of music differing from other forms was badly needed.[21]

Besides Sargeant's book, only a few others address specifically the musical materials of jazz: André Hodeir's *Hommes et problèmes du jazz* (1954; English translation, 1956); Marshall Stearns's *The Story of Jazz* (1956); and Leroy Ostransky's *The Anatomy of Jazz* (1960). The publication in 1968 of Gunther Schuller's *Early Jazz* was a landmark in jazz studies. In its preface he stated:

---

[21] Winthrop Sargeant, *Jazz: Hot and Hybrid* (New York: Arrow Editions, 1938; 3d ed., enl., New York: Da Capo Press, 1975), 7.

Although there is no dearth of books on jazz, very few of them have attempted to deal with the music itself in anything more than general descriptive or impressionist terms. The majority of books have concentrated on the legendary of jazz, and over the years a body of writing has accumulated which is little more than an amalgam of well-meaning amateur criticism and fascinated opinion.[22]

Since Schuller's book, which traces musical developments up through the early years, will be followed by a second volume, his publication will likely have gone further than its predecessors in depth and scope.

For the fall 1969 issue of *JAMS,* Dr. Friedrich Körner sent the following report on a so-called Jazz Musicology Congress held in Graz, Austria, sponsored by the Akademie für Musik und darstellende Kunst:

At the Jazz Institute of the Academy of Music and Theater Arts in Graz, the first Jazz Musicology Congress took place from April 16 to 20, 1969. After having spent the years since its founding developing a theoretical and practical curriculum for the training of jazz musicians, the Institute is now taking on its second field of endeavour: jazz musicology.

Until now the few scholarly publications on jazz musicology have been largely the result of private initiative. The Jazz Institute intends to form a Jazz Musicology Center. . . .

As part of the Congress, the first work session of the International Federation for Jazz Musicology (IGJ)—founded in Graz under the auspices of the Jazz Institute—took place. The IGJ is a fusion of both conventional and jazz musicologists, ethnologists, music educators, jazz musicians and those simply interested in jazz. It has taken upon itself the task of systematically working on a new area of musicology. In conjunction with the Jazz Institute the IGJ will sponsor the following publications:

1.) *Journal for Jazz Research* — annually in book form

2.) "Jazz-Research" — at irregular intervals

3.) Jazz musicological samples: records, sheet music (transcriptions, etc.) . . .

At the first work session of the IGJ it was decided to divide the giant field of Jazz into sections, so as to better define the various points of departure from which the work could proceed.

A mere glance at the categories is enough to see what work is to be done: 1.) bibliography, 2.) discography, 3.) historiography, 4.) terminology, 5.) methodology, 6.) ethnology, 7.) transcription, 8.) psychology, acoustics, technical aids and statistics, 9.) sociology, 10.) musical instruments, 11.) pedagogy, 12.) jazz related music, 13.) phenomenology, 14.) aesthetics, 15.) jazz and new

---

[22] Gunther Schuller, *The History of Jazz,* vol. 1: *Early Jazz* (New York: Oxford University Press, 1968), vii.

music. Those involved in this work will be in constant touch with each other through the Center in Graz.

The first large project will be the publication of the lectures held at the Congress as the first issue of the above mentioned *Journal for Jazz Research*.[23]

The first popular music papers read at national meetings of the AMS were presented in November 1971, when the meetings were held in Durham and Chapel Hill, North Carolina. Session II, designated "Urban Popular Music" (held jointly with the Society for Ethnomusicology) included:

Albert Goldman, "Pop-Cycles in American Music: Swing versus Rock"

Gerard Béhague, "Bossa and Bossas: Recent Changes in Brazilian Bossa Nova Repertoire"

These were followed at the national meeting in November 1972 in Dallas, by:

Richard Crawford, "It Ain't Necessarily Soul: *Porgy and Bess* as Symbol"

Laurence A. Gushee, "Frank Zappa: Unpopular Pop"

In the summer of 1977, when the International Musicological Society met in Berkeley, California, several sessions were devoted to "Worldwide Transmutations of American Popular Music." These were the introductory remarks by Andrew McCredie:

This afternoon's round table inaugurates the first of two sessions devoted to "Worldwide Transmutations of American Popular Music." The contents of today's session will comprise a brief anthropological and epistomological projection of the problem by Klaus Wachsmann to be followed by six regional case studies representing such areas as the Soviet Union, Central Europe, Great Britain, South Eastern Europe, Japan, and Mexico. At the conclusion of these papers we hope to invite further comment respectively representing anthropological and empirico music-sociological viewpoints from Wolfgang Laade and Peter Etzkorn. At Thursday's study session, in addition to discussing matters arising from today's meeting, we hope to shed light on such issues as the interaction of American popular music with those of Third World music cultures and the interaction of American popular music with traditional art musics as well as other Western art forms. In the process of this exercise, we hope to be able to locate some problem areas likely to attract future historiographers of popular music.[24]

---

[23] Friedrich Körner, "Communications," *Journal of the American Musicological Society* 22 (1969): 531-32.

[24] International Musicological Society, 12th Congress, Berkeley, 1977, *Report,* ed. Daniel Heartz and Bonnie Wade (Kassel: Bärenreiter, 1981), 570.

The sessions, covering as they did the worldwide spread of interest in jazz and other American popular music, liberally demonstrated a culmination of the influence that had been generated for more than three quarters of a century.

When the national meeting of the AMS took place in New York in 1979 the following papers were given:

> Paul Machlin, "Thomas 'Fats' Waller's Early Solo Recordings: The Quintessence of Stride"

> Terence J. O'Grady, "Jazz Improvisation in Rock Bands: The Early Attempts"

> Daniel Deutsch, "Miles Davis and Jazz-Rock Fusion"

> Peter Winkler, "Pop and Jazz Harmony since the 1960's: A New Language or a New Fashion?"

In a little over a decade, Schuller's *Early Jazz* (1968) was followed by three other major books in the jazz-pop field. These include Alec Wilder's *American Popular Song: The Great Innovators, 1900-1950* (1972), Frank Tirro's *Jazz: A History* (1977), and Charles Hamm's *Yesterdays: Popular Song in America* (1979). Of the four books, *Early Jazz* and *Yesterdays* were the results of truly thorough investigation. Schuller, although not primarily a scholar, adopted exhaustive methods of research and presentation; Hamm's approach was equally thorough and illuminating. Yet neither of these is pedantic, for the authors' enthusiasm for their subjects results in lively and imaginative writing. Wilder's and Tirro's books show less concern for methodical research, leaning heavily on more personal reactions, but even so, both authors exhibit a vast and detailed knowledge of their subjects.

There are many passages about popular songs in Charles Hamm's *Yesterdays* that are evocative of the times and sentiments that were once uppermost in our lives, especially when we were young. We are experiencing our "inner book of unknown symbols," as Richard Crawford has cited from Proust's *Remembrance of Things Past,* [25] and their power is as strong as ever. Another positive quality of the book is Hamm's device of setting the historical stage for whatever period he is writing about.

In *JAMS,* evidence of increasing editorial interest in jazz and other popular music began to accumulate in the late sixties and seventies. Shortly after Schuller's *Early Jazz* was published in 1968, *JAMS* published a lengthy review of it by William Austin. Frank Tirro's *Jazz: A History,* which came out in 1977, was reviewed in *JAMS* by Lawrence Gushee. Responses by John R. Shannon and by Tirro to that review also appeared in the journal. In the Spring 1978 issue, Nicholas Temperley, as the new editor, wrote an editorial spelling out his policies concerning the journal's scope. This clarified the changes that had been developing during the previous years.

---

[25] See above, pp. 347-48.

Editors of this JOURNAL have been concerned for some years with the need to broaden its base, so that it may more fully represent the discipline of musicology in all its aspects. They have wanted to publish more material dealing with the philosophy, psychology and sociology of music, with music theory and analysis, American music, popular and folk music, non-Western musics, and the music of the last hundred and fifty years. Yet these fields have continued to be under-represented in the JOURNAL. Some scholars working in these fields have mistakenly assumed that they were the victims of deliberate biás on the part of the editor.[26]

By the early 1980s most of the earlier outward conflicts were a thing of the past. The fact that the 1981 founding meeting of IASPM was held in Amsterdam symbolizes the paradox that recognition of the significance of America's jazz and other popular music came first in Europe and only later in the United States. If the signal events of 1983 are a true indication of the future, the study of American jazz and other popular music has achieved worldwide dignity and respect. In the April 1983 issue of *Early Music* there appeared an article by Patrick Little, "The Poet and the Duke," reflecting attitudes that are almost antithetical of some of the limited views we witnessed in the past. The poet is Guillaume de Machaut (the poet/composer) and the Duke is Edward Kennedy Ellington. The songs are Machaut's "Ay mi! dame de valous" and Ellington's "I Got It Bad and That Ain't Good" (lyrics by Paul Francis Webster). Little chooses to compare these two apparently unrelated songs because, contrary to one's likely first reaction, the words express very similar thoughts and feelings, despite being separated by six centuries and vastly different musical settings. The analysis of words and music is very detailed. The sections of the article quoted below demonstrate Little's clearheadedness and lack of bias in choosing these two songs for his study:

> It may be concluded therefore that Machaut on the one hand and Ellington and Webster on the other were engaged in writing what is essentially the same kind of thing. There is however a sense in which *Ay mi!* and *I got it bad* are emphatically not the same kind of thing. This can be summed up in the observation that Machaut is a composer whose music is the business of what we might call the mainstream musicologist — roughly defined as the sort of person who reads, and for the matter of that writes, articles in learned journals — and Ellington is not. This judgement is one which few would hestitate to make; and it may be instructive to consider what justifications there are for it.
>
> The mere matter of date can, of course, be immediately dismissed. *I got it bad* was copyrighted in 1941, some six centuries after Machaut, and this clearly argues against its classification as early music; but it has nothing to do with its academic respectability.

---

[26] One member of the Editorial Board during the years previous to 1974 commented to me that no articles had been submitted which showed adequate research and competent presentation on or about popular music.

Does the distinction, then, lie somewhere in the texts of the two songs? It is not, evidently, in the sentiments they express, since in translation they are virtually indistinguishable. I should admit here that I have altered the sex of the Ellington-Webster *persona* (which is of course frequently done in performance), and this casts an interesting light on the development of the notion of romantic love, since to do this to a medieval courtly poem would be almost literally unthinkable. But a change in socio-sexual attitudes can surely not be the basis of the distinction that we need to justify.

It may seem that there is an essential literary difference between Machaut's refined 14th-century French and Webster's uneducated 20th-century American, but this is an illusion. In each case the poet is speaking through a poetic *persona*, and clearly Webster himself cannot have been illiterate, any more than Machaut can have spoken habitually in rhyming tetrameters. Both poems are the work of highly skilled craftsmen, and the social status of their chosen *personae* is beside the point. In any case, we may cite such pieces as Lassus's *Matona mia cara*, with a text written in the appalling and obscene Italian of a Flemish mercenary, as evidence that the choice of literary style has no necessary effect on the academic acceptability of its musical setting.

Perhaps we should consider rather the intention of the music. Ellington's song is without question popular, in the sense that it is intended to have an immediate appeal to the musically unsophisticated; but then, this appears also to be true of Machaut's virelai. Its simple and repetitive structure, its largely syllabic wordsetting, and the self-sufficient nature of the melody, combine to give it an immediate appeal which is not shared by the far more sophisticated polyphonic ballades, such as *Quant Theseus* or *De toutes flours,* for example; and it is still further removed from the austerities of the Mass and most of the motets. It seems likely that the monophonic virelais were intended for dancing; this is avowedly the case with *Dame a vous sans retollir* from the *Remede de Fortune.* One possible implication of this is that the dancers themselves, or the spectators, were expected to join in the refrain, which also argues for a deliberate attempt on Machaut's part to write in a popular style. It would be dangerous to base our justification on the grounds of musical intention.

There is no serious possibility of claiming that the technical quality of Machaut's music is in some way superior to that of Ellington's. It has already been demonstrated that Ellington's melodic structure is at least as sophisticated as Machaut's; and his skill in handling what is essentially late-Romantic (or perhaps post-Romantic) harmony is such that any suggestion of incompetence would be both impertinent and silly.[27]

---

[27] *Early Music* 11 (1983): 219-20.

When the Sonneck Society was in its eighth year, 1983, its handsome journal *American Music* began publication. In the eighteen issues published so far (1987) we find a liberal number of articles and reviews on jazz, other popular music, and related topics.

During the meetings of the International Association of Music Libraries in May 1983 in Washington, D.C., there was one session devoted to "Jazz in Research Libraries." Richard Andrewes, President of the Research Libraries Commission, introduced the sessions with:

> I hope the title of our session today has attracted a few who might not normally find themselves amongst research librarians, and I also hope it has not frightened away any of our regular members! It must be admitted that the bias within our professional branch has been towards the sources of what is broadly called classical music, but this is only natural in an Association which has its roots in European culture. Our libraries contain, and we endeavour to preserve, the documents which our predecessors collected, and to which we have the privilege to continue to add. We preserve many kinds of musical material: medieval plainsong antiphoners, renaissance chansonniers, 16th century sets of madrigal partbooks, 17th century common place books, 18th century sets of orchestral parts, 19th century holograph scores. Each item represents only a single piece in an incomplete historical puzzle which it is nowadays the task of the research to attempt to put together. . . . There are new areas of research, and though we cannot hope to be specialists in all of them, we do need to know something about them. Plainsong; Asian musics; Musical sociology; Popular music: each has its primary sources for which we may at some time have responsibility. Since we are holding this meeting in the United States of America, it is right that we should place jazz in the limelight. What are its primary sources? How should we go about collecting them? What special problems do they present to the librarian? What does the jazz researcher require? These are a few of the questions which I hope our distinguished guests will answer.[28]

After Andrewes' introduction, three papers addressed the problem of resources to be sought in pursuing the studies of jazz. Derek Langridge's "survey" posed the proposition that in each country there be one central repository of materials, with more specialized collections being formed in other locales within the nation. Laurence Gushee, in "The Researcher's View," related his own experiences in finding some useful collections but also in finding that some other needs were not being adequately met in libraries he had visited. Paul S. Machlin's paper "Wallering in Muddy Waters" echoed concerns similar to those of Langridge and Gushee, with particular reference to his work on Fats Waller.

---

[28] *Fontes artis musicae* 31 (1984): 18-19.

The Winter 1983 issue of the *Drexel Library Quarterly* was devoted to "Collecting Popular Music"; it included:

"Understanding and Developing Black Popular Music Collection," by James Briggs Murray

"Jazz: An Afro-American Art Music," by Marie P. Griffin

"Rock Music's Place in the Library," by John Politis

"The Folk Music Revival on Records," by Christopher C. Swift

"The Last Days of the Avant Garde; or How to Tell Your Glass from Your Eno," by Lee David Jaffe

Because the aim of this paper has been to emphasize the importance of a relatively new organization which has deliberately chosen the words "popular music" for part of its name, it is again appropriate to stress the divergencies of musics IASPM has chosen to include. It would be safe to say that IASPM's interests range from the minstrel songs and parlor ballads of the nineteenth century down to the latest rock video and include every style of popular music in between. Charles Hamm, in his book *Yesterdays,* in discussing the styles of rock music from 1955-70, has called them "different dialects of the same language." In a similar way, the dialects of jazz have been variously called: Dixieland, New Orleans, Chicago, Kansas City, and St. Louis styles, Boogie-Woogie, Bop, Be-Bop, Re-Bop, Swing, Cool, Progressive, and so on. Rock music, originally called rock 'n' roll, has gone through stylistic dialects with numerous nicknames. Arnold Shaw has written "What started in 1955-1956 as an explosion of energy, musical primitivism, and youthful rebellion has through the years been transformed into an extremely complex organism. There are, and there have been, more varieties of Rock than there are Heinz products, and there are fusions of every conceivable kind."[29] Among these varieties are: Rhythm and Blues, Rockabilly, Doo-wop, Neo-doo-wop, Chicago, Memphis, New Orleans, and San Francisco sounds, Latin Rock, Folk Rock, Acid Rock/Psychedelic, Afro Rock, Glitter Rock, Heavy Metal Rock, Bubblegum, Funk, Disco, New Wave, and so on and on. Sometimes the distinctions in style have been sharp and sometimes not. Some of the strong personalities from the early days of rock, who created their own styles, include Little Richard, Elvis Presley, Chuck Berry, and Jerry Lee Lewis. As other composer/performers came along, the music grew and changed with the indelible sounds of the Beatles, the Rolling Stones, Simon and Garfunkel, Carole King, Janis Ian, Elton John, and many others. By the mid-seventies, the most successful of these artists, by virtue of the money and power they had earned, became virtual members of the "establishment" they had once disdained. *Rolling*

---

[29] Arnold Shaw, *Dictionary of American Pop/Rock* (New York: Schirmer Books, 1982), v.

Stone, which in the 60s had been the forum for the anti-establishment milieu, had become a chronicle of social and political thinking, strong enough to influence the press and even the legislators of the nation, while continuing to reflect the latest in popular entertainment.

The most recent direction of popular music has developed, with astonishing speed, in the direction of sound and sight. Video has arrived! At first, the legal roadblocks seemed virtually insurmountable, but the solutions released an avalanche of rejuvenated energy, interest, and widespread economic effect on the pop entertainment industry. The full implications for the future are impossible to predict. The only safe thing to say is that further developments will be anything but dull.

Appendix I

Among numerous American institutions, the Library of Congress and the New York Public Library have played leading roles in espousing the study of American music, through their collecting policies and publications. Oscar Sonneck in Washington and Carleton Sprague Smith in New York originally were responsible for these developments, as can be seen from some of the events and the publications listed below. It must be emphasized that this compilation does not purport to provide an exhaustive list of events or bibliography on the subject. Rather, only some of the highlights in events and publications appear here. Exhaustive coverage would necessitate citing many more equally important developments and publications than space permits in this article. Furthermore, I have abitrarily limited the list to a time period from the beginning of this century to the founding of the Sonneck Society in 1975.

1899

Oscar G. T. Sonneck returns from Europe and begins his East Coast travels.

1902

Sonneck becomes Chief of the Music Division of the Library of Congress.

1905

Sonneck, *Bibliography of Early Secular American Music* (Washington: Printed for the Author by H. L. McQueen).

1907

Sonneck, *Early Concert-Life in America (1731-1800)* (Leipzig: Breitkopf & Härtel).

1915

Sonneck, *Early Opera in America* (New York: G. Schirmer).

1917

Sonneck leaves the Library of Congress to become President of G. Schirmer, Inc.

1927-48

New Music: A Quarterly of Modern Compositions, ed. Henry Cowell.

1928

Sonneck dies.

1930

William Treat Upton, *Art Song in America* (Boston, New York: Oliver Ditson).

1931

John Tasker Howard, *The Music of George Washington's Time* (Washington, D.C.: United States George Washington Bicentennial Commission).

Howard, *Our American Music* (New York: T. Y. Crowell).

1934

Howard, *Stephen Foster, America's Troubadour* (New York: T. Y. Crowell).

1935

Grove's Dictionary of Music and Musicians: American Supplement (London: Macmillan).

John Tasker Howard, *Ethelbert Nevin* (New York: T. Y. Crowell).

1937

Henry Hadley founds the National Association of American Composers and Conductors.

1939

Richard S. Hill joins the staff of the Music Division of the Library of Congress where he ultimately becomes Head of Reference services.

1940

John Tasker Howard is appointed to the staff of the Music Division of the New York Public Library by Carleton Sprague Smith.

1941

Harry Dichter and Elliott Shapiro, *Early Sheet Music: Its Lure and Its Lore* (New York: Bowker).

Works Progress Administration, Historical Records Program, *Bio-Bibliographical Index of Musicians in the United States of America* (Washington, D.C.: Pan American Union).

John Tasker Howard, *Our Contemporary Composers* (New York: T. Y. Crowell).

1943

Americana Collection of the Music Division of the New York Public Library is established with John Tasker Howard as Head.

Music Library Association *Notes,* Second Series, begun in December, ed. Richard S. Hill.

1944-45

Dena Epstein, "Music Publishing in Chicago before 1871," a seven-part article in *Notes,* vols. 1 and 2. Reprinted in book form (Detroit: Information Coordinators, 1969).

1945

Oscar G. T. Sonneck, *A Bibliography of Early Secular American Music,* revised and enlarged by William Treat Upton (Washington, D.C.: Library of Congress, Music Division; reprint with introduction by Irving Lowens, New York: Da Capo Press, 1964).

1950

Rudi Blesh and Harriet Janis, *They All Played Ragtime: The True Story of an American Music* (New York: Alfred Knopf).

1951

Charles Haywood, *A Bibliography of North American Folklore and Folksong* (New York: Greenwood Press).

1955

James J. Fuld, *American Popular Music, 1875-1950* (Philadelphia: Musical Americana).

Gilbert Chase, *America's Music: From the Pilgrims to the Present* (New York: McGraw Hill).

1959-60

John Edmunds and Gordon Boelzner, *Some Twentieth-Century American Composers: A Selective Bibliography,* vols. 1-2 (New York: New York Public Library).

1960

John Kirkpatrick, *A Temporary Mimeographed Catalogue of the Music Manuscripts and Related Materials of Charles Edward Ives* (New Haven: School of Music, Yale University).

1964

Harold Gleason and Thomas Marrocco, *Music in America: An Anthology from the Landing of the Pilgrims to the Close of the Civil War, 1620-1865* (New York: W. W. Norton).

1964

Richard J. Wolfe, *Secular Music in America 1801-1825: A Bibliography,* introduction by Carleton Sprague Smith, 3 vols. (New York: New York Public Library).

1969

Louis Moreau Gottschalk, *The Piano Works of Louis Moreau Gottschalk,* ed. Vera Brodsky Lawrence; editorial advisor, Richard Jackson (New York: Arno Press).

1971

Eileen Southern, *The Music of Black Americans: A History* (New York: W. W. Norton).

Scott Joplin, *The Collected Works of Scott Joplin,* ed. Vera Brodsky Lawrence; editorial consultant, Richard Jackson (New York: New York Public Library).

1973

Inez Barbour Hadley bequest to the New York Public Library of Henry Hadley's music manuscripts, documents, correspondence, etc.

1975

Sonneck Society is founded; first president, Irving Lowens.

In fashioning a chronology of jazz and other American popular music, I have gleaned the following from sections of Nicolas Slonimsky's *Music since 1900*[30] and headlines from the *New York Times,* as they appear in the *New York Times Index.*[31]   Slonimsky citations are marked NS and those from the *Times* are marked NYT. The brevity of the headlines renders them only capsules of information; but, since most of them were probably skillfully written, they do give rather dramatic evidence of the range and direction of feelings prevalent in the public opinions of the moment.   These quotations range from extremely negative, even vicious, reactions in the first decades of the century, to the manifestly positive, even respectful, attitude as shown by the last Slonimsky entry, dated 17 May 1969, reporting on a United States postage stamp issued honoring W. C. Handy as the "father of the Blues."   One could base a detailed study of the sociology of popular music history largely on this sequence of widespread public reactions.

28 June 1904 – NS

Daniel Decatur Emmett, the Northerner whose song *Dixie* became the fighting hymn of the Confederacy during the Civil War, dies in his native Mount Vernon, Ohio, at the age of eighty-eight.

6 March 1913 – NS

The word jazz appears in print for the first time as a synonym for pep, in the *San Francisco Bulletin,* in a sports column written by "Scoop" Gleeson.

20 May 1913 – NYT

London Peeress shocked at modern dances.

21 May 1913 – NYT

Turkey trot banned at Panama.

28 May 1913 – NYT

Turkey trotting in New York City hotels condemned by Grand Jury in presentiment.

25 June 1913 – NYT

Donald D. Bartholomew ejected from high school dance for turkey-trotting.

10 July 1913 – NYT

Swiss hotels prohibit "American" dances, Austrian officer challenges daughter's American partner to duel.

---

[30] Nicolas Slonimsky, *Music since 1900,* 4th ed. (New York: Scribner's, 1971).

[31] *New York Times Index* (New York: New York Times, 1913-).

26 July 1913—NYT

Turkey-trot-Prussian officer killed by general in duel over its propriety.

16 December 1913—NYT

Bavarian King puts ban on tango; does not wish army officers to take part in festivities where it is danced.

9 November 1913—NYT

Society girls give lessons in tango; great demand for tango music.

18 November 1913—NYT

German Emperor forbids army and navy officers to dance tango, one-step, or two-step in uniform, Royal Opera warned.

30 November 1913—NYT

Tango banned at American Thanksgiving celebration until departure of official guests.

30 December 1913—NYT

Italian King forbids the tango at state ball.

13 November 1913—NYT

New York City restaurants cater to craze for modern dances.

21 November 1913—NYT

Tango prohibited by the Vatican.

25 January 1914—NYT

Eight bishops in Provinces of France ban tango.

13 February 1914—NS

The American Society of Composers, Authors and Publishers (ASCAP), established to protect performing rights and to distribute annual fees to members according to the frequency of performance of their music, is formally organized at a dinner meeting in the Hotel Claridge in New York under the directorship of Victor Herbert.

15 February 1914—NYT

President Poincaire bars dance at the Elysée.

2 March 1914—NYT

Dr. C. Campbell Morgan calls new dances a "reversion to monkeyism."

11 March 1914—NS

At Carnegie Hall, New York, Jim Europe conducts a Negro symphony orchestra in an instrumental ensemble anticipatory of jazz bands, sans oboes, bassoons or second violins, but with a cornucopia of clarinets, trumpets, trombones, banjos, a set of drums, and a phalanx of ten pianos.

7 June 1916—NYT

Vatican Consistory ruling against dancing at entertainments given under auspices of Church.

7 March 1917 – NS

The world's first jazz recording is issued by the Victor Company, with *Livery Stable Blues* on one side and *Dixieland Jazz Band One-Step* on the other.

6 April 1917 – NS

On the day of the declaration of war on Germany by the United States, George M. Cohan composes the famous song *Over There,* based on the three notes of the bugle call. (The song was copyrighted by Leo Feist, publishers, on 1 June 1917; Cohan received a check for $25,000 from the publishers on 31 October 1917 in full payment for the song; this money he gave to soldiers' funds and civic charities.)

10 December 1917 – NS

The Vatican issues a decree, signed by the Secretary of the Consistorial Congregation, enjoining Catholics against dancing the tango and the maxixe, at home, in public, in the daytime, or at night.

25 July 1919 – NYT

British Imperial Society of Dancing Teachers promises new dances; jazz doomed.

11 June 1919 – NYT

Jazz Band. Art in Paris Le Matin claims music originally made by French cats 120 years ago.

February 1920 – NYT

Pittsburgh dance hall proprietors form organization for suppression of jazz and improper dancing.

3 March 1920 – NYT

Demonstration of "shimmy" in White Plains Court barred.

19 June 1920 – NYT

Jazz denounced by Mrs. M. Obendorffer in speech at convention of General Federation of Women's Clubs.

28 March 1921 – NYT

Hungary bans fox trot, one step, and jazz.

19 September 1921 – NYT

Jazz barred from Louisville, Ky., Episcopal churches.

22 January 1921 – NYT

Dr. H. Beets says shimmy and jazz set Indians wild again.

16 May 1922 – NYT

Mrs. Bable Dorbandt fined for allowing 3-year-old daughter to dance in public.

12 February 1922 – NYT

Kansas City School Superintendant wants legislation to stop jazz as intoxicant.

7 April 1922—NYT
M. M. Wilson driven to suicide by jazz.

14 January 1923—NYT
Art of jazz craze in Japan.

22 August 1923—NYT
Kalamazoo, Michigan, amendment forbids dancers to look into each other's eyes.

12 February 1924—NS
George Gershwin, 25-year-old Brooklyn-born composer of inspired popular songs in an authentically modern American style, appears as piano soloist in the first performance, at a concert conducted by Paul Whiteman in Aeolian Hall in New York, of his epoch-making *Rhapsody in Blue,* completed by him in piano score on 7 January 1924, and arranged for piano and a jazz-type ensemble by Ferde Grofé.

18 November 1924—NYT
O. H. Kahn discusses possibility of producing American jazz opera at Met Opera House, talks with Irving Berlin, Jerome Kern, and George Gershwin on production.

1 December 1924—NS
Lady Be Good, musical revue by George Gershwin with lyrics by Ira Gershwin, containing one of his most important, musicologically speaking, songs, *Fascinating Rhythm,* in which an apocopated 7/8 theme generates off-beat ictuses as it overlaps the barlines in 4/4 time, is produced in New York.

2 January 1925—NYT
Nadia Boulanger predicts national school of American music, but says it will not be founded on jazz.

28 November 1925—NS
"Grand Ole Opry," a series of Saturday night broadcasts lasting 4½ hours each and embodying a medley of cowboy tunes, country ballads, and rustic jazz, is inaugurated in Nashville, Tennessee, on Radio Station WSM, under its initial appellation "Barn Dance."

4 February 1926—NYT
Cincinnati Salvation Army hinders erection of theater adjoining home for girls on grounds that music would implant jazz emotions in babies born at home.

14 June 1926—NYT
Cornetist to Queen Victoria dies on hearing American jazz.

28 June 1926—NYT
O. H. Kahn says adaption of classical airs to jazz has brought about increased interest in the classical originals.

15 August 1926—NYT
Maharajah of Kashmir imports jazz band to play at his court, Shalimar Gardens.

15 September 1926 — NS

Jelly Roll Morton and his Red Hot Peppers (George Mitchell, cornet; Kid Ory, trombone; Omer Simeon, clarinet; Johnny St. Cyr, banjo; John Lindsay, bass; Andrew Hilaire, drums) hold their first recording session in Chicago for R.C.A. Victor, cutting among other pieces their famous *Black Bottom Stomp,* whose rollicking swing beat artfully conceals the total absence of the tonic chord in the entire opening section.

3 March 1927 — NYT

Charleston not being danced in society circles in Spain at request of Queen Victoria.

13 November 1927 — NYT

American dances banned throughout province of Chieti in Italy.

31 March 1927 — NYT

Letter from Queen Mario expresses fondness for jazz while preferring opera.

28 April 1927 — NS

The first Russian jazz band ever to perform in public is introduced in a program of miscellaneous jazz numbers in Leningrad.

28 June 1928 — NS

Louis Armstrong and his Hot Five record *West End Blues,* a milestone in the history of jazz.

18 August 1930 — NYT

T. M. Sheehy sees doom of jazz and return to conservatism.

20 January 1930 — NYT

Mme. Galli-Curci likes it for dancing.

30 January 1932 — NYT

Mme. Alda deplores crooning and jazz.

15 March 1933 — NS

The Berlin radio issues an absolute ban on broadcasting of "Negro jazz."

17 March 1933 — NYT

Negro jazz banned by Hitlerites in Germany.

17 May 1933 — NYT

Popularity increases in Russia as ban is lifted.

31 December 1933 — NS

An anti-jazz parade is held at Mohall, Ireland, with banners proclaiming "Down with Jazz and Paganism."

1 January 1935 — NS

Swing appears in print for the first time in the American monthly *Down Beat,* defined as "a musician's term for perfect rhythm," with pragmatic connotations as a free improvisation on a clarinet or a jazz trumpet, accompanied by steady square beat in the piano and drums.

29 June 1936 – NS

The Congress of the United States presents a gold medal to George M. Cohan in recognition of his meritorious service as the composer of the rousing World War I song *Over There* and of the patriotic ballad *You're a Grand Old Flag*.

28 November 1938 – NS

The State Jazz Orchestra of the Union of Soviet Socialist Republics is inaugurated in Moscow, signalizing official Soviet acceptance of jazz as legitimate popular art, in a program of jazzified pieces by Tchaikovsky and Rachmaninoff, and a suite for jazz orchestra expressly written for the occasion by Dmitri Shostakovich.

24 August 1951 – NS

Modern Jazz Quartet is founded in New York by John Lewis (pianist), Milt Jackson (vibraphonist), Percy Heath (bassist) and Kenny Clarke (drummer), with the aim of establishing a fruitful coalition of classical music and jazz. (The official beginning of the Modern Jazz Quartet is reckoned from their first recording session of 22 December 1952.)

17 May 1969 – NS

The United States Post Office issues a six-cent stamp honoring W. C. Handy, "Father of the Blues," and concomitantly celebrating the sesquicentennial of the City of Memphis, the scene of Handy's early triumphs, in which he is portrayed playing trumpet in deep blue against a purple background.

Part VI

Tributes

Recollections of Richard Hill

by

Leonard Feist

The passage of years since Dick Hill's death and my involvement in quite different fields of musical activity than the type of publishing in which I engaged before the mid-60s had dimmed my memory. There are no contemporary colleagues with whom I might chat about the exciting post-war decades of serious music publishing and, thus, about people who had provided some special character to our little world. However, I was glad to discover that the invitation to contribute to this Memorial has loosened my retrospective juices which, in turn, have recaptured some of the color and restored some of the savor.

Still there are slightly hazy outlines. The memories, not in sharp focus, run something like this. Dick Hill was a most noteworthy although transitory participant in the music publishing scene of the late forties and fifties. Naturally, I knew him best as the advertising salesman for *Notes*. I doubt if a more unlikely space salesman existed — or a more elegant one. Or a more learned, literate, informed and charming one!

If the truth were to be told or admitted, there really was no need for Dick Hill to come to New York to solicit ads. For those publishers of the music that *Notes*' readers purchased, a telephone call or a note from Washington would surely have been enough. The space rates were reasonable. And *Notes* sold music! The number of advertising pages were a clear endorsement of that. As a matter of fact, even if it didn't deliver sales, many of us would have felt that as a unique journal *Notes* deserved our support.

I think many of my colleagues thought as I did that Dick used the solicitation of advertising as an excuse to visit New York and to spend time with the people who were part of the action and who were creating the materials of present and future music librarianship. It was quite apparent that he enjoyed our company, if only as a change of pace.

I'm quite sure that Dick, with his inate courtesy, always called in advance, but that was hardly necessary. We were always glad to welcome him. He brought news from the Library of Congress and about our mutual friends. He also brought an insatiable interest in publishing, here and abroad, old and new, serious and popular. Particularly the more esoteric.

Our discussions of the business of selling ads were barely noticeable if it occurred at all. Surely it was painlessly brief.* Perhaps it didn't really take place. What did take place was a free wheeling, broad-reaching, unhurried chat with few if any editorial restraints — news about musicians, gossip about friends, memories of good food and cookery and all the lively arts.

I don't recall when or how I met Dick Hill. I suspect that he came to my office. I don't remember how often we met over a decade and a half nor at what other places. Surely at the Coolidge Concerts. Yet all that remains as my specifics of Richard Hill seems like one long ranging visit and the pleasure of his company.

After Dick's death, Harold Spivacke called together a group of his publisher friends to seek their views on the future of *Notes* and, I suppose, to be assured of their continuing support and involvement. That wasn't necessary, but to me it was gratifying to think that I was in some way part of *Notes,* and Dick Hill's heritage.

---

* From Hill's letters and the memories of his *Notes* colleagues, not all of his adventures in selling advertising were as pleasant as those with Feist. Cf. pp. 35-36 above. — Editors.

Richard S. Hill and IAML:
A Love Affair

by

Virginia Cunningham

Dick Hill was a person who could keep numerous pots on front burners simultaneously, and tend them all lovingly. Such was the case with IAML. He became involved with the organization early on and gave it his strong support for the rest of his life.

Meetings preparing for the organization of IAML were held at Florence (October 1949) and Lüneburg (July 1950). Dick may have been present in Florence, but he was not at Lüneburg. Formal establishment of IAML took place at a meeting in Paris in July 1951, and Dick was elected president. He undoubtedly attended the meetings of the Executive Committee each year until Alec Hyatt King was elected president in 1954. Dick probably also attended the annual meetings and the triennial congresses from 1954 to 1960.

American participation in IAML was a matter of concern to Dick. He was influential in placing Americans on IAML commissions, and gradually American participation increased to where we played a leading role. IAML's *Bulletin d'Information* (vol. 1, no. 2, March 1952) lists eleven institutional members and thirty-nine individual members from the United States. In 1983 that number had grown to 229 institutional members and 182 individual members.

Dick was not a librarian; he was a scholar who happened to be working in a library. His scholarship clearly gained him the respect of his European colleagues, scholars all. Impressive, too, was his ability to articulate his concerns, whether speaking or writing. His article on the need for an international cataloging code is remarkable for its understanding of the subject and its vision for the future. He was often long-winded, as he recognized, but he was forgiven for that.

Dick loved people. In personal conversations he made it clear that he liked you, he respected you, and he was willing to listen to what you had to say. I can remember, however, that on more than one occasion we had a lively conversation that ended by our agreeing to disagree, no hard feelings. He established a loving relationship with the Europeans too, as is evidenced by their letters to him and his replies. Who else in the world would have had the temerity to address Vladimir Fédorov as "Honeybunch?"

His love for his European friends manifested itself in another way. After the war he bought stockings for his friends' wives, because stockings were difficult to come by in Europe. He brought back perfume for his American lady friends.

I selected the title for this article because I truly believe that Dick's relationship to IAML was a love affair. He contributed his time generously to organizing the association, he nurtured its growth carefully, and he used his formidable persuasive powers to get others to contribute. It is in large part due to Dick that we have IAML and IAML/US as flourishing organizations today.

Dick Hill Goes to "Work"

by

Gilbert Chase

It's more than possible — even likely — that I first met Dick Hill between the years 1935 and 1940, when I returned from my long stay in Paris. But the first meeting I can definitely recall is after I assumed my position as Latin American Music Specialist at the Music Division of the Library of Congress in 1940. The Music Division staff were a friendly and congenial group, and I still treasure the memory of my three years there. The luncheons we all shared were often unpredictably loquacious, sometimes controversial, but never expressively negative.

We all know, of course, how much Dick did, as both editor and contributor, to promote the prestige and growth of MLA *Notes*. It was also obvious that he knew the importance of advertisements to its continuous growth, and I can vouch from personal experience that he made every possible move to obtain its expansion. From the Library of Congress I went to work with the National Broadcasting Company in New York City and, as would be expected, Dick did his best to convince me that I could get the ad he wanted from NBC. Well, I tried my best, but there was no result, and before long I quit NBC and went to RCA-Victor in Camden, who was not interested in an ad either.

Nevertheless our friendship continued to the end. His memory remains as vividly as ever, and I could never imagine myself having read only *once* any article by Richard S. Hill. Thus it happens that I have chosen for this tribute to him "The Mysterious Chord of Henry Clay Work" (*Notes* 10, 1952/53).* To me it is illuminating and fascinating, both as biography *and* history — plus romance, which my out worn dictionary describes as "4. A novel or story dealing with a love affair"; and more succinctly as "5. A love affair." What would Dick think if he knew that I gave only one page of my own writing to Work,[1] plus another from the autobiography of George Root,[2] who describes Work as

---

* Subsequent quotations are identified by page numbers only.

[1] *America's Music: From the Pilgrims to the Present,* 2nd ed. (New York: McGraw-Hill, 1966).

[2] *The Story of a Musical Life: An Autobiography* (Cincinnati: John Church Co., 1891; reprint, New York: AMS Press, 1973).

a quiet and rather solemn-looking young man, poorly clad [who] was sent up to my room from the store with a song for me to examine. I looked at it and then at him in astonishment. It was "Kingdom Coming". . . .[3]

Anyhow, I'm sure that Dick knew all about *that,* plus everything else relating to Henry Clay Work, including the "Mysterious Chord" of his life and checkered career. The proof of this, obviously, is in the depth and scope of the article we are discussing. He sets the tone at the very beginning of his article, when he writes that such songs as *Wake Nicodemus* and *Grandfather's Clock* "may not be rated quite so highly as Foster, but neither does he deserve such a quick 'brush-off' as he is generally given" (p. 211). The "brush-off" may have diminished since Dick wrote his article but he also had something to say about that:

> Perhaps the fault for this neglect is not altogether ours. A composer who had the forethought to die near the peak of his career with one of the best of all song titles tucked away in his wallet is playing into the hands of his biographers. On the other hand, a song-writer who crowds his most creative period into four short years and then proceeds to outlive that period by twenty more years, broken only by the most sporadic and unequal efforts, tempts fate. When Work died on June 8, 1884, most people were surprised to find he had not died long before, and the obituary that appeared the next day in the *New York Daily Tribune* ran only to a routine five lines [p. 211].

It is not my intention to discuss in detail all that Dick has to say about Work in this extensive — and, I would say, "definitive" — article. My condensation seeks to be a tribute to Dick's genius and to apprise those unfamiliar with the original article.

The first part of Dick's article deals primarily with "the years of greatest productivity," the years between 1861 and 1866, then "a steady decline leading down to only one or two songs in each of the years from 1870 to 1872" (p. 215). After complete silence for a few years, "a sudden burst of energy takes the list to its peak in 1876 and 1877, only to relapse once more for the next four years, ending with a brief and chilly Indian Summer in 1882 and 1883" (p. 215). As Dick notes, "The vital statistics for his early years are sufficiently common to call for no elaboration" (p. 215). Though he goes on with the biographical chore, we need not necessarily go along with him — at least all the way. We know that Work "objected so violently" to being a tinker or tailer that "the plan had to be altered and the boy was allowed to become a printer" (p. 216). Denied thorough training in music, Work "did his best to teach himself the rudiments of music while he was being taught his trade" (p. 216). When he was only twenty-one he composed his first song. Thereafter came a contract with Root & Cady, his visit to Europe, followed by an investment of "all his savings in a fruit farm at Vineland, N.J." with one of his

---

[3] Ibid., 137.

brothers. The venture collapsed, so we may as well forget the fruit.
He "returned once more to his old trade of printer in Philadelphia"
and now, enter Susie! (pp. 216-17).

Susie was a member of the Mitchell family, which in spite of having
"four or five daughters and three songs" — or perhaps because of that
burden — found it necessary to take in boarders. We are told that

> Work was rapidly on the best of terms with the whole family,
> and the friendship was prolonged for many years after he
> had left Philadelphia, through a lively correspondence with
> all of its members [p. 217].

But there was a special affinity that developed, as Dick relates:

> With Susie, the situation was totally different. These
> forty odd letters from her girlhood which she preserved so
> carefully until her death in 1921 tell the story in reverse,
> reaching their climax and explaining many cryptic passages
> in the early letters only eight years after the correspondence
> began. To some extent it will be necessary to follow that
> pattern, but in one respect it seems essential to anticipate
> the letters by revealing that when Work left Philadelphia
> at the end of June, 1869, he was very much in love with Susie
> and thought that Susie returned his love. As a married man
> and a gentleman of the old school, none of this could be
> put into words. Instead, Work escaped — temporarily — on
> an extended trip to the Far West, taking his young son
> Waldo with him for company.
>
> Although Susie was already teaching a class of young
> girls at the Keystone School, she had only turned eighteen
> a week or two before Work left her home. Later, he was
> to comment facetiously on the difference in their ages — in
> the years he was married, she was just a quarter as old as
> he; by 1870, she was half as old. This changing ratio
> unquestionably conditioned the course of their relationship.
> A man of thirty-eight is practically doddering to a girl of
> eighteen, whereas when the girl reaches twenty-five, a man
> of forty-four may seem only somewhat mature. Even on
> Work's own evidence, therefore, there would seem to be
> grounds for suspecting the depth of Susie's affection for him
> during the first years, although she may well have sensed
> his love for her without any overt expression of it, and been
> greatly flattered at the attentions of so famous a personage.
> In his very first letter, written from Reno on July 6th, 1869,
> Work complains that there are two Susies and he is afraid
> that his letter may fall into the hands of the wrong one. She
> has given him permission to call her "Sister Susie," and his
> letters are invariably so addressed. Apparently, this is the
> spontaneous Susie, who acts without reserve and is kind to
> him, whereas "the other Susie" is somewhat more distant,
> since she has learned there are times when it is best not to
> encourage him too much [pp. 217-18].

I would very willingly go on with the rest of Dick's description
of the Susie and Work letters but my personal aim is two fold: to
arouse general interest in Dick's stupendous presentation of this

unconsecrated "love affair" carried on through the postal service, and to propose that the friends and followers of Dick Hill declare themselves able and willing to sponsor an up-dated publication of "The Mysterious Chord of Henry Clay Work."

Work's letters to Susie went on and on, mentioning virtually every topic that caught his interest, from his working hours to what he regarded as his "literary career." We are told that

> During the summer of 1873, Susie asked him what great mental effort—musical or literary—he had become involved with, and in a short note at the end of his letter he replied:

> > Oh, no! only mechanical. My attention is turning more and more in such directions—and I think wisely— although I am still often tempted or urged to wander in musical or literary fields. In five years, if I live, I shall have, all over the country, collections of wheels and levers, and rollers and cranks, in continual motion, doing that which I taught them to do, and doing it as machinery had never been able to do it. And I shall not be as poor then as now [p. 374].

And so it goes from one idea and one plan to another; but always with Susie on his mind. (Or is it deeper?) We are told that in his letters

> His most frequent refrain revolves about his desire to see her. Hardly a letter passes without either the suggestion that he visit her in Philadelphia or an elaborately concocted plan for her coming to New York [p. 375].

They met occasionally, but their correspondence continued to come and go, and eventually Work found himself writing about the man he thought would be her spouse, a certain "Mr. Scupham," whom he had met on his western trip in 1869. As we shall see, he was completely *on* the track, much to his deep regret.

Not to be too prolix, I shall skip the details of Work's problems with his wife and his great sadness when his young son Waldo died of consumption. Yet the correspondence continued, on and off, to the very end, with letters galore on both sides. It appears that Work had something to say about *everything,* including matrimony.

> With regard to engagements, my opinion is that just as soon as such a promise begins to feel like a chain—not a delicate gold chain, but that of a prisoner—there ought to be some way of breaking it or throwing it off. Provision at the outset should be made for such a contingency, and if frankness is ever desirable it is in the case of engagements where one or the other has the slightest hesitation as to the step they have agreed upon. One reason for there being so many mis-mated couples in the world is that incompatibilities were not corrected—or avoided—when they might have been—before marriage. People are apt to think that they are unfaithful to their vows if they make any attempt to reconsider their

engagement, whereas the contrary is true: they are unfaithful, in spirit at least, if they do not reconsider when changed circumstances or feelings prompt thereto . . . [p. 383].

Verily, a Daniel come to judge! No doubt he had in mind the engagement of Susie to the previously mentioned Mr. Scupham, and he ends the letter thus:

. . . Write to me next week: write "while the day lasts; for the night cometh, in which no man can"—be written to without permission,

with much love,

X. Y. Z.

The next letter to Susie is even longer and more intense in feeling: he *was* her lover in heart and mind:

. . . Once, at least, you stood before me just as you were in 1868-9, or as I saw you then, on rare and never-to-be-forgotten occasions—with a softened light flashing from your eyes, and a delicate tint of crimson over-spreading your cheeks. . . . But, since that Sunday night good-bye, when I felt the warm flush on your cheek instead of seeing it, I have not so much need of recalling the extreme past—have you? Oh! that sad and delightful good-bye! 'Twas so very short for such a long absence—the life-long separation that is to be! Why such haste? Why didn't I lengthen the happy moment? Why didn't I hold you fast in my arms forever, so that you couldn't be carried beyond the Rocky Mountains, or anywhere else? No! I don't mean that. If I can see you once more, I think I shall be able to see you go. A few days since, I thought that I could do so very calmly. I told you, I believe, that I shouldn't feel bad about your going, because I had always known that something of the kind must occur, or was liable to occur, and had prepared my mind to hear of it and be satisfied with it, or rather, reconciled to it. And that's what I thought then; but I miscalculated and under-rated the long-slumbering forces within. They had been pretty thoroughly quieted, as I thought, by the narcotic of absence, and I did not doubt my ability to control them. But the magnetism of personal presence, of sight, and of touch, has awakened them all again.

(The long letter continues, apparently *ad infinitum;* some further excerpts:)

At my age, a person has usually had the greater part of his self-conceit taken out of him by hard knocks and otherwise. In speaking of knowing your feelings as well or better than your words expressed them, I only meant that I interpreted your words by the light of all the various incidents of our long acquaintance. . . . I know that you love me, and knew it (though not so well) before I went to California. But just how much I couldn't then and can't now say. . . . However that may be . . . I can but tell you that your letters to me during this long period have given me a higher estimate and a more vivid realization of *woman's constancy* than I ever had before. There is certainly a mysterious chord connecting us, and, having lasted so long, it will probably never be entirely severed. But after this month, it must lie, like an ocean cable, deep out of sight. . . . Of all the motives that serve as main-springs for human action, the love of a woman has been with me the strongest — by far the strongest. Under such influence, but rarely otherwise, I can do my best. Oh! how differently I might have been situated today, had such an influence, like a beacon light, shone strongly and steadily on all the years of my manhood! Even leaving out of the question my earliest disappointments, misfortunes, successes and reverses, what different results might have been wrought out during the past few years. . . . My heart is full, and you are the only one in all the world to whom I can whisper or even hint my feelings. . . . In parting, it is the last scene that is most indelibly impressed upon the memory, so let me see you once more as I have always seen you — a girl — and let me forget that anyone claims you as a wife [pp. 385-86].

Very soon Susie replied to his letter; he immediately answered her "kind, sympathetic, and sensible letter," and in turn, contritely apologized for having assumed too much in his relationship with her.

. . . In spite of my regret, I can't in my heart retract the over-confident assertion I made. I dare not. 'Twould be sacrificing (in a way far worse than burning) the thirty-one letters that lie on the table before me, bearing your signature. 'Twould cruelly banish the spirit that now animates them, and leave them but cold corpses [p. 387].

The *Public Ledger* for 28 July 1877 formally records the Scupham-Mitchell marriage, and Dick Hill notes that "Quite properly," Henry Clay Work "was left to say his final good-bye in a song — *Farewell, my loved one!*"

What is perhaps not generally known is that Work seriously planned to return to music as a career. . . . Most of the letters of 1871, and some from 1872 and 1873, are written on paper with the letterhead: "Henry C. Work's Musical Studio / No. 769, Broadway" [p. 372].

But this proved to be mostly wishful thinking. As he wrote to Susie:

You ask what music I am writing. I have a sad report to make in this respect. You know what great aspirations I had in the spring — perhaps you did not know what important results I expected to accomplish this summer. But, Oh, what a failure — an almost total failure — I have made! [p. 372].

And at the very end of his tether:

I can't stand it much longer. I won't stand it. There'll be a general breaking up here of some kind before long. Although

I have read of the sad fate of fishes who jump from the frying-pan, I shall certainly jump. (Not from my window — if I can help it.) [p. 372].

He had at least not lost his sense of humor entirely!

Work then decided that a literary venture would be more productive; and so wrote to Susie on 11 June 1871:

> . . . I have some grand literary plans, in prose, stirring up a great commotion in my brain — which, combined with the musical din produced there is likely to set me crazy, unless I find an outlet for it.
>
> I'm something of an adept at Planning, you know; but astonishingly slow in writing up details. Well, I've thought that with the assistance of some other person who possessed a quicker perception, and a faculty of thinking more rapidly, we two might produce something that neither could alone. What do you say to *our* making an attempt of that kind, and writing a story to astonish the world! [p. 372].

This could be taken as both an impulse to somehow succeed at *something,* and his strong desire to be *with* Susie, in whatever manner that could be arranged. But it proved to be just another case of wishful thinking that led nowhere. When Susie asked him how he was getting on with his literary career, he replied: " . . . The topics upon which I am most internally-urged and strongly-impelled to write are those which the world is not now prepared to hear" [p. 373].

Work went on to try various projects that he thought might bring him good fortune, but with very little if any success. He never gave up — and that goes also for his attachment to Susie, as "His most frequent refrain revolves about his desire to see her" [p. 375]. He did his best in that direction, but not with total success, as she was seldom with him. So it is to the letters they exchanged that we must turn for the full picture of their relation.

But that is beyond the immediate scope of my present tribute to Dick Hill as friend, scholar, musician, and author. Thanks to him we have at hand the entire story of "The Mysterious Chord" of Henry Clay Work and the dearly beloved whom he could not marry, "Dear Sister Susie."

Richard S. Hill: Reference Librarian

by

Vincent H. Duckles

Richard S. Hill's total professional career could be summed up in his concept of the role of the reference librarian in the modern library structure. His official title at the Library of Congress during most of his 21-year tenure was Head of the Reference Section of the Music Division. That position enabled him to bridge the gap between the advanced research scholar and the amphorphous music-loving public.

As a "service librarian" he was known to the Washington cultural community and to the world beyond. At the time of his death, Paul Henry Lang wrote in the 19 February 1961 *New York Herald Tribune:* "There is scarcely a cultivated musician or scholar in this country who directly or indirectly did not receive valuable guidance or information from Mr. Hill." To this one might add that the indebtedness was shared worldwide.

Dick Hill was a man of many parts: reference librarian, musicologist, editor, and scholar with special interest in contemporary and early American music. His great concern was the journal *Notes,* from editorial policy to financial operation; he wrote endless reviews for it. He initiated bibliographical projects and gave support and encouragement to others to pursue such work. He was one of the founders of the International Association of Music Libraries, serving as its first president, and was one of the initiators of the International Inventory of Musical Sources (RISM)—and he made time for research and writing! Any one of these fields could consume the full energies of an ordinary man, but for Hill they were part of the daily routine. The focus of that daily routine was his work as a music reference librarian.

Much of his reference work was carried on by correspondence. One of the many letters I had from him, reprinted below on pages 386-88, was in response to a request for information on copyright restrictions on the performance of Schoenberg's works. The twelve-tone music of Schoenberg and his school was a special interest of Dick Hill. In the *Musical Quarterly,* January 1936, he published a pioneer article, "Arnold Schoenberg's Tone Rows and the Tonal System of the Future," and from 1945 to 1952 he wrote extensively of Schoenberg's work in reviews for *Notes.* His response to my request illustrates not only his prodigious knowledge, but his thoroughness as a music reference librarian. He tells all I might possibly need to know; he provides background, refers me to other sources, and suggests a variety of possibilities. Moreover, the style, which became famous among his friends, is typical. The letter runs on for three pages, typed single-space by his own hand, too hurriedly written to correct typographical errors except where facts are concerned. He complains about the work load and the rush for time, but takes the time to search out the answers and to write this lengthy reply. His genial nature and his warm friendship are evident throughout.

The Library of Congress
Reference Department
Music Division
May 19, 1952

Dear Vincent:

I started out to answer your letter right away because I thought it was one I could tend to without leaving my desk, but one thing led to another and I have been chasing around the building the entire afternoon looking up one thing here and checking something else there. And me with a stack of reference letters dating back to February still to tend to!

Some of the Schönberg songs were never registered for copyright [op. 1, *Zwei Leider;* op. 2, *Vier Lieder;* op. 3, *Sechs Lieder;* and op. 6, *Acht Lieder*—all published in Berlin by the Dreililien Verlag] and one item, op. 13, *Friede auf Erde,* did not have its copyright renewed and consequently now is free.[1] The main body of his music, however, is as you suspect thoroughly protected, and thus it can't be microfilmed without the written permission of the copyright claimant—who is usually the publisher. You and Mr. Cudworth agree, I understand, on the research value of microfilm, but when it comes to performing the stuff, I'll take printed music any time. It's clearer and by the time you have made enlargements, cheaper. Since you are going to have to right [i.e., write] around anyway to see if you can pick up copies of the protected publications, I should think it would only be sensible to see how many of the other things can also be had, and then have only those things microfilmed of which you haven't been able to locate copies.

Since Schönberg's principal publisher was the Universal Edition [op. 8, 10 (*Entrückung,* arr. by A. Berg), 12, 14, 20 *(Herzgewächse),* 27, and 28], you might as well start out with the Associated Music Publishers, Inc., 25 West 45th Street. I'm not certain of this, but they also used to represent Ed. Bote and G. Bock, who issued op. 35, *Sechs Stücke für Männerchor,* and you might as well ask them if they still do, since this is another of the protected works. Next, I'd

---

[1] Foreign titles have been italicized for easier reading. — The Editors.

try G. Schirmer, Inc., since the firm published many of Schönberg's later works, and while they still represented him, I would suppose it likely that they laid in a stock of works published by others. These [*sic*] may not be true, or they may have sold off the stock, but at least it is worth a try. In this country, there is no particular choice thereafter, but you should certainly ask Orpheus, Broude, the Music Exchange, and Joseph Patelson if they have anything you still need. Oh, yes! You don't list op. 15, 15 songs from Stephan Georg's *"Das Buch der hängenden Gärten."* Since this is one of Schönberg's most important collections of songs, your silence probably means that you have it. Just thought I ought to mention it. It was published by Universal, and the copyright was renewed.

There are two things which you can certainly get quite easily — four part songs published by E. B. Marks Music Corp. without an opus number, although I have seen them listed as Op. 49, and *Drei Lieder,* Op. 48, which is hot off the presses of Bomart Music Corp., of Hillside, New York. (They were advertised last September in *Notes,* but only just issued because Bomart got tied up on getting the words cleared. I [i.e., I've] reviewed them in the June issue, but you don't have to wait for the review, since there is not one word of qualitative appreciation — just some history and the row business. Actually, the songs were written in Berlin in 1933, just before Schönberg got run out, and by the time he got over here, he [is] said to have "forgotten" them. It is so unlike the gent to forget anything having to do with A. Schönberg that I have another theory, but you will have to read the review to find out what it is.)

Lastly, there is your "Op. 58 *(Dreimal 1000)."* On the theory that this was a typo for Op. 48 — since 58 is impossible — I almost missed this one completely, but after chasing all over both buildings, I finally caught up with it. It's a music insert in the course of an article by Krenek called: *"Arnold Schönberg sjuttiofen aar,"* and consists of a facsimile of Schönberg's autograph of a short chorus for mixed voices entitled: *"Dreimal Tausend Jahre, Dikt av Dagobert D. Runer* [the gent that owns Philosophical Library and published the English translation of the *Harmonielehre* and Schönberg's *Style and Idea*] *för blandad kör av Arnold Schonberg,* op. 49 B." At the end of the piece Schönberg has written: "Copyright by Arnold Schönberg Apr. 20, 1949," and a printed copyright claim is given below. I don't understand about the "B" after Op. 49, unless perhaps the four Marks' quartets are actually Op. 49A. In any case, I haven't seen any indication that Op. 49B has been published elsewhere, and in spite of the fact that *Prisma* nor the quartet seem not to have been actually registered for copyright, the printed claim ties them up, and you will either have to get written permission from Mrs. Schönberg or buy a copy of the magazine. The supplement is bound in between pp. 40 and 41 of Vol. 2, Nr. 4, 1949. The editorial offices are P. A. Norstedt and Söners Förlag, Stockholm. No street address is given in the magazine, and so I suppose this must be enough.

And then after you have been a good boy and done all of the things I've told you to, you will still not have found copies of everything — although perhaps you will have found enough. If you want more, try ordering microfilms of Opera 1, 2, and 3 at $1.00 each—the minimum fee per item handled. You may get stuck for two, four, or six dollars respectively, since the songs are published separately, and if anyone in Photodup decided to get technical, he could figure it that way. Since the songs in each opus are in a folder, however, it is possible to consider the folder as an item handled. Op. 13 (call no. M1584.S) will also cost you a dollar, but op. 6 (call no., like the early three opera, M1621.S), with all eight songs in the same cover, will cost $1.28. For any of the others, you will have to have written permission from the copyright claimant, and I haven't tried to make cost estimates until you have seen whether copies can be bought or you have obtained the necessary permissions. Most of the estimates will be around a dollar, but if your University is putting through the order, they won't have to pay in advance, and estimates won't be necessary. If your order division insists, however, let me know and I'll send you something more specific.

The article[2] is at the printers. Popping something into the middle of a long paragraph normally means that the balance of the paragraph has to be re-set. I liked Cudworth's suggestions, however, and with a few adjustments in the text of the additions, I think I've fixed their length so that they will require just the right space to make a set of full lines, and therefore the balance of the paragraph wont have to be reset. I doubt if you will notice the changes in most instances, but I thought I ought to tell you anyway.

A letter from Manfred [Bukofzer] says that he is definitely going to Utrecht. I suppose I shall have to go, too, but I don't know where the money is going to come from and consequently there is nothing set definitely yet. Inventory plan, but I'm so far behind, I doubt if I get a chance to do it soon. I'd much rather talk things over with him, and if he expects to be in Washington on his way over, will you let me know. I thank you.

Sincerely yours,

Richard S. Hill

Mr. Vincent Duckles
The Music Library
University of California
Berkeley 4, California

---

[2] Vincent Duckles, "Some Observations of Music Libraries at Cambridge," *Notes* 9 (1951-52): 388-94.

Epilogue: In His Own Words

[On stationery of the Grand Café Glacier, Dijon]

Dijon, le 11 Mars 1926

Dear Pete:

No letter has come yet from you, but since I have not kept Paris posted as to my whereabouts, and since I am returning tomorrow, and especially since monstrous pleasant things have been happening to me of late, I have decided to write again anyhow; and perhaps it is just as well, for in a couple of weeks, I shall be back in Oxford again where I shall have to stay for at least twelve weeks, and from where, lacking the inspiration to be found in French cafés, I seldom am moved to write anything but the most necessary of letters. . . .[sic] But to the tale.

A week ago tomorrow, I arrived in Milan with my *belle ami,* Julie Lincoln. She had decided, when she was given a vacation from Brentano's, that she would like to see Italy — and so she started off. I think you would like her, for she's always doing things like that. Can you imagine seeing Italy in two weeks? However, she decided that it was too much of a strain travelling alone, so we joined forces, and had a very pleasant time. I'd send her places during the day while I was at the library, and in the evening we would play around, or read. We got along splendidly with Benvenuto Cellini, whom, after our first reaction against his bumptiousness, we found right amusing. A week in Rome, a glorious Saturday night and Sunday wandering about Orvieto, two days in Florence (where Julia broke the record by drinking two cups of chocolate and eating five grafins at one sitting), Pisa, Genoa, and then as I said, we arrived Saturday morning in Milan. The first thing we did was to rush to La Scala to get seats for that night, and what should we find to be on the bill but The Martyrdom of Saint Sebastian by d'Annunzio, Debussy, and Leon Bask (? spelling) [Leon Bakst]. Can you feature a better trio? And then to cap it all, St. Sebastien [sic] was to be played by

Ida Rubenstein. I turned handsprings all over the street while Julie held my hat and cheered. I had completely given up all hope of ever seeing the thing, since it had been forbidden in Paris until last year, and there seemed to be no hope of getting it produced again even though the ban was removed. Once I thought I was going to hear selections from it at the Concert Collonne, but the Saturday night before had been big and something happened to my watch which I didn't discover until nearly four Sunday afternoon. I rushed to the Chatelet then, but the only number left on the program was Scherezada (?). Consequently, as I have intimated, my joy knew all kinds of bounds, leaps, and skips, when I found I was going to see the thing *tout complete*. As a matter of fact, it was not quite complete — one act was omitted — but since even then it lasted for three and a half hours, I could hardly find it in me to ask for more. The scenery and costumes were excellent, the music uneven, sometimes as perfect as anything he has done and again quite unintelligible even though I was reasonably familiar with it from the piano transcription. It only occasionally reached the steady high level of *Pelleas*. And the play itself is hopeless. They say that as poetry it is remarkably good, but since I am not in a position to appreciate poetry in French, especially when it is fired at me rapidly, I can only speak for the plot. Now the plot does very nicely in the Golden Legend, but when I read that Sebastian danced on the burning coals, I can reasonably accurately imagine his discomfort but I am left completely cold when I see Ida jump upon a marble slab heated by strips of paper, an electric fan, and red lights where she postures and cuts graceful capers. I did get reasonably excited in the next act where Sebastian lays himself down at the feet of Cesare, and six women of Biblos, *les plus belle,* come and tempt him. Especially, when six very black men came in carrying trays of roseleaves on their heads with which the women buried Sebastian. In short, the thing is an accurate — as far, at least, as is possible in a play — transcription of the legend, which only goes to prove that d'Annunzio is not a genius, for if he was, he would have changed the legend to fit his own time, as did another writer I might name. He should have known, moreover, that the supernatural is never convincing on the stage. Either you must leave it to the imagination entirely, or realize it perfectly. The first automatically eliminates it from the stage, and until actors are willing to let their feet be blistered for the sake of art, the second does, too. When I get back to Paris, I shall buy the play and see if it makes better reading than it does acting, but just at present I can't hand it a thing.

The next day, Julie had to leave so as to be back at work Monday, so I've been playing around alone since. Sunday afternoon, I went to seen another comparatively new opera — Kovanschina by Moussorgski (at least I think that was it). It was unfinished when he died, so Rimsky-Korsakoff put an ending on it, but even then, for some reason, it only seems to have [been] given once in Paris and not at all in Italy. It is decidedly something as a drama, and the music is sufficient, so I had a beautiful time although I couldn't for the life of me figure out what it was all about. In the third act, the scene is laid in a beautiful red Russian-type of room belonging to some noble. After dinner, his harem performs and some lovely Persian ladies dance for him. He mauls one of them for awhile on a couch. And then a messenger comes in, and he luckily desists, for if it came to a show-down, I'm afraid the girl would have been completely squashed, as he weighed at least two hundred and fifty pounds. Anyhow, a string of servants come in bearing a huge brass bowl in which he bathed his hands, then an embroidered table cover on which he dried them, a pillow on which rested a comb with which he straightened his beard and hair, a perfectly glorious silver brocaded coat, and a white fur hat at least two feet high. When he was already, he started for the stairs at the back which led to the door. When he was at the top, a serf suddenly came through, stabbed him, and disappeared. The duke calmly fell over backwards down the stairs. I wouldn't have done it for the opera house, and what it must have meant to him with his 250 pounds, I should hate to have to discover. Anyway, I sincerely hope that at least part of those excess pounds were padding. If not, I think, when I give the American production of St. Sebastien, I'll negotiate with him to dance on my burning coals. It was about this time that I decided that the gist of the play was that the people didn't care much for the Duke, and were trying to get the Czar to do something about it. About the only people who did care for him it seems, were some monks and nuns, and in the next scene they were neatly arranged for — why I'm not exactly sure, but as you will discover, they didn't seem to be very chummy with the Czar. The scene was laid in a pine forest, at the back, the entrance to the monastery partially hidden by the trees. On either side, were huge piles of underbrush. It was night, and the moon helped little against the obscurity. The monks and nuns filed out of the monastery. A herald arrived, announcing the victory of the Czar's troops and their approach. The leader sent them back into the monastery to put on their festal robes. After a short development of the minor love story of the plot, they returned, dressed all in white — and bearing lighted tapers. Slowly they climbed up on the brush — seventy monks on one side and seventy nuns on the other. The head monk went about lighting the pine, and soon smoke began twisting about them and the fire turned their white robes red. A trumpet had been blowing behind in the woods. Gradually it came nearer until the Czar's troops rushed in at the back. They stopped in horror. The monks were writhing and falling down dead in the flames. Yes, a very nice opera! And La Tosca hasn't a thing on it.

That night, I went to *Orfeo,* and since I had a seat in the front row of the gallery and wasn't sleepy, I enjoyed it even more than last time. The last two acts are as good as anything I know. Monday, the place was closed, but Tuesday night I saw *The Martyrdom* again to see if my first impressions had been correct.

They were for the most part. Somebody spotted d'Annunzio in a box, and he was clapped until he gave a little speech. As a matter of fact, it was the only time during the performance that the audience got at all vociferous.

The next morning I left for Turin early, spent the day at the library, took the night train for Lyon, again spent the day in the library, and late in the afternoon took the train to Bourg. You will perhaps remember that I spoke rather highly of the food at Bourg. Well, after living on what I could get for three months, I decided since I was within sixty kilometers of the place to go there and see if the place always had as good meals as I had that one night. When I first stepped into the hotel, I realized something had happened. The dinning [sic] room had been shifted to the other side of the hotel, and right opposite the main entrance were two glass doors through which the stoves with chefs busy about them could be seen. They took me to my room, a large affair with a private bath. I was on the point of telling them that I was not accustomed to such splendor, but then I says to myself, "No, Hill, you will make a night of it. This is your first night in France after three long months. You will take this room, and not even ask the price of it, for if you did, you might feel compunctions. No, you will go down and have a perfect meal, and then after your café and cognac, you will come up here, fill the tub with nice hot water, and soak for a least two hours." All of which I did. When I got to the dinning [sic] room, my suspicions were confirmed. Dinner had gone up over ten francs and the wine eleven. But I was feeling reckless, and by continually reminding myself that the franc had fallen considerably, I kept up my spirit, ordered the things I wanted, and a half bottle of Romanée for twenty francs. Everything was perfect, and the *poulet en Breese roti* was an event. It was young, tender, but firm. They brought in half a chicken, and I said this is absurd—no one can eat half a chicken. But I proceeded to fool myself and ate every scrap. Everything was marvellous. One couldn't ask for better. And I sat there and gorged myself, thinking the while that although I was sorry the place had been "discovered," it was some satisfaction to know that I had found it even before. The next morning, I went to the Church of Bron and took some pictures of the carvings on the choir stalls which had particullarly [sic] delighted me on my previous visit. Then back for an excellent lunch and a cold bottle of Chablis, after which I called for the bill with fear and trembling. My splendid room and bath had cost twenty-five francs. When I considered that I had had to pay 75 piasters (which are worth more than a franc) for a room with a wash basin & pitcher in Cairo, I realized one of the greatest blessings of *la douce France.* My whole splurge had cost 139 francs, about five dollars. And then although I wanted to finish my days there, I came on here where I shall start in again tomorrow hunting through manuscripts for Thais. Best, Dick

The December 1954 issue of *Notes* carried Hill's review of the fifth edition of *Grove's Dictionary of Music and Musicians;* the review took editor Eric Blom to task for nationalism, reprinting obsolete information, omission, and haphazard coverage of American topics. Shortly thereafter a reader suggested *Notes* print a second review which would emphasize some of the fifth edition's "positive factors." This is Hill's response to that suggestion.

February 9, 1955

. . . I couldn't agree more that some of the "positive factors" should be stressed, and consequently did so. Right in the first paragraph, I wrote: "there is a goodly stand of sturdy new timber"; and indeed not until one gets halfway down the first column on the second page is there any stress placed on "negative factors." Then, on page 88, with the paragraph beginning: "Although the effect of these principles has naturally altered the fundamental character of the new edition, they have, of course, only decreased and not eliminated its usefulness," I returned again to the positive aspects. After a page of noting points that called for praise, I pulled the passage together by stating: "This listing of individual articles could go on indefinitely, but I hope the point has now been established that there are a goodly number of excellent things to be found in the new Grove." From here on to the end of the review, the good and bad points are intermixed in too rapid a succession to disentangle them now, but I insist that the good is stressed quite as much as the bad. In fact, the picture I was trying to put together was that of a publication which had some excellent material weighted down unfortunately by too much very inferior new material and a reprint job from earlier editions of just about half of the whole book, much of which was wholly out-of-date, and the rest poorly and inadequately revised. Having no axe to grind, I was trying to give a balanced picture, and I'm sorry if your unidentified "they" feel that I should have glossed over the bad and written up only the good. Frankly, I felt it my duty to the music librarians to give them both sides of the coin, and I would not like to see the balance upset — as it surely would be if someone so closely associated with Blom that he was presented with a free copy of the *Dictionary* by its editor were to write a sequel stressing *only* the "positive factors."

As a matter of fact, I have an idea that you might find it difficult to find anyone who is not a friend of Mr. Blom that would go to bat for the new Grove. I've written a good many reviews in my time, but never has the reaction to a review been so completely in agreement with the sentiments expressed and so vocal in letting me know about it. You are the only one out of at least two dozen who has come to the defense of the new Grove. Some of the comments have been merely verbal and I've discounted them on the basis that they could be merely polite and friendly remarks. But three or four people have taken time out to write letters entirely devoted to expressing their agreement with my picture of the dictionary, and a surprising number have made some comment in the course of writing on other subjects.

For example, Oliver Strunk wrote: "Many compliments on your review of the new Grove!!" Geraldine de Courcey showed the review to Professor Misch, who was annoyed with me previously because I refused to let him make some comments (which seemed ill-advised) in response to the "Notes" review of his book. Under the circumstances, Misch could hardly be said to be prejudiced in my favor. But Geraldine quotes her telephone call from him: "Misch went into an extasy! You must have innocently ruffled his feathers on some occasion, since after reading the review he telephoned me that 'this magnificent review' had entirely reconciled him with Mr. Hill, since anyone who could write such a masterpiece 'könnte sich alles erlauben.'" And Carroll Pratt wrote: "Your review of Grove's Dictionary is a masterpiece. I read with great delight and profit, admired your felicitous and pungent comments, and decided to keep an eye out for more of your writings."

I quote these not to spread the praise about, but only to demonstrate that most people seem to feel much the same as I do. Under the circumstances, two points occur to me. You write that "they feel the positive factors should have been stressed too," and since I most certainly stressed many positive factors, I cannot help but wonder whether you have yourself read the review or depended largely on what "they" told you about it. Secondly, just how much time have you spent digging around in the new Grove yourself? You blithely state that "the new edition contains a high percentage of accurate and hitherto unpublished information." How high is "high"? Mr. Blom states in his preface that only about half the edition consists of new articles (or at least one can deduce this from what he does say). I admit in my review that by no means all the reprinted material is inadequate, but likewise a really appalling amount of the new stuff is excessively poor to middling. Naturally, with so many contributors writing new articles, it would be phenomenal if some were not extremely fine, but to magnify this into a "high percentage" is, I'm afraid, just plain nonsense — and you can tell ____ so for me. Before getting too involved, I suggest you do some extensive checking and see then which side you wish to be on.

I don't mean by any of this to close the door to further comment on the new Grove in "Notes." Being editor as well as author, I would feel it incumbent to lean over backward and give any qualified person who isn't involved in the writing of the dictionary the opportunity to speak his or her piece. But I tried to be as careful and objective as I knew how to be, and to give a thoroughly balanced description of the new Grove. It would be absurd knowingly to unbalance that picture by asking someone who was associated with the production of the thing and who must necessarily be "emotionally involved" to carry on the discussion with "a further critique." If you know of someone not "emotionally involved" who can contribute facts not already implied or stated, *that* would be an entirely different matter.

How about it?

Sincerely yours,

Richard S. Hill
Editor

During a New York trip to sign up *Notes'* advertisers, Hill learned of the impending switch from monaural to stereophonic records. This excerpt from a multi-paged letter dated 2 July 1958 to Kurtz Myers discusses the implications of that switch for the "Index of Record Reviews" and the Supplement to *Record Ratings.* (Cf. pp. 38-40 above.)

. . . My week in New York turned up some other considerations, one of which is pretty devastating. Talking to quite a few record people, it gradually became clear that one and all consider that the switch to stereo is rapidly going to be as complete and thorough as the switch from the 78 rpm discs to the LPs, and that very soon it will be impossible to buy a monaural recording. The bigger companies are busily engaged in replacing all of their monaural releases with the same recording in stereo form. Presumably most of these will be phonies, since they couldn't possible [*sic*] re-record everything from fresh performances, and obviously no one can actually get two soundtracks out of a single track. The little fellows, of course, are completely non-plussed, since their small catalogs have been built up over a period of years and none of them have the capital to re-issue everything all at once, but the big companies apparently like this, since they seem to feel that, although stereo will give them a big shot in the arm, it will quickly wipe out a large part of the competition from the smaller firms.

Personally, I'm not at all convinced that this switch to stereo is going to come as quickly or as completely as the big companies seem to think. It is by no means comparable to the switch from 78's to LP's. In that case, the record collector only had to buy an inexpensive turn-table and pick-up in order to get cheaper records and a truly vast improvement in recording technique through the uninterrupted playing of longer compositions. With stereo, it is only the turn-table that can still be used, and all other equipment has either to be replaced or duplicated. The only thing gained in the process is an increase in "presence" and reality, and those qualities can only be gained if one is willing to sit still in a rather restricted area between the speakers. It will do me no good to put on a record in the living room and listen to it in the study while typing letters (which, shameful as the procedure may be, is one of the chief ways in which I listen to records). Still, Bob Carneal, the engineer of our Recording Laboratory, insists that stereo will sweep the country. That the record companies have already sunk too much money in it to allow it to fail—they'll have to make their investment good by plugging it in ads and magazines until it catches on. He claims that there is already over a thousands [*sic*] stereo discs that have been released, and that come autumn this number will be multiplied many times.

What does this mean so far as we are concerned? In *Notes,* of course, it means relatively nothing, since you can index stereo discs just as well as monaural ones as soon as reviews begin appearing in any quantity. If the same review covers both the monaural and stereo versions, it will introduce further complications, but you can use the double-entry system for this just as you have always done for splits on foreign releases. But with the Supplement, we're stuck. Crown [Publishers] is only interested in bringing it out because they hope that in bringing RR [Record Ratings] up-to-date they will be able to continue to sell copies of RR along with copies of the Supplement. But if no one is interested in monaural releases any more, they aren't going to buy even the supplement, let alone RR. Does it make any sense for us to put a lot of time into preparing the Supplement, and for MLA and Crown to sink money into it in view of a greatly reduced interest in monaural recordings? The answer to this obviously hangs on the "greatly reduced interest." If stereo is actually going to sweep the country, then obviously it would be silly for us to continue with the Supplement; if it isn't, then the book would still be useful. It thus becomes essential for us to get a reasonably correct answer to that question. What has your experience been in Detroit and on your travels? I had hoped to be able to discuss the problem with [Robert] Simon [of Crown Publishers] while in New York, since he is undoubtedly the gent who will make the final decision. Worse still, we have no specific contract with Crown, and thus we can prepare the whole book and have him turn it down at the last minute. In that case, we would have no recourse whatsoever, and would have to swallow Crown's decision. Unfortunately Simon is in Mexico on a month's vacation, and we can probably get no answer from him until the end of August. The real hell of the situation is that, if we are going ahead at all, we ought to go ahead just as fast as possible in order to cash in on whatever lingering interest there may be in our fine collection of monaural entries. If the shift to stereo comes gradually, a sufficient number of copies of the Supplement may perhaps be sold to cover its cost, whereas every day we wait may mean a lessening market for back copies of RR and of the new copies of the Supplement. It's one of the nastiest situations I've ever been in.

At one point, I hoped we could bale ourselves out of this by getting Crown to agree to an increase in the investment permitting us to add the new stereo numbers to the old releases. This would complicate the assembling and pasting almost passed all bearing, but it would extend the usability of the Supplement for a little longer. The chief drawback to the idea is that I can't seem to get any dope on the new numbers. God knows, a lot of new stereo discs are being issued, but I can seem to get no proof that the old discs are actually being re-issued in stereo form. Various people have *said* that this was going to happen, but thus far I haven't seen one. Have you? In any case, I'm not altogether sure that the simple addition of a new stereo number to an old entry would answer the problem, since the stereo version may solve the technical problems so inadequately that reviews of the old version may be rhapsodic whereas the new reviews, written by stereo fans, will turn thumbs down on the new version. Unless we could incorporate some reviews of the stereo version the entry might not serve any useful purpose. Besides, if the companies have already brought out a thousand stereo releases so far this summer, the magazines will naturally have to pick and choose, since they certainly won't have enough space available to cover such a tremendous quantity of discs. They will almost surely choose the new releases rather than the re-issues, and hence it may be months before we get enough new reviews of stereo re-issues to make any difference. Got any good hunches on this aspect of the situation?